# THE CELL BLOCK PRESENTS...

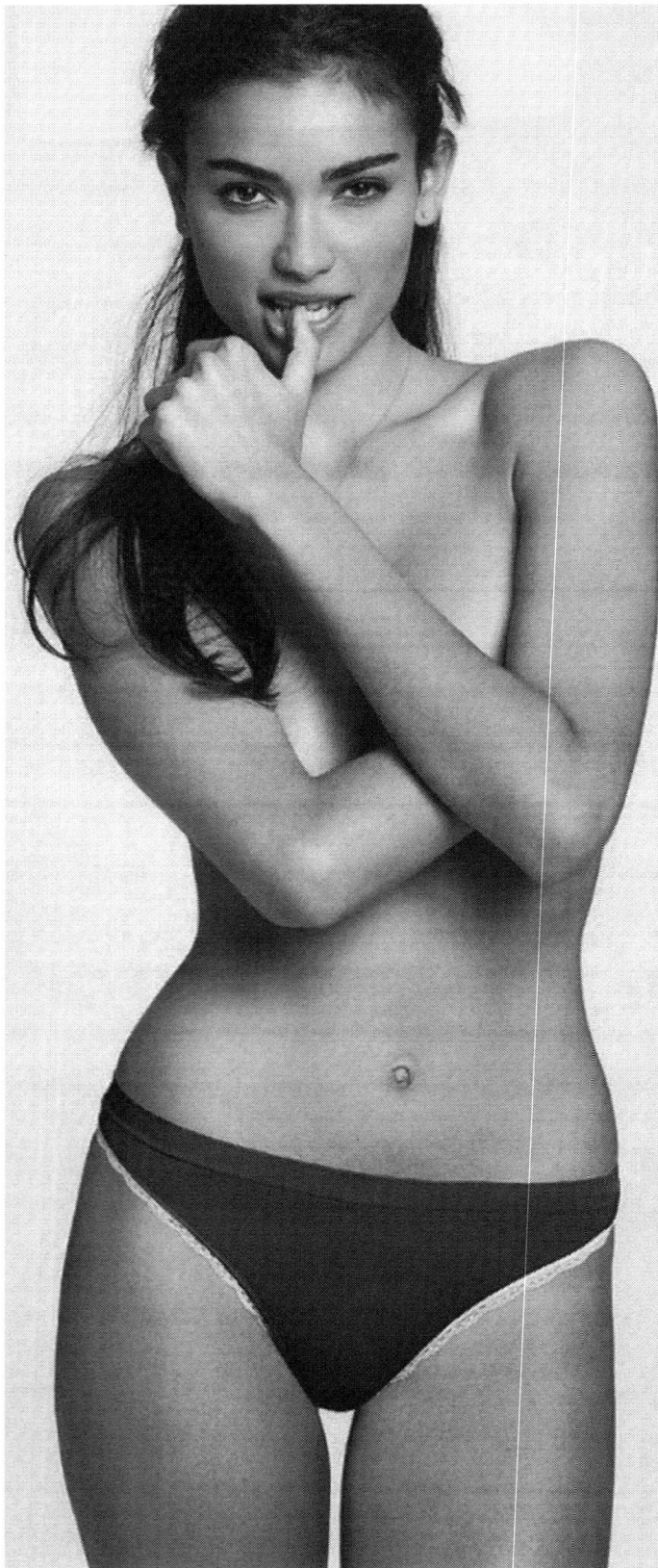

WANT TO SEE MORE OF ME AND MY FRIENDS? STAY TUNED!

# THE BEST RESOURCE DIRECTORY FOR PRISONERS

## TABLE OF CONTENTS

Published by: The Cell Block™

The Cell Block
P.O. Box 1025
Rancho Cordova, CA 95741

Facebook.com/thecellblock.net
Website: thecellblock.net
Corrlinks: thecellblock.net@mail.com

Copyright © 2017 by Mike Enemigo


Cover Design: Mike Enemigo

Send comments, reviews, interview and business inquiries to: thecellblock.net@mail.com

# A Letter From The Cell Block:

Despite being sentenced to life in prison in 2002, I stay trying to make something happen; whatever it may be. I've never been one to let things – even prison walls, steel bars and razor wire – stop me from doing what I set out to do. And in order to be successful, I've had to build up a network of relationships and resources. After all, especially when trying to accomplish something from inside a prison cell, where you're forced to rely on assistance from other people on the outside, it is *all* about networking, relationships, and resources.

During the time I've spent doing the various things that I do and gathering up the much needed resources, I learned that there are actually a lot of things prisoners have available to them and can do, that most just don't know about. But with the proper information, some creativity (you *must* learn to think outside of the box when you live in one) and determination, there are many, *many* things that can be done. And yes, right from the inside of *your* prison cell, too....

This realization is what inspired me to create this book. Whether it's a lawyer to help you with your case, either for a fee or pro bono, or a place for artists to sell their art so they can make better money than a fellow prisoner can often pay; whether it's a typist, agent, or self-publishing service to help authors get their books or poetry published, or a pen pal service or club that can help one make friends from all over the country – all over the world, even – right from their cell; whether it's a place that will sell prisoners books and magazines or send them for free, or an advocacy/organization to assist with an injustice; whether it's a school that offers correspondence courses, or a company that offers a personal assistant service, sells sexy pictures, or gifts we can buy and send to our loved ones, and much, much more; I have done all I can to think of what a prisoner could possibly want to do from their cell, and provide the necessary resources in order to do so. Again, be creative, determined and willing to work hard, and you may be surprised of just what you can do.

Now, it should be noted that The Cell Block does not cosign any of the companies in this directory. We are only notifying you of them and what resources they promote to offer. And though we've done our best to weed them out, some of these companies may no longer be in business anymore or have changed their mailing address. Some may even be scams looking to take advantage of us – kick us while we're down. One can never be certain. However, whatever experiences you have with any of these businesses, we want to know about it. If they're scams, write and tell us. We'll put them on blast in our next edition – let our fellow prisoners know they're bad business and shut 'em down. If their business is 100, we want to know that, too. We'll notify everybody of who is solid in the next edition and encourage them to deal with those companies. Companies that treat us well deserve to be rewarded by getting our business, companies that are foul deserve to get shut down; our fellow prisoners deserve to be made aware of who's who. This is all a part of the network.

For this latest edition of *The Best Resource Directory For Prisoners*, I've cut out a lot of the nonsense; filler other companies -- freeworld companies who wish to exploit our struggle for their profit, as this is the *only* directory created entirely by inmates – use to bulk up their books in order to make them seem more than what they are. I've sent over 400+ letters, myself, just this year to make sure the information is current, and that's not including the 500-plus sent by my teammates and a few other helpful friends from around the country. I've compacted the text as much as possible and made everything nice and clean. It's pure, useful information. Remember, this directory is a living entity; it is constantly evolving. We are constantly making adjustments that improves its quality, and I thank those of you who have participated in letting me know where weaknesses are, and how we improve them. So if you have any suggestions or requests for resources that would assist you with your objectives, I welcome them gladly.

Sincerely,

Mike
The Cell Block

**Resource 1:** a source of supply or support **2:** available funds **3:** a possibility of relief or recovery **4:** a means of spending leisure time **5:** ability to meet and handle situations **6:** something to which one has recourse in difficulty

# WANT MONEY?

# INDEX OF RESOURCES

Internationalist Prison Books…
Midwest Books to Prisoners
NYC Books Through Bars
Portland Books to Prisoners
Prison Book Program
Prison Library Project
Prisoners Literature Project
Providence Books Through …
Read Between the Bars
Spring Grass Book 'Em
Urbana- Champagne Books …
Wisconsin Books to Prison…
Women's Prison Book Project

## BOOK PUBLISHERS
Beginning on page 138.

## BOOK SELLERS

A Book You Want
Acclaimed Books
American Correctional…
BBPD
Black Star Music & Video
The Cell Block
Direct Access
Groundwork Books Collective
L33t Gaming
Left Bank Books
Lighthouse Resource Center
The Osborne Association
Pathfinder Press
PM Press
Prison Professor
South End Press
Sureshot Books
Third Coast Gifts & Books
Wall Periodicals

## CHRISTIAN

Amazing Facts
American Bible Academy
American Bible Society
American Rehabilitation Ministries
Ben & Ima Prayen
Berean Prison Ministry
Bible Helps
Christian Pen Pals
Christianpenpals.org
Crossroads Bible Institute
Grace Ministries Bible College…
Global University
International Bible Society
International Christian College...

Joyce Meyers Ministries
Message of the Cross Ministries
Mike Barber Ministries
Mount Hope Prison Ministry
The Missing Link
Moody Bible Institute
Mt. Hope Prison Ministry
Our Daily Bread
Prisoner Fellowship Ministry
Prison Outreach Worldwide
Prisoners for Christ Outreach ...
Rock of Aged Prison Ministry
St. Dismas Guild
United Prison Ministries
International

## CLEAR PLASTIC PRODUCTS

See package companies.

## CLOTHES/SHOES

See package companies.

## CUSTOM CDs

See package companies.

## DISCOUNT CALLS

Affordable Inmate Calling Services
Callsfromwalls.com
Cons Call Home
Freedom Line
FREE JAIL CALLS
Get Connected
GTI Voice
Inmate Toll Busters
Jail Calls
JailCallsUSA.com
Local123.net
Ocslocal.com
Save on Prison Calls
SP Telecom
Tim's Inmate Mail Service
VFC

## EDUCATION

Adams State College
American Rehabilitation …
Arts in Criminal Justice
The Asian Classics Institute…
Bard College
bestgedtutor.com

Blackstone Career Institute
Boston University Prison Education
College in Prison
College Level Exam Program
Complete GED Preparation
CORE
Cornell Prison Education Program
Education Behind Bars
Education Justice Project
Global University
Grace College Prison Extension…
Graduate School USA
Hudson Link for Higher Edu…
Indiana University
International Christian &...
International Sports Sciences...
Lansing Correctional Facility
Maine State Prison College
Programs
NCJRS – The National Instit…
New Freedom Collage
Oakland City University Prison…
Ohio University College Prog…
Operation Outward Reach, Inc.
The Paralegal Institute
PASS Program
Penn Foster Career School
Prisoners' Guerilla Handbook
Prison University Project
Project Rebound
Purdue University Northern …
SJM Family Foundation, Inc.
Spanish for Prisoners
St. Mark's School of Legal Studies
Stratford Career Institute
University Beyond Bars
University of North Carolina
Upper Iowa University
Windham School District

## ELECTRONICS

See package companies.

## E-MAIL SERVICES

Conpals Inmate Connections
Inmate Classified
Inmate Scribes
Internet Access Through Mail

## FAMILY-BASED SERVICES

About That Life Publications
Amachi Program

Casa Frontera Visitor Center
Center for the Children of Incarcera
Children of Incarcerated Parents
Edwin Gould Services for Children
Families of Parchman Prison …
Family and Corrections Network
Families United
FamliySupportAmerica.org
Forever Family, Inc
Friends outside
From Here to the Streets
Hour Children
Legal Services for Prisoners with ...
Matthew House
Middle Ground Prison Reform
National Center for Youth Law
National Fatherhood Initiative
National Incarcerated Parents …
National Institute of Corrections
PB&J Family Services, Inc.
Pelipost.com
PictureDoney.com
Prison Information Network
Prison Place
San Francisco Children of …
South Dakota Prisoner Support …
Spletter
Support for Kids with Incarc…
United Shuttle

## FAMILY/FRIEND LOCATORS

U.S. Mint Green

## GIFT SHOPS

ATS
Basket Boutique
Bottled Thoughts
Brilliance Audio, Inc.
Cell Shop
Elegant Roses
Elija Ray Gifts
Free-world Services
From Inside Out
Harvest 21 Gifts
infoLINKS
Inmate Scribes
Jaden Moore of New York
Julie's Gifts
Loving a Convict
Millennial Masterpieces
Special Miracles

## FOOD

See package companies.

## GREETING CARDS

Acclaimed Books
Ajemm Brothers Greeting Cards
Ashley Rice Collection
Diversified Press
Freebird Publishers
Millennial Masterpieces
Occasion Gallerie
Wistful Expressions

## HEALTH

AIDS in Prison Project
AIDS Law Project of Pennsylvania
Aids Treatment News
Alianza
Allegheny County Department of ...
American Diabetes Association
AMFAR Aid Research
Cell Workout
Centerforce
Center for Disease Control's Natio…
Center for Health Justice
Correct Help
Disability Rights Texas
Drug Policy Alliance
Hepatitis and Liver Dis...
Hepatitis C Awareness Project
Hepatitis C Support Project
Hepatitis Prison Coalition
HIV/Hepatitis C Prison Committee
Hepatitis, AIDS, Research Trust…
Institute For Criminals Justice Healt
International Sports Sciences...
Latino Commission on AIDS
Lesbian AIDS project
Medical Malpractice Experts
National AIDS Treatment Advoc…
National Health Prison Project
The National Hepatitis C Prison...
Our Bodies, Ourselves
Positively Aware; National
Magaz…
Prison AIDS Resource Center
Prison Diabetes Handbook...
Prison Health News
Prisoners with AIDS Rights Advoc…
San Francisco AIDS Foundation
Services to Elder Prisoners, PA
The Wrongful Death Institute

## INMATE SERVICES

ATS
Dean's Books
Help From Beyond the Walls
JAD Enterprises

## INTERNET RESEARCHERS

A Book You Want
ATS
CIPS - Certified Internet...
EPS
Help From Beyond the Walls
Internet Access Through Mail
Just Us Investigation
LRM
Package Trust
Prison Bay

## ISLAMIC/MUSLIM

About That Life Publications
Alavi foundation
Assisting Incarcerated Muslims
Conveying Islamic Message Society
Council on American Islamic...
Crescent Imports and Publications
Diamma Akhewel
Islamic Ahlulbayt Association
Islamic Center
Islamic Center of Springfield
Missouri
Islamic Circle of North America
Muslims for Humanity
Why Islam

## LATINO

Barrios Unidos
Centro Legal de la Raza
Chican@ Power & Struggle…
La Raza Centro Legal, Inc
La Voz de Esperanza
Latino Commission on AIDS
Latino on Wheels
Legal Publications in Spanish, Inc

## LEGAL BOOKS/ SELLERS

A Jailhouse Lawyers Manual
Actual Innocence
Advanced Criminal Procedure...
Arrested: What to do...
Arrest-Proof Yourself

## LEGAL HELP/SERVICES

Susan L. Burke
Sylvia Rivera Law Project
Texas Center for Actual Innocence
Texas Innocence Network
Timberwolf Litigation & Research
Timothy C. Chiang-Lin
Thurgood Marshall School of Inn..
Transformative Justice Law Project..
TR&R
University of Baltimore Innocen…
University of Miami Law Innocen…
University of Texas Center for…
Uptown People's Law Center
Wesleyan Innocence Project
West Virginia Innocence Project
William L. Schmidt
Winning Writ Writers

**Note:** For more legal help resources
see our list of over 130 pro bono
attorneys starting on page 130

## LEGAL INFORMATION

American Bar Association
Bar None
Battered Women's Justice Project
Carolina Case Law
Center for Constitutional Rights
Central Texas ABC
Columbia Human Rights Law Rev
Georgetown ARCP
Legal Information Services Assoc…
National Criminal Justice Refere…
National Legal Aid and Defend…
PLN Accumulative Index
Prisonlawblog.com
Prisoner Rights Information Sys…
Prisoners' Rights Research Project
Sentencing and Justice Reform…
The Sentencing Project
Set My Way Free Ministries, Inc
TR&R
W. Barron

## LEGAL WEB PAGES

Conpals Inmate Connections
Friends Beyond the Wall

## LGTB

Black and Pink
Gay and Lesbian Advocates and…
Gay Identity Center of Colorado

Gender Muting Collective
Lesbian AIDS Project
Lesbian and Gay Insurrection
Midwest Pages to Prisoners Project
Midwest Trans Prisoner Penpal …
National Center for Lesbian Rig…
National Gay and Lesbian Task…
The Network/La RED Ending…
Out of Control Lesbian Commit…
Pace Post Conviction Project
Prisoner Correspondence Project
Sinister Wisdom, Inc.
Sylvia Rivera Law Project
The Transformative Justice Law…
T.I.P. Journal
Transformative Justice Law Proj…
Transgender, Gender Variant,…
Transition of Prisoners, INC
Tranzmission Prison Books
Wisconsin Books to Prisoners…
Women's Prison Book Project

## LIFERS/DEATH PENALTY

American Civil Liberties Union…
California Lifer Newsletter
Campaign to End the Death Penalty
Citizens United for Alternati…
Death Penalty Focus
Death Penalty Information Center
D.R.I.V.E. Movement
Fair Chance Project
Fight for Lifers West
Incarcerated Citizens Council
Juvenile Lifers
L.I.F.E. Association
Lifeline
Lifers to be Free
Lifers United
The Moratorium Campaign
Muncy Inmate Coordinator
The National Coalition to Abolish…
National Death Row Assistance…
Oregonians for Alternatives to the…
PA Lifers Association
The Other Death Penalty Project
The Voices.Con Newsletter

## LITERARY AGENTS
Beginning on page 142

Alive Communications, Inc.
Betsy Amster Literary Enterprises
B.J. Robbins Literary Agency
Bookends, LLC

Briar Cliff Review
Browne & Miller Literary…
Castiglia Literary Agancy
Concho River Review
Curtis Brown, LTD
Defiore & Co.
Diana Finch Literary Agency
Dunham Literary, Inc.
Dystel & Godrich Literary…
The Evan Marshall Agency
Fineprint Literary Management
Jeany Naggar Literary Agency. Inc.
Jodie Rhodes Literary Agency
The Joy Harris Literary Agency...
Loretta Barrett Books, Inc.
Lowenstein Associates, Inc.
Mendel Media Group, LLC
Michael Larsen/Elizabeth Pomada,
Philip G. Spitzer Literary Agency...
Richard Henshaw Group
RLR Associates, LTD
Robin Straus Agency, Inc.
Rosalie Siegel
Russell & Volkening
Sandra Dijkstra Literary Agency
Sanford J. Greenburger Associates...
Sheree Bykofsky Associates, Inc.
Trident Media Group
Veritas Literary Agency
Victoria Sanders & Associates
The Wendy Weil Agency, Inc.
WM Clark Associates
Writers House

## LITERARY PUBS/REVIEWERS
Beginning on page 144

African American Review
AGNI Magazine
Alaska Quarterly Review
Alligator juniper
American Literary Review
The American Scholar
The Antioch Review
Apalachee Review
ARC Poetry Magazine
Arion
Arkansas Review
Ascent; English Dept.
The Awakening Review
Baffler
The Bayou Review
Bellevue Literary Review
Bellingham Review
Bellowing Ark

Beloit Poetry Journal
The Bitter Oleander
Blackbird
Blue Mesa Review
Boston Review
Boulevard
Brain, Child
Briar Cliff Review
Brilliance Corners
Callaloo
Calyx
Capilano Review
The Caribbean Writer
Carolina Quarterly
The Chattahoochee
Chicago Review
Cimarron Review
College Literature
Colorado Review
Columbia
Commentary Magazine
The Comstock Review
Conjunctions
Connecticut Review
Court Green
Crab Orchard Review
Crazyhorse
Creative Nonfiction
Cutbacks
Daedalus
Denver Quarterly
Descant
Eclipse; A Literary Journal
Ecotone
Epoch
Eureka Literary Magazine
Event
Fantasy & Science Fiction
Faultline
Fiction; Mark J Mirksy, Editor
Fiction International
Fiddlehead; Campus House
Field
The First Line
Florida Review
Folio
Fourteen Hills
Fourth Genre
Georgia Review
Gettysburg Review
Grain
Green Hill Literary Lantern
Greensboro review
Gulf Coast
Harper's Magazine

Harpur Palate
Harvard Review
Hawaii Pacific Review
Hayden's Ferry Review
The Healing Muse
Hiram Poetry Review
Hotel Amerika
Hudson Review
Hunger Mountain
Idaho Review
Iris, UVA Women's Center
Iron Horse Literary Review
Isotope; Utah State University
Italiana Americana, University of
Rhode Island
Jabberwock Reviews
Jewish Currents
The Journal
Karanu
Kenyon review
Land Grant College Review
The Laurel Review; Dept. of
English
Literal Latte
The Long Story
Louisiana Literature
Louisville Review
Malahat Review
Massachusetts review
McSweeney's
Meridian, University of Virginia
Michigan Quarterly Review
Mid-American Review
Midstream
Missouri Review
Natural Bridge
New Delta Review
New England Review
New Letter, University of Missouri
New Ohio Review; English Dept.
New Orleans Review
The New York Quarterly
Nimrod International Journal
Ninth Letter
North Carolina Literary Review
North Dakota Quarterly
Northwest Review; The Editor,
NWR
Notre Dame Review
Nylon
Oklahoma Today
Oxford American
Painted Bride Quarterly
Pearl
Phoebe; George Mason University

MSN 206
The Pinch, Dept. of English
Pleiades
Ploughshares, Emerson College
Poet Lore
Potomac Review
Pottersfield Portfolio
Prairie Fire
Prairie Schooner
Prism International
Quarterly West
Raritan, Rutgers University
Rattle
Rattapallax
Redivider, Emerson College
RHINO
Room
The Saint Ann's Review
Salmagundi; Skidmore College
Salt Hill; English Dept.
Santa Monica Review
Seattle Review
Seneca Review
Seven Days
Sewanee Review; Univers…
Shenandoah
Sonora Review
So-To-Speak
The South Carolina Review
South Dakota Review
Southeast Review, English Dept.
Southern Humanities Review
The Southern Review
Southwest review
Speakeasy; The Loft Literary Center
The Spoon River Poetry Review
St. Anthony Messenger
Sun
Swivel
Sycamore Review
Talking River Review
Tampa Review; The University …
The Texas Review; English Dept.
Thema
Threepenny Review
Tikkun
Tin House
Transition Magazine
Turnrow; English Dept.
War, Literature, and the Arts; Engl..
Wascana Review
Washington Square Creative Writ…
Watchword
Witness
Xavier University

Yale Review
Zahir; Sheryl Tempchin
Zoetrope
Zyzzyva

## MAGAZINES

American Indian Art Magazine
Auto Restore
Auto Week
Baseball America
Bead and Button
Blade Magazine
Crime Magazine
Don Diva Magazine
The Editorial Eye
ESPN
Esquire
Forbes
Friction Zone
Hollywood Scriptwriter
Home Business Magazine
In the Wind
Indian Life Magazine
In-Touch Ministries
Latino on Wheels
LLG
Lowrider Magazine
National Geographic
The Order of the Earth
Outlaw Bikers
Robert Kennedy Publishing
Slingshot Magazine
SMOOTH
Sports Illustrated
Sports Weekly
Sunshine Artist
Tattoo Review
Time Magazine
Writer's Digest

## MAGAZINE SELLERS

Alice S. Grant Publications
American Magazine Service
Black Star Music & Video
Direct Access
Discount Magazine Subscriptions …
Girls & Mags
Inmatemags.com
Inmate Magazine Services
The Magazine Wizard
Magazine City
Munhall, Bob & Colette
Sanders, Ms. Julia A.

Tightwad Magazines
Wall Periodical

## MAIL FORWARDING

Help From Beyond the Walls

## MEDITATION

Amitabha Buddhist Society of USA
Association for Research and En…
Baus Book Circulation
Bridge Project
Buddhist Association of the Unite…
Chuang Yen Monastery
Buddhist Churches of America
Dallas Buddhist Association
Dharma Seeds Foundation
Freeing the Mind / Kadampa
Gassho Newsletter/Atlanta Soto …
Heart Mountain
Inside Dharma
Insight Meditation Society
International Buddhist Meditation
…
Liberation Prison Project
National Buddhist Prison
Sangha/Zen
Prison Dharma Network
PSSC/Parallax Press
Snow Lion Publications
Sravasti Abbey/Ven Thubten
Chodron
Strawberry Dragon Zendo
The Sutra Translation Committee …
Syda Foundation Prison Project
Tricycle Magazine: The Buddhist …
Upaya Prison Outreach Project

## MISC.

60 Minutes
American Motorcyclist Association
Camelback Group
Catalogchoice.ord
CDCR, office of Ombudsman
Cheaters
Death Before Dishonor
Exotic Fragrances
Fox Broadcasting
Freedom of Information Act
Genealogical Research, Refere…
Getgrrandpasfbifile
Gold Star Fragrances
In Scan Document Service

InsightCrew
Internal Affairs, CDCR
L33t Gaming
Library of Congress
Military Records; National Person...
National Directory of Catalogs
Trump, President Donald
PARfessionals
PETA
Prism Optical, Inc
Prison Mindfulness Institute
Prisonnewsnetwork.us
The Massachusetts Chess Ass…
Thomas Merton Centre
PREP
U.S. Dept. of Justice
U.S. Small Business Association

## MISC. RELIGIOUS/SPIRITUAL

Association of Happiness for …
BTP
Dharma Garden Newsletter
Greenman Ministry
Human Kindness Foundation
Inner Traditions
In-Touch Ministries
Jewish Prisoners Assistance
Foundation
Jewish Prisoners Services …
Kabbalah Research Institute
Miracles Prisoner Ministry
Prison Ashram Project
Prison Fellowship
Prison Library Project
Susman, Eli
Watchtower

## MUSIC SELLERS

Music By Mail
Pack Central Music
Walkenhorst's

## NATIVE AMERICAN

American Indian Art …
Bayou La Rosa
Indian Life Magazine
Mettanokit Outreach
National Native American Prison…
Native American Pride Committee
Native American Prisoners' …
Navajo Nation Corrections Project

## PACKAGE COMPANIES

Access Securepak California
Bust the Move
Golden state Packages
Union Supply Direct California
Walkenhorst's

## PARALEGAL SERVICES

A&K Paralegal Services
Angres, Robert L., Esq.
Butler Legal Group
Inmatenavigator.org
Miller Paralegal
Ms. Tahtianna Fermin
Y.S.E. Administration Services

## PAROLEE/EX-OFFENDER

Better People
Catholic Charities USA
Cleveland Career Center
Conquest House
Conquest Offender
Correctional Library Services
D&D Worldwide Services
Dress for Success
Energy Committed to Offenders
Evolve
Exodus Transitional Commun…
Ex-offender Re-entry Website
Fair Chance Project
From Jail to a Job
From Here to the Streets
Homeboy Industries
Impact Publications
Justice Watch
Justice Works!
Legal Action Center Services
LWPP
Making Career Connections
The Missing Link
Open, Inc.
Philadelphia Brotherhood Rescue …
Prison Fellowship Ministry
Project Return
Salvation Army
Second Chance Act
SJM Family Foundation, Inc.
St. Patrick Friary
Support Housing & Innovative …
Task Force on Prisoner Re-entry
Transitional Housing for Georgia

## PEN PAL CLUBS

Bhandari, Suresh
Christian Pen Pals
Inside Out
Lifeline
Nubian Princess Ent…
Reaching Beyond the Walls
Sylvian Clarke
Write4life

## PEN PAL LISTS

Co-Sign Pro
ESCTS
Girls & Mags
Marjorie Lee Publishing
Meet-A-Mate

## PEN PAL MAGAZINES

Cosmic Cupid
The Fog Corporation

## PEN PAL WEBSITES

B.F.I.A.
Christianpenpals.org
Con Pals
Conpals Inmate Connections
Convict Mailbag
Diversified Press
DRL
Exclusiverprisoner.com
Friends Beyond the Wall
Inmate Classified
Inmate Connections
Inmateconnection.com
InmateNHouseLove.Com
Inmate Pen Pal Connection
Inmate Scribes
Inmates in Waiting
JAD Enterprises
LostVault.com
Loveaprisoner.com
Meet-An-Mate
Nubian Princess Ent.
Outlaws Online, Inc.
Penacon.com
Prison Connection
Prison Pen Pals
Prison Inmates Online
Prisonerpal.com
Prisonpenpalmingle.com
Prisonerlife.com

Prisoner Promotions
Prisonvoice.com
Sexyprisoners.com
South Beach Singles, Inc
Tele-pal.com
Texas Prisoners Network Support
Waitingpenpals.com
Writeaprisoner.com
Writesomeoneinprison.com
Writetoinmates.com

## PERSONAL ASSISTANTS

Escape Mate
Leonard's Mom Enterprises
LRM
TFL

## PHOTO DUPLICATION / MANIPULATION

Con Pics
Flikshop.com
Inmate Photo Provider
Package Trust
Pelipost.com
PicturDonkey.com
Prison Bay

## PHOTOCOPIES

IPP

## PRISON(ER)-BASED PUBS

4strugglemag
AFCS
Alabama Prison Project
Angolite
The Beat Within
The Best 500 Non-Profit…
California Lifer Newsletter
California Prison Focus
The Cell Block
The Cell Door
The Celling of America
Coalition for Prisoners'…
Dharma Garden Newsletter
Fanorama Society…
The Fire Inside
The Fortune News
Freebird Publishers
Graterfriends
Inmate Shopper
Internationalist Prison…

Journal of Prisoners on Prisons
Justice Denied
La Voz de Esperanza
Mennonite Central …
MIM Distributors
The New Abolitionist
Open, Inc
Phantom Prisoner
Prison Focus
The Prison Journal
Prison Legal news
The Prison Mirror
Prison Outreach Worldwide
Prisonworld Magazine
Prisoner Solidarity
Prisoner's Right Union
San Quentin News
Southland Prison News
The Voices.con Newsletter
Tri-State Legal Journal
Turning the Tide: Journal...

## PRO BONO ATTORNEYS

See our listing on page 126

## SEX ABUSE

An End to Silence
Association for the Treatment….
Prison Rape Elimination…
The Safer Society Foundation
Sex Abuse Treatment…
Stop Prisoner Rape

## SEXY PHOTOS

ATS
Branlettes Beauties
Butterwater, LLC
Cameltoe Photo
Cheryl Johnson Company
CNA Entertainment
Co-Sign Pro
FIYA Girls
Flix 4 You
F.O.S.
Free-World services
Grab Bag Hot Pics
Ghost Photos
Hot Dreams
HotFlixx
Inmate-Connection.com
Inmate Scribes
Kill Shot King

Krasnya, LLC
Meshell Baldwin Publications
Millennial Masterpieces
Moonlite Productions
Nubian Princess Ent.
On Demand Inmate Services
Package Trust
Photo Tryst
Photoworld
Picmate.net
Picture Entertainment
Poplar Enterprise
Prison Publications
The Senza Collection
Sexy Girl Parade
Shots That Rock
Soiled Doves
South Beach Singles, Inc.
Special Miracles
Summerbunnies.com
Suthern Cumfort
Total Access Services
UVP
Villa Entertainment

## SOCIAL NETWORK SITES

See website builders.

## SONGWRITER RESOURCES

International Acoustic Music
Awards
USA Songwriting Contest

## SPORTS

African America Golf Digest
Baseball America
Dallas Cowboys Football Club
ESPN
San Francisco Forty …
Sports Illustrated
Sports Weekly

## STAMP BUYERS

Cash For Your Stamps
Great Goods
The Greenback Exchange
Help From Beyond …
Prison/Inmate Family Service

## STATIONARY

Bare Expressions
H. Avery

## SUPPORT GROUPS (NA/AA)

Alcoholics Anonymous General…
Association for the Treatment …
Atkins House
Baitil Salaam Network
Baker Industries
Bayou La Rosa
Catholic charities USA
Georgia Justice Project
ISO World Services, Inc
Narcotics Anonymous
Project Blanket

## TYPING SERVICES

Ambler Document Processing
Buck Co. Secretarial
Gillins Typing Service
Jeff Vincent
Let My Fingers do your Typing
Liz's Paper Jungle
The Office
Sanders, Louise S.
Sandra Z. Thomas
TJL

## URBAN BOOKS/ PUBLISHERS

4orPlay Publications
A Million Thoughts…
Anatomy of Hip-Hop...
A New Quality Publishing
Badland Publishing
BHU Publishing
The Cell Block
DC Book Diva
Envisions Publishing
Fast Lane Entertainment
Final Round
Gorilla Convict …
G Street Chronicles
Harris Publications
King Poe Publishing
LC Devine Media, LLC
RJ Publications
Sisyphen Tasks, LLC
Street Life Publishers
Wahida Clark Presents…

## VIRTUAL ASSISTANTS

See personal assistants.

## WEBSITE BUILDERS

Help From Beyond the …
Inmate Pen Pal Connection
Inmate Web Sites

## WOMEN ONLY

The Action committee…
Battered Women's Justice..
California Coalition for…
Chicago Books to Wo…
Hasting Women's Law…
Justice Now
Keeping the Faith: The …
Ms. Magazine
NASW Women's Council..
National Clearinghouse…
Off Our BacksPower Inside
Our Bodies, Ourselves
Women and Prison: A Site women.

## WRITER/AUTHOR

21st Urban Editing…
4orPlay Publications, LLC
APWA
Ashley Rice Collection
Association for Authors…
The Blue Book of Grammar...
The Blumer Literary…
Children's Book Insider
Cimarron Review
Damamli Publishing…
Defiore and Company
The Editorial Eye
Everyday Letters For Busy People
Freebird Publishers
Freelance Success
Get Your Poetry Pub…
Hawkeye Editing

Helping Hands' Inmate Publishing
Hollywood Scriptwriter
Infinity Publishing
Info
INKWELL Magazine
LeNoir Publications
Locus
Manning Document Publishing
Manuscripts To Go
The Marshall Project
Occasion Gallerie
Outlook on Justice
Pen American Center
The Poetry Wall…
Poets and Writers, Inc
The Poet Workshop
Poetry Society of America
The Prison Journal
Professional Press
Randy Radic
Rolling Stone – Letters
Sagewriters
Sanders, Louise S.
Sentinel Writing Competitions…
Shotcaller Press
Sinister Wisdom, Inc
Skin&Ink Letters
Slipstream Poetry contest
SMOOTH Fiction
SMOOTH Talk
Teachers and Writers Corroborative
The ThreePenny Review
Thousands Kites
Tri-State Legal Journal
Women and Prison: A Site.
Writer's Digest
Writer's Guild of America
Writer's Market Companion
Writing To Win

**Writers/Authors**: Also see Literary
Pubs/Reviews, Literary Agents and
Book Publishers for more
information!

## ZINES

Bernard Library Zine…
East Bay Prisoner Support
Fanorma Society Pub…
Worker's Vanguard

# GENERAL RESOURCES

## #

**4orPlay Publications, LLC**
4100 Esters Rd. #286
Irving, TX 75038

This is an urban publishing company. They publish books like "East Boogie," "Silence is Secrecy," "4orPlay" and more.

They are now also accepting manuscripts for possible publishing. They want you to send the first 7 chapters, which are not to exceed 70 pages, and a synopsis.

Website: 4orPlayPublications.com

**4strugglemag**
PO Box 97048
RPO Roncesvalles Ave.
Toronto, Ontario M6R3B3 Canada

Views, thoughts and analysis from the hearts' and minds' of North American political prisoners and friends. **FREE** to prisoners.

**21st Street Urban Editing and Publishing**
P.O Box 2033
Perris, CA 92572

This is an urban editing and publishing company, here are their submission guidelines: manuscript must be complete/ query letter/ synopsis/ submit first 5 chapters only – will request completed version if interested/ complete contact information including name, address, contact number, and email/ use 10 pt. font, double spaced, in manuscript-style format/ email all submissions/ allow up to 30 days for a response/ any manuscript not following these guidelines will be discarded immediately.

Website: 21streeturbanediting.com

Email: submissions@21streeturbanediting.com.

**60 Minutes**
51 West 52nd Street
New York, NY 10019

News show.

## A

**A Book You Want**
PO Box 16141
Rumford, RI 02916

Barbara runs this company. She does all kinds of services for a fee; search for hard- to-find books, internet searches, etc. Write/Send SASE for **FREE** information.

**About That Life**
PO Box 517
Saranac, MI 48881

Resources for inmates and families. New Islam book available now -- "A Moor's Point of View" Koran. 101 Q&A's broken down. Send $20 check or money order.

**ACCESS SECUREPAK**
P.O. Box 50028
Sparks, NV 89435

Package company that sells food, CDs, shoes, clothes, appliances and more. Write for a **FREE** catalog.

**Comment:** This used to be my go - to place for packages. They had a bunch of mixtapes I just had to have, plus the food is priced decently, so I usually went to them. However, they no longer sell mixtapes (I read in PLN that they got sued) and I couldn't get shoes from them for pretty much all of 2016. Weird. I've also heard recently that they're making some lame substitutions that folks are not happy with. - - Mike

**Acclaimed Books**
Box 180399
Dallas, TX 75218-0399

Can provide full color scripture greeting cards, Mother's Day cards, Father's Day cards, general assorted cards and holiday cards for as low as 5¢ per card.

**A Jailhouse Lawyer's Manual**
435 West 116th Street
New York, NY 10027

A Jailhouse Lawyer's Manual publishes three books designed to explain your rights and help you navigate the justice system.

The JLM 10th Edition (2014) ($30 for prisoners) is the main volume of the JLM. It is a 1288 page book that can help you learn about: Researching the law; Appealing your conviction or sentence; Receiving medical care; Protecting your civil liberties; and more.

The Immigration Supplement (2011) ($5 for prisoners) is a 116 page supplement to the main JLM containing information about immigration and the rights of non-citizens.

The Texas Supplement (2014) ($20 for prisoners) is a 408 page supplement to the main JLM containing information specific to Texas state prisoners.

To order the JLM, send a check or money order (no credit cards or stamps accepted) and your shipping information. For institutional prices or questions, contact jlm.board.mail@gmail.com.

**A Million Thoughts Publishing**
POB 872002
Mesquite, TX 75187

This company publishes/sells urban books, they ship **FREE** to prisoners. Write for a catalog.

**A New Quality Publishing**
POB 589
Plainfield, NJ 07061

This is an urban book company that ships **FREE** to prisoners. All books are $15; write for a catalog.

**ACLU of Idaho**
P.O. Box 1897
Boise, Idaho 83701

The ACLU of Idaho is a non-partisan organization dedicated to the preservation and enhancement of civil liberties and civil rights. They believe that the freedom of press, speech, assembly, and religion, and the rights to due process, equal protection and privacy, are fundamental to a free people.

Phone Number: 208.344.9750
Fax: 208.344.7201

**ACLU LGBT Rights / AIDS Project**
125 Broad St, 18th Floor,
New York, NY 10004

Experts in constitutional law and civil rights, specializing in sexual orientation, gender identity, and HIV/AIDS.

**ACLU of Montana**
PO Box 1317
Helena, MT 59624

Phone Number: (406) 443-8590

**ACLU NPP**
915 15th St. NW, 7th Fl.
Washington, DC 20005

The National Prison Project seeks to create constitutional conditions of confinement and strengthen prisoners' rights through class action litigation and public education. Their policy priorities include reducing prison overcrowding, improving prisoner medical care, and eliminating violence and maltreatment in prisons and jails, and minimizing the reliance on incarceration as a criminal justice sanction. The Project also publishes a quarterly journal, coordinates a nationwide network of litigators, conducts training and public education conferences, and provides expert advice and technical assistance to local community groups and lawyers throughout the country. The NPP is a tax exempt foundation funded project of the ACLU Foundation.

**ACLU of Northern California**
39 Drumm Street
San Francisco, California 94111

The ACLU of Northern California works to preserve and guarantee the protection of the Constitution's Bill of Rights.

Phone Number: 415-621-2493

## ACLU of San Diego & Imperial Counties
P.O. Box 87131
San Diego, CA 92138-7131

The ACLU of San Diego and Imperial Counties fights for individual rights and fundamental freedoms for all through education, litigation, and policy advocacy.

Phone Number: 619-232-2121

## ACLU of Texas
Executive Director: Terri Burke
P.O. Box 8306
Houston, TX 77288

Phone Number: (713) 942-8146
Web: http://www.aclutx.org

## ACLU of Texas Prison and Jail Accountability Project
P.O. Box 12905
Austin, TX 78711-2905

Phone Number: (512) 478-7300

## ACLU Reproductive Freedom Project
Reproductive Freedom Project
American Civil Liberties Union
125 Broad Street 18th Fl
New York, NY 10004-2400

Phone Number: 212-549-2633
Website: aclu.org/reproductive-freedom

## ACLU of Washington
901 Fifth Avenue, Suite 630
Seattle, WA 98164

## Actual innocence: When Justice Goes Wrong and How to Make it Right

This book describes how criminal defendants are wrongly convicted, DNA testing and how it works to free the innocent, devastating critique of police and prosecutorial misconduct. The book is 403 pages, $16.00, and can be bought from Prison Legal News.

## Adams State University
208 Edgemont Boulevard
Alamosa, CO 81102

They offer associates, bachelors, and master's degrees via correspondence. Since they are regional accredited, their credits should transfer to most colleges and universities in the United States. Three credit hour courses cost around $500 plus books.

## Adopt An Inmate
PO Box 1543
Veneta, OR 97487

"We began our work after a family member was incarcerated, and discovered how difficult it is for to remind the world and these caught in the grip of the justice system that both accused and adjudicated are human.
To provide relief, comfort, and hope to these facing judgement, and to help these sentenced emerge from prison while, knowing they are part of a larger family that loves and cares for them.
Ultimately, Adopt an Inmate would seek to change prison itself from an arbitrary system of cruelty and punishment to one which internally recognizes the humanity of its charges and treats them accordingly such that recidivism is rare, rather than a feature of our current system's design.
Write for an Inmate Survey for you to complete and return. Please note that the survey is net an "application" that requires approval. We do not collect fees or put ads on our site for individual inmates. We want every inmate to be "adopted," and match people up based on their location and gender preference, and any ether useful information we have from both adopter and adoptee. Your name will be added to the waiting list as seen as we receive your completed survey (if it indicates you want to be adopted). We are a small organization and don't have the resources to reply in writing to your completed survey. If you have further questions, please write to us and include a SASE
If you can provide email addresses of family member(s) or friend(s), we will add them to the mailing list for our quarterly newsletter, which is produced for family and advocates of inmates. You can also give them our contact info, adoptaninmate.com, and info@adoptaninmate.org.
We welcome your stories from the inside for our "Letters From Prison" series, poems, and artwork, including "welcome" banners' for our website, to publish on our website. A SASE is most appreciated if you require a reply. We love to get jail, but please be

3

patient and expect delays in our replies while we are focusing on getting all of you adopted."

## Advanced Criminal Procedure in a Nutshell

This book is designed for supplemental reading in an advanced criminal procedure course on the post-investigation processing of a criminal case, including prosecution and adjudication. It's 505 pages, $43.95, and can be bought from Prison Legal News.

## AFCS
2161 Massachusetts Ave
Cambridge, MA 02140

They have a 24-page quarterly magazine titled "Outlook on Justice." It's $2 per year.

## Affordable Inmate Calling Services

Keeping you connected while saving you money! No hidden fees. One flat monthly rate. **FREE** setup with referral information. No charges to add/remove numbers. No transfer fees. 100% BOP compliant! Currently only available for federal prisoners. 450 minutes, 2 numbers; $15 + tax a month. Additional numbers for $1.50 each. Get $5.00 for each referral you send to them. Additional minute plans available.

Inmates Contact: inmates@alcsllc.net or 303-214-0097
Families Contact: www.aicsllc.net, bllling@aicsllc.net, or 866-645-9593

## AFSC Prison Watch Project
89 Market Street, 6th Floor
Newark, NJ 07102

American Friends Service Committee Prison Watch Project has published the Fifth Edition of the Survivors Manual: Surviving in Solitary, by Bonnie Kerness, (June 2012, 94 pages), which is **FREE** to prisoners and $3 for all others. This book is a powerful collection of voices from solitary, as people currently or formerly held in isolation vividly describe their conditions and their daily lives.

Phone Number: 973-643-3192
Website: afsc.org/story/survivors-manual-those-suffering-solitary

## Ahrony, Graham, & Zucker, LLP
## 401 Wilshire Blvd., 12th Floor PH
## Santa Monica, CA 90401

This is an appellate and post-conviction law firm. They specialize in appeals, Habeas Corpus Writs (Factual Innocence), parole hearings, SB 260 hearings, MDO hearings, re-sentencing, probation violations, rap sheet correction, prison and parole issues, 115 discipline issues, for California and federal courts. California cases only.

Unsolicited documents will NOT be returned.

Phone: 310-979-6400 or 310-288-0319
Website: AhronyGraham.com

## AIDS Law Project of Pennsylvania
1211 Chestnut Street, Suite 600
Philadelphia, PA 19107

Phone 215-587-9377
Website: http://www.aidslawpa.org

## AIDS Project of L.A.
1313 N. Vine Street,
Los Angeles, CA 90028

Resource guide for inmates living with AIDS called "Be Good to Yourself" that discusses nutrition, exercise and self-massage for people incarcerated. **FREE** to inmates.

## Aid to Inmate Mothers
PO Box 986
Montgomery, AL 36101-0986

AIM provides services to Alabama's incarcerated women with emphasis on enhancing personal growth and strengthening the bonds between inmate mothers and their children.

Phone Number: 334-262-2245
Website: inmatemoms.org

## AIDS ARMS Network, Inc
351 West Jefferson Blvd., Suite 300
Dallas, Texas 75208-7860

Supports victims.

Phone Number: (214) 521-5191

## AIDS in Prison Project
The Osborne Association
809 Westchester Ave.
Bronx, NY 10455

Brochures for HIV-positive people. Info hotline in English and Spanish. Also provides transitional housing with case management for recently released and ex-prisoners.

Phone Number: (718) 707-2600
Email Address: info@osborneny.org

## AIDS Treatment News
AIDS.ORG
PO Box 69491
Los Angeles, CA 90069

## AIM
765 McDaniel Street
Atlanta, GA 30310

An advocacy group for incarcerated mothers. AIM can provide helpful information for all women in prison who have children but can only provide social services in the Atlanta area.

Phone Number: (404) 658-9606

## Ajemm Brothers Greeting Cards
PO Box 10354
Albany, NY 12201

They sell greeting cards for all occasions and circumstances. Write/Send SASE for **FREE** information.

## AK Press
674-A 23rd St
Oakland, CA 94612

AK Press publishes and distributes a wide variety of radical literature and audio, many directly relating to prisoner and policing issues. Certain titles are written by prisoners themselves. Offers prisoners a 40% discount on any/all purchases. Distributes some Spanish language titles but do no have a Spanish language catalog.

Phone Number: (510) 208-1700.

## A&K Paralegal Service
13017 Westeria Dr. Suite 382
Germantown, MD 20879

15 years experience, specializing in prison litigation – single cell negotiation, ICC transfer, internet research, copies, sentence reduction/modification, parole

biography and more. "We have the winning strategies because we research each and every case effectively and efficiently." Any state, reasonable fees. Send SASE for brochure.

Phone Number: (240) 246-7857
Website: andkparalegal.com

## Alabama Prison Project
215 Clayton St
Montgomery, AL 36104

They sell a newsletter for $4 a year and will accept stamps for payment. Write/Send SASE for **FREE** information.

## Alba Morales
Florida Direct File Project
Human Rights Watch
350 5th Ave., 33rd Floor
New York, NY 10118

Were you under 18 at the time of your offense? Were you prosecuted in adult court in Florida? Human Rights Watch is conducting an investigation on how Florida prosecutors use direct file and how this process affects juveniles. If your case got to adult court in Florida via direct file, contact this person.

## Alaska Innocence Project
PO Box 201656
Anchorage, AK 99520-1656

Provides legal, educational, and charitable services to identify and exonerate individuals who have been wrongfully convicted in Alaska. AIP suggests and implements policies, practices and reforms that will prevent wrongful convictions and hasten the identification and release of innocent persons.

Phone Number: 907-279-0454
Website: alaskainnocence.org

## Alavi Foundation
500 Fifth Avenue, Suite 2320
New York, NY 10110

Write for more information to get **FREE** Qurans and Islamic Literature.

Phone Number: 212-944-8333.

## Alexander Byrd Optics
PO Box #1063

Richland, WA 99352

This is an eyeglass company that offers a single vision eyeglass special -- $36.99 plus S/H. Upgrade to transition by adding $69.99. Contact them on CorrLinks at: abyrdopticsligmail.com or write to receive order form and details.

## Alianza
PO Box 63396
Washington, DC 20009

They provide information on AIDS in Spanish.

## Alcoholics Anonymous General Service Office
PO Box 459 Grand Central Station
New York, NY 10163

**FREE** information, local phone lines, meetings in most communities.

Phone Number: (212) 870-3400

## Allegheny County Department of Aging
441 Smithfield Street Building
Pittsburgh, PA 15222

They provide a broad range of human services for persons over age 60, the handicapped and the needy. Information and referral, care management, senior center-based services, senior employment program, home help, congregate/home delivered meals and emergency housing assistance. *Former* **inmates**, victims and families living in Allegheny County may obtain additional program information and assistance in accessing services by contacting the Department of Aging.

## Alice S Grant Publications, INC
PO Box 28812
Greenfield, WI 53228

## All Of Us or None
C/O Legal Services for prisoners with children
1540 Market St. 490
San Francisco, CA 94102

Organizes to build political power and restore the civil and human rights of people who have been in prison or who have past convictions. Write for more information.

Phone number: 415-255-7036 X337
Website: allofusornone.org.

## Alliance of Incarcerated Canadians/Foreigners in American Prisons (AICAP)
C/O NMB INC
131 Bloor St. W. Ste 200
Toronto, M5R 2E3 Canada

Phone Number: (416) 968-9417

## Amachi Program
Big Brothers and Big Sisters of Greater Charlotte
3801 E Independence Boulevard, Suite 101
Charlotte, NC 28205

Phone Number: 704-910-1301

## Amazing Facts
PO Box 909
Roseville, CA 95678

Write for a **FREE** sample magazine and **FREE** bible studies.

## Ambler Document Processing
Jane Eichwald
PO Box 938
Darien, CT 06852

They type manuscripts and screenplays (only) with prices starting at $2 per page. Write/Send SASE for **FREE** information.

Phone Number: (203) 849-0708
Website: jane@protypeexpress.com

## American Bar Association
321 N. Clark St.
Chicago, IL 60610

Allows site-users to search for a list of resources available in their state, including pro bono or inexpensive lawyers, help in dealing with lawyers, legal information, and self-help materials.

Phone Number: (800) 285-2221

## American Bible Academy
P.O. Box 1627,
Joplin, MO 64802 – 1627

**FREE** English and Spanish Bible Correspondent Courses for prisoners. All courses are 120 pages in length.

## American Bible Society

1865 Broadway,
New York, NY 10023 – 7505

Works directly with correctional chaplains. If your chaplain needs **FREE** Scriptures (**FREE** Bibles in English and Spanish) for your facility, please contact.

## American Civil Liberties Union
**Capital Punishment Project**
201 West Main Street, Suite 402
Durham, N.C. 27701

Partnering with ACLU affiliates in death penalty states, and with coalition partners nationally, CPP promotes both abolition and systemic reform of the death penalty.

Phone Number: 919-682-5659

## American Civil Liberties Union
125 Broad Street, 18th Fl.
New York, NY 10004

Helps prisoners who are facing discrimination because they are transgender, lesbian, gay, bisexual or have HIV.

## American Correctional Association
206 N. Washington Street
Alexandria, VA 22314

Sells publications, including self-help books.

Phone: (703) 224-0000
Website: aca.org

## American Diabetes Association
ATTN: Center for Information
1701 North Beauregard Street
Alexandria, VA 22311

You can also call their Center for Information and Community Support at 1-800-DIABETES (1-800-342-2383). Their hours of operation are Monday - Friday, 8:30 a.m. - 8:00 p.m. EST.

Website: diabetes.org

## American Indian Art Magazine
7314 East Osborn Drive
Scottsdale, AZ 85251

For more than 35 years, American Indian Art Magazine has been the premier magazine devoted exclusively to the great variety of American Indian art. This beautifully illustrated quarterly features articles by leading experts, the latest information on current auction results, publications, legal issues, museum and gallery exhibitions and events.

Phone (480) 994-5445
Website: aiamagazine.com

## American Magazine Service
1042 Fort Union Blvd. #387
Midvale, UT 84047

Phone Number: (800) 428-6242

## American Motorcyclist Association
13515 Yarmouth Dr
Pickerington, OH 43147

## American Rehabilitation Ministries
P.O. Box 1490
Joplin, Missouri 64802-1490

They offer bible correspondence courses **FREE**.

## AMFAR AIDS Research
120 Wall Street, 13th Floor
New York, NY 10005-3908

## Amitabha Buddhist Society of USA
650 S. Bernardo Ave.
Sunnyvale, CA 94087

Phone Number: 408-736-3386

## Amnesty International, USA
5 Penn Plaza
New York, NY 10001

Phone Number: 212-807-8400
Email: aimember@aiusa.org

## Amnesty Mid-Atlantic Regional Office
600 Penn. Ave., SE 5th Floor
Washington, DC 20003

Phone Number: (202) 544-0200

## Anatomy of Hip-Hop Volume 1

This book is by Erskine Harden and Anthony Booth, AKA "The Hip-Hop Connoisseurs", and available from Lavish Life 88 Entertainment.

Synopsis: Enough of the ungratifying fables, and bold face lies about the movement called Hip-Hop! This book takes the reader on an in depth history lesson from the mid-70s to the present, including every element of the genre, giving the much deserved respect to the founding fathers (Kool Herc, Grandmaster Caz and Busy Bee to name a few), in a secure effort to educate the youth and misinformed. This book shines a light on aspects of hip-hop that unfortunately aren't usually mentioned; breakdancing, graffiti and fashion were just as important in the foundation, along with rap music. We, the Hip-Hop Connoisseurs, decided to tell the whole story from conception, growth, and dominate existence of the global phenomenon we love and respect.

Comment: As a Hip-Hop connoisseur myself, reading this book was like going on a fun ride down Hip-Hop Memory Lane. Things I haven't thought about in years were mentioned; as were a few things I didn't know about - - both events and artists. There are a few things I think could and should have been included, but it's probably due to where I'm from verses where they're from - - our respective underground scenes, etc. For example, Brothe Lynch Hung and C-BO were not mentioned at all. Both Bo and Lynch were fuckin' with Master P at his hottest, and Bo was on two songs on Pac's "All Eyes On Me". There probably could have been more on Mac Dre, too, being he's had such a huge impact on the culture where he's from and beyond.

Any fan of hip-hop will appreciate the ride this book takes you on; any upcoming hip-hop artist should be obligated to read it as a history lesson. I don't know everything, but it's at least 95% accurate. Good read. - - Mike

## An End to Silence
College of Law
4801 Massachusetts Ave NW
50th Street Building
Washington, DC 20016

The Project on Addressing Prison Rape is committed to eliminating sexual abuse for individuals in custodial settings. The Project on Addressing Prison Rape is a leader in addressing the implications and implementation of the Prison Rape Elimination Act of 2003 (PREA) and its forthcoming standards. Since 2000, the Project on Addressing Prison Rape has provided training; technical assistance and legal guidance for correctional agencies, advocates and survivors who want to effectively prevent, respond and eliminate sexual abuse in custodial settings.

Phone Number: 202-274-4385

## Angel Tree; IDSI
510 SE Delaware Ave
Bartlesville, OK 74003

Through Angel Tree, a program of prison fellowship, your child(ren) can receive gifts at Christmas, with love, from you. To share the love of Jesus Christ, church volunteers buy gifts and give them to your child(ren) with age-appropriate presentation of the gospel. Contact your prison's chaplain to request a participation form, or write to them directly.

## The Angolite
Louisiana State Penitentiary
Angola, LA 70712

To subscribe, send your name and address to:
The Angolite
C/O Cashier's Office Louisiana State Prison
Angola, LA 70712 USA

The Angolite is the inmate published and edited magazine of the Louisiana State Penitentiary (Angola) in West Feliciana Parish, Louisiana. Each year, six issues are published. Subscriptions are $20 per year.

Phone Number: (504) 655-4411

Comment: This is an award winning magazine of interest to Louisiana State Prisoners. It's a very high quality publication, even if its target demographic is limited. - - Mike

## Angres, Robert, L. Esq.
4781 E. Gettysburg Ave., Suite 14
Fresno, CA 93726

Personalized service at reasonable rates with office conveniently located in the Central Valley near seven California State Prisons. 14 years of experience in criminal law. Contact for post-conviction remedies – CA cases only.

Phone Number: (559) 348-1918

## Another Chance 4 Legal, LLC
PO Box 78
Mullins, SC 29574

"AC4L is the only **FREE** interactive post-conviction web site! Ask us any question you have about post-conviction or prison issues for **FREE** at: ANOTHERCHANCE4LEGAL@GMAIL.COM.

Trust in AC4L to solve your legal query. AC4L has been doing effective, affordable and credible post-conviction litigation with over 25 years of experience."

Phone Number: 843-879-8361

## Anti-Recidivism Coalition
448 South hill Street, Suite 908
Los Angeles, CA 90013

This company goes hard for California lifers and are working hard on things like getting our family visits back, getting better good time credits for all Cali inmates and supporting things like SB260, SB261 and SB9. They are always in need of signatures for their Petitions. Please write and ask how you can assist, and/or have your family go to safetyandrehabilitation.com. This organization is supported by actors Jake Gyllenhaal and Jonah Hill, and rappers like Nas and Common, plus many other people.

Raising Awareness Through Art...

"Our team at ARC has been looking for ways to bring new supporters into this movement, to help us fund reentry programs, housing, mentoring, job training and support for people coming home. Having seen the incredible artists behind the walls, we are proposing doing a huge and high profile art auction to raise funds and awareness for this movement. It would not be your traditional art auction, it would be at a major museum, with celebrity art auctioneers, and the ability to raise tremendous awareness, bring in massive press and a considerable amount of funding, all to benefit a nonprofit organization and also the artist inside (50/50). We have many board members with powerful connections in the art world, and believe art from inside could sell for 5x or 10x what it traditionally would get.

So, if you are interested in having us sell your pieces to benefit a nonprofit organization as well as support your rehabilitation and reentry, please send a photograph of your piece. (if you're able) or contact us to receive your piece and figure a starting amount for the auction."

Phone: 213-955-5885

Comment: This is a great organization /movement. They cannot be supported enough. By the time this is published, the Raising Awareness Through Art auction written about will probably have taken place. HOWEVER, if you are interested in participating, I suggest you write them and ask about it anyway. They may do more than one, especially if the one they do is successful. In addition, if enough people ask about it, they may do something more consistent to help us prison artists, like start a great website that is supported by their celebrity contacts and board of Directors. We can petition" them to do something like this for us, just like they petition for law/policy changes. Think outside the box! –Mike

## Appalachian Prison Book Project
P.O. Box 601
Morgantown, WV 26507

Sends **FREE** books to: KY, MD, OH, TN, VA, and WV only.

Website: aprisonbookproject.wordpress.com.

## Appellant Research Services, LLC
PO Box 0337
Emmett, MI 48022

These guys do research. Write/Send SASE for more information.

## Appeals Law Group
33 E. Robinson Street, Suite 220
Orlando, FL 32801

"Aggressive appellate and post-conviction relief attorneys. We specialize in U.S. Supreme Court Appeals, Direct Federal and State Appeals, post-Conviction Relief Motions, Writs of Habeas Corpus, Writs of Error Coram Nobis, Motions for Certificate of Appealability, Pardon and Commutation Petitions, Clemency Petitions, Sentencing Petitions, 2254 and 3355 Petitions, 3582 Petitions, Federal Drugs -2 Motions, Rules 60(b)Motions, Actual Innocence Claims. Call today for a **FREE** consultation!

Due to high volume, unsolicited documents will not be returned. Serious financial inquiries only. Payment plans available on a case by case basis. This is an advertisement for legal services. Offices located in FL, NC and MN."

Phone Number: 1-800-411-6898

## APWA
198 College Hill Road
Clinton, NY 13323-1218

The American Prison Writing Archive Is an Internet-based, non-profit archive of first-hand testimony to the living and working conditions experienced by Incarcerated people, prison employees and prison volunteers. Anyone who lives, works or volunteers Inside American prisons or jails can contribute non-fiction essays, based on first-hand experience: 5,000 word limit (15 double-spaced pages); a signed APWA permission-questionnaire must be Included In order to post on the APWA. All posted work will be accessible to anyone in the world with Internet access. For more Info and to download the permissions-questionnaire, go to www.dhinitiative.org/projects/apwa, or write to the address above.

## Archipelago
13017 Wisteria Dr. #310
Germantown, MD 20874

This company offers affordable gifts inmates can buy and have sent to loved-ones. Send a first-class stamp for their catalog.

## ARE Prison Program; Assn
215 67th St
Virginia Beach, VA 23451

They send religious books to prisoners. Write/Send SASE for more information.

## Arab-American Anti-Discrimination Committee
1732 Wisconsin Ave, NW
Washington, D.C. 20007

Provides advice, referrals, and full-time staff attorneys to help defend interest of the community. Also serves as a vital clearing house of accurate information on Arab culture and history for education and school systems.

Phone Number: 202-244-2990

## Arizona Justice Project; Arizona State University
MC 4420
411 N. Central Avenue, Suite 600
Phoenix, AZ. 85004-2139

The Arizona Justice Project is primarily a volunteer-based organization that reviews and assists in cases of actual innocence, or cases in which a manifest injustice has occurred. Accepts both DNA and non-DNA cases and represents indigent Arizona inmates whose claims of innocence have gone unheeded. Conducts post-conviction DNA testing in cases of forcible rape, murder, and non-negligent homicide cases, shaken baby syndrome and arson and other cases where the testing might demonstrate actual innocence.

Phone Number: 602-496-0286
Website: azjusticeproject.org

## Arrested: What to Do When Your Loved One's in Jail

Whether a defendant is charged with misdemeanor disorderly conduct or first-degree murder, this is an indispensible guide for those who want to support family members, partners or friends facing criminal charges. It's 240 pages, $16.95, and can be bought from Prison Legal News.

## Arrest-Proof Yourself

This essential "how not to" guide written by an ex-cop explains how to act and what to say when confronted by the police to minimize the chances of being arrested and avoid additional charges. Includes information on basic tricks that police use to get people to incriminate themselves. It's 288 pages, $14.95, and can be bought from Prison Legal News.

## Arts in Criminal Justice

Phone Number: (215) 685-0759
info@www.artsincriminaljustice.org
www.artsincriminaljustice.org

## Asheville Prison Books Programs
67 N. Lexington Ave.
Asheville, NC 28801

Sends **FREE** reading material to indigent inmates in facilities in North Carolina, South Carolina, Georgia and Tennessee. Can sometimes provide books in Spanish. Donations gladly accepted!

Email Address: prisonbooks31@hotmail.com

## Ashley Burleson
Attorney and Counselor at Law
1001 Texas Ave., Suite 1400
Houston, TX 77002

Post-conviction State and Federal Habeas Corpus, Parole Representation, and Family Law for Texas inmates.

## The Asian Classics Institute (ACI)
PO Box 144,
New York, NY 10276, USA

Phone Number: (212) 475-7752
Website: www.acidharma.org
E-mail: aci@world-view.org

## Ashley Rice Collection
Blue Mountain Arts, Dept. WHIM
P.O. Box 4549
Boulder, CO 80306

This is a greeting card company. Send card material that is light, lively and very original with SASE.

## Assisting Incarcerated Muslims (AIM)
PO Box 460
Clayton, LA 71326

Phone Number: (318)757-0557

## Association For Research & Enlightenment
c/o Prison Outreach,
215 67th St,
Virginia Beach, VA 23451

Books about the life and work of Edgar Cayce, meditation, and reincarnation. Prisoners are limited to one book every two months.

## Association of Happiness for All Mankind
4368 NC Highway 134,
Asheboro, NC 27205

Spiritual books and newsletter.

## Association for the Treatment of Sexual Abusers
4900 S.W. Griffith Drive, Suite 274
Beaverton, Oregon 97005, USA

Phone Number: (503) 643-1023
E-mail: atsa@atsa.com

## Athens Books to Prisoners
30 1st Street
Athens, OH 45701

Email:athensbooks2prisoners@gmail.com
Website: athensbookstoprisoners

## Atkins House
313 E. King Street
York, PA 17403

Atkins House, located in York, PA, is a residential and outpatient treatment center for women offenders providing counseling for drug, alcohol and sexual abuse as well as victim awareness, life skills and mother-child transition after incarceration. Atkins House is a non-profit service organization.

Phone Number: (717) 848-5454
Website: www.atkinshouse.org

## A Touch of Light
300 Lenora Street, Ste #311
Seattle, WA 98121

A Touch of Light is a not-for-profit organization dedicated to featuring and promoting the artistic creations of Captive Artists (TM.) from around the world. Our missions is to use the Arts to promote social change, help the families of prisoners stay connected to their incarcerated loved ones, and create second chances for prisoners being released with little or no support. Our organization is building both nationally and internationally, working to promote prisoner-created Captive Art of any kind. We represent sculpture, jewelry, paintings, sketch art, woodcraft, metalcraft, music, and more -- any form of medium of Art is accepted.

Submissions of Captive Art to A Touch of Light are featured at no charge on our website and promoted aggressively via social media. We build a page unique to each artist, featuring each piece they submit, a picture of themselves (or an image of their choice, if they prefer not to submit a personal photo), and a short biography about their involvement in the arts, what inspires them, and any additional information they wish to share about how the art has impacted their time in prison and what they hope to achieve. We already feature a number of Captive Artists on our website, atouchoflight.org, and are seeking additional artists in the United States and internationally who would be interested in working with us to represent their art.

Interested artists of their family/supporters can contact us for more information at: info@atouchoflight.org or 206-245-4037. Please note that while we are not presently able to accept calls directly from incarcerated persons, we are more than happy to speak with family or other supporters calling on an artist's behalf. Our office hours are Mon-Fri, 10 am -1 pm EST.

**Comment:** This guy sent me his info to include him in my Directory. It looks like something decent, but I've written him once or twice and haven't received a response. I hope it's legit, but I haven't had the chance to have my team check out his website so proceed with caution. - - Mike

## ATS
Box 530367
Henderson, NV 89053

Inmate services. Great prices. Photos of models, pen pals, copy service, VIP services, gifts to friends and family, internet searches, etc. Send SASE for complete info.

## Attorney Ivy McCray

Civil Litigation, Family Law, Probate, Appeals. "If you don't see it here, let's talk."

Phone Number: (415) 306-0888

## Auto Restore
3 Burroughs
Irvine, CA 92618

Auto Restorer is a monthly how-to newsletter with in-depth articles and step-by-step photos on auto and truck restoration, written by people experienced and knowledgeable on the subject. It serves as a forum for readers to interact with experts and other restoration enthusiasts. 12 issues for only $20.

Phone Number: (949) 855-8822
Website: autorestoreermagazine.com

## Auto Week
1155 Gratiot Avenue
Detroit, Michigan 48207-2997

This is the #1 auto magazine in the USA. It's $29.95 for a 1-year subscription; 26 issues per year.

Phone Number: (313)446.6000
Website: http://www.autoweek.com

## B

## Badland Publishing
POB 11623
Riviera Beach, FL 33419

They sell urban books. Write for a catalog.

Phone Number: (561) 842-4746
Website: badlandpub.com.

## Baitil Salaam Network
675 Village Square Dr. LL1,
Stone Mountain, GA 30021.

If you are a woman needing transitional housing or a place to parole, call or write.

Phone Number: 770-255-8500
Email:haleem1@aol.com

## Baker Industries
184 Pennsylvania Avenue
Malvern, PA 19355

Baker Industries is a unique 501(c)(3) nonprofit organization that promotes a work rehabilitation program employing an overlooked and underutilized workforce population. "We focus specifically on four groups of vulnerable adults: people with disabilities, recovering substance abusers, individuals on parole, and homeless persons, and give them all the opportunity to learn the importance of a solid work ethic in a real work environment."

Phone Number: 610-296-9795
Website: http://bakerindustries.org.

## Ball State University Correctional Education Program
Online and Distance Education
Carmichael Hall Room 200
Muncie, IN 47306

Offers degree programs for men incarcerated at Pendleton Correctional Facility.

Phone Number: 765-285-1593

## Banks, Jeffery S., Esq.
485 West 5th St.
Reno, NV 89503

Post conviction filings, appeals, writs, petitions, placement, immigration removal and more.

Phone Number: (775) 324-6640

## Bard Prison Initiative
Bard College
 PO Box 5000
Annandale-on-Hudson, NY 12504-5000

Phone Number: 845-758-7308
Website: bpi@bard.edu

**Comment**: This is a terrific in - prison college program. They offer a select group of New York state prisoners the opportunity to earn college degrees for FREE - - Mike

## Bar None
PO Box 1
Arcata, CA 95518

Info packets available from Bar None: Art & Radio & Writing, Civil case forms, Complaints channel to conditions of confinement, Distance Learning, Latest legal, Legal resources, LGBT Resources, LIRA Brief & Decision, Medical Advocacy / Hep C, acupressure, Medical surveys, Parole Resources, Pro Bono Lawyers, Resource Guide, Sample Advocacy Letters, SHU, Transfers.

Email: barnonearcata@gmail.com

## Bare Expressions
PO Box 1043
Mathis, TX 78368

This company sells stationary supplies and more. Write/Send SASE for more information.

## Barrios Unidos
1817 Soquel Avenue
Santa Cruz, CA 95062

## Baseball America
4319 South Alston Avenue, Suite 103
Durham, NC 27713

Since 1981, Baseball America has been finding the prospects and tracking them from high school to the big leagues. That means you get comprehensive coverage every step of the way, from high school and colleges to the minors and the majors. 26 issue subscription for $92.95.

## Basket Boutique
PO Box 352
Sparta, TN 38583

They offer unique and affordable gift baskets. For a FREE brochure, send a SASE.

## Battered Women's Justice Project
1801 Nicollet Ave South, Suite 102
Minneapolis, MN 55403

Provides assistance/info to battered women charged with crimes and to their defense teams. **FREE** newsletter. No direct legal representation.

Phone Number: 800-903-0111 x1
Website: bwjp.org

## Battling The Administration

This book, by David Meister, is an "inmate's guide to a successful lawsuit." Written from a prisoner's perspective, this book is excellent for both the first-time litigant and the old hand when it comes to navigating the strange world of prisoner's rights. Its 555 pages, $34.95, and available from Wynword Press.

## BAUS Books Circulation
2020 Route 301
Carmel, NY 10512

Buddhist books, only $1-2 postage fees. Write for list of books.

## Bayou La Rosa
302 NJ St. #13
Tacoma, WA 98403

Native American Indian support.

## B.B.P.D.
PO Box 248
Compton, MD 20627

This company offers over 1,000 books. From the look of their list it seems as if they offer all the most popular genres and titles amongst prisoners: Classical African Civilizations; Antebellum/General History; Civil Rights/ Black Liberation; African/Indigenous Religions; Modern Black Religious Thought; Islam Related; Religious "Anthropology"; Spiritual Philosophy;

13

Political Issues; Masonry/Secret Societies/Conspiracies; Sociology/Family/Love; Psychology/Education; General Health and Nutrition; Business/Economics/Motivational; Law/Reference; Street Life/ General Literature; Prison Life; Languages; Books in Spanish; and even some specials/used and out-of-print titles. The prices are typical. They also offer a few urban style magazines. Send them a SASE for a **FREE** catalog

Website: bookstoinmates.com

## Bead and Button
Kalmbach Publishing Co.
21027 Crossroads Circle
P.O. Box 1612
Waukesha, WI 53187-1612

This magazine is full of materials, ideas, supplies, and accessories. 6 issues for $26.95.

Phone Number: 1-800-533-6644
Website: beadandbutton.com

## The Beat Within
PO Box 34310
San Francisco, CA 94134

"We're a nonprofit organization that publishes the writing and artwork of incarcerated youth throughout the country. The Beat Withins' mission is to provide incarcerated youth with consistent opportunity to share their ideas and life experiences in a safe space that encourages literacy, self-expression, critical thinking skills, and healthy, supportive relationships with adults and their community. Outside of the juvenile justice system, The Beat Within partners with community organizations and individuals to bring resource to youth both inside and outside of detention. We are committed to being an effective bridge between youth who are locked up and the community that aims to support their progress towards a healthy, non-violent, and productive life.

The last few pages of our publication are dedicated to writing from incarcerated individuals outside of juvenile hall, which includes writing from jails, camps, ranches, prisons, etc., which is where your writing can be published.

We understand that in the past, subscriptions have been free. We regret to inform you that with such high demand, the cost of publication and postage, and the nature of our business (non-profit supported by a limited number of grants), we can no longer provide free subscriptions. Should you desire a specific copy or a subscription, please inquire and send a SASE. You can receive a **FREE** issue, however, if you are published. If published, we will send you the issue your writing appears in.

We look forward to reading your work and passing along your words to the youth and all Beat readers!"

## Behive Books Behind Bars
c/o Weller Book Works
607 Trolley Square
Salt Lake City, UT 84102

Sends books to prisoners in these western states only: AZ, CA, CO, ID, MT, NM, NV, OR, UT, WA, and WY.

## Bee Smith
PO Box 60156
San Diego, CA 92166

Copies law and does web searches.

## Caught: The Prison State and the Lockdown of American Politics

This book is by Marie Gottschalk. Its $35.00 and available from Princeton University Press at press.princeton.edu. Here are a few blurbs…

"Caught may well be the best book on this subject to appear in decades." -- Glen C. Altschuler, Huffington Post

"Devastatingly persuasive." -- Stephen Lurie, Los Angeles Review of Books

"A searing critique of current Incarceration policies and prevailing approaches to prison reform… Caught is brilliantly argued, breathtakingly capacious In Its Informational reach, and intellectually bold. A stunning achievement." -- Mary Falnsod Katzenstein, Cornell University

## Ben and Ima Prayen
PO Box 211
Raymond, WA 98577

They provide **FREE** bible study for new believers.

## Benjamin Ramos, Attorney at Law
705 E Bidwell, Suite 2-359

Folsom, CA 95630

Experienced Habeas Corpus practitioner admitted in all California state and Federal courts. Gives parole representation, challenges bogus gang validation and more.

Phone: 916-358-9842

## Berean Prison Ministry
PO Box 761
Peoria, IL 61652

They provide **FREE** bible study material and KJV bibles.

## Barnard Library Zine Collection
3009 Broadway
New York, NY 10027

They provide photocopies of zines written by women with an emphasis on zines by women of color. The more specific your question or request the better the assistance they will be able to provide.

## BESTGEDTUTOR.COM

Expert online tutoring, has coached over 1200 students to successfully pass the GED, and specializes in biggest challenges on GED tests -- math and essay writing. Personalized training for about $1.00 a day. Contact Janice Chamberlin.

## Better People
3711 NE Martin Luther King, Jr. Blvd.
Portland, Oregon 97212

Better People is an established employment and counseling program solely dedicated to helping individuals who have legal histories find, keep and excel in well-paying jobs with fair, decent employers. Servicing the Portland metropolitan area.

Phone Number: (503)281-2663
Website: betterpeople.org

## Bhandari, Suresh
Top Floor Udar Guest House
Malvi 313203
Udaipur, India

This company can hook you up with a woman in India who wants to get married. Send them a photo, a full matrimonial bio and $5.

## BHU Publishing
55 Public Square, Suite 1500
Cleveland, OH 44113

They publish/sell urban books. Write for a catalog.

Phone Number: (216) 856-4340.

## Bible Helps
PO Box 391
Hanover, PA 17331

They provide **FREE** bible tracts.

## Black and Pink
Community Church of Boston
Black & Pink
614 Columbia Rd
Dorchester, MA 02125

A volunteer organization that lists queer and transgender prisoners on a pen-pal website, distributes a monthly newsletter of primarily queer/trans prisoner writing, and advocates for specific prisoner needs when possible while also working to abolish the Prison Industrial Complex as a whole.

Phone Number: 617-942-0217

## Black Star Music & Video
PO Box 449
New York, NY 10027

These guys sell urban books and mags. Send them a SASE and ask for their one-sheet book/mag list.

Phone Number: 888-252-2595

**Comment:** I need you to write these guys and request books by Mike Enemigo and The Cell Block. I need them to realize how many people want my/our books so they will sell them through their company. - - Mike

## Blackstone Career Institute
1011 Brookside Rd, Ste 300,
P.O. Box 3717
Allentown, PA 18106 – 3717

Low-cost paralegal course by mail.

"Blackstone Career Institute's distance learning program enables students to learn about the law and the paralegal field by studying at their own pace and at their facility. No computer, proctors, or facility institutors are required. Upon completion, graduates will have obtained a paralegal certificate and gained knowledge they can use now and in the future.

Here are five reasons why Blackstone is the best choice for paralegal training:

1. Students learn from the best.

Blackstone is nationally accredited by the Accrediting Commission of the Distance Education Accrediting Commission (DEAC), regionally accredited by the Middle States Commission on Secondary Schools, and has been privately licensed since 1984. Our 915-clock hour program meets the educational requirements to sit for the Certified Paralegal/Certified Legal Assistant (CP/CLA) Exam sponsored by the National Association of Legal Assistants and administered at testing centers across the country. As BCI Graduate A. Vasquez says, "I have gained knowledge and practical skills that will help me far into the future. BCI sets the standard for excellence in paralegal education."

2. Students start their own library.

As part of the tuition, students receive ten volumes of our Modern American Law series as well as four more exclusive Blackstone study units to guide them through their studies. But that's not all; students will also receive two additional reference resources to assist them throughout the program -- the Blackstone Law Glossary and Merriam-Webster's Dictionary of Law — as well as the book Writing to Win: The Legal Writer upon graduation.

3. Students get everything they need -- for less.

Blackstone's Paralegal Studies Certificate Program remains one of the most reasonably priced in the country. Everything students need to graduate is included with their tuition -- textbooks, study guides, exam services, and student support delivered through the mail. We also offer a BCI Interest-free payment plan, and our career program is approved for GI Bill Education Benefits.

4. Students decide when and where to study.

Students set their own schedule and progress at their own pace. They can finish as quickly as they wish or take the full two years they are permitted.

5. Students prepare to follow their dream!

Our paralegal program will give students the opportunity to enhance their knowledge, help others, or acquire new skills they can use in the future. In addition to our Modern American Law series, we have included research, ethics, and Job search skills in our 915-clock hour program.

With BCI, incarcerated individuals will be taking an important step towards a better future. Send for full information now!"

Phone Number: 800-826-9228
Website: blackstone.edu

**Comment:** While not very challenging casework, they are a quality, dependable and affordable company that offers correspondence courses to prisoners. -- Mike

## BLADE Magazine
700 E State St.
Iola, WI 54990

BLADE Magazine – The World's Number One Knife Publication.

Phone Number: (715)445-2214
Website: www.blademag.com

## The Blue Book of Grammar and Punctuation

A guide to grammar and punctuation by an educator with experience teaching English to prisoners. It's 110 pages, $14.95, and can be bought from Prison Legal News.

## Book'em
P.O. Box 71357
Pittsburgh, PA 15213

**FREE** books to PA prisoners only. Focuses on educational and non-fiction books.

## Books Between Bars
1117 Peach Street
Abilene, Texas 79602

Books Between Bars can provide one book every 60 days to Texas prisoners who write to request it. Each request takes 7-14 days to process. The requests can be fiction, nonfiction, biography, self-help, parenting religious, etc. Write for a copy of an application form, which needs to be filled out and sent back to Books Between Bars.

## Book to Prisoners
c/o Left Bank Books
92 Pike St., Box A
Seattle, WA 98101

Request by subject. Very limited legal and religious material available. Cannot pay postage to prisons in CA, or to prisoners requiring "New Books."

Phone Number: (206) 442-2013
Website: bookstoprisoners.@live.com

## Books To Prisoners
c/o Groundwork Books,
0323 Student Center
La Jolla, CA 92037

**FREE** books. Serves all states

## Books Through Bars
4722 Baltimore Ave
Philadelphia, PA 19143

Provides books to prisoners in PA, NY, NJ, DE, MD, WV, and VA. Please request books by subject or topic rather than by specific titles. They generally have little to no legal materials.

Phone Number: (215) 727-8170
Website: booksthroughbars.org

## Books Through Bars – NYC
c/o Bluestockings Bookstore
 172 Allen St
New York, NY 10002

Ships to prisoners nationwide. Specializes in political and history books. Occasionally sends fiction and educational books. No religious literature. Donations of stamps and cash are appreciated.

## Books Through Bars / Providence
c/o Paper Nautilus Books
5 Anqell St.
Providence, RI 02906

Nationwide. Write with a list of subjects you're interested in.

## Boston University Prison Education Program
808 Commonwealth Avenue
Boston, MA 02215

Phone: (617) 353-3025
website: prisoned@bu.edu

**Comment:** This is another terrific in-prison college program that's allows Massachusetts state prisoners to earn associates, bachelors, and master's degrees for free. This is a terrific organization. – Mike

## Bottled Thoughts
P.O. Box 110752
Carrollton, Texas 75011-0752

Bottled Thoughts is committed to providing unique gifts to express your love for that special someone. "Our customer service department aims to achieve the highest possible standard in all that we do. Our number one priority is helping our customers execute a heartfelt reaction with creativity and flair."

Your message will be beautifully printed on themed paper and placed in a glass bottle with sand and sea shells, tied with a ribbon. They also have a few gifts you can order, as well as gift packages for children. Write/Send SASE for more information.

Phone Number: 1-877-705-0425

## Boulevard
PMB 325
6614 Clayton Rd
Richmond Heights, MO 63117

## Brain, Child
The Magazine for Thinking Mothers
PO Box 714
Lexington, VA 24450

## Branlettes Beauties
PO Box 5765
Baltimore, MD 21282

Our prices are simple:

1-4999 photos = 0.45 cents each
5000+ photos = 20% discount

1-9 catalogs: $3.00 each (+SASE)
10 catalogs: $25.00 + SASE (4 stamps)

Select your favorite:

White catalogs (60 volumes), Black catalogs (60 volumes), Asian and Latino catalogs (60 volumes). Please state what style photos -- provocative poses or nude.

**FREE** catalog? Yes! Just send us 2 US Forever stamps and a SASE and we will send to you one nude or BOP-friendly sample catalog (1 per customer) with 84 gorgeous girls in full color. Act now as this offer will not be around long!!

Branlettes Breathless Beauties Bag: A random selection of 50 of the rare and exotic. Yes, 50 beauties all posing just for you! Plus 2 of our finest color catalogs! Only $19.99! Did you read that right? Yes, only $19.95 for 50 of Branlettes breathless beauties (please specify nude of BOP-friendly)! Plus two of our finest color catalogs **FREE**! (You pick the volumes) Our regular shipping/handling policies apply.

All sales are final! Each catalog has 84 gorgeous ladies to choose from. High quality prints on 4X6 glossy photo paper.
Shipping and handling:

Due to various prison policies regarding how many pictures can be sent in one envelope, our policy is as follows:

01-5 photos - $1.00 per envelope
06-15 photos - $1.50 per envelope
16-25 photos - $2.00 per envelope

Our simple policies: Special requests are not permitted and all models are of legal age. Due to tremendous time and cost answering letters, unless you are placing an order or a question regarding your order, we will not reply to any other questions. A SASE is required for any inquiries or concerns!

You and you alone are responsible for your selections being allowed into your facility! Know your institution's policies as to what image content is allowed. Returned orders are non-refundable. They will be held for 14 calendar days in order for you to send self-addressed stamped envelopes (3 first-class stamps per envelope), with a street address for every 20 pictures. All returned images held after 2 weeks will be resold and we will return to our stock.

All payments are by institutional checks or US postal service or Western Union money orders! These payments are processed immediately and shipped in less than 3-4 weeks. Any other company money orders delay shipment 8-10 weeks or until that money clears our bank. Yes, we deal with people that are, while in prison, still trying nickel and dime scams.

**Bridge Project**
Center For Community Service and Justice
4501 N. Charles St
Baltimore, MD 21210

**FREE** brochure of contemplative meditation.

**Brilliance Audio, INC**
1704 Eaton Dr.
Grand haven, MI 49417

These guys sell gifts. Write/Send SASE for more information.

**Brothers Against Banging Youths**
632 Harden Dr. #2
Inglewood, CA 90302

"We are an alternatives option program for 'Youth at Risk. The mission of Brothers Against Banging Youths (B.A.B.Y.) is to prevent and deter young people in the South Los Angeles area from joining gangs by educating them and their parents on the recruitment strategies of gangs, as well as provide counseling services to those 'At Risk' youth whom are prime targets of gang recruitment. Additionally, we will provide before and after school activities for youth, thus keeping them engaged in positive activities and programs decreasing the likelihood of them turning to gangs to participating in other negative activities."

**BTP**
92 Pike Street Box A
Seattle, WA 98101

Books on spiritual growth and Edgar Cayce. Prisoners may receive 2 **FREE** books per month. Request books by topics not titles.

Email Address: bookstoprisoners@cs.com

**Buck Co. Secretarial**
PO Box 8
Shippack, PA 19474

This is a typing service. Write/Send SASE for more information.

Phone Number: (610)287-0122
email: eenewwhart@verizon.net.

## Bud Plant Comic Art
PO Box 1689
Grass Valley, CA 95945

The Bud Plant Incredible Catalog is published 3 times a year. These 248-page monsters cover everything from the upper levels of the underground to mainstream comic art. The first copy is three bucks (redeemable on your first order) and then continuously as long as you keep ordering from them. They also send smaller update catalogs every couple of months. Many of the comics included in Beyond Cyberpunk! are available through *Bud Plant*. The service is prompt, the calls are toll-free, and your comics come tightly wrapped in protective paper. *Bud Plant* also carries lots of adult comics and how-to art books.

Phone Number: 1-800-242-6642

## Buddhist Association of the United States
Chuang Yen Monastery
2020, Route 301
Carmel, NY 10512

**FREE** books.

Phone: 845-228-4287
Email:book@baus.org

## Buddhist Churches of America
1710 Octavia Street
San Francisco, CA 94109

Phone Number: (415) 776-5600 x11
Website: buddhistbookstore.com

## Bust The Move
PO Box 1026
Point Pleasant Beach, NJ 08742

"Our mission is to serve the incarcerated and their family members by providing quality merchandise, competitive prices and excellent customer service. We have designed our catalog and website to be your one stop shopping resource by including clothing, underwear, outerwear, domestic items, footwear, personal products, electronics, books and a wide selection of food. We also offer a gift section so that an inmate can send a gift to a love one for that special occasion, or just because."

Phone Number: 800-676-0286
Email: btmcustserv@aol.com

## Butler Legal Group
818 18th St. NW, Suite 630
Washington, DC 20006

These guys will type your briefs or help you write a motion. Write/Send SASE for more information.

Phone Number: (202)223-6767

## Butterwater, LLC
PO Box 669
Mathews, NC 28106

Catalogs:
The Butterwaters 1&2: $2.50 or 5 stamps (with SASE). **FREE** online!
The Butterwaters 3&4: $2.50 or 5 stamps (with SASE). **FREE** online!
The Butterwaters 5: $2.50 or 5 stamps (with SSE). **FREE** online!
The Butterwaters 6: $2.50 or 5 stamps (with SASE).
The Butterwaters 7: $2.50 or 5 stamps (with SASE).
White Pages 1: $2.50 or 5 stamps (with SASE).
White Pages 2: $2.50 or 5 stamps (with SASE).
Pink 11 (nude): $5.00 or 10 stamps.
Pink 12 (nude): $5.00 or 10 stamps.
The "B" side: **FREE** online.

Send SASE today for a **FREE** catalog!

4X6 color photos. One dollar ($1.00) per photo. Minimum order is ten (10) photos for ten dollars ($10.00), plus $2.50 shipping and handling. Orders can be shipped as per facility rules (5 per envelope, etc...). We do not accept cash. Please send money order or Corr. facility check. Use order form or create your own list.

Website: thebutterwaters.com

## Buzz Photo
PO Box 255
Webb City, Missouri 64870

E-mail: buzzphotos045@yahoo.com
Legal name: Brandon Persinger

## The Buzz Report

Subscribe today and get all of your sports scores and lines delivered conveniently to your email inbox, every day! Add infosportzzbuzz.com to your Corrilinks email subscription list for info on how to get The Buzz!

## C

### California Coalition for Women Prisoners
1540 Market St. Suite 490
San Francisco, CA 94102

Runs action center and produces newsletter "The Fire Inside."

### California Families to Abolish Solitary Confinement

Website: http://www.abolishsolitary.com/

### California Innocence Project
California Western School of Law Institute for Criminal Defense Advocacy
225 Cedar Street
San Diego, CA 92101

Cases Accepted:
DNA and non-DNA cases from Southern California: Imperial Co., Kern Co., Los Angeles Co., Orange Co., Riverside Co., San Bernardino Co., San Diego Co., San Luis Obispo Co., Santa Barbara Co., and Ventura Co., sentence of more than 3 years will consult.

Phone Number: 619-525-1485

### California Lifer Newsletter
PO Box 277
Rancho Cordova, CA 95741

CLN is a newsletter published six times per year, with reviews of the latest published and unpublished state and federal cases concerning parole issues and many more topics of interest to prisoners. CLN for prisoners are $30 or (60 First Class Forever Stamps) per year.

Phone Number: (916) 402-3750
Website: lifesupportalliance.org

### California NORML
2215 R Market St. #278
San Francisco, CA 94114

This is a national organization working to change laws that criminalize marijuana sales, possession, and use. Write/Send SASE for more information.

Phone number: (415)563-5858
Website: canorml.org

### California Prison Focus
1904 Franklin Street, Suite 507
Oakland, CA 94612

"Our newsletter magazine is primarily by prisoners and for prisoners, their friends and families. The current and past issues are available **FREE** for download. You can also receive a paper copy at your home (or send one to your relative or friend in prison). We request a donation of $20 or more for four issues to help cover editing, printing, and mailing costs. Write/Send SASE for more information."

Phone Number: (510) 836-7222
Website: www.prisons.org

### Callsfromwalls.com
PO Box 459
New Milford, NJ 076461

**FREE** 60 minute trial offer! Call or write for details!

Phone Number: (888) 828-6168

### The Camelback Group
1220 South Almar Circle
Mesa, AZ 85204

Phone number: (602) 535-1298
thecamelbackgroup .com

This is an internet public relations group that will help remove unwanted, negative postings for when you are Googled, etc.

### Campaign to End the Death Penalty
P.O. Box 25730
Chicago, IL 60625

A national grassroots abolitionist organization that works with prisoners, family members and organizers. CEDP publishes a newsletter called The New Abolitionist (**FREE** to prisoners).

Phone Number: (773) 955-4841.

### Carbone, Charles

PMB 212
3128 16th St.
San Francisco, CA 94103

This is an attorney that specializes in prison rights. CA only.

Website: prisonerattorney.com

## Carolina Caselaw
5401 A South Blvd #281
Charlotte, NC 28217

Write/Send SASE for more information.

## Casa Frontera Visitor Center
PO Box 70407
Riverside, CA 92513

These guys provide transportation (by reservation) from Ontario Airport to the CA Institution for Women, as well as provide visiting families with proper visiting attire, information, light refreshments, and a place to rest.

Phone Number: (909)597-7845.

## Cash for your Stamps
P.O. Box 687
Walnut, CA 91788

Get the highest return for all your stamps. Send SASE for brochure.

## Catalogchoice.org
They list thousands of catalogs on their website. Some cost money but others are **FREE**.

## Catholic Charities USA
P.O. Box 17066
Baltimore, MD 21297-1066

They provide a host of services including emergency services, food banks, soup kitchens, home delivery meals, clothing assistance, disaster response, transitional housing, temporary shelter, counseling and mental health services, substance abuse treatment and recovery services and adoption services.

Phone: 703-549-1390
Website: www.catholiccharitiesusa.org

## CDCR, Office of the Ombudsman
1515 S. St. Room 540 North

Sacramento, CA 95811

## Celebrity Tattoo
Attn: Brian
11730 West Colfax Ave.
Lakewood, CO 80215

These guys buy and sell tattoo line art. Write for more information.

Phone Number: (720)436-2912
Website: findthattattoo.com

## The Cell Block
PO Box 1025
Rancho Cordova, CA 95741

The Cell Block is an independent multimedia company with the objective of accurately conveying the "street/prison" experience and LIFE$TYLE, with the credibility and honesty that only one who has lived it can deliver, through literature and other arts, and to entertain and enlighten while doing so.

Available titles:

- The Best Resource Directory For Prisoners, by Mike Enemigo
- The Art & Power of Letter Writing for Prisoners, by Mike Enemigo
- Thee Enemy of the State, by Mike Enemigo
- Conspiracy Theory, by Mike Enemigo
- BASic Fundamentals of The Game, by Maurice "Mac BA$" Vasquez
- Loyalty & Betrayal, by Mike Enemigo & Armando Ibarra
- A Guide to Relapse Prevention for Prisoners, by Charles Hottinger Jr.
- Money IZ the Motive; By Mike Enemigo & Ca$ciou$ Green
- Money IZ the Motive 2; By Mike Enemigo & Ca$ciou$ Green
- Mob$tar Money; By Mike Enemigo & Ca$ciou$ Green
- Block Money; By Mike Enemigo & Ca$ciou$ Green
- Underworld Zilla, by Mike Enemigo & Guru
- How to Hustle & Win: Sex, Money, Murder; by Mike Enemigo & Guru
- This is my Life, by Crow

Website: thecellblock.net
Facebook: facebook.com/thecellblock.net
E-mail: thecellblock.net@mail.com

CorrLink: thecellblock.net@mail.com

### The Cell Door Magazine
149850 Road 40.2
Mancos, CO 81328

Mission Statement: Articles are written by prisoners or people who are closely associated with the prison experience. Our goal is to acquire readers who choose Cell Door for its quality and educational/entertainment value, learning in the process that prisoners are intelligent, personable, talented human beings.

Comment: This mag is a 5.5 x 8.5 color booklet with articles and art by prisoners. It's nice and it's FREE. You can also submit writings and art of your own, too. - - Mike

### CELLBLOCKART.COM

Email: frank@mesaart.net

Comment: These guys are not connected to my company, The Cell Block. I'ma have to check them out, though. They offer fine art prints, digital prints, posters (12" X 18"), and t-shirts. - - Mike

### The Cellings of America

This is PLN's first anthology and it presents a detailed "inside" look at the workings of the American criminal justice system. It's 264 pages, $22.95, and can be bought from Prison Legal News.

### Cell Workout

This book, written by a former prisoner (L.J. Flanders), is a bodyweight training guide designed for use in a prison cell without the need for actual weights. This program is suitable for any age, ability and fitness level and promises results for everyone who tries it. There are step-by-step instructions of how to do the exercises, photographs and sample workouts to follow. The aim of this book is to benefit the physical and mental health of people in prison and outside. Get the body you want -- inside and out!

Cell Workout is 215 pages, and $35 from Prison Legal News. Inmates can pay with new postage stamps, or check, money order, or credit card.

### CellPals!
PO Box 13278
Las Cruces, NM 88103

### Cell Shop
PO Box 1487
Bloomfield, NJ 07003

This company sells gifts that prisoners can buy for their loved-ones. Write/Send SASE for more information.

Phone Number: (973)770-8100
Website: cellshopgiftshop.com

### Centerforce
PO Box 415
San Quentin, CA 94964

Community-based organization providing HIV-related education for inmates.

### Center for the Children of Incarcerated Parents
P.O. Box 41-286
Eagle Rock, CA90041

Provides FREE educational material for incarcerated parents and their children, as well as therapeutic services, family reunification services, and related information. Many services are FREE.

### Center for Constitutional Rights
666 Broadway, 7th Fl.
New York, NY 10012 NY

CCR is a non-profit legal and educational organization committed to the creative use of law as a positive force for social change and dedicated to advancing and protecting rights guaranteed by the US Constitution.

Phone Number: 212-614-6481
Website: ccrjustice.org

### Center for Disease Control's National Prevention Information Network
P.O. Box 6003
Rockville, MD20849-6003

Provides info, publications, and technical assistance on HIV/AIDS, STDs, and TB M-F 9am-6pm (Eastern Time.) Se habla espanol. General medical info hotline on ALL medical questions is 1-800-CDC-INFO.

### Center for Health Justice

900 Avila Street, Suite 301
Los Angeles, CA 90012

This is a hotline for prisoners with HIV and Hep; collect calls accepted.

Phone Number: 213-229-0985
Website: centerforhealthjustice.org

## Center on Wrongful Convictions
Northwestern University School of Law
375 East Chicago Avenue
Chicago, Illinois 60611-3069

Phone Number: (312) 503-2391
Website: law.northwestern.edu

## Central Texas ABC
PO Box 7187
Austin, Texas 78713

They have D.I.Y. legal booklets and some anarchist literature. Write/Send SASE for more information.

## Centro Legal De La Raza
3022 International Blvd, Suite 410
Oakland, CA 94601

Provides many services for immigrants and helps with detention cases.

## Centurion Ministries, INC
221 Witherspoon
Princeton, New Jersey 08542-3215

A private non-profit organization that will ONLY consider cases of wrongful conviction in the U.S. and Canada that involve a sentence of life in prison or death. CM does NOT consider self-defense or accidental death cases. Do not call or email, ONLY submit a written summary of the facts of a case and the facts supporting your innocence. All letters are responded to. Submit a case for consideration to the address listed. For submission procedures and guidelines:
http://www.centurionministries.org/criteria.html

Phone Number: (609) 921-0334

## Chandra Yoga Resources
1400 Cherry St
Denver, CO 80220

FREE books on devotional yoga and mantra meditation.

## Channel Guide Magazine
PO Box 8501
Big Sandy, TX 75755

This TV guide offers daily schedules for over 120 channels, weekly TV best bets, over 3,000 movie listings, TV crossword, Sudoku, celebrity interviews and more. For one year (12 Issues), send $30.00 check or money order.

Phone Number: 866-323-9385

## Cheaters
4516 Lovers Lane, Suite 104
Dallas, TX 75225

Comment: You know she's cheating, bruh. You might wanna write these fools. - - Mike

## Cheryl Johnson Company
215 W. Tray St. #2004
Ferndale, Ml 48220

This is a non-nude photo company. You can buy your Cheryl Johnson Company catalog packed with plenty of sexy, non-nude women for $9.00. Cheryl offers various specials when you buy her catalog – photos in bulk, etc.

## Chicago Books to Women in Prison
4511 N. Hermitage Ave
Chicago, IL 60640

FREE books to women prisoners in AZ, CA, CT, FL, IL, IN, KY, MO, & OH.

## Chicago Innocence Project
205 West Monroe Street, Suite 315
Chicago, IL 60606

The Chicago Innocence Project investigates cases in which prisoners may have been convicted of crimes they did not commit, with priority to murder cases that resulted in sentences of death or life without parole.

Phone: 312.263.6213

## Chican@ Power and the Struggle for Aztlan

This book is by a MIM (Prisons) Study Group. It costs $20 + s/h ($10 for prisoners), and the production costs are huge. Chican@ Power is an invaluable resource for anyone struggling for liberation of the internal semi-colonies of the United States. They don't want anyone to be prevented to read the book for lack of funds, so they're asking anyone who can contribute $10 for their copy, or more to cover for others, to please step up and send in your donations today! If your facility allows, you can send them stamps. To send a check, they need to send you their instructions so write and tell them first. Send to Under Lock & Key.

### Chicken Soup for the Prisoner's Soul
P.O. Box 7816
Wilmington, DE 19803

Inspirational seminars and books. Seminar: "A Winning Recipe for Success Behind Bars." Books include: "Chicken Soup for the Prisoner's Soul," "Serving Productive Time," Serving Time, Serving Others" and "Chicken Soup for the Volunteer's Soul."

Phone Number: 302-475-4825
Website: www.tomlagana.com

### Children of Incarcerated Parents
PO Box 41-286
Eagle Rock, CA 90041

Works to stop intergenerational incarceration. Provides resources in three areas: education, family reunification, and services for incarcerated parents and their children.

### Children's Book Insider, LLC
901 Columbia Road
Fort Collins, CO 80525

Questions & Information: 970-495-0056

### Christian Pen Pals
PO Box 11296
Hickory, NC 28603

### Christian Prison Pen Pals
P.O. Box 333
Inverness, FL 34451

Personal ads start at $10. Send SASE for complete info.

### ChristianPrisonPenPals.org

Post your profile immediately, just like any dating website, and edit it any time of day or night. Friends and family can register, pay for your ad with PayPal, and upload your photos, address, description and bio.

### CIPS -- Certified Internet Provider Service

4733 Torrance Blvd. #738
Torrance, CA 90503

"Submit your request, we search, locate and download the most current/accurate information available on the Internet and mail it back to you within three (3) BUSINESS DAYS from receipt of your order. We use the most popular search engines: Yahoo, Google, Bing, Ask, Lycos, AOL, Web Crawler, etc. Now just $15 for 10 page minimum for black and white print. Add 50 a page for color print.

### Citizens Against Recidivism
P.O. Box 9 - Lincolnton Station,
New York, NY 10037.

They work to achieve the restoration of all the rights of citizens among people in prison or jail, as well as those who've been released, in collaboration with other community and faith based organizations.

Phone Number: (212)252-2235
Website: www.citizensinc.org

### Citizens United for Alternatives to the Death Penalty
PMB 335
2603 Dr. Martin Luther King Jr. Hwy
Gainesville, FL 32609

The Religious Organizing Against the Death Penalty Project seeks to build a powerful coalition of faith-based activists. Nationally, it works with official religious bodies to develop strategies and to promote anti-death penalty activism within each faith tradition. At the grassroots level, the Project links with individuals and faith communities, establishing "covenant" relationships to foster local abolition efforts.

Phone Number: (800) 973-6548

### Citizens United for Rehabilitation of Errants
### National CURE
PO Box 2310
Washington, DC 20013-2310

CURE is a membership organization. "We work hard to provide our members with the information and tools necessary to help them understand the criminal justice system and to advocate for changes."

Phone Number: 202-789-2126
http://www.curenational.org

**The Classroom and the Cell: Conversations on Black Life in America**

This book is written by Mumia Abu-Jamal and co-authored by Columbia University professor Marc Lamont Hill. It's available from Third World Press -- TWPBooks.com. For Mumia's commentaries, visit www.prisonradio.org. Keep updated on him at freemumia.com. Encourage the media to publish and broadcast Mumia's commentaries and interviews.

**Cleveland Career Center**
C/O Edward Little
1701 E 13th St.
Cleveland, OH 44114

These guys have a project called PROES – providing real opportunities for ex-offenders to succeed. PROES focuses on immediate employment, augmented with support services, and they work in conjunction with employment solutions programs of Alternatives Agency, Inc., a halfway house for formally incarcerated individuals.

Phone number: (212) 664-4673

**CNA Entertainment, LLC**
PO Box 185
Hitchcock, TX 77563

"Hey there! We are a visual media entertainment mail order LLC that distributes photos of a large variety of models to the prison population across the country. We currently have over 180 non-nude catalogs with a variety of different themes. We also offer custom printing and personal photo reproduction. For more information about any of our services or products, please drop us a line and we will fill you in. Hope to hear from you soon and have a great day."

Website: CNAEntertainment.com
Email: CNATexas@live.com

**Comment**: This company has a lot going on - - pictures, custom calendars, bookmarks, 20 - photo "proof" sets, and more, all with bad bitches on them. This is one of the biggest, most serious non-nude photo companies I've seen and they are well organized. - Mike

**Coalition for Jewish Prisoners**
1640 Rhode Island Avenue NM
Washington, DC 20036

**Coalition For Prisoner's Rights Newsletter**
Box 1911
Sante Fe, NM 87504-1911

Prisoners' Rights - Prison Project of Santa Fe. Monthly newsletter **FREE** to currently and formally incarcerated individual and family members. Stamps and donations needed.

Phone Number: (505) 982-9520

**College Level Exam Program**
CN 6600
Princeton, NJ 08541

College credits for self-taught knowledge.

**College In Prison**

Written by Bruce Michaels, this book is $14.95 and can be purchased at barnsandnoble.com.

**Colorado Innocence Project**
Wolf Law Building | 401 UCB
2450 Kittredge Loop Drive
Boulder, Colorado 80309

Phone Number: 303-492-8047
Website: colorado.edu/law/academics/clinics/colorado-innocence-project

**Colorado Criminal Justice Reform Coalition**
1212 Mariposa St., #6
Denver, CO 80204

The mission of the Colorado Criminal Justice Reform Coalition is to reverse the trend of mass incarceration in Colorado. They also strongly oppose the for-profit, private prison industry and its presence in Colorado.

Phone Number: (303) 825-0122
Email: info@ccjrc.org

**Colossal Book of Criminal Citations**
c/o Barkan Research
PO Box 352
Rapod River, MI 49878

3700+ citation references for Supreme, Circuit, District and State courts; Sample Federal and State; Jury instructions; District court addresses; 100+ topics; 500+ legal definitions. Prisoner price is $54.95. You can also order the PDF file online at Barkanresearch.com for $19.95.

## Columbia Human Rights Law Review
Attn: JLM Order
435 West 116th Street
New York, NY 10027

The *JLM* Eighth Edition main volume is $30. The *Immigration & Consular Access Supplement* is $5. The books may be ordered together, or either book may be ordered separately. First-class shipping is included in both prices. **They do not accept postage stamps as payment.**

Phone Number: (212) 854-1601

## Columbia Legal Services, Institutions Projects
101 Yesler Way, Suite 300
Seattle, WA 98104

Phone Number: 206-382-3399
Website:www.columbialegal.org

## Cosmic Cupid
PO Box 383
Cookville, TN 38503

This is a worldwide pen-pal newsletter. Ads are only 10¢ per word.

## Commentary Magazine
165 East 56th St.
New York, NY 10022

## Committee for Public Counsel Services Innocence Program
Lisa Kavanaugh, Program Director
CPCS Innocence Program
21 McGrath Highway, 2nd floor
Somerville, MA 02143

Phone Number: 617-623-0591
Website: lkavanaugh@publiccounsel.net

## Community Alliance on Prisons
PO Box 37185
Honolulu, HI 96837

A coalition that focuses on alternatives to incarceration, prison reform legislative issues, community education, and effective interventions for Hawaii's non-violent offenders.

## Compassion Works for All and Dharma Friends Prison Outreach Project by mail:
Compassion Works for All
Attn: Anna Cox
PO Box 7708
Little Rock, Ar. 72217-7708

Website: JUSTUSFRIENDS.org

## Complete GED Preparation

This useful handbook contains over 2000-GED-style questions to thoroughly prepare students for taking the GED test. It offers complete coverage of the revised GED test with re- testing information, instructions and a practice test, its 922 pages, $24.99, and can be bought from Prison Legal News.

## Con-Art
PO Box 61
Lankin, ND 58250

Want to see your arts and crafts? These guys specialize in selling work by incarcerated people. They accept all art, from any institution. Contact Colten Pede or Kellie Warner.

Phone: 701-331-2518

## CONPALS / InmateConnections.com
465 NE 181st Ave, 0308
Portland, OR 97230

"92% response rate! 75,000 hits daily! A+ rating with the BBB!

Ready to go online? Sign up now! Choose the basic webpage for $45 and get your first-contact emails all year long! Or, choose the Deluxe Webpage for $65 and got ALL your emails from everyone, including friends and family, all yearlong!

We offer personal, Legal, and Art & Business webpages.

Basic webpages are $45. Deluxe webpages are $65. Add another $10 to either page option and receive our brochure, 'How to Write a Better Pen Pal Ad'. You may submit your statement after you've had a chance to review our brochure. Brochure only available with purchase of web page and cannot be purchased separately.

Our service includes: Maximum 150 word statement and 2 scanned images displayed on your page; OR, Maximum 250 words statement on your page a 1 scanned image displayed on your page. Your professionally-designed web page on the inmateconnections.com website for a full year. Photo re-touching and enhancement. Personal web pages for male prisoners: Your linked photo placed in directories for state or federal prisoners; in age directory, alpha directory, photo gallery and in directory of newly-listed prisoners for the first 30 days. Your linked photo placed in directories for lifer, gay/bisexual, and death row prisoners, if applicable. Personal web pages for female prisoners: Your linked photo placed in directories for female prisoners and in our directory of newly-listed prisoners for the first 30 days. Legal web pages for male and female prisoners placed in our directory of legal web pages and newly-listed prisoners for the first 30 days. Art & Business web pages placed in directory of Art & Business web pages and newly-listed prisoners for the first 30 days. If you purchase a Legal or Art & Business web page it is recommended that you also purchase a personal web page. You will get more exposure to your Legal or Art & Business web page this way. With any of these options you will also get a printout of your page mailed to you, as well as Email messages (if any) mailed to you each week.

EXTRA EXPOSURE & MORE...

Front Page Placement: 4 weeks, $20; 12 week, $50; 1 year, $150. This gets your photo on the first page visitors see after entering the site.

Landing Page Placement: 4 weeks, $30; 12 weeks, $75; 1 year, $225. This gets your photo on the Home page.

Pen Pal Express: 4 weeks, $60; 12 weeks, $150; 1 year, $450. This gets your photo on the left-hand side of every page on the site.

Triple Exposure: 4 weeks, $75; 12 weeks, $175; 1 year, $525. This gets your photo in all three of the above areas!

Hit Counter: $20 per year. This is so you know how many visits your page has received.

URL Submission: $10 per year per URL. This is a hand submission of your URL to Google, Yahoo and MSN.

Language Translation: $15 per language. You get an auto-translation of your page into any major language so your page is in English AND other languages.

Linked Photo Rotation: $25 per year. Rotates 2 photos of you in the directories. Each additional photo added to rotation is $10.

Extra Words: $5 per 50 words.

Extra Photos: $10 per photo.

Personal Email Address: $60 per year. You get your own personal email address at yourconpals.com. Your family and friends can contact you without having to go to your web page. Email messages downloaded and mailed to you each week.

Payment Options: We accept personal checks, institution checks and money orders. We accept all major credit cards as well as PayPal. To pay these methods, you will need to have someone on the outside go to our web site to pay online. STAMPS: We accept new, unused stamps. When paying with stamps, please send as many books and whole sheets, and as few loose stamps as possible. Do not put tape on stamps. The easy formula for calculating payment for stamps; DOLLARS X 3 = NUMBER OF STAMPS. For example, a payment of $10 would be 30 stamps."

### Connecticut Innocence Project
c/o McCarter & English
Cityplace I
185 Asylum Street, 36th Floor
Hartford, CT 06103

Phone: 860-275-6140

### Conpics

"We print your pictures and send them to you! We print: Friends List, Social Media Profiles, and profiles of your friends on regular paper or photo paper! Wherever you have pictures, we can send them to you! Email us at conpics616@gmail.com for all pricing info.

### Conquest House
7101 7th Street NW
Washington, DC 20012

A Washington, DC- based ex-prisoner Christian ministry working with local church and area corrections officials to provide support and options to those affected by, or at risk of being affected by the criminal justice system. Through its Reintegration of Ex-Offenders project and its transitional housing center, CORM seeks to help ex-prisoners turn their lives around and avoid repeat criminal activity.

Phone: 202-723-2014
Website: www.conquesthouse.org.

## Conquest Offender Reintegration
PO Box 73873
Washington, DC 20056-3873

Federal prisoners, who want to be released to DC, write for an application for transitional housing.

Phone Number: (202)723-2014

## Cons Call Home
12748 University Drive
Fort Myers, FL 33907

They provide discount calls.

Toll Free 888-524-6151
Website:ConsCallHome.com
ConsCallHome.com®
A Millicorp™ Division

## Contemporary Verse 2
502-100 Arthur St.
Winnipeg, Manitoba R3B 1H3 Canada

## Contexts Art Project
4722 Baltimore Ave.
Philadelphia, PA 19143

The Contexts Collective hopes to represent to the public through the artwork of prisoners some of the realities of prison life; instill in the artist the sense of accomplishment and pride evoked by an exhibit of their own art; and raise money for Books Through Bars.

Phone Number: 215-727-8170 #5.
contexts@booksthroughbars.org

## Conveying Islamic Message Society
PO Box 834
Alexandria, Egypt

## Convictmailbag.com
Po Box 661
Redondo Beach, CA 90277

This is a pen pal website. They accept stamps for payment. Write/Send SASE for more information.

## Convicts for Christ
3651 N.W. 2nd Street
Fort Lauderdale, FL 33301

Inmate/prison advocacy. Individual & group counseling. Mail prison counseling, Christian & otherwise. Housing & job referrals.

Phone Number: 954-931-3292

## CORE
P.O. Box 1361
W. Sacramento, CA 95605

Self-help courses!

- Mindset Makeover: Changing your thoughts, change your ways!
- Biological Blueprint: What qualities you've inherited!
- Self-Awareness: Nurture your good qualities!
- Goal Gaining: Setting your goals and making them achievable!
- Perspective Personified: Seeing the world through more eyes!
- Dreaming in Color: Making your dreams a reality!
- Each completed course is awarded a certificate and letter of recognition. Each course is $20.95. Payment may be made by money order, institutional check, or stamps (3 complete books). For more info or to order, send SASE.

Email: CORE.educators@gmail.com

## Cornell Prison Education Program
Cornell University
115 Day Hall
Ithaca, NY 14853

Phone Number (607)255-4338
Website: http://cpep.cornell.edu/

## CorrectHelp
1223 Wilshire Boulevard, #905
Santa Monica, CA 90403

Phone Number: (310)399.8324

## Correctional Association of New York
2090 Adam Clayton Powell Blvd., Suite 200
New York, NY 10027

Have four working project groups: the Public Policy Project, the Women in Prison Project, the Prison Visiting Project, and the Juvenile Justice Project.

## Correctional Library Services
The New York Public Library
455 Fifth Avenue, 6th floor
New York, NY 10016

Phone Number: 212-592-7553

## COSIGN PRO
PO Box 1530
Port Richey, FL 34673

They provide "jailhouse services for the incarcerated." Send $10 to get their new catalog, which comes with 4 FREE sexy photos. The catalog has over 2000 photos of sexy girls to choose from, and offers only available through their catalog. They have an introductory offer of "25 (4x6) glossy photos for $20 of assorted provocative honeys" that they pick themselves. Cosign also offers a discount phone services, as well as a list of "over 40 female pen pals waiting to correspond with inmates" for $39.95. The females are USA based names and addresses. Must add $2 s/h for all orders.

Website: cosignentertainment.com

**Comment:** This company looks exactly like what Cold Crib and Prison Official were doing. Even the graphics of the catalog cover and the ad they put out look the same. I wouldn't be surprised if it was the same person (or people) doing it, just under a new name. - - Mike

## Council on American Islamic Relations
453 New Jersey Avenue, S.E.
Washington, DC 20003

Phone Number: 202.488.8787
Website: www.cair.com

## Cox, Harvey
PO Box 1551
Weatherford, TX 76086

This guy specializes in helping prisoners with transfers, grievances, and parole. Write for details.

Phone Number: (817) 596-8457

Website: prisonconsultant.com.

## CPCS Innocence Program
ATTN: Lisa Kavanaugh, Program Director
21 McGrath Highway, 2nd floor
Somerville, MA 02143

The purpose of the CPCS Innocence Program is to obtain exonerations for indigent Massachusetts state defendants who are actually innocent of the crimes of which they have been convicted. Defendants are actually innocent if no crime was committed or if someone else committed the crime in question.

Phone Number: 617-623-0591
Website: publiccounsel.net

## Crescent Imports & Publications
PO Box 7827
Ann Harbor, MI 48107

They sell tons of Islamic materials; books, oils, prayer rugs, jewelry, greeting cards and more. Write for a **FREE** catalog.

Phone Number: 1 800 521-9744
Website: halalcatalog.com.

## Criminal Defense Consultant
720 Washington St.
Standish Exec. Building 1$^{st}$ floor
Hanover, MA 02339

These guys specialize in getting sentences reduced or eliminated and have an 80% success rate. Write for more information.

Phone Number: (866)322-1906
Website: criminaldefenseconsultants.com.

## Criminal Injustice: Confronting the Prison Crisis

This remarkable anthology exposes our increasingly conservative and punitive justice system and uncovers the economic and political realities behind the imprisonment of large numbers of the working class, working poor and people of color. It's 374 pages, $19.00, and can be bought from Prison Legal New.

## The Criminal Law Handbook: Know Your Rights, Survive the System

This book was written by attorneys Paul Bergman and Sara J. Berman-Barrett. It breaks down the civil trial process in easy-to-understand steps so you can effectively represent yourself in court. The authors explain what to say in court, how to say it, etc. It's 528 pages, $39.99, and can be bought from Prison Legal News.

## Criminal-Law in a Nutshell, 5th Edition

Provides an overview of criminal law, including punishment, specific crimes, defenses and burden of proof. It's 387 pages, $43.95, and can be bought from Prison Legal News.

## Criminal Procedure: Constitutional Limitations, 7th Edition

Intended for use by law students, this is a succinct analysis of constitutional standards of major significance in the area of criminal procedure. It's 603 pages, $43.95, and can be bought from Prison Legal News.

## Critical Resistance - National
1904 Franklin St., Suite 504
Oakland, CA 94612

Critical Resistance works to build an international movement to end the Prison Industrial Complex by challenging the belief that caging and controlling people makes us safe. If you are not already familiar with this group, you should check 'em out. Please do not contact CR for legal help.

Phone Number: (510)444-0484

## Critical Resistance - NYC
451 West Street
New York, NY 10014

Phone Number: (212)462-4382
Website: criticalresistance.org/crnyc

## Critical Resistance – Southern Regional Office (reopened)
P.O. Box 71553
New Orleans, LA 70172

Phone Number 504-304-3784
Website: crsouth@criticalresistace.org

## Crossroads Bible Institute
PO Box 900
Grand Rapids, MI 49509-0900

They offer bible correspondence courses to inmates for FREE.

## Crusade 4 Hope
PO Box 27231
Raleigh, NC 27811

"Diamonds Beyond the Wall" by Miss Veronica. Poems and essays on prison life from a woman's view. Positive and uplifting. Send SASE for more information.

## Crystal Clear Express Images
PO Box 816
Rossville,GA 30741

Send SASE for FREE catalog and pic!

## Cutbank
University of Montana Dept. of English
Missoula, MT 59812

## DC Book Diva Publications
#245 4401 – A Connecticut Ave, NW
Washington, DC 20008

This is an urban book publishing company that sells books for $15 plus $3.99 for S/H, but she will sell them to prisoners for $11.25 + $3.99 S/H.

## DC Prison Book Project
PO Box 34190
Washington, DC 20043-4190

Sends donated reading material to prisoners and educates the public about issues surrounding prisoner education and literacy. Give about a 3 month turnaround time.

## DC Prisoners' Project
Washington Lawyers' Committee for Civil Rights and Urban Affairs
11 Dupont Circle NW, #400
Washington, DC 20036

Advocates for humane treatment and dignity of people charged under Washington, DC law -- even if you're being held anywhere in the federal system. They focus on health and medical issues, abuse, religious rights, mental Health, deaf issues and some parole matters.

Letters should provide as much detail and chronology of the situation as possible. They sometimes accept collect calls, but .mail is better

## D&D Worldwide Services, L.L.C.
P.O. Box 40081
Houston, TX 77240

Need help with your parole review? This company has 14 years of helping those in prison obtain another chance. Their parole plan shows you as a favorable candidate for parole!

Phone Number: (281)580-8844
Website: myparol.info

## Dallas Cowboys Football Club
1 Cowboys Pkwy
Irving, TX 75063

Write for **FREE** fan information on the team.

## Damamli Publishing CO
11 Greyfell Place
Pleasant Hill, CA 94523-1713

Phone Number: (925) 705-1612

## David Rushing
723 Main St. Ste. 816
Houston, TX 77002

This law office does federal writs, Texas parole and Texas writs.

## Dean's Books
420 SE 29th St.
Topeka, KS 66605

Inmate services. Send SASE for a list.

## Death Before Dishonor
Nkosi Shake Zulu -- El 369182
Washington Corrections Center
PO Box 900
Shelton, WA 98584

This is DC street legend Wayne Perry. He gives only Eyone Williams permission to speak on his behalf.

Instagram: Wayne_silk_perry

## Death Penalty Focus
5 Third Street, Suite 725
San Francisco, CA 94103

Phone Number: 415-243-0143
Website: deathpenalty.org

## Death Penalty Information Center
1015 18th Street NW, Suite 704
Washington, DC 20036

DPIC focuses on disseminating studies and reports related to the death penalty to the news media and general public covering subjects such as race, innocence, politicization, costs, of the death penalty, and more. Most of their publications are freely downloadable from their website, Or available for a small fee in printed format. Request a copy of their "Resource Order Form," and also a current list of their publications concerning individual state death penalty issues.

Phone Number: 202-289-2275
Website: deathpenaltyinfo.org

## Defense Investigation Group
PO Box 86923
L.A., CA 90086

$500 post-conviction investigations, locates up to three people in Los Angeles/Orange counties.

## Denver Anarchist Black Cross
PO Box 11236
Denver, CO 80211

The Denver Anarchist Blck Cros exists to contribute to the defense of social movements, both internally and externally, working against oppression everywhere. Questions, concerns, comments, ideas, and/or wishes to collaborate to participate, please contact Denver ABC at the above address.

## Deposition Handbook

How-to handbook for anyone who conducts a deposition or is going to be deposed. It's 352 pages, $34.99, and can be bought from Prison Legal News.

## deviantart.com

They sell and post art for artists. At 14 million members, they attract all kinds of businesses looking for various styles of art. If you are an artist and looking to make some real money, have your people contact them for details.

**Dharma Companions**
PO Box 762
Cotati, CA 94931

**Dharma Friends Prison Outreach Project**
Compassion Works for All
PO Box 7708
Little Rock, AR 72217-7708

**Dharma Garden Newsletter**
1 Fairtown Lane
Taneytown, MD 21787

Dharma Letter is a high-quality newsletter published by a consortium of Buddhist prisoners and outside advocates. Dharma Garden offers formal Buddhist studies from Prison Dharma Network and other resources for incarcerated Buddhists.

Website: Facebook.com/DharmaGardenSangha
E-mail: DharmagardenSangha@gmail.com

**Dharma Publishing**
35788 Hauser Bridge Rd.
Cazadero, CA 95421

Phone Number: 1-800-873-4276

**Dharma Seed Archival Center**
P.O. Box 66,
Wendell Depot, MA 01380

**Dharma Seeds Foundation**
PO Box 61175
Oklahoma City, OK 73146-1175

Dharma Seeds is a non-profit organization that produces a newspaper about meditation with a Catholic and Zen focus to those in jail, incarcerated within state or federal prisons. All subscriptions are **FREE** of charge to those incarcerated.

**A Dictionary of Criminal Law Terms**

This handbook contains police terms such as preventive detention and protective sweep, and phrases from judicial-created law such as independent-source rule and open-fields doctrine. A good resource to help navigate your way through the maze of legal language in criminal cases. It's 768 pages, $33.95, and can be bought from Prison Legal News.

**Disability Rights Education and Defense Fund Inc.**
3075 Adeline St, Suite 210
Berkeley, CA 94703

CA Prisoners Only. DREDF takes on very few cases each year. "We receive far more requests for assistance than our resources allow us to take on. If we cannot take your case we can provide you with referrals to other organizations. Please do not send original supporting materials. Please note, we do not provide assistance with disability benefits such as denial of Social Security Disability benefits."

**Disability Rights Texas**
2222 West Braker Lane
Austin, Texas 78758

Phone Number: (512) 454-4816(Voice)

**Discount Magazine Subscription Service, INC.**
PO Box 60114
Fort Myers, FL 33906

If a publisher authorized agency offers a lower current price on any magazine this company offers, they will match the price, guaranteed. Write/Send SASE for a **FREE** catalog.

**Diversified Press**
PO Box 135005
Clermont, FL 34713

This company offers a pen pal page, customized greeting cards and more. They are willing to accept stamps as payment. Write/Send SASE for more information.

**Don Diva Magazine**
603 W. 115th Street, #313
NY, NY 10025

Don Diva is an urban magazine – "the original street bible." A yearly subscription is $20.00; 4 issues a year. Single issues are $5.99 each. Send SASE for order form and info.

Website: dondivamag.com

**Dr. Lee Vernon Warren, Ph.D.**
15692, 2727 Hwy K
Bonne Terre, MO 63628-3430

Certified Paralegal, Legal Advocate, Mitigation Specialist.

"Are you locked up and looking for a chance at freedom? If you are serving a lot of time and need serious litigation, write and tell me what I can do for you. Be aware I cannot work for free. Include your outside info and telephone number. Never include anything in your inquiry but why you think your conviction is wrong or unconstitutional."

## Dress for Success
3820 Walnut St. Suite 2
Harrisburg, PA 17109

Provides professional attire and career support services to disadvantaged women.

Phone Number: (717) 657-3333

## D.R.I.V.E. Movement

Founded by Death Row prisoners, the DRIVE movement seeks to unite the Death Row community to push forward and initiate change in the conditions. Through a group of passionate prisoner activists who have put aside all barriers of ethnicity, creed, color and beliefs, to focus on the injustices forced upon us by this system. Resists by means of inner-resistance, outer-petition drives, direct actions, and hunger strikes.

Email Address: drivemovement@yahoo.com

## DRL
PMB 154
3298 N. Glassford Hill Rd, Suite 104
Prescott Valley, AZ 86314

This company offers a pen pal service with a lifetime membership for $40. Write/Send SASE for more information.

## Drug Policy Alliance
131 West 33rd Street, 15th Floor
NY, NY 10018

DPA is the nation's leading organization promoting drug policies that are grounded in science, compassion, health and human rights. DPA is putting out a call for drug war stories. If you would like to be profiled in the media, your story would be entered in a data base for possible use. They want you to send your name, current prison, ethnicity, kind of drug involved, whether or not a weapon was involved, contact information for outside

representative if possible (phone number and/or e-mail), and a short story of your case to "Drug War Stories! DPA" at the address above.

## Drug Policy Alliance
131 10th Street
San Francisco, CA 94103

One of the leading U.S. organizations promoting alternatives to the war on drugs, with extensive on-line library, reports on drug policy reform by state, public health alternatives to criminalization, and more.

## Durham Law Office
Craig H. Durham
910 W. Main Suite 328
Boise, ID 18370

Appeals, post- conviction, habeas, and parole services for Idaho inmates.

**E**

## East Bay Prisoner Support
PO Box 22449
Oakland, CA 94609

"We disseminate fiery ideas. We want this fire to spread from the pages of our zines to the architecture of their system. We hope these ideas can foment rebellions across the walls that divide us. Coordinated, these rebellions can shake the foundations of law and order that keep us down. This is our propaganda. This is our project. We share it with our comrades inside. We reach out to places they don't want us to find and contact people they don't want us to meet. We no longer wish to obey laws, punch clocks, pay rent, compete against each other, follow orders, bow to authority, appeal to moralities, ask for permission, always knowing that to resist is to end up in cages, like all those inside."

This is an anarchist zine publisher that will send zines once a month to prisoners in CA, AZ, NM, TX, UT, and NV. They will send to queer, trans, and women prisoners in any state. The zines are **FREE** and they will fill orders once a month. Each order is any one zine or a combination of zines up to 30 sheets. Send SASE for **FREE** catalog.

## EPS

I DO NOT RECOMMEND DOING BUSINESS
WITH THIS COMPANY!

**The Editorial Eye**
66 Canal Center Plazas, Suite 200
Alexandra, VA 22314

This is a magazine that covers standards and practices
for writers and editors.

**Education Justice Project**
University of Illinois at Urbana-Champaign
805 W. Pennsylvania Ave. M.C. 058
Urbana, IL 61801

They demonstrate the positive impacts of college-in-
prison programs and organize educational programming
at Danville Correctional Center through the University
of Illinois.

Phone Number: 217.300.5150
Website: educationjustice.net

**Edwin Gould Services for Children**

Phone Number: 212-437-3500
Website: info@egscf.org

**Elegant Roses**
PO Box 133342
Spring, TX 77393

Premium long-stem roses, chocolates, teddy bears, etc.
Send SASE for brochure and order forms.

Phone Number: (832) 618-2955

**Elite Services Group, LLC**
1240 Winnowing Way Suite 102
Mt. Pleasant, SC 29466

"Apply for dual citizenship now! Qualify for early
release, restore your rights, live abroad after your
conviction and get a new start on life! This offers many
benefits. Not all applicants qualify, however a criminal
record does not disqualify an application or possible
acceptance. Send SASE for more info."

**Elija Ray Gifts**
PO Box 3008
La Grande, OR 97850

They have over 2,500 gifts to choose from that you can
send to your loved ones. Send for a **FREE** 32-page
catalog, or $9 for a full 370-page catalog.

Website: elijahray.com

**Elmer Robert Keach, III, PC**
1040 Riverfront Center
P.O. Box 70
Amsterdam, NY 12010

This experienced civil rights attorney is dedicated to
seeking justice for those who are incarcerated;
reasonable hourly rates for criminal defense, appeals,
post-conviction relief and habeas corpus. Send SASE
and request inquiry guideline for whatever it is you wish
to hire him for.

Phone Number: 518-434-1718
Website: keachlawfirm.com

**End Violence Project**,
P.O. Box 1395,
Bryn Mawr, PA 19010

Committed to ending violence without violence (This
group has worked with PA Lifers in the past).

Phone Number: (610)-527-2821

**Energy Committed to Offenders**
P.O. Box 33533
Charlotte, NC 28233-3533

Provides services to inmates, ex-offenders and their
families. INMATES: pre-release planning, ECO
presentations about ECO services and pre-release
planning, correspondence support, half-way house for
female offenders completing their prison sentence -
referrals from NC Department of Correction only. Will
accept collect calls from inmates.

Phone Number: (704) 374-0762.
Website: ecocharlotte.org

**Envisions Publishing**
PO Box 451235
Houston, TX 77245

This is an urban book publishing company with a
catalog that includes: Dark Horse Assassin, World War
Gangster, MVP, MVP Reloaded, Wild Cherry,
Preacherman Blues, Preacherman Blues 2, The
Message, all by author Jihad; and Dynasty, Dynasty 2,

Dynasty 3, and Que, all by author Dutch. All books are $12.00 each. Buy 3, get a 4th **FREE**. Get a 15% discount on any of these books if you order from the website Jihadwrites.com.

## Equal Justice Initiative
122 Commerce St.
Montgomery, AL 36104

Legal representation for indigent defendants and those denied fair treatment in the legal system (such as trials marked by blatant racial bias or prosecutorial misconduct). They mostly help death-row prisoners and children prosecuted as adults. They usually don't answer unless they are interested in the case.

## Escape Mate

This is an online concierge service for those of you who have Corrlink accounts. They have plans as low as $29.99 for 3 months.

Website: escapemate.com

## ESPN
935 Middle St.
Bristol, CT 06010

This is a sports news magazine.

Website: espn.com.

## The Essential Supreme Court Cases: The 200 Most Important Cases for State Prisoners

This 2015, 330 page "indispensable reference book" is by Ivan Denison and costs $19.95.

## ETC Campaign
C/O Michigan CURE
PO Box 2736
Kalamazoo, MI 49003

ETC campaign is a national effort to reduce the high cost of prison phone calls.

Website: ectcampaign.com

## Everyday Letters for Busy People

Hundreds of sample letters that can be adapted for most any purpose, including letters to government agencies and officials. Has numerous tips for writing effective letters. It's 287 pages, $18.99, and can be bought from Prison Legal News.

## Evolve
1971 Stella Lake Dr.
Las Vegas, NV 89106

Evolve offers motivational counseling, case management, vocational education, and job placement to individuals with criminal histories.

Phone Number: (702) 638-6371

## Exclusiveprioner.com
PO Box 533
Madison, AL 35758

They provide a pen-pal service. Write/send SASE for details.

## Executive Prison Consultants
2384 Oaktrail Drive, Suite 2
Idaho Falls, ID 83404

Executive Prison Consultants is the nation's leading prison preparation and survival consultancy. Specializing in the needs of federal prisoners, Executive Prison Consultants regularly assists clients with disciplinary appeals, transfer requests, RDAP eligibility, medical care, and other specialized, individualized client concerns.

Website: executiveprisonconsultants.com
E-mail: info@executiveprisonconsultants.com

## Exodus Transitional Community, Inc.
2271 3rd Avenue
New York, NY 10035-2231

Fellowship of formerly incarcerated individuals that helps people coming out of prison build stable lives and fully reintegrate back into society.

Phone Number: 917-492-0990
Website: www.etcny.org

## Ex-Offender Reentry Website

This site has lots of books and resources for ex-offenders, how to search for a job, write resumes, etc., all geared to ex-offenders. All info must be bought in the form of books.

Website: exoffenderreentry.com

### The Exoneration Initiative
233 Broadway
Suite 2370
New York, NY 10279

Phone: 212.965.9335
Website: http://exonerationinitiative.org

### The Exoneration Project
312 North May Street, Suite 100
Chicago, IL 60607

The Exoneration Project is a non-profit organization dedicated to working to **FREE** prisoners who were wrongfully convicted. The project represents innocent individuals in post-conviction proceedings; typical cases involve DNA testing, coerced confessions, police misconduct, the use of faulty evidence, junk science and faulty eyewitness testimony, and effective assistance of council claims.

Exotic Fragrances
1645 Lexington Ave
New York, NY 10029

Write to receive FREE 30 page catalog. No SASE needed.

Comment: One of the biggest catalogs I've seen. You name it, they've got it, and they respond pretty fast. --
Robert Bennett

### FACTS: Families to Amend California's Three Strikes.
3982 S. Figueroa Street #209
Los Angeles, CA 90037

A coalition working to change the "three strike" rules. Membership is $10 per year, and includes a subscription to the quarterly newsletter – The Striker. Ask for prisoner membership options, FACTS Works to amend California's Three Strikes law to target violent felonies only. Quarterly newsletter (by donation). Print return address exactly if you want a response. Flyers printed in English and Spanish.

Phone Number: (213) 746-4844.

### Fair Chance Project
1137 E Redondo Blvd
Inglewood, CA 90302

Fair Chance Project represents a movement led by liberated lifers, their families and concerned community members advocating for just sentencing laws and fair parole practices. The group seeks to integrate newly liberated lifers back into their communities enabling them to become valuable resources towards the development of self-sustaining communities. Send $5 or $5 worth of stamps for your prisoner membership, which includes a newsletter titled Fair Chance News.

### Families Against Mandatory Minimum
1100 H Street NW, Suite 1000
Washington, DC 20005

FAMM is a national advocacy group that focuses on mandatory minimums and offers a quarterly newsletter –FAMMgram. $10 per year for prisoners.

Website:famm.org

### Families of Parchman Prison Inmates
P.O. Box 2174
Starkville, MS 39760

"We serve as a support center to anyone who has a family member incarcerated or recently released from Parchman and any other prison in Mississippi."

Phone Number: (662) 323-5878.

### Family and Corrections Network
93 Old York Road Suite 1 #510
Jenkintown, PA 19046

The mission of Family and Corrections Network (FCN) is to uphold families of prisoners as a valued resource to themselves and their communities in order that the criminal justice system, other institutions and society become supportive of family empowerment, integrity, and self-determination. FCN works alongside families of prisoners, program providers, policy makers, researchers, educators, correctional personnel and the public by: convening national meetings for mutually respectful learning, interaction and dialogue; distributing information through FCN's publications, web site, and speakers' bureau; designing and supplying technical materials, tools and services; advocating criminal justice policy reform that upholds the value of families; encouraging networking among families of prisoners for mutual support and cooperative action; and creating opportunities for linking with and learning from families of prisoners.

Phone Number: (215) 576-1110

## Families United
P.O. Box 9476
Philadelphia, PA 19139

For children with a loved one incarcerated. After-school and other programs for kids.

Phone Number: 215-604-1759.

## FamilySupportAmerica.org
307 W 200 S, Suite 2004
Salt Lake City, 84101

"Here at Family Support America, we are dedicated to providing the information, support, and connections that families need to survive. Whether you have questions about child abuse, alcoholism, disciplining children, divorce, or other topics related to families, we can help. And if we cannot help, we will direct you to someone who can."

## Fanorama Society Publisher and Prisoner Zine Distro
109 Arnold Ave.
Cranston, RI 02905

Publishes zines created by people in prison and provides these zines to other prisoners. Several are queer/trans. Payments may be made in cash, state money orders, or postage. Write for list.

## Fast Law Publishing
Po Box 577
Upland, CA 91785

They publish how-to legal books. Write/Send SASE for more information.

## Fast Lane Entertainment
#245 4401-A Connecticut Avenue, NW
Washington, DC 20008

This is the urban publishing company owned by national bestselling author Eyone Williams. Eyone is the official spokesman for the legendary DC thug Wayne Perry. Fast Lane offers titles 'Secrets Never Die,' 'Lorton Legends,' 'Money Ain't Everything', 'Never Lay Down' and more. Books are $15.00 with shipping.

## FCPS.
74 Garilee Ln
Elizabethtown, PA 17022

Forensic Clemency and Parole Services. They can assist you in preparing petitions for filing by collecting needed information for you. For more info, contact them.

## Federal Receiver, J. Clark Kelso
California Prison Receivership
PO Box 588500
Elk Grove, CA 95758

In 2002, California settled a class-action lawsuit by agreeing to reform their medical care system, and the federal court appointed a federal Receiver to oversee the reform process. The receiver's job is to bring the level of medical care in California prisons to a standard which no longer violates the U.S. Constitution. Prisoner patients under the control of the CDCR and their families may write to the above address with concerns about health care issues (except for mental health, dental, or substance abuse and treatment). Some patient-care issues brought to the Receiver's attention may prompt clinical investigation and action. All information provided to the Receiver is considered in implementing systemic improvements.

Phone Number: 916-691-3000
Website: cphcs.ca.gov
Felonism: Hating In Plain Sight

What's the real cause of the oppression you experience? What are some real solutions? Felonism: Hating in Plain Sight has the answers. Available on Amazon, or send $15 to Linda Polk, Book; PO Box 128071; Nashville, TN 37212.

## Feria & Corona
10 Universal City Plazas, Suite 2000
Universal City, CA 91608

This is a law firm; it accepts California cases only.

Phone Number: (818)905-0903.

## Fight for Lifers West
P.O. Box 4683
Pittsburgh, PA 15206

Dedicated to supporting people sentenced to life without parole and their loved ones, while striving to improve the criminal justice system and building positive community relationships.

Phone Number: 412-361-3066
Website: fightforliferswest.mysite.com

**The Fire Inside**
1540 Market St. #490
San Francisco, CA 94102

This is a quarterly newsletter of the California Coalition for Women Prisoners; **FREE** to women.

**FIYA GIRLS**
PO Box 112118
Houston, TX 77293

"Check us out! We are the best in the game! Here we have the sexiest and hottest babes. We have plenty of nail-biting catalogs, with different types of breath-taking women of all races to choose from. Fiya girls catalog has the biggest selections to choose from.

1. Send $2.00 or 5 stamps to receive hi gloss color catalog #19. It has over 450 white girls, coeds and Spanish girls. All hot poses in bras, G strings and panties. It also comes with 1 **FREE** pic.

2. Send $2.00 or 5 stamps to receive hi gloss color catalog #18. It comes with 1 **FREE** pic. It has over 440 new black, white and Spanish girls. All have super big apple bottoms! You don't want to miss out on catalog 18 and 19. ALWAYS SEND AN ALTERNATE ADDRESS WITH YOUR ORDER IN CASE YOUR ORDER IS REJECTED. WE WILL SEND IT TO THE STREET ADDRESS THAT YOU PROVIDED US WITH.

3. If your jail or prison is strict on sexy photos, send $3.00 along with SASE for the get-in cat #1. They will let it in and the photos too.

4. Send $13.00 to get non-nude 10 pic get-in set. Make sure to say if you want black or white girls when you want a get-in 10 pic set.

5. Send $20.00 to get the 30 pic get-in set and a **FREE** get-in #1 cat. It contains all races wearing bikinis on beaches and beside pools. Get the all NEW supervised high gloss color VIP catalog #4. Over thousands to choose from. All races! Non-nude strippers, porn stars and all!!! Only $15.00 (**FREE** s/h). Includes 2 **FREE** pics. Price on all pics in VIP cat #4 is now only $1.00 each. Must choose at least 15 pics. And send a SASE

for each envelope. We ship up to 22 pics per envelope. You need to put 2 postage stamps on each envelope.

6. ALL NUDE BIG BUNDLE CATALOG PACKAGE ONLY $15.00. Comes with **FREE** pics.

7. Get mail get paid book is still only $10.00.

8. We have over 100 10-pic sets of black, white and Asian women in sets of 10 different poses. They are very hot 10-pic sets. Only $13.00 a set or you can choose 3 sets for $23.00.

9. VIP yearly membership is only $45.00.

10. Send $5.00 to get one of the hottest all white girls coed catalogs on the market --cat #11. It has over 450 to choose from.

11. Cat #20 has over 400 sexy white girls to choose from. Send $3.00 to get it.

12. The 5 pack has a large selection of ebony women with apple bottoms mixed with Asian and white women. It's hot!! Send only $7.00. It comes with 2 **FREE** pics. It has hundreds to choose from.

13. 50 PICS OF HOT NON-NUDE WITH THE BEST QUALITY ASIANS WEARING LINGERIE AND BIKINIS FOR ONLY $25.00 **FREE** SHIPPING.

14. VOL #1. 50 PICS OF HOT NON-NUDE BEST QUALITY MIXED SET OF WHITE, BLACK AND SPANISH GIRLS AND PORN STARS WEARING STRIPPER OUTFITS ONLY $25.00. **FREE** SHIPPING.

15. VOL #2, 3, 4 AND 5 HAVE 50 PIC SETS OF WHITE, BLACK, AND LATIN GIRLS! EACH 50 PIC SET IS ONLY $25.00. **FREE** SHIPPING.

16. BUY ALL 5 GRAB BAG SETS. EACH SET HAS A MIX OF RACES. THEY ARE ONLY $25.00 A SET. **FREE** SHIPPING! THERE ARE A TOTAL OF 10 SETS. VOL #1-10. BUY ALL 10 NUDE SETS AND GET 50 **FREE** SHOTS!

VIP cat 5 has over a couple thousand choices. Only $15.00. **FREE** s/h. Cats 27-32. VIP cat 6 has over a couple thousand choices only $15.00. **FREE** s/h 33-cat 38). VIP cat 5 and 6 consist of white camel toe shots, bikini shots, curvy models, petite models, Latino models, beach shots, bedroom shots, G string shots, mini skirts, latex, spandex, fitness models, armature porn stars, micro thongs, booty shorts, tight jeans, blondes, redheads, brunettes, big breast, slim waist, big booties, erotic poses, college coeds, huge camel toes. New anmie sluts. They are super hot! VIP cat #5 and #6 are non-nude catalogs."

**Comment:** I wrote their ad they way they wrote it so you can judge for yourself. In addition, though I have seen guys get their orders from them, I ordered some pics and the "Get Mail Get Paid" book and never got it. ~ Mike

## flikshop.com
1-855-flikshop

Your family can download their **FREE** app, then send you pictures of friends, family, etc., in the form of a postcard for as low as 79 cents each.

## Flipping Your Conviction: Post-Conviction Relief for State Prisoners

This 2013, 449 page book by Ivan Denison has instructions, rules, forms and examples and costs $49.95.

## Flipping Your Habe: Overturning Your State Conviction in Federal Court

This 2014, 336 page book by Ivan Denison has instructions, rules, forms and examples and costs $34.95.

## Flipping Your Conviction: State Post-Conviction Relief for the Pro Se Prisoner

Step-by-step instructions on how to successfully challenge a state conviction. Analysis and framing of legal issues; sub claims under ineffective assistance; state appeals; 33 forms and more! This book, by Ivan Denison, is 500 pages, $49.99.

## Flix 4 You
PO Box 290249
Sandhills, SC 29229

"Get them cuz they're hot! Flix 4 You is often imitated, but can't be duplicated! We offer the best quality photos and fastest service in the game! Only .75 per photo! New Deal: order 10-14 photos, get 1 photo **FREE**; 15-19 photos, get 3 photos **FREE**; order 20-24 photos, get 5 photos **FREE**; order 25 or more, get 10 photos **FREE**. Over 100 catalogs to choose from, all just $5.00 each or

20 stamps! Black, Latin, Asian, White, celebrity, pornstars, club scenes, bikini shots, iPhone cuties, selfies and more! From fully clothed to fully nude! We otter photos that will satisfy everyone's needs!!

Overstock special: 20 photos for $7.50. You choose race, front shot or back shot, and we will choose from our overstock collection. You cannot choose from any specific catalog.

Shipping and handling is $2.20 per envelope. Each envelope only hold 25 photos, if you need more than 1 envelope, you must send additional shipping and handling. New policy as of January 1, 2015: we will no longer be responsible for rejected catalogs or photos! Be sure to order according to your facility's mailroom policy."

**Comment:** Flix 4 You sent me a couple of their catalogs -- 'Insta-grammy 2' and 'Legs, Tights, Assets 2'. The catalogs are printed in color and offer several choices each. Their images are some of the best I've seen. The baddest bitches on the planet. ~ Mike

## Florida Institutional Legal Services
14260 West Newberry Road #412
Newberry, FL 32669

Florida Institutional Legal Services, Inc. (FILS) is the only statewide legal services program in Florida dedicated to serving people who are institutionalized.

Phone Number: 352-375-2494
Website: floridalegal.org/newberry.htm

## Florida Justice Institute
3750 Miami Tower
100 S.E. Second Street
Miami, FL 33131-2309

They are a nonprofit public interest law firm that conducts civil rights litigation and advocacy in the areas of prisoners' rights, housing discrimination, disability discrimination, and other areas that impact the lives of Florida's poor and disenfranchised.

Phone: 305-358-2081; 888-358-2081
Website: info@floridajusticeinstitute.org

## Flying Over Walls Penpal Project
PO Box 401014
San Francisco, CA 94140

**The F.O.G. Corporation**
PO Box 17733
Honolulu, HI 96817

This is a Vietnam friendship magazine. Send SASE for details.

**Forbes Magazine**
PO Box 5471
Harlan, IA 51593

Note: This address is for subscription services only. This is a financial information magazine.

**Forever Family, Inc.**
387 Joseph Lowery Blvd.
2nd Floor, Suite A
Atlanta, GA 30310

Forever family works to ensure that, no matter what the circumstances, all children have the opportunity to be surrounded by the love of family.

Phone Number: 404-223-1200
Website: http://foreverfam.org/

**The Fortune News**
53 West 23rd Street, 8th Floor
New York, NY 10010

Phone Number: (212) 691-7554

**The Fortune Society**
29-76 Northern Blvd,
Long Island City, NY 11101 – 2822

Helps ex-prisoners break the cycle of crime and incarceration, and educates the public about prison and the causes of crime. **FREE** newsletter for prisoners.

**F.O.S.**
PO Box 42922
Phoenix, AZ 85080

"Hey guys, I'm back!!!! We finally relocated to Phoenix, AZ. I've missed you all!!! In case you haven't figured it out, it's me again. I've been gone for a while now and I feel it's time to make you guys REALLY happy. While I was gone, I was bust doing photo shoots! For you guys who don't know me, you can call me MOMS. I'm the one who is always wanting to do something "nice", a "little extra"; just my soft heart, I guess. I've been around the block a couple of times and I know just about every scam there is, so don't even start with me. Just remember, I want your money, not your nonsense, and we'll get along fine. You do your part and I'll do my part to deliver a professional, satisfactory product. Deal? Now for the BEST part; we have produced a NEW LINE OF FLIERS which will feature EXCLUSIVE photos. They're originals, NOT computer copies. This line of photos will be introduced by our company only. These photos absolutely cannot be purchased anywhere else.

The new flier series feature 59 flyers of assorted photos each. There are 40 photos to a page. Each flyer costs $1.50 or 5 stamps a flyer and are in color. Request the flyer you want by number.

The semi-nude flyers are as follows...

Hispanic girl flyers: 1, 2, 19, 20, 21, 32, 36, 46, 47, 52, 53, 54, 55. Same girl (Cuba, who is from Cuba) flyers: 22, 23, 24, 25, 26, 27. Hispanic and white girl photos are: 3, 4, 6, 7, 9, 12, 13, 14, 15, 17, 35, 38, 48, 49. Hispanic and Black girl flyers are: 8, 10, 11, 16, 18, 28, 30, 31, 45, 50, 51. Mixture of ladies: 5, 29, 37, 41. Chubby Chaser's girl flyers: White 39, 40, 42. White only flyer: 49. American Indian Flyers: 33, 34, 43, 44 (in flyer 33 she is wearing a see-through top so don't order if you can't get flyer). Flyer 56 is the flyer for guys who love feet. Flyer 57 is a big butt flyer. Flyer 58 is camel toe and Flyer 59 is a very tame flyer for guys who have a hard time getting photos and/or flyers in.

There are 33 nude flyers. The flyers and photos are the same price as the semi-nude. Nude flyers 1, 3, 4, 5, 7, 8, 9, 10, 11, 12, 13, 14, 17, 18, 21, 22, 23, 24, 25, 26, 27, 28, 29, 30, 31, 32, 33, 34 are mixed Hispanic and White girls. Nude flyer 2, 15, and 16 are Black girls and nude flyers 6, 19, and 20 are mixed Hispanic and Black. Sample nude flyer 40 is mixed girls.

Please notify us to whether or not you can have front shots only. This way we will delete the images not allowed from the print process before sending it to you. However, you are agreeing to receive less than 40 images per catalog by doing so. Remember, it's up to you to keep us informed of your institution's rules and regulations!

Photo and flyer prices are $1.00 each or 2 Forever stamps. Any checks $50.00 and over, photos are $.75 each which would be 67 photos. A stamp worth $1.15 gives you one photo. If you can receive 10-25 photos per envelope, 2 stamps must be included for each envelope. For 3-5 photos per envelope, 1 stamp per envelope.

We now have an email address for your family to contact us if they need to:
Freedomofspeech@gmail.com

Hugs and Kisses,
Moms"

## Fox Broadcasting
PO Box 900
Beverly Hills, CA 90213

## Free Battered Women
1540 Market Street suite 490
San Francisco, CA 94102

"In California, the majority of women prisoners are survivors of domestic violence; some are doing time for defending themselves and their children, or were forced to confess to crimes. Join the movement to **FREE** battered women from prison."

Phone Number: (415) 255-7036 x320

## Freebird Publishers
Box 541
North Dighton, MA 02764

They offer a bunch of services, products and publications. They "Service All Your Outside Needs With Inside Knowledge". Send SASE for more information.

Email: Diane@FreebirdPublishers.com,
Web: FreebirdPublishers.com

## Freedom Line
Box 7 – WCB
Connersville, IN 47331

Local phone numbers for $2.50 a month, anywhere in the USA, only 50¢ a minute. 15¢ a minute to Mexico. No sign-up or hidden fees. Send SASE.

WebSite:freedomline.net

## Freedom of Information Act
General Counsel's Office
Legal Services Corp Rm 601
733 15 St. NW
Washington, DC 20005

They provide printouts of unclassified government documents – your FBI file, Whitehouse emails, UFO sightings, etc.

Phone number: (202) 272-4010.

## FREE Jail Calls

Get a **FREE** guaranteed ConsCallHome number and 20 minutes of **FREE** talk time every month.

Phone: 855-232-2012
Website: freejailcalls.com

## Freeing the Mind / Kadampa Buddhism
KelsangTekchog
C/OSaraha
Buddhist Center
PO Box 12037
San Francisco, CA 94112

The New Kadampa Tradition (NKT) is an association of Buddhist Centers and practitioners that derive their inspiration and guidance from the example of the ancient Kadampa Buddhist Masters and their teachings, as presented by Geshe Kelsang Gyatso. Please write to request a correspondence program or **FREE** books offering the teachings of Geshe Kelsang Gyatso.

Website: kadampas.org.

## Freelance Success
32391 Dunford St.
Farmington Hills, MI 48334

This is an e-letter. It's $99 for a year subscription. 52 issues per year.

Phone Number: 1-877-731-5411
Website: freelancesuccess.com.

## Free-World Services
703 N. Mavis, #1
Anaheim, CA 92805

This company carries a large selection of sexy pictures, gifts, flowers, teddy bears, parole clothes, etc. Write/Send SASE for more information.

## Friction Zone
60166 Hop patch Springs Rd.
Mountain Center, CA 92561

This magazine costs $30 for a 1-year subscription; 12 issues per year.

Phone Number: (909) 659-9500
Website: frictionzone.com.

## Friends and Family of Louisiana's Incarcerated Children
1600 Oretha C. Haley Blvd.
New Orleans, LA 20005

FFLIC is fighting for the closure of Swanson and Jetson Centers for Youth and for an increase in community-based services that help our children grow and thrive in their own homes and communities.

Phone Number: (337) 562-8503.

## Friends & Lovers Magazine
Luigi Spatota
Suite 46 McCreary Trail
Bolton, Ontario L7E 2C9 Canada

This is a pen pal magazine. Write for details.

## Friends Beyond the Wall, Inc.
55 Mansion St., #1030
Poughkeepsie, NY 12602.

"Since 1999, Friends Beyond the Wall has been connecting our members with the outside world through our Friendship, Romance and Legal Connection Service. Our talented New York Graphic and Web Designers create your beautiful, full-color web site ad profile, using the photo and message you provide. Your web site is available on the Internet to a worldwide audience of millions, and web site visitors may simple 'click' to send you a response!"

The ads range from $29.95 - $59.95. They have a guarantee that, if you follow ALL their tips and suggestions and do not receive a response to your ad in six months of publication, your ad will be extended by a full six months, and your photo link will be displayed **FREE** in their special sections Headline Ads, New and Featured Ads, and the No Response Sections for specified times to be of further assistance.

For a **FREE** brochure/application listing all of their ad options, prices and suggested tips, send them a SASE.

Website: friendsbeyondthewall.com

## Friend Committee on Legislation of California

926 J St. #707
Sacramento, CA 95814

This is a Quaker founded group that advocates and lobbies for CA state laws that are just, compassionate, and respectful of the inherent worth of every person. It's $12 for a 1-year membership, which includes their newsletter. However, no direct services to prisoners.

Phone Number: (916) 443-3734

## Friends Outside
Po Box 4085
Stockton, CA 95204

They provide services to prisoners and their families. They also provide pre-release and parenting programs at all California State Prisons (through case management). They operate visitor centers at all California State Prisons too. Write for a **FREE** publication – "Children of Incarcerated parents," "The Bill of Rights," and "How to Tell Children about Jail and Prisons."

## From Jail to a Job

This is said to be the best ex-offenders job search manual available.

Website: jailtojob.com

## From Here to the Streets
P.O. Box 24-3664
Boynton Beach, FL 33424

"We provide information & services for inmates and their families. Our Website contains vital tools and information for successful reentry, pre-release and employment. We offer **FREE** book downloads available on our website."

Website: fromheretothestreets.com

## Fulton & Welch
10701 Corporate Dr., Ste. 390
Stafford, TX 77477

These ladies are Texas parole attorneys. And they look good, too.

**GainPeace**
1S270 Summit Ave, Suite 204
OakBrook Terrace, IL 60181

Questions about Islam? Islam is a religion of inclusion. Muslims believe in all the profits in both testaments. Read Quran, the original and unchanged word of God, the last and final testament. Watch Peacetv.tv.

Website: Gainpeace.com

**Game Informer Reader Art Contest**
724 First Street North, 3rd Floor
Minneapolis, MN 55401

Game Informer is a video game magazine. They run an art contest. Most of it is video game related, but I've seen pieces that aren't. "Submit your art to win our monthly prize. Please include your name and return address. Entries become the property of Game Informer and cannot be returned."

**Gassho Newsletter/Atlanta Soto Zen Center**
1404 McClendon Ave
Atlanta, GA 30307

Website: www.aszc.org

**Gay and Lesbian Advocates and Defenders**
Gay & Lesbian Advocates & Defenders
30 Winter Street, STE 800
Boston, MA 02108

Phone Number: (617) 426-1350

**Gay Identity Center of Colorado**
1151 South Huron Street
Denver, CO 80223

Phone Number: (303) 202-6466
Website: www.gicofcolo.org.

**Genealogical Research, Reference Service Branch**
National Achieves & Records Admin
8th and Pennsylvania Ave. RM 205
Washington, DC 20408

If you are interested in researching your family history, this is a good place to start. Write and request their **FREE** 20-page booklet.

Phone Number: (202) 523-3218

**Gender Mutiny Collective**
P.O. Box 0494
Chapel Hill, NC 26514

**Georgetown ARCP**
600 New Jersey Ave. NW
Washington, DC 20001

The Georgetown Law Journal Annual Review of Criminal procedures is a topic-by-topic summary of criminal procedures in the United States Supreme Court and each of the twelve Federal Circuit Courts of Appeals. The publication costs $15.

**Georgia Innocence Project**
2645 North Decatur Road
Decatur, GA 30033

Phone Number: 404-373-4433
Website: ga-innocenceproject.org/Alabama

**Georgia Justice Project**
438 Edgewood Ave.
Atlanta, GA 30312

GJP combines legal and social services. Staff attorneys and social workers develop long-term relationships with clients who must make a commitment to rehabilitation before being accepted as clients.

**Get Connected**
2127 Olympic Parkway; Suite 1006-248
Chula Vista, CA 91915

This is a discount call service. Write/send SASE for more information.

Phone Number: (866) 514-9972
Website: getconnectedus.com.

**getgrandpasfbifile.com**
This is an online FBI-file service.

Website: getmyfbifile.com

**Get Your Poetry Published**

"Be Published Now. Our Services Can Help. Request **FREE** Publishing Kit!"

Website: be-published.com

**Ghost Photos**
PO Box 1591

Rocky Mount, NC 27802

They offer non-nude photos, including special requests. MP3 photos, too. For a catalog, send $2.00, for a FREE brochure, send SASE

## Gillins Typing Service
229-19 Merrick Blvd. Suite 228
Laurelton, NY 11413

They offer reliable and prompt service typing manuscripts and legal material for $1.75 per page w/ line editing. Send SASE for brochure.

Phone Number (718) 607-9688

## Girls and Mags
3308 Rte. 940; Ste. 104-3018
Mt. Pocono, PA 18344

50 verified mega church addresses who offer pen pals: only $8.98 with sample letter. 67 churches that offer a mix of FREE publications: $6.00 or 20 F/C stamps. 200 pen pal addresses off the interweb (some photos and over half USA); $19.98.

Write your favorite celeb for FREE photos! Choose from models, athletes, TV stars, musicians: $10.00 per list or 3 for $25.00. Each list contains 75 addresses.

600 FREE magazines: Brand-new exciting catalog of magazines you may order FREE! Verified snail mail addresses and complete directions. Huge variety (80 pages): $15.98.

New female pen pal ads! With bio and color photos. 100 recently posted Latina Lovers. 100 just posted Black Beauties: $12.00 each.

44 verified pen pal magazines who offer free pen pal ands by snail mail: $14.00 each. Just posted 130 Asian Angels: $12.00. 329 mixed overseas: $18.00.

**Comment:** Girls and Mags is a new company by George Kayer. George is the founder of Inmate Shopper. He's now retired from Inmate Shopper and has sold it to Freebird Publishers. George is a true hustler, and I have a tremendous amount of respect for that. - - Mike

## Global University
Beren School of the Bible
1211 South Glenstone Avenue

Springfield, MO 65804

Highly recommended career school offering religious studies.

## Gold Star Fragrances
100 West 37th St.
New York, NY 10018

This company carries over 1,000 imported perfume oils; as well as soaps, massage oils, body lotion, shower gels and more. Write/send SASE for **FREE** catalog.

## Golden State Packages
212 E. Rowland St. #424
Covina, CA 91713

Sells food, clothes, shoes, CDs and a bunch of other shit.

## Gorilla Convict Publications
1019 Willott Rd.
St. Peters, MO 63376

Gorilla Convict is the publishing company operated and owned by incarcerated author Seth Ferranti. He's written such books as Prison Stories, Street Legends volume 1 and 2, and The Supreme Team, among others. His books are $15 each, plus $5.25 for s/h for the first book, and $2.25 for each additional book.

**Comment:** When I first decided books are what I'ma do I ordered two from Seth - - Prison Stories and Street Legends (the first one). He wrote and published them from his prison cell so they inspired me and let me know it can be done. He's out now and runs the website gorillaconvict.com. I'll be sending him all my books this year in hopes of reviews. - - Mike

## Grab Bag Hot Pics

20 sexy photos for $10. **FREE** s/h, but add $3 for tracking. You choose the category, they choose the photos. All pics are 4x6 glossy, non-nude. No duplicates in entire order. Choose from Asian, White, Latino, Black, Straight Stuntin, Football Babes and Western Chicks.

This deal is available from Freebird Publishers. Send $10 per set ordered with info on paper. They are not responsible for mailroom refusals and they will give no refunds, only credit vouchers.

**Grace College Prison Extension Program**
200 Seminary Dr
Winona Lake, IN 46590

Grace College and the Indiana Dept. of Corrections Offer Associate of Science and Bachelor of Science degrees to individuals who are incarcerated in maximum security units in the following facilities: Indiana State Prison, Miami Correctional Facility, Wabash Valley Correctional, Facility, and Pendleton Correctional Facility.

Phone Number: 800-544-7223
Website: grace.edu

**Grace Ministries Bible College & Institute**
PO Box 291962
Dayton, OH 45429

This study is highly recommended for the serious student. Diplomas and certificates offered for various Christian Theological Studies. Must be able to receive cassettes and/or CDs. **FREE** tuition available. Donations are accepted to help off-set costs.

**The Graduate Group**
PO Box 3703751
West Harford, CT 06137

They publish books that are helpful to prisoner/parolees at a discounted price of $22 each. Write/send SASE for **FREE** catalog.

Website: graduategroup.com.

**Graduate School USA**
600 Maryland Avenue, S.W.
Washington, DC 20024-2520

Website: customersupport@graduateschool.edu.

**The Granite Publishing Group**
PO Box 1429
Columbus, NC 28722

Inmates may write to receive **FREE** books on subjects that support the cultivation of planetary consciousness. The metaphysical/transformational subject of our books range from Native American spirituality to the extraterrestrial presence. Please send postage if possible.

Phone Number: (828) 894-8444

**Graterfriends**
Pennsylvania Prison Society
245 N Broad St., Suite 300
Philadelphia, PA 19107

This is a newsletter relating to prisons and prisoners' issues. Subscriptions are $3 (for prisoners).

Website: prisonsociety.org.

**Comment**: This is a terrific newsletter which publishes prisoners' writing in each and every issue. -- Mike

**Great Goods**
PO Box 2027
Bloomington, IN 47402

Stamps for cash! Great Goods will buy your stamps! 70 of face value: Complete books, sheets or rolls of Forever Stamps and Global Forever Stamps.

"We will send your funds as a money order or electronic payment to anywhere you designate. Great Goods can also send payment to an approved package vendor. Please provide complete name and address of where to send your funds. Also include any required forms or special instructions.

Minimum order of $20. No quantity of stamps too big. No taped or stapled stamps. Used, damaged, or torn stamps are not accepted and cannot be returned. Stamps MUST be on original postal backing. Only new stamps accepted. Singles and partials are accepted as a lower rate and cannot be returned. Please inquire for a complete list of rates."

**The Greenback Exchange**
PO Box 11228, Dept. NLN 5
Costa Mesa, CA 92627

They buy unused stamps. Send SASE for details.

**Greenman Ministry**
310 Morton St Ste. 390
Richmond, TX 77469-3119

Promotes Wiccan, Heathen and other Pagan religious practices, with emphasis on serving TX-based prisoners. Write for a sample newsletter, catalog of books, pamphlets & religious items, and a list of TX prisons where they hold rituals. Does not have the resources to give **FREE** books.

## Greeting Cards by Freebird Publishers

"We provide a hassle-free way of sending greeting cards to your loved ones. We create and mail custom cards printed with your loved one's name, your closure and name. We also offer signature and custom message services. Choose from 100's of cards by name brands.

General Card Catalog: Includes romance, missing you, birthday and anniversary. Holiday Card and Gift Catalog: Includes everything from Halloween to New Years. Valentine Day Card and Gift Catalog: filled with love, romance, affections and more. Easter Card and Gilt Catalog: Includes cards for everyone on your list and gifts too. Mother's Day Brochure: beautiful, heartfelt cards that is sure to please her.

Send $2 or 6 f/c stamps for each catalog, and $1 or 3 f/c stamps for each brochure to Freebird Publishers."

## Groundwork Books Collective
0323 UCSD Student Center
La Jolla, CA 92037

They carry books on the following subjects: Africa, African-Americans, Asia, Asian-Pacific Islander, Chicano/a, China, CIA, FBI, Police, Cultural Criticism, Ecology, Education, Feminist Theory, Labor, Latin American/Caribbean, Native American, Political Theory, Racism, United State history, Political Economy and Imperialism and much, much, more. Books are 40% off for those who can afford to pay. 2 **FREE** books will be given per person for those who are indigent.

Phone Number: 858-452-9625.

## G Street Chronicles
PO Box 1822
Jonesboro, GA 30237

They publish/ sell urban books. Send SASE with a request for their catalog.

## GTI Voice
PO Box 178171
Nashville, TN 37217

Save up to 95% on calls. Send SASE.

Phone Number: (866) 484-8642
Website: gtivoice.com

## The Habeas Citebook: Ineffective Assistance of counsel.

This is PLN'S second published book, which exclusively covers ineffective assistance of counsel-related issues in federal habeas petitions. Great resource for habeas litigation with hundreds of case citations. It's 200 pages, $49.95, and can be purchased from Prison Legal News.

## Hamden Consulting
1612 Homestead Rd.
Chapel Hill, NC 27516

Their objective is to end abusive prisoner phone service.

## Harris Publications
P0 Box 28773
Philadelphia, PA 19151-773

They publish the book 'Young & Incarcerated' by E.E. III -- an "inspiring and powerful success guide". Street Talk magazine says "This book is a must read for all former and currently incarcerated individuals who are truly committed to the pursuit of happiness and fulfillment." Philadelphia Chronicles says: "Simply put, this is the best book of its kind on the subject matter from inmate to boss." Its $15 plus $3 s/h, but **FREE** s/h for inmates. E-book is available.

## Harvest 21 Gifts
PO Box 3472
Modesto, CA 95353

"Best gifts, service, and price. **FREE** 30 day e-mail account. No risk!"

email: harvest21gifts@gmail.com

## Harvest Time Books
Altamont, TN 37301

Address it exactly like that. Ask for their catalog and they'll send you a list of FREE books.

**Comment:** I sent for a lot of their books when I was doing a SHU and they sent 'em, but they were just way too religious for me. - - GURU

### Hasting Women's Law Journal
100 McAllister, Suite 2207
San Francisco, CA 94102

HWLJ seeks submissions from women in prison about their experiences for publication. Write/Send SASE for more information.

### H. Avery
8280 SW 24th St., Apt. 7111
Pompano Beach, FL 33068

H. Avery sells address labels. It's $7 for 500, and $12 for 1,000; 3 lines of text.

### Hawaii Innocence Project
Attention: Prof. Hench
University of Hawai`i School of Law
2515 Dole Street
Honolulu HI 96822

The Hawaii Innocence Project (HIP) provides **FREE** legal assistance to Hawaii prisoners with substantiated claims of actual innocence in seeking exoneration, including investigating and obtaining DNA testing.

Phone Number: (808) 956-6547
Website: http://www.innocenceprojecthawaii.org

### Hawkeye Editing
PO Box 16406
St. Paul, MN 55116

Editing and typing services. Reasonable rates and rapid response. FREE evaluation of and manuscript, plus FREE proofreading and corrections on a single-page personal letter. Just enclose a SASE for return of your document. For quickest response, their service is also available through CorrLinks.

### Heart Mountain
1223 South St. Francis Dr. #C
Santa Fe, NM 87505

**FREE** meditation manual – doing your time with peace of mind. Comes in English, Spanish, and tape versions.

### Helping Hands' Inmate Publishing
PO Box 1793

Gastonia, NC 28054

"Inmate Publishing $99 EBook $299 Print. Includes: editing, format fb page, cover. We need crochet & art Artist for gala send SASE & $1foror contract w/pic & bio writers send intro. Payment plans."

**Comment:** I wrote their ad exactly as they did. Need I say more? - - Mike

### Help From Beyond Walls
POB 185
Springvale, ME 04083

This is a prisoner services company that does it all: pen pals ads, stamp reimbursement, photo editing, gift ordering, internet reach, letter forwarding, website creation and much more. Write/Send SASE for more information.

### Help From Outside
2620 Bellevue Way NE #200
Bellevue, WA 98004

Phone Number: 206-486-6042
Website: helpfromoutside.com

This company will help you accomplish the things you need to get done on the outside but can't -- finance and business, social networking, phone calls, information, administrative work and more. Send SASE for a brochure and application.

### Helping Educate to Advance the Rights of the Deaf (HEARD)
PO Box 1160
Washington, D.C. 20013

HEARD is an all-volunteer nonprofit organization that provides advocacy services for deaf, hard of hearing and deaf-blind inmates across the nation. HEARD's mission is to promote equal access to the justice and legal system for deaf defendants, detainees, prisoners, and returned citizens. HEARD can train and correspond with wardens, corrections officers and directors of departments of corrections; and can refer cases to our network of attorneys.

Phone Number: 202-455-8076
Website: behearddc.orp

### Hepatitis C Awareness Project
PO Box 41803

Eugene, OR 97404

**FREE** information, treatment options.

## Hepatitis and Liver Disease: What You Need to Know

Describes symptoms and treatments of hepatitis B & C and other liver diseases. Includes medications to avoid, what diet to follow, exercises to perform and a bibliography. It's 457 pages, $17.95, and can be bought from Prison Legal News.

## Hepatitis C Support Project
PO BOX 15144
Sacramento, CA 95813

The Hepatitis C Support Project (HCSP) is a registered nonprofit organization founded in 1997 to address the lack of education, support, and services available at that time for the HCV population.

Website: www.hcvadvocate.org

## Hepatitis Prison Coalition
Hepatitis Education Project
911 Western Avenue, Suite 302
Seattle, WA 98104

Provides hepatitis and blood born infection classes in all WA state prisons. Links prisoners with medical care upon release. Their newsletter, HEP News, is **FREE** to prisoners subject to available funding. Send SASE for more details.

Phone Number: (206) 732-0311

## HIV/Hepatitis –C Prison Committee
California Prison Focus
1904 Franklin Street, Suite 507
Oakland, CA 94612

Phone Number: (510) 836-7222
Website: www.prisons.org

## Hepatitis, AIDS Research Trust
513 E. 2nd St
Florence, CO 81226

Write for a monthly newsletter.

## Hollywood Scriptwriter
PO Box 10277
Burbank, CA 91510

If you want to start writing movie scripts, order this magazine. It's $36 for a 1-year subscription, 6 issues.

## Homeboy Industries
130 West Bruno Street
Los Angeles, CA 90012

"Homeboy Industries is a re-entry and rehabilitation program for formerly gang involved and previously incarcerated men and women. We offer FREE services, including: tattoo removal, employment services, twelve step meetings (AA/NA/CGA), educational classes, case management, mental health counseling, legal services, solar panel installation training etc.
These post release services will aid you in your transition to life on the outside. For instance, you can receive assistance with: 1) obtaining your Social Security card, Driver's License or California ID; 2) creating a resume, searching for employment, learning interview techniques, building job skills; 3) obtaining your GED through prep classes and one on one tutoring; 4) learning life skills, anger management, parenting, building healthy relationships, interpersonal communication, leadership, alternative to violence, etc. All of our services and classes are offered in-house at our headquarters in downtown Los Angeles. We cannot put you on a waiting list, since you have to come in person to participate.

It is my sincerest hope that you will consider us in your plans to get on the right track upon your release, and that you come become a part of the Homeboy family."

Phone: 323-526-1254
Website: HomeboyIndustries.org

## Home Business Magazine
PO Box 807
Lakeville, MN 55044

Even from a prison cell, this is a good magazine if you want to start your own business. It's $15 for a 1- year subscription, 6 issues.

Website: homebusinessmag.com

## Hot Dreams
PO Box 112118
Houston, TX 77293

"Get your new non-nude cat #31 and **FREE** photo. You must send a SASE along with 5 stamps or $2.00. Hundreds to choose in bikini and panties.

Get the non-nude super catalog package #1 that has over 2000 hot White babes in panties, lingerie and thongs. Your favorite types of shots only $15.00 **FREE** s/h. Comes with 5 **FREE** pics.

To receive a 30 pic set of cameltoe shots and coeds of all sexy, hot White babes, send only $20.00 along with 4 stamps! They are hot! In panties, bras, thongs and G strings.

Got stamps? Send 50 stamps to get 10 non-nude hot pics. Send $20.00 to get non-nude catalogs 2-11. Comes with 5 **FREE** pics.

Send $2.00 to get non-nude catalog #30.

Send only $15.00 to get the all nude big pack catalog #1. Has thousands to choose from. Comes with 5 **FREE** pics."

**Comment:** They definitely offer some great images. A lot of pussy shots. It looks like this company is either affiliated with FIYA Girls, or was bought out by them because they changed their address to theirs.

## HotFlixx
PO Box 137481
Fort Worth, TX 76136

Catalogs are $3 each + SASE

Action Shots 1
Women Vol. 1, 2, 3, 4, 5, 6, 7
Black Women Vol. 1
Tattoo Girls Vol. 1
Plumpers Vol. 1, 2
Boobs Vol. 1, 2, 3
Camel Toe Vol. 1, 2
Asian Vol. 1
Booty Vol. 1
Topless Vol. 1, 2
Latinas Vol. 1
Men Vol. 1, 2, 3, 4, 5
Transsexual Vol. 1

Pics are $1 each, 10 pic minimum per order. **FREE** shipping. Not responsible for rejected photos.

## Hour Children
36-11 12th St.
Long Island City, NY 11106

Phone Number: (718)-433-4724

## How to Win Your Personal Injury Claim, 7th edition

While not specifically for prison-related personal injury cases, this book provides comprehensive information on how to handle personal injury and property damage claims arising from accidents -- including dealing with doctors, attorneys and insurance companies. It's 304 pages, $34.99, and can be bought from Prison Legal News.

## Hoy, Marion
PO Box 833
Marble Falls, TX 78654

This is a legal consultant that specializes in whether or not you have a case against your arresting officer.

## Hudson Link For Higher Education
PO Box 862
Ossining, New York 10562

Phone Number: 914-941-0794

They offer **FREE** college courses to prisoners in select New York state prisons.

## Huffman Services
2503 Station Road, Suite 206
Erie, PA 16510

"We reduce your charge/sentence using confidential information that we find. Pre and post-conviction results. We're negotiators, not lawyers.

E-mail: huffmansservices18@gmail.com
Phone: 814-350-6898

## Human Kindness Foundation
P.O. Box 61619
Durham, NC 27715

Two **FREE** books or catalogs of other hard to find spiritual books. Sends spiritual books **FREE** to prisoners.

## Human Rights Coalition
4134 Lancaster Ave
Philadelphia PA 19104

Phone Number: 267.293.9169

## Human Rights Pen Pal Program
1301 Clay Street, PO Box 71378
Oakland, CA 94612

This is an all-volunteer group that will put you on their list for a pen pal. However, it may take a while, so please be patient.

## Human Rights Watch
1630 Connecticut Avenue N.W. Suite 500
Washington, D.C. 20009

Stands with victims and activist to prevent discrimination, to uphold political freedom, to protect people from inhumane conduct in wartime, and to bring offenders to justice. Investigates and exposes human rights violations and hold abusers accountable, challenges governments and those who hold power to end abusive practices and respect to International Human Rights Law. They work on a variety of prison issues.

Phone Number:202-612-4321.

## Hungry Robot

"There are 1.7 million children who have a parent In prison In the U.S. (Bureau of Justice Statistics). If you are one of the 357,300 parents held in state or" federal prison, then stop and consider the importance of gilding your child's growth. Hungry Robot displays the destructive habits of materialism, selfishness, and more, with a simple message -- 'find a purpose'. It's a perfect bed-time story, easy to read, fully illustrated with colorful action … and something worth thinking about!"

This book is by author Anthony Tinsman. It's only $2.99 and it's available on Kindle only. ASIN: B001P1CAK4, 30 pages.

**Comment:** Anthony is a personal friend of mine who genuinely cares about working for and contributing to 'the greater good'. If you have a child, it is your duty as a parent to spend the low $2.99 price to provide your child(ren) with this invaluable lesson. - - Mike

## Idaho Innocence Project
Boise State University
1910 University Dr
Boise, ID 83725

Focuses on cases where DNA evidence would change the outcome. Write for more criteria. Do not send transcripts or legal documents. Idaho only.

## Illinois Innocence Project
University of Illinois Springfield
One University Plaza
Springfield, Illinois 62703-5407

Phone Number: 217-206-6600

## I'm Not Crying

This book is by Michael Norwood aka Minkah Abubakar. It's $15.00 plus $3.95 for shipping and can be ordered from Don Diva Magazine.

"A story by an African-American ex-professional bank robber, now jailed for life, for a robbery he did not commit."

## Image; Center for Religious Humanism
3307 Third Ave West
Seattle, WA 98119'

Literary publication.

## Immigration Service
105 East Grant Rd
Tucson, AZ 85705

Phone Number: (520)620-9950.

## Impact Publications
9104 N Manassas Dr.
Manassas Park, VA 20111

They publish the "Ex-Offender's Job Hunting Guide"; it's $17.95.

## Incarcerated Citizens Council
Richard Carter 310 Morea Road
Frackville, PA 17932

**Indiana University**
Owen Hall 001
790 E. Kirkwood Avenue
Bloomington, IN 47405

Highly recommended career college.

**Indian Life Magazine**
PO Box 32
Pembina, ND 58271

This magazine has a lot of Native American resources.
Send $1.50 or 4 stamps and they'll send you a sample.

Phone Number: (204) 661.9333
Website: indianlife.org.

**Infectious Diseases In Corrections Report**
146 Clifford St
Providence, RI 02903

Publication edited and written by prison health care
providers discussing HIV/AIDS and hepatitis care for
incarcerated people.

**Infinity Publishing**
1094 Dehaven St. Suite 100
Attn: **FREE** Guide
West Conshohocken, PA 19428

This is a book publishing company. Write and request
their **FREE** guide on how they can help you publish
your book(s).

Phone Number: (877) buy-book
Website: infinitypublishing.com.

**Info**
PO Box 64
Darien, CT 06820

Looking for a writing coach to help you with your
literary works? Write/Send SASE for more information.

**InfoLINKS, L.L.C.**

Offers daily sports info and updates, photo forwarding
from your family to you, gifts and flowers sent to your
family from you, **FREE** horoscopes and quotes and
**FREE** legal news. Sign up now at info@infolincs.com.

**Ink From The Pen Magazine**
1440 Beaumont Ave., Suite A2-266
Beaumont, CA 92223

Ink From The Pen Mag is a mag full of prison art. You
can order an issue for $12.95 plus $5.95 for s/h.

How to submit artwork:
"Submission of artwork to be considered for publication
may be done one of several different ways

You may submit original artwork, and if you would like
it sent on to a loved one please include a SASE. After I
have scanned and made a complete electronic file of the
artwork I will then send it on to your requested
designation.

You may also submit either good-quality copies, or you
may have a loved one email JPEG files to
inkfromthepen@yahoo.com.

Any original artwork submitted without a SASE with
where to send it will be considered a gift, and will be
kept to display at the several different art expos I have
planned for the upcoming year.

To be considered as a feature artist and not just a guest
artist, I must have a minimum of 10 pieces of artwork,
because the collectible trading cards in each issue are
made from featured artists' artwork.

I do not need 10 pieces to publish as a guest artist.

I look forward to seeing your work. I'm very excited
about this project and really hope you will come aboard
with us."

Website: inkfromthepenmagazine.com
Email: inkfromthepen@yahoo.com

**Comment**: I've only seen one issue. It was decent
quality but I'm not sure how stable the
business/magazine is. Their communications is not
that good either, but if you're a struggling artist
trying to get your work out there, you gotta take
advantage of all you can. - - Mike

**INKWELL Magazine**
Manhattanville College
2900 Purchase Street
Purchase, NY 10577

Mail Entry Guidelines: Entry fee: $5 for the first poem,
$3 for each additional poem. Include your name,
address and email in a cover letter or on each poem.

Phone Number: (914) 323-5239
Email: inkwell@mville.edu

**Inmate Alliance, LLC**
PO Box 241
Lebanon, OR 97355

Your pen pal connection. Send SASE for more info.

**Comment:** Some new shit I ain't checked out yet. But I will. - - Mike

**InmateConnections**
465 NE 181 St. #308
Portland, OR 97230

Pen pal company that runs the sites
inmateconnections.com
and convictpenpals.com. Send SASE for **FREE** brochure.

**InmateNHouse love .com**
4001 Inglewood Ave. Suite 10 Dept. 144
Redondo Beach, CA 90278

Pen pal Company. Send SASE for details.

**InmateMAGS.com**
4208 University Way NE
Seattle, WA 98105

Will send a printed catalog with descriptions of 1200+ magazines and 1200 newspapers from over 70 countries for 10 stamps or $3.00. Write/Send SASE for more information.

Website: inmatemag.com

**Inmate Classified**
PO Box 3311
Granada Hills, CA 91394

This is a pen pal website. They also offer email forwarding. Write/Send SASE for more information.

**Inmateconnections.com**
465 NE 181st Ave. #308
Portland, OR 97230-6660

Pan pal hookups for prisoners! 92% response rate in 20141 75,000+ hits daily! A+ rating with the BBB! Accepts checks, credit cards, stamps, Moneygram and

Trugram. Write for a **FREE** brochure/application. Send SASE or stamp for fast reply.

**Inmate-Connection.com**
PO Box 83897
Los Angeles, CA 90083

"Only the best and hottest photos! We have the newest, most sensational and exclusive photos on the planet! To order our **FREE** catalog, send SASE or $1.20. All photos are prison friendly. All photos are 4X6, high quality and glossy!

Photo prices:

12 photos for $10
16 photos for $15
22 photos for $20
28 photos for $25
35 photos for $30
45 photos for $35

Minimum order is $10. Additional pics with any set are $.80 each. Add a flat rate of $2.20 for shipping on all orders. We will not ship your order without payment for postage. We do not accept stamps for payment. We have been in business since July 2002."

**Comment:** Good images. – Mike

**Inmate Magazine Services**
PO Box 2063
Fort Walton Beach, FL 32549

They sell magazines at a discount. Write/Send SASE for more information.

Website: inmatemagazineservice.com.

**InmateNavigator.Org**
827 Missouri St., Suite
Fairfield, CA 94533

Community services, E-mentorship, Legal document assistance.

Phone: 707-877-6060

**Inmate Pen Pal Connection**
Attn: Ralph Landi
49 Crown St. 20B
Brooklyn, NY 11225

Pen pal ads, personal webpage, MySpace, Facebook and Craigslist ads. They do it all for one low price. Send 6 stamps for more information.

## Inmate Photo Provider
PO Box 2451
Forrest City, AR 72336

"Don't miss another special moment or event! Stay in the loop!

Have your FAMILY/FRIENDS text you UNLIMITED photos to (870) 317-7561 or email them to you at info@inmateprovider.com. All EMAIL/TEXT PHOTOS must include your full name, inmate number and address in the subject line in order for delivery to occur. If you ever go to the SHU, HOLE, or on LOCKDOWN at your facility, NO PROBLEM! We will continue to process your orders as long as funds are available in your prepaid account. Start your prepaid account today!) Minimum $10 deposit required.)

All photos are .50 cents per copy plus tax, shipping and handling. We also print social media photos from your Facebook page, Instagram account, Tagg, and the likes for .89 cents per copy, plus tax, shipping and handling! Our prices are based on the quality of service we provide. Photos are received and processed 24/7, seven days a week with quality service guaranteed for all local, state, federal and international inmates. Send your deposit to the above address today!

All deposits received will go toward processing your orders. For additional payment options, email us. Our representatives are standing by to assist you! We ACCEPT Money Orders, Institutional checks, JPay, MoneyGram (contact us for outside representative information to use this feature via email), family/friend debit or credit PayPal deposits are accepted. We do not accept personal checks. '

EXCLUSIVE FEATURE...

Add backgrounds, clothes and your loved ones to your photos! Starting at $15 (charges may vary according to your request and detail). Add $2.50 per additional photo used to create your photo. You must number your photo(s) and explain which features you want applied to your photo(s) on an additional sheet of paper. Based on your request, an additional 2-3 days may be needed to fulfill your order. For more information, see our Product & Service Description Pages in our catalog.

SOCIAL MEDIA...

SM Page Monitoring Packages available (prices vary). Email us at socialmedia@inmateprovider.com with questions.

NOW PROVIDING LOCAL NUMBERS ...

Affordable Inmate Calling Services, keeping you connected while saving you money! 100% Compliant! Make your everyday long distance calls into local calls today! Receive (3) local numbers for only $22. With signing up today, earn (1) FREE MONTH of service ($10 activation fee included). You must provide us with the" first and last name of the contact personal for each line of service requested for verification and security purposes! Once payment is received, we will contact your family/friend to activate your account. We will email or mail you your local landline number after your account is set up.

Let IPP copy, Enlarge, and Collage your Photo(s) Today! 4x6, 5x7, 8x10 and wallet size services available, color or black and white!

To learn more about our magazine subscriptions, product, services, features and rates, simply write or email us at info@inmateprovider.com. To receive information from IPP, you must provide a SASE with your request, and if you are requesting our magazine listing, please send in (3) postage stamps

**Comment:** I received their catalog of photo manipulation examples. The quality looks pretty decent, especially for the price. They can take your head and put it on a body wearing a suit, or some other outfit that's better than your prison clothes. They can cut the background out of your prison photo and have you standing in front of a Bently, or in your city, whatever. - - Mike

## Comment: This is a good business. -- Jesse Mason
## Inmate Scribes
P.O. Box 371303
Milwaukee, WI 53237

Offers e-mail, facebook, dating sites, pen pal sites, social media, research, friend finding, lyrics and tabs, personal gifts, photo editing, sexy photos and more. Send SASE for a **FREE** brochure.

## Inmateservices.net
13017 Wisteria Dr. #310
Germantown, MD 20874

Affordable gifts. Send a first-class stamp for catalog.

## Inmate Toll Busters

Discount inmate telephone calling services for federal and state prisons, county jails and INS detention centers nationwide. **FREE** same day installation, only $1.25 per month and 6¢ per minute. They send to cell phones. International call service available.

Phone Number: (888) 966-8655
Website: inmatetollbusters.com

## Innocence and Justice Project

Univ of New Mexico School of Law 1117 Stanford NE
Albuquerque, NM 87131-0001

Phone Number: 505-277-2671

## Innocence Matters

PO Box 1098
Torrance, CA 90505

Phone Number: 310-755-2518
Website: innocencematters.us

## Innocence Project

40 Worth St., Suite 701
New York, NY 10013

Provides advocacy for wrongly convicted prisoners whose cases Involve DNA evidence and are at the post-conviction appeal stage. Maintains an online list of state-by-state innocence projects.

Phone Number: 212-364-5340
Website: Innocenceproject.org

## Innocence Project For Justice (New Jersey Cases)

Rutgers University School Of Law Constitutional Litigation Clinic
123 Washington St.
Newark, NJ 07102

INNOCENT, a Christian-based non-profit organization refers prison inmates and their families to a national network of Innocence organizations following receipt and review of claims of wrongful conviction. Utilizing expertise in the media and in community organization, INNOCENT increases public awareness of legitimate claims of innocence and problems associated with wrongful convictions. (Founded by an innocent who was released in 2004 after fighting 10 years.)

## Innocence Project NW Clinic

University of Washington School of Law
William H Gates Hall, Suite 265
PO Box 85110
Seattle, WA 98145

They will only consider cases from Washington in which actual innocence is claimed. Write for questionnaire to fill out about your case.

Website: law.washington.edu/ipnw.

## Innocence Project of Florida, Inc.

1100 East Park Avenue
Tallahassee, FL 32301

The Innocence Project of Florida (IPF) is an IRS-certified 501(c) (3), non-profit organization founded in January 2003 to help innocent prisoners in Florida obtain their freedom and rebuild their lives

Phone (850) 561-6767
Website:floridainnocence.org

## Innocence Project of Iowa

19 South 7th Street
Estherville, IA 51334

Website: iowainnocence.org

## Innocence Project of Minnesota

Hamline University School of Law
1536 Hewitt Avenue
St. Paul, MN 55104

Phone: 651-523-3152

## Innocence Project of New Orleans

4051 Ulloa Street
New Orleans, LA 70119

E-mail: info@ip-no.org
Website: http://www.ip-no.org

## Innovative Sentencing Solutions

78 DeepwoodDr
Avon, CT 06001

They offer a nice variety of services for federal prisoners. Write/Send SASE for details.

Phone Number; (860)922-7321
Website: innovativesentencing.com.

**Innocence Project (National)**
40 Worth Street, Suite 701
New York, NY 10013

Only handles cases where post-conviction DNA testing of evidence can yield conclusive evidence of innocence. Currently not accepting new cases from California, Ohio, Washington, or Wisconsin (check state listings for those states)

Website: innocenceproject.org.

**The Innocence Project of Texas 1511**
Texas Ave.
Lubbock, Texas 79401

Phone: (806) 744-6525
Website: http://www.ipoftexas.org/

**In Scan Document Services**
401 Wilshire Blvd, 12th Floor PH
Santa Monica, CA 90401

This is a nationwide document scanning service for inmates. "Never fear losing your documents during a search or being transferred!"

You mail them your documents. Their attorney-based service will ensure that you documents will be safely secured.
They scan the documents. The documents are scanned into a secure digital file in which you will have access to. Ask about their printing fees.
They mail you back the originals. Shipping fees will apply. They can also shred the originals per your request.

Only $59.99 -- onetime fee, permanent storage.

Scanning fees do apply: up to 500 pages is $0.30/PG; over 500 pages is $0.25/PG.

Founded and powered by attorneys who understand the value of your documents! Write today!

Phone: 800-470-5338
Website: inmatescan.com

**Inside Books Project**
C/O 12th St Books
827 W 12th St
Austin, TX 78701

All volunteer, non-profit organization that sends **FREE** books and educational materials to people in prison in the state of Texas.

Phone Number: (512) 647-4803

**Inside Dharma**
PO Box 220721
Kirkwood, MO 63122

Offers a bi-monthly Buddhist newsletter for prisoners. Write/Send SASE for details.

**Inside Out**
PO Box 29040
Cleveland, OH 44129

Pen pal services. Write/Send SASE for details.

Website: insideout.com.

**Inside-Out Prison Exchange Project**
University of Oregon
1585 E 13th Ave
Eugene, OR 97403

Phone Number: 405-208-6161

**INSIGHTCREW**

Market indexes and currency prices. Includes a stock watch list (make your own watch list). List emailed to you Mon-Fri. Two FREE weeks when you sign up!

Email: Mkinsightcrew@gmail.com

**Insight Meditation Society**
1230 Pleasant St.
Barra, MA 01005

Website: www.dharma.org

**The Insight Prison Project**
PO Box 151642
San Rafael, CA 94915

Communication training in nonviolence in correctional facilities; expanding to include post-release training.

Phone Number: (415) 459-9800

**Inspector General Hotline**

State Capitol, Room 160
900 Court Street
Salem, OR 97310

Inmates who are currently being sexually assaulted are encouraged to talk to a staff member. This will allow for the quickest response. Each institution has a Sexual Assault Response Team that can respond and ensure needed services are afforded. Inmates may report in person, through an inmate communication, or through the grievance system.

The Governor's Citizen Message Line: (503) 378-4582

## Institute For Criminals Justice Healthcare
1700 Diagonal Rd Ste 110
Alexandria, VA 22314

Phone Number: (703) 836-0024
Website: institute-for-criminal-justice-healthcare.

## Institute of Children's Literature
93 Long Ridge Rd.
West Reddington, CT 06896

This is a writing school that will help if you are serious about writing children's books. Write and request their **FREE** catalog.

Phone Number: (800) 243-9645
Website: theinstituteofchildrensliterature.com.

## Intelligent Solutions

I DO NOT RECOMMEND DOING BUSINESS WITH THIS COMPANY!

## International Christian College & Seminary
PO Box 530212
Debary, FL 32753

Correspondence courses via mail. Tuition as little as $12.95 per month. FREE evaluation! Send a SASE. Associates -- Pd.D. Accredited.

## Internal Affairs, CDCR
10111 Old Placerville Rd., Suite 200
Sacramento, CA 05827

## International Acoustic Music Awards
2881 E. Oakland Park Blvd, Suite 414
Ft. Lauderdale, FL 3306, USA

IAMA offers a songwriting contest. Send SASE for flier with details.

Website: inacoustic.com

## International Association of Sufism Prison Project
14 Commercial Blvd. Suite 101
Novato, CA 94949

A program of the IAS; also runs the Sufi Women Organization Prison Program. Correspondence opportunities and a quarterly newsletter.

Phone Number: 415-382-7834.

## International Bible Society
1820 Jet Stream Dr.
Colorado Springs, CO 80921-3696

Inmates can receive **FREE** on the inside Bible (English or Spanish) and a booklet for women or men. No large print inmate bibles.

## International Buddhist Meditation Center
928 South New Hampshire Ave,
Los Angeles, CA 90006

IBMC is primarily oriented toward Zen but teaches all schools of Buddhism. "We can send our quarterly newsletter c/o the prison library or chaplain. You may write to request the newsletter. We will send a maximum of 4 copies to each prison."

Phone Number: (213) 384-0850
Website: www.ibmc.info.

## International Christian College and Seminary
P.O. Box 530212
Debary, FL 32753

Correspondence courses via mail, associates through PhD, credit for life experience, tuition as low as $19.95 a month. This school is not regionally credited. Send SASE for a **FREE** evaluation.

## International Food Information Council Foundation
1100 Connecticut Ave., NW, Suite 430
Washington, DC 20036

IFIC, the International Food Information Council Foundation provides food safety, healthy eating and nutrition information.

Website: foodinsight.org.

**International Prison Ministry**
PO Box 2868
Costa Mesa, CA 92628-2868

"IPM has available FREE of charge to prisoners all over the US when requested and if there is time to get materials there before a release or transfer: Bibles (KJV regular print or the New KJV in regular print). The Practical Bible Dictionary/Concordance, Testimony and Devotional books. We do not send lists of our books because the inventory changes without notice. We send a list of organizations who have Bible Study Correspondence Courses, but we do not have correspondence course as such, just books which help you study the Bible. We do not send you monthly newsletters or magazines to inmates. In order to get literature, one must write and request it. We are happy to answer prisoner letters and send what we can when we can. We send New Testaments to short term facilities such as jails, reception centers, etc. No Pen Pal programs available that we know of. We are sorry we cannot fulfill the requests for different Bibles and books other than those above. "

**International Prison Watch Project**
PO Box 674
Las Cruces, NM 88004

An international coalition of advocates dedicated to shedding a spotlight inside our prison walls.

**Internationalist Prison Books Collective**
405 West Franklin Street
Chapel Hill, NC 27514

Volunteer collective that sends books to prisoners in Mississippi, Alabama, and parts of North Carolina. Has fiction as well as political and legal nonfiction. Also prints prisoners' art, writing, and news in a regular biannual publication.

Phone Number: (919) 942-1740

**International Sports Sciences Association**
1015 Mark Avenue
Carpentaria, LA 93013

The International Sports Sciences Association acts as a teaching institution and certification agency for fitness trainers, athletic trainers, aerobics instructors, and medical professionals in every field of health care. All seven training courses can be completed entirely through the mail. Each program costs $600

**Inner Traditions, Bear & Co**
One Park St.
PO Box 388
Rochester, VT 05767

They send inmates various religious publications. Write for more details.

**Internet Access Through Mail**
4600 Monterey Oaks Blvd., #235
Austin, TX 78749

This company provides internet searches, as well as some email services. Write/Send SASE for more information.

**In The Wind**
PO Box 3000
Agoura Hills, CA 91376

This magazine is about custom Harleys and events. It's $16.95 for a 1-year subscription, 4 issues per year.

Phone Number: (818)889-8740
Website: easyriders.com

**In-Touch Ministries**
P.O. Box 7900
Atlanta, GA 30357

**FREE** *"In Touch"* religious magazine.

**Islamic AhlulBayt Association**
12460 Los Indios Trail
Austin, TX 78729

**Islamic Center**
2551 Massachusetts Ave, NW
Washington, DC 20008

They provide **FREE** Koran and study guides. Can send through Chaplain.

**Islamic Center of Springfield Missouri**
2151 East Division St.
Springfield, MO 65803

Provides **FREE** Qur'an and will write letters to prison authorities and to politicians about conditions in prisons for prisoners in Missouri and adjacent states.

**Islamic Circle of North America**
166-26 89th Ave

Jamaica, NY 11432

They provide Islamic material and guidance.

**ISO of SAA Inc**.
PO Box 70949
Houston, TX 77270 USA

Website: saa-recovery.org.

# J

**Jackson & Associates Law Centers**
402 W. Broadway, POB 81609
San Diego, CA 92138

This firm calls themselves the "Freedom Angels." Their goal is to get you an evidentiary hearing. They look for new evidence, witness, etc. They make a lot of nice claims; might be worth writing for more Info.

Phone: 1-855-411-2643
Website: 411FreedomANGELS.com

**Jackson & Reed**
601 Sawyer Ste. 105
Houston, TX 77007

Attorneys that offer compassionate defense, parole, and post-conviction work. Parole representation from $1500.

Phone Number: 713-429-1405
Website: jacksonandreed .com

**JAD Enterprises.**
4409 Birdsong
Plano, TX 75093

"100% guaranteed pen pal locator! We have a large database of available men and women seeking prison pen pals. Tell us what you're looking for and we'll make a connection for you. We also offer other services. Sens a SASE for more info!"

**Jaden Moore of New York**
2600 south Rd., Suite 44-258
Poughkeepsie, NY 12601

This company sells tons of gifts that you can purchase and send to your loved ones. Send $2.50 or 5 stamps for a full color catalog.

Website: jadenmooreofnewyork.com.

**Jaguar Books**
7271 Garden Grove Blvd. E
Garden Grove, CA 92841

Order a 40 page, full color, magazine-type catalog by sending $1 or 3 f/c Forever stamps. Hundreds of books – fiction, nonfiction, novels, religious cards, pastimes – English and Spanish.

**Jail Calls**
PO Box 271
Cedar Brook, NJ 08018

This company provides phone calls at a discount. Write/Send SASE for more information.

Phone Number: (888)892-9998
Website: jailcalls.com.

**JailCallsUSA.com**

$9.95 a month for unlimited calls for federal, state, and county inmates. They'll give you a local number and make it to where inmates can call your cell phone.

Phone Number: 888-776-2012

**Jail House Lawyers Guild**
1734 Summit
Mount Holly, VT 05785

Website: justicepersued.com.

**Jailhouse Lawyers: Prisoners Defending Prisoners v. the USA**

In "Jailhouse Lawyers," Prison Legal News columnist, award-winning journalist and former death-row prisoner Mumia Abu-Jamal presents the stories and reflections of fellow prisoners-turned-advocates who have learned to use the court system to represent other prisoners, and in some cases have won their freedom. A must-read for jailhouse lawyers! This book is 280 pages, $16.95, and can be bought from Prison Legal News.

**JDM**
PO Box 130063
Dallas, TX 75313

Write for a **FREE** Kings James bible.

**Jeff Vencent**
109 Post Oak Circle
Hurst, TX 76053

This is a typing service. Write/Send SASE for more information.

Phone Number: (817) 282-1392.

**Jewish Prisoners Assistance Foundation**
770 Eastern Parkway
Brooklyn, NY 11213

Publishes The Scroll, **FREE** weekly newsletter for Jewish prisoners.

Phone Number: 718-735-2000

Website: www.prisonactivist.org/resources

**Jewish Prisoners Services International**
PO Box 85840
Seattle, WA 98145

They offer religious materials and support for Jewish prisoners and their families.

Phone Number: (206) 985-0577
Website: jewishprisonerservices.org.

**John's Services**
601 Mackenzie St. NE #209
Warroad, MN 56763

Send one F/C stamp for details.

**Jokes**
Po Box 3000
Agoura Hills, CA 91301

Easyrider magazine pays $40 for good jokes, old or new, on biker oriented subjects.

**Journal of Prisoners on Prisons**
c/o Justin Piche, PhD
Department of Criminology
University of Ottawa
Ottawa, Ontario, Canada
K1N 6N5

General Information...

The JPP is a prisoner written, academically oriented and peer reviewed, non-profit journal, based on the tradition of penal press. It brings the knowledge produced by prison writers together with academic arguments to enlighten public discourse about the current state or carceral institutions. This is particularly important because with few exceptions, definitions of deviance and constructions of those participating in these defined acts are incompletely created by social scientists, media representatives, politicians and those in the legal community. These analyses most often promote self-serving interests, omit the voices of those most affected, and facilitate repressive and reactionary penal policies and practices. As a result, the JPP attempts to acknowledge the accounts, experiences, and criticism~ of the criminalized by providing an educational forum that allows women and men to participate in the development of research that concerns them directly. In an age where 'crime' has become lucrative and exploitable, the JPP exists as an important alternate source of information that competes with popularly held stereotypes and misconceptions about those who are currently, or those who have in the past, faced the deprivation of liberty.

History...

The JPP grew out of presentations at the International Conference on Penal Abolition (ICOPA) III held in Montreal in 1987, where participants were concerned with the lack of prisoner representation. It subsequently emerged in 1988, and has since published over 30 issues featuring prison writers from many different countries who discuss a broad range of topics pertaining to imprisonment. Articles are used regularly in university courses, and are frequently reprinted in books and cited in academic works. Readership includes prisoners, former prisoners, activists, academics, as well as community and justice workers amongst many others. The Editorial Board that produces and manages the journal is comprised of university professors, prison justice activists, and current and former prisoners who voluntarily contribute time and effort, The JPP is funded through subscriptions and sales and is not dependent on any outside sources. It is currently published through the University of Ottawa Press in a bi-annual format. Many past contributors have received awards for their writing (e.g. PEN) and also have gone on to publish books. Writing as Resistance: The JPP Anthology 1988-2002 (Gaucher, Ed. 2002) won silver prize for book of the year in Foreword Magazine's annual awards in 2002.

Submission Guidelines...

- Prisoners and former prisoners are encouraged to submit papers, collaborative essays, discussions transcribed from tape, book reviews, and photo or graphic essays.
- The Journal will not publish any subject matter that advocates hatred, sexism, racism, violence or that supports the death penalty.
- The Journal does not publish material that usually focuses on the writer's own legal case, although the use of the writer's personal experience as an illustration of a broader topic is encouraged.
- The Journal does not usually publish fiction and does not generally publish poetry.
- Illustrations, drawings and paintings may be submitted as potential cover art.
- Articles should be no longer than 20 pages typed and double-spaced or legibly handwritten. Electronic submissions are great fully received.
- Writers may elect to write anonymously or under pseudonym.
- For references cited in an article, writers should attempt to provide the necessary bibliographic information. Refer to the references cited in past issues for examples.
- Editors look for developed pieces that address topics substantially. Manuscripts go through a preliminary reading and then are sent to review' by the Editorial Board. Those that are of suitable interest are returned to the author with comments or suggestions. Editors work with writers on composition and form, and where necessary may help the author with referencing and bibliographic information not readily available in prisons. Selected articles are returned to authors for their approval before publication. Papers not selected are returned with comments from the editor. Revised papers may be resubmitted.
- Please submit biographical and contact information, to be published alongside articles unless otherwise indicated.
- If interested in making a submission we appreciate the enclosure of a brief abstract, with clear and accurate contact details for the author.

## Journal Broadcasting and Communications
PO Box 3084
Pittsburgh, PA 15230

This company sells a book titled "Writing for Lawyers," by Hollis T. Hurd, for about $6.

## Joyce Meyers Ministries
PO Box 655

Fenton, MO 63026

Write to request their **FREE** monthly magazine and a **FREE** one-time-only hygiene gift.

## Julie's Gifts
PO Box 1941
Buford, GA 30515

This company has a lot of nice gifts for sale. Write/Send SASE for more information.

**Comment:** I've never ordered gifts from Julie, but I have ordered her magazines (she runs Tightwad) and her business there was all the way straight. Fast and accurate. She gets an A+ from me for sure. - - Mike

## Just Detention International
3325 Wilshire Blvd., Suite 340
Los Angeles, CA 90010

This is a human rights organization that seeks to end sexual abuse against men, women, and youth in all forms of detention.

Phone Number: 213-384-1400

Website: justdetention.org

## Justice Brandeis Law Project
(formerly the Justice Brandeis Innocence Project)
Schuster Institute for Investigative Journalism
Goldfarb 69-19, MS 043
415 South Street
Waltham, MA 02453

Phone Number: (781) 736-4953

## Justice Denied
P.O. Box 66291
Seattle, WA 98166

Although no longer publishing a print magazine, Justice Denied continues to provide the most comprehensive coverage of wrongful convictions and how and why they occur. Their content is available online and includes all back issues of Justice Denied magazine and a database of more than 3,000 wrongly convicted people.

Phone Number: 206-335-4254
Website: justicedenied .org

**Just Us Investigation**
191 North Ave., Suite 236
Dunellen, NJ 08812

They provide internet searches.

**Justice Now**
1322 Webster Street Suite 210
Oakland, CA 94612

Focuses solely on the needs of women prisoners. They work on alternative sentencing, document human rights abuses in prison, and their Building a World without Prisons project (works with women prisoners to get their words and art in the media).

Phone Number: (510) 839-7654

**Justice Watch**
1120 Garden Street
Cincinnati, OH 45214

Works to eliminate classism and racism from prisons and opposes the death penalty. Operates Garden Street Transitional House for parolees. Publishes quarterly newsletter.

Phone Number: (513) 241-0490

**Juvenile Lifers**
P.O. Box 8077
Pittsburgh, PA 15216

This is a not-for-profit organization dedicated to juveniles in the state of Pennsylvania and across the country who are serving sentences of life without parole. "Our purpose is to educate the public and legislators and to reach out to juveniles and their families."

Website: juvenilelifers.org

If you have your own stories about lifers for publication email them to: lifex@prisoners.com.
http://www.prisoners.com/life.html#life

# K

**Kabbalah Research Institute**
ATTN: Mikhail Plaksin

PO Box 670263
Flushing, NY 11365

Would you like to study Kabbalah? For a **FREE** interactive correspondence course, write to them.

**Keeping the Faith: The Prison Project**
606 Maynard Ave, Suite 201
Seattle, WA 98104

Founded in 1995, "Keeping the Faith: The Prison Project" is a series of workshops with incarcerated women in WA, MA, FL, and Brazil focusing on writing, movement, and performance skills provided through lecture demonstrations, performances, and classes.

Phone Number: (206) 522-8151

**Kenneth Passaro**
PO Box 1799
Patterson, NJ 07509

Email, Internet, phone, etc. Send SASE.

**Kentucky Innocence Project**
Department of Public Advocacy
100 Fair Oaks Lane, Ste. 302
Frankfort, KY 40601

Phone Number: 502-564-3948
Website: dpa.ky.gov/kip

**Kill Shot King**
PO Box 81074
Corpus Christi, TX 78468

"Are you in prison, or do you have a homeboy in prison? Kill Shot King is what you need! Kill Shot King has made thousands of men in prison happy with our shots of sexy females! If you have a homeboy in prison, show him some love by getting him a $10 VIP gift card at KillShotKing.com! All our shots are 30 each or less until September 1, 2015! WE DO NOT ADD TAX, SHIPPING, OR ANY OTHER BS CHARGES TO OUR PRICES! All our shots are high gloss 4x6 photos and are 100% waterproof.

Use code BatmanBMPagasus to get 50 shots for $10! Good until September 1, 2015. You pick 'em and we ship 'em!

Send us a SASE for a **FREE** catalog with 396 images! Just let us know if you went 'action' or 'non-action' type catalog because we know some prisons don't allow 'action shots.' Download and print all our catalogs for **FREE** at KillShotKing.com!

Don't want to wait for your withdraw request to be approved or do you have a limit of how many shots you can order at once? Solve both problems by purchasing one of our VIP gift cards! Spend what you want when you want! Stop paying more with the other guys! Enter our $500 art contest! Go to KillShotKing.com or send us a SASE for more information.

**Comment**: Every other year or so I see an add from this company. I've seen them in PLN, and I've also seen a full-page ad in BlackMen Magazine. But they have never responded, even though I included a SASE. That is a problem for me. - - Mike

### King Poe Publishing
817 Bridle Drive
Desoto, TX 75115

Floyd "Poe" Simms is the author of 'How to Became a Millionaire Buying and Renting Properties in the Hood,' and 'Lil Poe: Drug Kingpin.' Each book is $15.99 plus $4.00 for s/h. You can order them direct.

### Kira International
PO Box 2839
North Babylon, NY 11703

Discount phone service.

Phone Number: (631)983-3719
Website: kiraintl.com.

### Krashna Law Firm, LLP
Omar Krashna, Attorney at Law
7700 Edgewater Drive, Suite 1030
Oakland, CA 94621

Personal injury attorney.

Phone Number: (510) 836-2999

### Krasnya LLC
PO Box 32082
Baltimore, MD 21282

"Welcome to Krasnya Babes and Krasnya Studs worldwide. Tens of thousands of the hottest and most scandalous babes and dudes found on the planet. Each catalog has 120 beautiful girls or boys posing just for you! Order one catalog page for only $4.50 or 10 U.S. Forever stamps with a SASE. We will send you volume one. Each additional volume is the same price. We are more than happy to answer e-mail inquiries; however, due to mailing costs of 49¢ a letter, enclose a SASE with all inquiries sent through the mail. Otherwise, no replies! Prices and policies? Color prints on 4x6 glossy photo paper as low as 35¢ per print on orders over 500, shipped according to policy: 25 pictures shipped every 24 hours. S/h is $2.00 per envelope. Method of payment: U.S. Postal Service money orders or state and federal correctional checks made out only to Krasnya, LLC.

Send $24.95 for a grab bag of 50 photos. You specify race and main area of your interests; we will pick selection for you. We will also throw in a bonus catalog of 120 babes, nude or BOP-friendly.

Send 3 brand-new flat books of 20 U.S. Forever stamps for a grab bag of 45 photos. You specify race and main area of interest, we will pick selection. We will also throw in a bonus color catalog page of 120 babes of studs. Please include 6 forever stamps with this order for s/h.

For Krasnya clients who work the yards, have we got a great deal for you... Mr. Hustle Grab Bag Bargain Days, only 250 per babe/print. 5 grab bag minimum purchase required. $2.00 s/h per bag. 25 awesome babes per bag at only $6.25. You must buy at least 5 grab bags for this deal. You may want to sit down for this bonus bargain... Our Babes catalog special of the decade! 5 color catalogs for $6; 10 color catalogs for $12; 15 color catalogs for $18; 20 color catalogs for $24. Our catalog special is available only when you purchase the 5 grab bag minimum. The price includes **FREE** shipping on the catalogs. Because of shipping terms, all catalogs sold in multiples of 5 for $6 only. You choose male or female, nude or non-nude.

Want a **FREE** sample catalog from Krasnya? Send a BASE with 2 first class stamps. 120 babes in each catalog. You choose male or female, nude or non-nude."

E-mail: krasnyababes@hotmall.com

### KYTE Magazine

I DO <u>NOT</u> RECOMMEND DOING BUSINESS WITH THIS COMPANY!

## L33t Gaming
PO Box 30362
Midwest City, OK 73140

Comics, novels, magic, war craft gear, etc. To order full catalog, send $5.99

## La Raza Centro Legal, INC.
Lawyer Referral Service and Pro Bono Project
474 Valencia Street #295
San Francisco, CA 94103-3415

This is mainly for Spanish-speaking prisoners. They handle all types of legal problems, civil and criminal. All attorneys are located in San Francisco, but no geographic requirements for clients.

## La Voz de Esperanza
C/O The Esperanza Peace and Justice Center
922 San Pedro
San Antonio, TX 78212

This is a bilingual publication (English/Spanish) that's **FREE** to prisoners.

## Latino Commission on AIDS
24 W 25th Street, 9th Floor
New York, NY 10010

Provides education and training for treatment for all those in need with the HIV virus. Offers written information and resources in Spanish.

Phone Number: (212) 675-3288

## Latino on Wheels
585 E Larned St. Suite 100
Detroit, MI 48226

This magazine is about the latest automotive trends. 4 issues per year.

Phone Number: (313) 962-2209
Website: latinosonwheelsinc.com.

## Law Dictionary

Comprehensive up-to-date law dictionary explains more than 8,500 legal terms. Covers civil, criminal, commercial and International law. This book is 525 pages, $19.95, and can be bought from Prison Legal News.

## Lawful Remedies
3300 Bee Cave Road Suite 650-1185
Austin, TX 78746

"Your indictment is defective!! You were indicted under the wrong statue. This issue can be raised at any time. Our firm is now in the Supreme Court on this matter. Join the petition or have us file a claim in district court. With over 80 wins, a history of relief and years of experience, this issue has provided the highest rate of successful litigation on behalf of prisoners in 146 years!! Our investigative team has discovered the proof needed. Government has waived argument."

Website: lawfulremedies.com
E-mail/Corrlinks: lawfulremedies594gmail.com

## Lawyers Committee for Civil Rights Under Law
1401 New York Ave., NW, Suite 400
Washington, DC 20005

Phone Number: (202) 662-8600 or (888) 299-5227.

## Law Offices of C.W. Blaylock
401 Wilshire Blvd., Floor 12
Santa Monica, CA 90401

C.W. Blaylock has been selected as a "Rising Star" by Super Lawyers. He represents inmates for Direct Appeals, Petition for Writ of Habeas Corpus, Parole Hearings, State and Federal Admission.

Phone: 310-496-4245
Website: ChrisBlaylockLaw.com

## Law Office of David Rushing
PO Box 431649
Houston, TX 17243

David Rushing is the President of the National Association of Parole Attorneys, and the Chairman of the National Convention on Post-Conviction Relief.

Parole: packets, hearings, revocations, time, classification, medical, hardship, disciplinary and more!

Writs: state writs, federal writs, DNA writs, actual innocence, direct appeal and more!

Serving almost all state and federal jurisdictions -- local counsel who knows local in-and-outs, but who work for us nationally instead of for their local friends.

Great pricing options -- payment plans available.

STILL fighting endlessly for your rights – now almost everywhere.

Wrongful conviction is the worst crime of all! Contact us today, time may be running out!

Phone Number: 713-671-1300
Website: doctorhabeas.com

## Law Office of Donald R. Hammond
222 W. 6th Street, Ste. 400
San Pedro, CA 90731

Attorney Don Hammond is a member of Fair Chance Project.

Phone Number: 323-529-3660
Email: don@donhammondlaw.com
Website: donhammondlaw.com

## Law Office of Stanley Goff
15 Boardman Place
San Francisco, CA 94103

Police Misconduct, Criminal Defense (Prop 47 Petitions), Personal Injury, all other Civil Rights Violation.

Phone Number: (415) 571-9570
E-mail: scraiggoff@aol.com

## Law Offices of Jan Karenina Jemison, MBA
A Professional Law Corporation
3738 Park Blvd. Way
Oakland, CA 94610

Advising entrepreneurs, business owners and nonprofits.

Phone Number: (510) 530-3352

## The Law Office of William Savoie
909 Texas Ave, Ste. 205
Houston, TX 77002

Parole, post-conviction, pardons, prison planning (powers of attorney, probate/trusts for families).

Phone: 832-341-4802
Email: WLsavoielaw@gmail.com

## LC DeVine Media, LLC
P.O. Box 4026
Flint, Ml 48504

"Welcome! The Internet has changed how we do business and have created new avenues for business owners to bring the world to their place of business, searching for new ways to keep growing and earning profits. In the 21st Century a high percentage of people in the world have access to the Internet, businesses can virtually put their products and services online and have customers come to them from all over the world, instead of just their local communities. If you are a small store front, a progressive church, a company or a sole proprietor, let us help you do business 21st Century Style! That's doing business smarter, not harder! Some of the low cost, affordable services we include: Online advertising; unique website design; logo design; brochure design; business cards; post cards; signs; editing services; self-publishing; one-of-a-kind artworks.

Services/Prices: Typing, $1 per page; general editing, $2 per page (grammar and spelling clarity only); Copying, .15 for black and white, .30 for color (per page); Facebook page, $25 set-up only (you provide pic and info); Twitter page, $25 set-up only (you provide pic and info); Websites/Blogs, $200.00 set-up only (you provide pic and info); Website (3 pages), $350.00 set-up only (you supply picture and Info); E-book publishing, $500.00 complete set-up --copyright, ISBN, all profits yours; Printed book, $500.00 service fee, you pay all other expenses; E-book or printed paperback with company paying all costs, 50/50 contract deal. Fees are payable before work is done.

Please feel free to contact me if you desire any of the above services, or have any other services that I may assist you with. Sincerely, DeVine"

## Left Bank Books
92 Pike St., Box A
Seattle, WA 98101

This company carries thousands of books. Write/send SASE for more information.

## Legal Action Center
225 Varick St. 4th Floor
New York, NY 10014

Non-profit organization providing **FREE** legal services to formerly incarcerated people, recovering alcoholics, substance abusers, and people with HIV.

Phone Number: 1-800-223-4044

## Legal Action Center Services
153 Waverly Place.
New York, NY 10014

Publications about looking for work when you have a criminal record. Publication and information clearinghouse.

## Legal Aid Society Prisoner's Rights Project
199 Water Street
New York, NY 10038

Priority is to address guard brutality and sexual abuse, other unsafe physical conditions, disability discrimination, lack of mental health and medical care, and lack of educational programs for young prisoners.

Phone Number: (212) 577-3300

Legal Assistance to Minnesota Prisoners
William Mitchell College of Law
875 Summit Ave., Room 254
St Paul, MN 55105

Phone Number: 651-290-6413
Website: wmitchell.edu/legal-practice-center

## Legal Information Services Associates
PO Box 636
Norwalk, Ohio 44867

Attention Federal Prisoners! If it happened last week in the courts or in congress, you'll know about it first thing Monday morning. Our no-cost email newsletter focuses on what you care about -- Federal post-conviction cases, Sentencing Guidelines action and Capitol Hill sentence reform.

To receive our FREE newsletter, send a corrlinks invitation to newsletter@lisa-legalinfo.com.

## Legal Insights Inc
25602 Alicia Parkway, Suite 323
Laguna Hills, CA 92653

Phone Number: 775-301-3588
Website: infolegalinsights.com

Professional specialists with extensive post-conviction experience. They do Just about any type of appeal and they cover all 50 states. **FREE** initial consultation.

## Legal Liability Protection

Criminal arrest insurance coverage. Benefits: Immediate cash bail; criminal defense attorney coverage; expert eyewitness; reimbursement of lost wages while attending court; civil suit damage protection. Emergency Resources: 24/7 emergency hotline; local attorney referral within 24 hours; nationwide attorney network; expert witness coordination. Protect your constitutional rights!

Phone: 855-440-2245
Website: LegalLiabilityProtection.com

## Legal Move Logistics
PO Box 211
Lincoln, IL 62656

"Need criminal defense paralegal help or case review? Helping to overturn wrongful convictions since 1975! Send copies of paperwork and $35.00 to initial review. Need help understanding your case? I can help! Send SASE! All payments should be made out to Fonda Robbins."

## Legal Publications in Spanish, Inc.
7 E 94th St,
New York, NY 10128

## Legal Research: How to Find and Understand the Law

Comprehensive and easy to understand guide on researching the law. Explains case law, statues and digests, and much more. Includes practice exercises. This book is 568 pages, $49.99, and can be bought from Prison Legal News.

## Legal Services for Prisoners with Children
1540 Market St. #490
San Francisco, CA 94102

## LeNoir Publications
350 Bay St, Suite 100-361
San Francisco, CA 94133

This is a company that provides publishing services and specializes in catering to incarcerated individuals. To request a full list of their services, write/send SASE.

## Leonard's Mom Enterprises
PO Box 5415
Apache Junction, AZ 85278

This company provides personal assistance to prisoners. Write/Send SASE for more information.

Website: leonardsmomenterprises.com

## Lesbian AIDS Project
446 West 33rd Street c/o GMHC
New York, NY 10001

Information and support for women and lesbians living with HIV.

## Lesbian and Gay Insurrection
3543 18th Street, Suite 26
San Francisco CA 94110

Phone Number: 510-434-1304
Website: lagai.org

## Let My Fingers Do Your Typing
Sandra Z. Thomas
PO box 4178
Winter Park, FL 32793

This company provides typing services. Write/Send SASE for more information.

## Levin, Michael R, ESQ.
1001 SW 5th Ave. Suite 1414
Portland, OR 97204

Mr. Levin is the author of "138 Mitigating Factors" and offers a newsletter. Write/Send SASE for more information.

Website: services-commerce.com.

## Lewisburg Prison Project
PO Box 128
Lewisburg, PA 17837

Publishes a number of low-cost materials for prisoners, including "legal Bulletins," "Prisoner's Guide to Federal Parole," and "Due Process Standards for Administrative Detention." Provides direct legal service to all federal prisoners in Central Pennsylvania, including those at USP Allenwood and USP Lewisburg. Send SASE for publication and price list.

Phone Number: (570) 523-1104
Email Address: prisonproject@dejazzd.com.

## Liberation Prison Project

P.O. Box 31527
San Francisco, CA 94131

The prison project offers **FREE** Buddhist books, prayers and practice booklets, practice items, Mandala subscriptions and video and audio tapes of teachings to individuals and Buddhist study groups in over a hundred prisons in the United States.

Website: www.liberationprisonproject.org

## Library of Congress
101 Independence Ave., SE
Washington, DC 20540

Write and request copyright forms needed for books, screenplays, music, etc.

## L.I.F.E. Association
Thomas Rovinski CAM
Attn: Michael Moore #AY 5139; SCI-Dallas
1000 Follies Road
Dallas, PA 18612

## Lifeline
63 Forest Rd
Garston, Watford WD25 7QP, UK

International pen pal for death row prisoners only. Waiting list is 3-4 months. Postage for international is 90 cents.

## Lifers to be Free
C/O NedraStribling
3982 s. Figueroa St. #210
Los Angeles, CA 90037

Families and friends of long-term lifers and liberated lifers. Current campaign to influence the Governor to not override the Board's decision to parole.

## Lifers United
Dale Gardner BI
5107 Route 26, Box A
Bellefonte, PA 16823-0820

Pennsylvania has over 4,300 lifers and they want to see more of their lives profiled on this site. Friends and family of lifers need to have these stories told of what got their loved ones in prison, what have they done since their arrest to better themselves and their environment, and how would society benefit upon their release. For those who don't know, life in Pennsylvania means for the rest of their life. So push Pennsylvania's lifers to share their stories. You'd be surprised to hear what they have to say.

Ideally the profiles should not exceed 3 pages. One does not have to go into specific details of their crimes, admit guilt or identify victims. Also include a small photo. Once these are scanned they will be returned along with a printout of how it looks. This is all **FREE**. You will NEVER be charged.

Website: lifers.talkspot.com

## The Lionheart Foundation
PO Box 170115
Boston, MA 02117

They send a FREE resource guide. with books and organizations for prisoners.

**Comment:** I like it and have used the resources that they sent on several occasions. Send for it, you won't regret it. - - GURU

## Litigation Support
PO Box 100
Myrtle Beach, SC 29578

They offer case review, motions, and more. Send F/C stamps for details.

## Liz's Paper Jungle
This is a typing service. Contact for **FREE** estimates.

Phone Number: (949) 481-3571

## L.L.G.
PO Box 7207
Tampa, FL 33673

Subscription to Onslaught magazine and 2 year membership in the L.L.G. is $40. Write/Send SASE for more information.

## Local123.net

Discount phone calls.

## LostVault.com
PO Box 242
Mascot, TN 37806

This is a pen pal website that you can have your family post your profile on for FREE (one ad per inmate!). If you do not have someone on the outside to do it for you, LostVault will do it for $10, or FREE if you are on death row. Fees are to be made payable to LostVault and need to be on a prison-issued check or money order only. Please note that we will not return your photos or send an ad copy if you do not send us a SASE! Photos without a SASE will be held for 30 days and then destroyed.

AD RULES ...

You may not update your ad for free during the 1 year on our website except for address changes, or unless we make an error on your ad. The only exception is for death row inmates, who may update their ad after each 1-year anniversary. If any inmate wants to update the text or photo in his or her ad prior to the 1-year date, the ad will be considered new and the $10 fee will be imposed for a rewritten ad, death row included. If you do not have a photo when your ad is posted and you wish to add one later, no fee will be assessed and the ad will run for the remainder of the 1-year cycle. Bottom line: we don't have time to redo your ad over and over. If you update your ad for any reason, even an error on our part, and wish to have a copy on your new ad, you must include a SASE.
• Your ad must be under 150 words and not contain sexually explicit or foul language.
• You may send us one photo for your ad. Note that ads with photos are viewed at least 10 times more than those without.
• If you know an inmate who wishes to send us a mail ad, they must send a SASE or stamp for application.
• Please allow 45 days before you inquire about the status of your ad or photo. Mail takes time to get back and forth and to process; ads are placed in the order they are received.

**Comment:** I'm not sure if you can add more words/photos if you have someone on the outside post your profile, but I plan to check soon. Also, I've seen inmates get hits off this site. - - Mike

## Louisiana Books 2 Prisoners
1631 Elysian Fields Ave. #117
New Orleans, LA 70117

Sends **FREE** books prisoners in the following states: VA, WV, KY, TN, AR, NC, SC, LA, MS, AL, GA, and FL. Women and LA prisoners are prioritized.

## Locus

PO Box 13305
Oakland, CA

This is a newspaper that covers the sci-fi writing field. It's $60 for a 1-year subscription; 12 issues per year.

Phone Number: (510) 339-9198
Website: locusmag.com.

## Looking for a WAY OUT

This book is by Michael Norwood aka Minkah Abubakar. It's $15.00 plus $3.95 for shipping and can be ordered from Don Diva Magazine.

"An African-American legal consultant explains in easy-to-read terms how simple it is to get yourself out of prison."

## Loveaprisoner.com
PO Box 112118
Houston, TX 77293

"Inmates! Get on board today! Join Loveaprisoner.com! A year is only $25 for 1 photo and a 250 word bio. Send SASE with $2 of 5 stamps for brochure."

## Lowrider Magazine
PO Box 420235
Palm Coast, FL 32142

National and international coverage of Lowrider car shows. It's $35 for a 1-year subscription; 12 issues per year .(Note: look around because you can often find Lowrider for less than $35.)

Website: lowridermagazine.com.

## LRM
PO box 145
Hillsboro, OR 97123

This is a personal assistance company – internet searches, shopping, etc. They also offer celebrity photos. Write/Send SASE for more information.

## L.W.P.P.
10155 Greenwood Ave. N, #231
Seattle, WA 98133

They provide a cell phone service for ex-offenders. Send SASE for details.

## Lycoming County Pre-Release Center

546 County Farm RD.
Montoursville, PA 17754-9208

**M**

## The MacArthur Justice Center's Northwestern University School of Law
375 E. Chicago Ave
Chicago, IL 60611

Impact litigation on criminal justice issues, focused specifically on Illinois. Individual prisoner cases are rarely accepted.

Phone Number: 312-503-1271
Website: law.northwestem.edu/macarthur

## The Magazine Wizard
PO Box 1846
Bloomington, IN 47402

They sell magazines at a discount.

Phone Number: (800) 936-0053
Website: magwiz.com.

## Magazine City

They have magazines subscriptions at a discount, but offer no printed catalog.

Phone Number; (800) 787-1414
Website: magazinecity.com.

## Maine Books to Prisoners
c/o Norris
PO Box 12
Fairmington, ME 04938

## Maine State Prison
Gary Upham, Principal
807 Cushing Road
Warren, ME 04864

Phone: 273-5300
Email: Gary.upham@maine.gov

## Marjorie Lee Publishing
PO Box 66921
Portland, OR 97290

Majorie has been in business since 1979. See offers a bunch of pen pal lists. Send her a SASE for a complete list.

**Making Career Connections**
278 Clinton Ave
Albany, NY 12210

They help individuals with criminal histories find employment.

**Malcom X Grassroots Movement California Office**
PO Box 3585
Oakland, CA 94609

The Malcolm X Grassroots Movement is an organization of Afrikans in America/New Afrikans whose mission is to defend the human rights of our people and promote self-determination in our community.

Phone Number: (877) 248-6095.

**Maloof, Michael W.**
215 N. McDonough St.
Decatur, GA 30030

Laywer.

Phone Number: (404) 373-8000

**Manning Document Processing**
PO Box 641
Norwalk, CT 06856

They type, design and prepare manuscripts for self-publishing. Reasonable, accurate and fast.

**Manuscripts To Go**
16420 Cooley Ranch Rd.
Geyderville, CA 95441

This company will help you with your manuscript(s). Write/Send SASE for more information.

**Maoist International Ministry of Prisons**
PO Box 40799
San Francisco, CA 94140

**FREE** subscriptions to "Under Lock and Key," the voice of the anti-imperialist prison movement. Offers study courses and **FREE** books on topics including;

current events, revolutionary nationalism (BPP, YLP, Etc.) and Marxist classics.

Website: prisoncensorship.info.

**Marijuana Law**

Examines how to reduce the possibility of arrest and prosecution for people accused of the use, sale or possession of marijuana. Includes info on legal defenses, search and seizures, surveillance, asset forfeiture and drug testing. This book is 271 pages, $17.95, and can be bought from Prison Legal News.

**Marilee Marshall & Associates, Attorneys at Law**
523 West Sixth St., Suite 1109
Los Angeles, CA 90014

Certified criminal law and appellate law specialists for California inmates. 29 years of success.

Phone Number: 213-489-7715
Website: marileemarshallandassociates.com

**The Marshall Project**
156 West 56th St., Suite 701
New York, NY 10010

The background of The Marshall Project is that former New York Times Editor Bill Keller left the Times to start a new nonprofit news organization reporting solely on criminal justice, because he and many of the reporters now at The Marshall Project believed it was a pressing national issue that deserved an exclusive focus.

They launched in 2014, and the majority of their readers tend to be experts, advocates, practitioners, etc., with a direct interest in criminal justice. However, they do get a lot of readers from the general public, primarily because they co-publish many of their articles with publications like The Washington Post, The New York Times, Atlantic, Slate, Vice, etc.

ATTENTION ALL WRITERS!

Want your thoughts to be read in newspapers like The New York Times and The Washington Post? It can happen if you submit your writing to The Marshall Project. This is a call for submissions for The Marshall Project.

"The Marshall Project is a news organization that reports on the criminal justice system, including what happens inside jail and prisons. We have over 10,000 daily readers.

Part of what we do is publish first-person writing and reporting from inside jail and prisons, written by prisoners themselves. We want to give readers a sense of what life is like inside jails and prisons, and we believe that those who are actually inside are the best people to tell us.

If you are interested in writing for us – and reaching an audience of thousands of readers on the outside who want to know what life is like on the inside -- here is some information about the type of writing we are looking for.

What we are looking for: Nonfiction writing about a specific aspect of life inside. Try to focus on one specific topic and tell a story about that topic. For example, tell us a story about a friendship you've made while inside; or a story about food or going to mess hall or commissary; or about how you get exercise; or about getting an education or having a job; or how you maintain relationships with family on the outside; or a story of your relationship with staff members; or the experience of solitary confinement or other forms of punishment.

The topic could be almost anything. The most important thing is to choose a very specific part of your experience and to write us a story about it.

What we are NOT looking for: Poetry, fiction, stories about your whole life (rather than a specific topic), essays about anything outside of your direct experience."

Length: 500-2,000 words

Please include your full name, how to contact you, and the url facebook.com/thecellblock.net

## The Massachusetts Chess Association
Steve Frvmer, Prison Chess Coordinator
64 Asbury St.
Lexington, MA 02421-6521

"The MCA runs a prison chess program. We have chess magazines and chess books that we mail to both prison facility libraries and recreation coordinators in bulk, the method we prefer, and to individual prisoners. Donations are welcomed but NOT solicited.

We have a mailing list for our periodical, Chess Horizons, which is published 2-3 times per year. A yearly subscription for inmates is **FREE**.

I can evaluate one's chess skill if I'm sent a couple of games in algebraic notation."

## Matthew House
PO Box 201
Monroe, WA 98272

This is a hospitality house that provides temporary housing for families visiting prisoners in Monroe, bus service to other Washington prisons, programs for children of prisoners, prison ministry, and more.

Phone Number: (360) 794-8720.

## Medical Malpractice Experts
106 Mayfield Ave.
South Shore, Kentucky 41175

Negligence? Pain and suffering? Wrong diagnosis? Need treatment? Send SASE.

Email: baddocs2015@gmail.com

## Medill Justice Project Northwestern University
1845 Sheridan Road
Evanston, IL 60208

The Medill Justice Project investigates potentially wrongful murder convictions. The case must meet all the following criteria to be considered:
- The crime took place within 250 miles of Evanston IL
- Charges include murder
- Case heard by the appellate court and sentence confirmed
- Prisoner must claim actual innocence

Phone Number: 847-491-5840
website: medilljusticeproject.org

## Meet-A-Mate
Box 128
Coalton, OH 45621

"**FREE** ads! No forwarding fee! Send just 2 f/c stamps!"

## Meet-An-Inmate
Attn: Arlen Bischke

PO Box 1342
Pendleton, OR 97801

Pen pal service.

Website: meet-an-inmate.com

## Melvin Macomber, Ph. D.
PMB 316
8789 Auburn Folsom Road, Suite C
Granite Bay, CA 95746

Private Psychological Evaluation for Lifers.

"Many lifers are receiving CDCR/BPH FAD psychological evaluations indicating a moderate or high risk that they do not deserve, based upon the misuse of actuarial measures. This will result in a BPH lengthy denial and many more years of suffering.

A private psychological evaluation, arranged with the help of your attorney, will correct this injustice and in many cases result in your deserved release. If you have such a denial, a new psych report is new evidence, allowing you to go back to the board sooner. I have over 40 years of experience (over 3000 reports) evaluating lifers and my reports are recognized by the courts."

Phone Number: 916-652-7014
See: reports@drmelmac.com

## Meshell Baldwin Publications
14801 CR 438
Lindale, TX 75771

"Meshell Baldwin Publications is home to the most unique fetish pictures in the country. We cater to the man who craves more than your standard girly picture. We have older ladies, fat ladies, midgets, trannies, gay twinks, action shots, pregnant ladies, foot fetish and much more. Pictures are printed at a professional photo lab and are only 500 each plus shipping. Catalogs are black and white and are 3 Forever stamps or $1.00 each. Catalogs come in volumes of over 100 pictures. Mention that you saw our ad in **The BEST Resource Directory For Prisoners** and get your catalog for 2 stamps or 50¢ each! You will also get 5 **FREE** pictures when you order 10 or more pictures on your first order!

25¢ grab bag special! You tell us the type of flix and we'll pick them for you. No more than 25 flix per order. Cannot be combined with 50¢ regular f lix. Example: say you want older women, or blondes with big asses, that is what you will get. If you tell us you want gays with colored hair, we will get that for you. Keep in mind, if you order these a lot, you may get some duplications as we don't keep track of your orders. Grab bags are only from the following catalogs Fattie Action, Tranny Action, Old Lady Action, Barely Legal Action, Goth Action, Latinas Action, Asians Action, Arabs Action, or Pregnant Action.

The following catalogs are $1 each. Most have masturbation, naked butts, and lesbian/gay kissing. If this will be a problem at your institution, let us know so we can delete them before we print your catalog...

Asians vol. 1, 2
Hot Chicks 1-9, lots of camel toes and asses
Barely Legal vol. 1
Fatties vol. 1, 2
Black Babes vol. 1
Facials vol. 1, 2, 3
Older Ladies vol. 1, 2, 3, 4
Pregnant vol.1
Cigarette Smoking Gals vol. 1
Goth Gals vol. 1
Latinas vol. 1, 2
Arabians vol. 1
Foot Fetish Girls vol. 1
Cat Fight Girls vol. 1
Girl on Girl vol. 1

Single page catalogs, 250 or 1 stamp: Men Foot Fetish, Black Men, Midget Girls, Golden Showers, Hairy Muffin, Dildo Freaks, Bottle Page, Nina Hartley, Spanking, New Facials, Twink Selfies, Women Body Builders, Latino Boys, NEW Shemales.

Action Shots (Risky), 250 or 1 stamp: White 1-20, Interracial 1-12, Black 1-3, Boy On Boy 1-12, Fem Don, Bisexual, Blow Jobs 1-2, Bikini Riot Blurred, Butt Sluts Blurred.

We take institutional checks, personal checks, money orders and cash. Please make all checks out to Meshell Baldwin. S/h is as follows: 5-30 flix, $4; 31-50, $5; 51-70, $6; 71-100, $7 101-130, $8; 131-150 $9; 151-170, $10; 171-200, $11, 201-230, $12; 231-250, $13; 251-300, $14."

## Message of The Cross Ministries
PO Box 9992
Colorado Springs, CO 80932

They will send you **FREE** biblical information (Christian). Write and tell them what you're interested in learning about.

**Metropolitan Prison Consulting Service**
554 North Fredrick Ave., Suite 225
Gaithersburg, MD 20877

Phone Number: (301) 556-7741.

**Mettanokit Outreach**
173 Merriam Hill Road Attn: Medicine Story
Greenville, NH 03048

Native American circles in 9 prisons in New England. Booklet describing the program and post-prison group called Ending Violent Crime.

Phone Number: (603) 878-2310

**Mennonite Central Committee, US Office of Justice and Peace**
PO Box 500
Akron, PA 17501

**FREE** publications for prisoners and their families.

Phone Number: (717) 859-1151.

**Mexican American Legal Defense and Educational Fund (MALDEF) National Office**
634 S. Spring St., 11th floor
Los Angeles, CA 90014

Has a regional office in GA, IL, TX, CA, and DC. Largest Latino civil rights organization. MALDEF litigates large class action cases; cannot take individual cases, nor criminal cases. Write for more info. Provides referrals. Best to use online contact form.

Phone Number: (213) 629-2512.

**Miami Law Innocence Clinic**
3000 Biscayne Blvd., Suite 100
Miami, FL 33137

The Innocence Clinic is dedicated to identifying and correcting wrongful convictions.

Phone: 305-284-8115

**Michigan Innocence Clinic**
1029 Legal Research Building
625 State Street
Ann Arbor, MI 48109

Phone: 734-763-9353

**Mid-Atlantic Innocence Project**
(**District of Columbia, Maryland** and **Virginia** Cases)
American University - Washington College of Law
2000 H Street, NW
Washington, D.C. 20052

Phone Number: 202-995-4586
Website: exonerate.org

**Middle Ground Prison Reform**
139 East Encanto Drive
Tempe, AZ 85281

Working for Arizona's prisoners and their families since 1983. Main areas of activity are: 1) public education about the need for criminal justice reform 2) legislative advocacy on behalf of prisoners and their visitors 3) litigation to protect and define the rights and responsibilities of prisoners and their supporters 4) referral to community resources for ex-offenders. Spanish-speaking volunteers available.

Phone Number: (480) 966-8116.

**Midnight Express Books**
PO Box 69
Berryville, AR 72616

"We've helped inmate author's self-publish books for over 10 years. We are the preferred service company helping inmate authors self-publish their work and the only company that publishes inmate's books full time. Helping inmate authors is all we do!

**FREE** standard ebook format included with every paid paperback book project!

2014 catalog of our authors' books available. To get your copy, send FIVE unused first class postage Forever stamps with your mailing address. Please print clearly.

Do you Corrlinks? We do! Sign up for our **FREE** monthly writing tips email programs. Only available via email; sorry.

Services/Prices...

Typing Services, starting at $3.50 per page: MEB is really excited to announce that we have put together a database of typists for our authors' use. Typing projects will be quoted individually and will be based on the quality of the handwriting and the documents themselves. That is to say that if the paper the project is written on is crumpled, torn or the handwriting is light, those projects will incur a higher rate. If you want you project quoted, please send in a complete copy along with any formatting requirements. We now also accept legal document typing and typing for documents other than manuscripts to be published.

Spanish Conversion, starting at $300.00: A new service we offer to authors we've already published. We'll take your book and cover and convert them to Spanish, assign them a new ISBN for a new paperback book and ebook. There are no proofs or drafts with this service.

Digital Covers, starting at $250.00: MEB will now provide access to our group of artists to prepare covers on book projects when we are not doing the entire book project. Prices will be more for just cover projects and will be quoted individually based on design concept submitted.

ISBN and Bar Codes; $200.00 with project, $250.00 without project: Authors who only need us to provide an independent ISBN registered to them or their company, with or without an entire project assignment.

Ebooks, starting at $200.00: For authors who have previously had a print book prepared by a company other than MEB and who can provide the digital text file for the insides and pdf or indesign file for the cover, we will prepare an ebook for them and list it on Amazon for Kindle and Smashwords for distribution to other ebook retailers. Each project will be quoted independently."

Phone Number: 870-210-3772

Email: MEBooksl@yahoo.com

## Midwest Books to Prisoners
1321 North Milwaukee Ave, PMB 460
Chicago, IL 60622

**FREE** books to Midwest prisoners.

## Midwest Innocence Project
605 West 47th Street
Kansas City, MO 64113

The MIP is dedicated to the investigation, litigation and exoneration of wrongfully convicted men and women in the following states: AR, KS, MO, IA and NE. Applicant must claim actual innocence in other words, that he/she did not participate in the crime; has more than ten years left to serve on his/her sentence and/or the applicant must register as a sex offender; is not currently represented by an attorney and has NOT received the death penalty. MIP does NOT accept cases of self-defense

Phone Number: 816-221-2166
Website: themip.org.

## Midwest Pages to Prisoners Project
c/o Boxcar Books
118 S. Rogers, Suite 2
Bloomington, IN 47404

Great resource for queer studies, gender and sexuality. No California prisoner requests.

Phone Number: (812) 339-8710

## Midwest Trans Prisoner Penpal Project
c/o Boneshaker Books
2022 23rd Avenue South
Minneapolis, MN 55404

## Mike Barber Ministries
PO Box 1086
De Scto, TX 75123

Write for information on prisoner services.

## Military Records; National Personal Records Center
One, Archives Dr.
St. Louis, MO 63132

If you're interested in obtaining your military records, send a request and include your last duty station and military I.D. number.

## Millennial Masterpiecs
285 Bridger Dr.
Logan, UT 84321

"Babes 'R' Us is a division of Millennial Masterpieces. This service is not to be confused or associated with any other Babes 'R' Us online sites or services. We have established this service primarily for inmates at correctional facilities who do not otherwise have access to pictures of beautiful, non-nude women available to them. We do not have a website. All orders are by mail only, using our order form. You may duplicate your order form by hand so you have the original to refer to for subsequent or future orders.

Due to the fact that these non-nude photos might still be deemed 'inappropriate' by some facilities, you should be aware of your institutional rules and not order if you think the photos will be denied by your mailroom staff. Quantity is another factor you'll need to consider in regards to your institutional rules. NOTE: Any orders which are rejected by your facility will still be charged $1.50 for p/h costs and be deducted from any refunds! Check/ money orders must be made out to Millennial Masterpieces. Be sure to calculate the proper amount of your order, as any incorrect orders will be returned.

Photos are now printed on standard 8.5" x 11" sheets of paper, and are slightly smaller than a standard 4"x6" photo (4 pics per page, or as many as ordered). The price is $1.00 for each photo printed. Be sure to indicate by photo ID number which photo(s) you are ordering and please write legibly to avoid any mistakes in filling your order. Be sure to calculate the proper amount of your order, as any incorrect orders will be returned."

**Comment:** They currently offer a catalog of 54 Babes 'R' Us girls. All the Babes look good and the pictures themselves look like they were taken by professional photographers. - Mike

### Miller Paralegal
PO Box 687
Walnut, CA 91788

Legal research, copies, decisions, statues, and regulations, etc. Write/Send SASE for more information.

### MIM Distributors
PO Box 40799
San Francisco, CA 94140

They publish "Under Lock and Key," an anti-imperialist newsletter. Write for details.

Website: prisoncensorship.info.

### Minkah's Official Cite Book

This book is by Michael Norwood aka Minkah Abubakar. It's $15.00 plus $3.95 for shipping and can be ordered from Don Diva Magazine.

"Written by America's top jailhouse lawyer for prisoners, lawyers, and paralegals looking for a fast, inexpensive means of locating case citations that favor criminal defendants."

### Miracles Prisoner Ministry

501 E. Adams St
Wisconsin Dells, WI 53965

**FREE** spiritual recovery reading materials. Chaplains may request DVDs. Send for catalogue.

### The Missing Link
PO Box 40031
Cleveland, OH 44140

Life-changing, Christian residential programs.

### Mission Statement of the Free Speech Society

The Free Speech Society is a movement that is dedicated towards protecting and defending the First Amendment rights of imprisoned activists. As imprisoned activists, we are embedded reporters for the people. We are the eyes and ears for the people -- for the taxpayers -- articulating the human atrocities that plague the prison industrial slave complex with impunity in your name.

Human atrocities compelled by racial oppression can only flourish when silence permeates the corridors of the vortex of torture, the PISC, necessitating the manifested destiny of a collective insurgence of voices of resistance forged by the rediscovery of our humanity.

Though our endeavor is just, the agents of torture and repression -- the OCS (Office of Correctional Safety), SSU (Special Services Unity), IGI (Institutional Gang investigations) and ISU (Investigations Services Unit) -- have dedicated their resources towards silencing our voices and suffocating the true spirit of free speech.

This mission statement is only a brief invite designed to both captivate and solicit free speech loving people to join our movement and assist us in mobilizing against the forces of oppression. If you are interested, please contact Steve Martinot at martinot4gmail.com

### Mississippi Innocence Project
University of Mississippi School of Law
P.O. Box 1848
University, MS 38677

Phone: 662-915-5206

### MNN, Inc.
Shani Bruton, ESQ
244 5th Ave., Suite B-230
New York, NY 10001

This is a non-profit legal organization.

**Montana Innocence Project**
P.O. Box 7607
Missoula, MT 59807

Phone: 406-243-6698

**Moody Bible Institute**
Moody Distance Learning
820 N. LaSalle Boulevard
Chicago, IL 60610

Religious studies.

**MoonLite Productions**
PO Box 1304
Miami, FL 33265

"You've seen all those videos and TV shows that show you all the beautiful girls at South Beach, partying at the hottest clubs in Miami. Now you can see for yourself, let us show you, just how hot the girls in Miami really are. We have a huge selection of hot, sexy girls showing off their beautiful bodies for you. We try our best to have something to please every taste.

Some companies sell poor quality pictures, some you can even tell they are taken from pages of magazines or posters. We offer excellent professional quality. We have girls wearing the smallest G-string bikinis, sexy outfits, lingerie or spread nude. We also have pictures with penetration, and hot XXX action. We have whatever your institution allows! Make sure you know what you are allowed to receive. If any pictures we send you within the rules are rejected by the institution, we will exchange them when you send us a SASE and we get the originals back. If you have a question and write without an order, you MUST include a SASE or DO NOT expect a reply.

Half sets are 5 pictures for $7.49 or 25 stamps. Full sets are 10 4X6 pictures for $14.98 or 45 stamps. Get 15 pictures (a full set and a half) for $22 or 65 stamps. Get 20 pictures (2 full sets) for $29 or 85 stamps. Penetration/action sets are 8 for $14.98. Individual pictures are $1.50 each. Payment in stamps includes shipping. NO loose stamps please. Join our VIP Club and get **FREE** shipping on ALL orders while you are a member.

Sorry but we don't offer **FREE** samples. You can request a **FREE** catalog of almost 100 models when you send a $25 order or higher (not including shipping).

If ordering less than add $1 to get it. To order just the catalog send $1.50 or 5 stamps. We are always looking for hot new models to add, so there are more girls which do not appear in the catalog. We can make your first order a variety set of beautiful girls. Then you could tell us who you'd like to see more of, or if you want another variety set the next time. We have a high volume of sales. Some models are so popular that it's really hard to keep their pictures in stock. You can request your favorite models, but we reserve the right to substitute if we don't have pictures that would be allowed of the girls you ask for. We suggest you give us second and third choices just in case."

Shipping/Handling for pictures:

1-5 pictures --$1.00
6-10 pictures -- $2.00
11-15 pictures -- $3.00
16-20 pictures -- $4.00, etc.
Order $100 or more and get **FREE** shipping.

**Mount Hope Prison Ministry**
25 Summit Ave
PO Box 1511
Hagerstown, MD 21741

They offer bible correspondence courses to inmates FREE.

**The Moratorium Campaign**
586 Harding Blvd.
Baton Rouge, LA 70807

Contact us at info@moratoriumcampaign.org

**MS. Magazine**
ATTN: MS. In Prison Program
1600 Wislon Blvd., Suite 801
Arlington, VA 22209

Ms. is a feminist publication covering current events, politics, and culture. Women in prison can obtain a **FREE** membership by writing to the address above.

**Ms. Tahtianna Fermin**
387 Shepard Ave., Suite 3A
Brooklyn, NY 11208

Specializes in all prison litigation, civil and criminal. Info on anything. Inexpensive.

**Mt. Hope Prison Ministry**
PO Box 1511

Hagerstown, MO 21741

**FREE** bible studies.

**Muncy Inmate Coordinator**
Mr. Campbell Staff Liaison
ATTN: Tanya Dacri (MIO President)
PO Box 180
Muncy, PA 17756

**Munhall, Bob & Colette**
PO Box 2107
San Marcos, CA 92079

They provide a discount magazine service. Write for a **FREE** catalog.

**Music By Mail**
PO Box 329066
Bush Terminal
Brooklyn, NY 11232

They sell CDs. Write for a **FREE** catalog.

**Muslims for Humanity**
12346 McDougall St., Suite 200
Detroit, MI 48212

A resource for emergency services.

Phone Number: (313) 279-5378
Website: helpinghandonline.org.

**MSU College of Law**
610 Abbot Rd.
East Lansing, Ml 28823

They publish the "Disciplinary Self-Help Litigation Manual" that helps guide prisoners through the misconduct and disciplinary litigation process.

**N**

**NA World Services, INC**
PO Box 9999
Van Nuys, CA 91409

Quarterly recovery oriented newsletter, **FREE** to incarcerated addicts.

Website: na.org.

**NAACP Legal Defense & Educational Fund Inc**.
99 Hudson Street, Suite 1600
New York, NY 10013

Non-profit law firm which deals only with cases of obvious race discrimination, handles small number of death penalty & life w/o parole cases.

Phone Number: (212) 965-2200.

**NAACP National Prison Project**
4805 Mt. Hope Drive
Baltimore, MD 21215

Website: naacp.org/programs/prison.

**Narcotics Anonymous**
**World Services Main Office**
PO Box 9999
Van Nuys, California 91409

Phone Number: (818) 773-9999
Website: NA.org.

**NASW Women's Council Prison Project**
204 Ave B
Redondo Beach, CA 90277

They provide social services for women in prison and recently released, educate social workers about prison conditions and imprisoned women's needs, advocate for prison alternatives. Write for information on special services.

Phone Number: (310) 540-3715.

**National Action Network**
Crisis Department
106 W. 145th St.
Harlem, NY 10039

To seek their assistance in a crisis, send them a letter 3 pages or less, printed or typed. Include your name, address, and contact information.

Phone Number: (212) 690-3070.

**National AIDS Treatment Advocacy Project (NATAP)**
580 Broadway #1010,
New York, NY 10012

Will mail Hepatitis C and Hepatitis C Co-Infection Handbook.

**National Alliance for the Mentally Ill**
3803 N. Fairfax Dr. #100
Arlington, VA 22203

Seeks equitable services for people with severe mental
illnesses. Promotes treatment alternatives to
criminalization of people with severe brain disorders.

Phone Number: (703) 524-7600

**National Buddhist Prison Sangha/ Zen Mountain
Monastery**
NBPS
P.O. Box 197
Mount Tremper, NY 12457

Phone Number: (845) 688 2228
Website: nbps@mro.org.

**National Center for Lesbian Rights California Office**
870 Market Street suite 370
San Francisco, CA 94102

Provides legal referrals for LGBTQQI.

Phone Number: (415) 392-6257.

**National Alliance of Black Panthers**
339 Elm Street NW
Washington, DC 20001

Phone Number: 202-413-0255 or 202-271-0031
Website:nabp.zoomshare.com.

**National Center for Youth Law**
405 14th Street, 15th Floor
Oakland, CA 94612

Provides information, referrals, technical assistance, or
written materials; serves as co-counsel in cases affecting
a large number of children and families. Assists lawyers
who are directly representing at-risk or incarcerated
youth. Publishes Youth Law News.

**National Center on Institutions & Alternatives
(NCIA)**
7222 Ambassador Road
Baltimore, MD 21244

Provides criminal justice services to defense attorneys,
defendants, inmates and court systems throughout the
country. "We have worked with more than 10,000
clients in all 50 states. When assisting defense attorneys

or defendants facing sentencing, we provide assistance
in understanding the applicable sentencing statues or
guidelines and design individualized sentencing reports
or memoranda, which include specific sentencing
proposals. When permitted by the applicable State or
Federal law, our sentencing proposals frequently
include the use of creative public service that draws on
the offender's strengths and background, substance
abuse counseling, work-release, home confinement and
community confinement. In addition to sentencing
advocacy, we also provide capital case mitigation
services, parole release advocacy, institutional
designation and transfer and release planning."

Phone Number: 410-265-1490
Email: aboring@ncianet.org
Website: www.ncianet.org
Contact: Alice Boring.

**National Clearinghouse for the Defense of Battered
Women**
125 South 9th St., Suite 302
Philadelphia, PA 19107

"We accept collect calls from incarcerated battered
women."

Phone Number (215) 351-0010.
Website: ncdbw.org

**National Clemency Project**
8624 Camp Columbus Rd.
Hixon, TN 37343

35 years of clemency, parole assistance, and transfers
under the International Prisoner Treaty. Write/Send
SASE for more information.

Phone Number: Phone: (423) 843-2235

**National Clemency Project**
3907 N. Federal Highway, #151
Pompano Beach, FL 33064

Contact them for info on sentence reduction through
executive clemency. 36 years of experience.

Phone Number: 954-271-2304

**The National Coalition to Abolish the Death Penalty**
1620 L St, NW, Suite 250
Washington, DC 20036

Phone Number: (202) 331-4090

Website:info@ncadp.org.

**National Commission on Correctional Heath Care**
1145 W. Diversey Pkwy
Chicago, IL 60614

Phone Number: 773-880-1460

**National Criminal Justice Reference Service**
P.O. Box 6000
Rockville, MD 20849-6000

Phone Number: (800) 851-3420
Website: www.ncjrs.org

**National Death Row Assistance Network**
*Summer* June - Sept
NDRAN Claudia Whitman
6 Tolman Rd
Peaks Island, ME   04108

Phone Number: (207) 766-2418

*Winter* Oct - May
NDRAN Claudia Whitman
12200 Rd 41.9
Mancos, CO  81328

Phone Number (970) 533-7383

**National Directory of Catalogs**

They list over 12,000 catalogs.

Phone Number: (612) 788-4197
Website: nmoa.org/catalogmailorder

**National Fatherhood Initiative**
101 Lake Forest Blvd., suite 360
Gaithersburg, MD 20877

They offer parenting education. Write/Send SASE for more information.

Phone Number: (301) 948-099
Website: fatherhood.org.

**National Federal Legal Services**
2392 N. Decatur Rd.
Decatur, GA 30033

• Federal Appellate Representation for all Circuits and Supreme Court.

- Member of all Federal Circuits and Supreme Court
- Over 150 appeals filed.

• Federal 2255 Habeas Petitions anywhere in the United States.
- Representation.
- Pro Se Litigation; assistance or representation.
- Over 200 Habeas represented

Experienced attorneys make the difference, winning cases throughout tne United States for over 20 years.

Website: federalappealslawyer.com

**National Gay and Lesbian Task Force**
2684 Lacy Street
Suite 210
Los Angeles, CA 90031

Phone Number: 323.539.2406
Website: thetaskforce.org.

**National Geographic Magazine**
PO Box 64116
Tampa, FL 33664

Write for information.

Phone Number: (800) 647-5463.

**National Health Prison Project**
32 Greenwood Ave. #4
Quincy, MA 02170 -2620

Covers wide range of topics. Will answer personal questions. **FREE** subscription to prisoners.

**The National Hepatitis C Prison Coalition**
Phyllis Beck, Director
PO Box 41803
Eugene, OR 97404

Offers **FREE** newsletters.

Phone Number: (541) 607-5725

**National Incarcerated Parents and Families**
PO Box 6745
Harrisburg, Pennsylvania 17112-6745

Website: incarceratedparents.org.

**National Innocence Network**

This organization responds to claims of innocence and assists prisoners in locating appropriate help. If your case is accepted by a member of the Nation Innocence Network, they will offer support services.

Website: innocencenetwork.org

**National Institute of Corrections**
11900 E Cornell Ave, Unit C
Aurora, CO 80014

Provides the directory of programs servicing families of adult offenders; research and publications about other prison topics. May only be available online. Write/Send SASE for more information.

Phone Number: 800.877.1461
Website:nicic.gov

**National Lawyers Guild (Philadelphia)**
924 Cherry St.
Philadelphia, PA 19107

Phone Number: (215) 592-7710

**National Lawyers Guild Prison Law Project**
132 Nassau Street, Room 922
New York, NY 10038

The National Lawyers Guild (NLG) helps publish the Jailhouse Lawyers Handbook on bringing civil rights claims alleging violation of constitutional rights in prison or jail. NLG does not provide lawyers or legal assistance, but does provide **FREE** membership for jailhouse lawyers.

Phone Number: 212-679-5100
Website: www.nlg.org

**National Legal Aid and Defenders Association**
1625 K St, 8th Floor, NW Ste. 800
Washington, DC 20006

They provide referral to legal programs and services in your area.

**National Minority AIDS Council**
1931 13th Street NW
Washington, DC 20009-4432

Develops leadership in communities of color to address the challenges of HIV/AIDS. Has a **FREE** online resource library. Helps community and faith-based organizations, correctional facilities and health

departments evaluate, improve and implement effective discharge planning for HIV positive prisoners and former prisoners.

Phone Number: (202) 483-6622

**National Native American Prisoners Rights/Advocacy Coalition**
c/o Len Foster Navajo Nation Corrections Project
PO Drawer 709
Window Rock, AZ 86515

**National Network for Immigrant and Refugee Rights**
310 8th Street suite 303
Oakland, CA 94607

Helps monitor and share information to build campaigns against immigration raids, police collaboration with immigration enforcement, abuses by immigration police or other law enforcement agents, and BICE and other DHS activity in workplaces, neighborhoods, and public spaces.

Phone Number: (510) 465-1984

**National Prison Hospice Association**
11 S. Angell St. #303
Providence, RI 02906

NPHA helps to develop and implement hospices and better end-of-life care for terminally ill prisoners and their families. Also publishes a newsletter.

**Native American Pride Committee**
3256 Knight Court
Bay City, MI 48706

**Native American Prisoners' Rehabilitation Research Project**
2848 Paddock Lane
Villa Hills, KY 41017

**Navajo Nation Corrections Project**
PO Drawer 709
Window Rock, AZ 86515

They visit and provide spiritual counseling for prisoners, including death row prisoners.

**Nebraska Innocence Project**
P.O. Box 24183
Omaha, NE 68124-0183

**The Need to Abolish the Prison System**

This is a book by Steve Martinot -- a human rights activist, organizer and writer and retired machinist, truck driver and professor, most recently at San Francisco State University. He has organized labor unions in New York and Akron and helped build community associations in Akron. He was a political prisoner in New York State charged with contempt of grand jury. He has published 8 books.

Email: martinot4@gmail.com

**The Network/La RED Ending Abuse in Lesbian, Bisexual Women's and Transgender Communities**
PO Box 6011
Boston, MA 02114

Services include confidential hotline, emergency shelter, advocacy, and **FREE** support groups for lesbians, bisexual women, and transgender folks fleeing domestic violence.

Hotline number: 617-423-SAFE

Phone Number: (617) 695-0877

**The New Abolitionist**
P.O. Box 151 F
Fennimore, WI 53809

Newsletter of Prisoners Action Coalition –good contact for prison issues in Wisconsin has experience dealing with super max issues.

**New Beginning**
1865 Big Tree Drive
Columbus, OH 43223

New Beginning: Guidelines for Offering to Ex-Offenders Radical Hospitality in Faith Communities furnishes evidence that supports the fact that the leadership of faith communities offering radical hospitality to ex-offenders can reduce recidivism. Hope can be restored, damaged and broken relationships can be mended, forgiveness from both sides can be made, and the returning citizen remain a law-abiding member of society. Order book by calling 614-266-3387.

**New England Innocence Project**
160 Boylston Street
Boston, MA 02116

Phone Number: (857) 277-7858

**New Freedom College**
1957 W. Burnside St. #1660
Portland, OR 97209

"New Freedom College is designed for inmates, so our 2-year and 4-year programs offer a wide range of classes and majors that can all be completed in prison. At only $33-$55/credit, NFC will save you over $20,000 compared to traditional schools like Adams State ($165/credit + books = about $25,000 for 120 cr).

New Freedom has: Majors you want like Business and Psych; multi-class and referral discounts; lots of feedback; flexibility to meet your needs and openness to your ideas; low rates that include books, study guides, etc. You can get a 4-year diploma for as low as $3,960. We have a Certificate Program so everyone can participate, plus a monthly payment plan to best meet what you're able to afford! Write now for into guide and enrollment form!"

Web Site: NewFreedomCollege.org

**New York State Prisoner Justice Coalition**
33 Central Avenue
Albany, NY 12210

Phone Number: 518-434-4037
Website: http://www.nysprisonerjustice.org/

**NFC**
1957 W Burnside #1660
Portland, OR 97209

Inmate anthology seeks authors and cover artist. Send up to 2 poems (must be signed) and 1 prose piece (10 pg max) and cover art.

**Nicole M. Verville**
Attorney at Law
PO Box 2817
Chula Vista, CA 91912

Case Review, Writs of Habeas Corpus, Prop. 47, Transfer Request, Discrimination, Lifer Hearings. California cases only! Send SASE.

**NJ Office of the Corrections Ombudsman**
P0 Box 855
Trenton, NJ 08625

Phone Number: 609-633-2596

## No Equal Justice: Race and Class in the American Justice System

This book is a devastating critique that shows how the criminal justice system perpetuates race and class inequalities, creating a two-tiered system of Justice. This book is 232 pages, $19.95, and can be bought from Prison Legal News.

## Nolo's Plain-English Law Dictionary

Find terms you can use to understand and access the law. Contains 3,800 easy-to-find definitions for common (and not so common) legal terms. This book is 496 pages, $29.99 and can be bought from Prison Legal News.

## Nolo Press
950 Parker St.
Berkeley, CA 94710

Publishes self-help material such as "Legal Research," "The Criminal Law Handbook" and "Represent Yourself in Court." Write for a catalog.

## North Carolina Center on Actual Innocence
PO Box 52446
Shannon Plaza Station
Durham, NC 27717

Phone: 919-489-3268

## Northern Arizona Justice Project
Department of Criminal Justice
Northern Arizona University
P.O. Box 15005
Flagstaff, AZ 86011-5005

Working to help with the wrongfully convicted.

Phone Number: 928-523-7028

Website: http://jan.ucc.nau.edu/d-najp

## Northern California Innocence Project
Santa Clara Law; Santa Clara University
500 El Camino Real
Santa Clara, California 95053

The mission of the Northern California Innocence Project (NCIP) is to promote a fair, effective and compassionate criminal justice system and protect the rights of the innocent.

Phone: (408) 554-4361

Website: lawadmissions@scu.edu

## The November Coalition
282 West Astor
Colville, WA 99114

An organization of drug war prisoners and their loved ones. Their goal is to enlighten the public about unjust sentencing laws and the destructive increase in the US prison population. They publish "The Razor Wire", $6/yr. for prisoners.

Phone Number: (509) 684-1550

## Nubian Princess Ent.
PO Box 37
Timmonsville, SC 29161

This company is ran by porn star Chanail. For $25 inmates can get exotic letters from her. For $27 you can get your pic and contact info on her facebook. Send SASE for details.

facebook.com/chanail.paree
Website: writesomeoneinprison.com.

## NW Immigrant Rights Project
Eastern Washington Office
212 Sunnyside Ave.
PO Box 270
Granger, WA 98932

They promote justice for low-income immigrants by pursuing and defending their legal status. They also focus on direct legal services, supported by education and public policy work.

Website: nwirp.org.

## NW Immigrant Rights Project
Western Washington Office
615 2nd Ave., Suite 400
Seattle, WA 98104

Phone Number: (206) 587-4009.

## NY Campaign for Telephone Justice
666 Broadway 7th floor
New York, NY 10012

Main Office Line: 212-614-6464.

**NYC Books Through Bars**
C/O Bluestockings Bookstore,
172 Allen St.
New York, NY 10002

**FREE** nationwide, except MI. Specializes in political and history. Also literary fiction and other educational books. No religious books.

**NYC Jericho Movement**
PO Box 670927
Bronx, NY 10467

Phone Number: 718-325- 4407
Website: jerichony.org

**Oakland City University Prison Ministries Project**
Oakland City University
138 North Lucretia Street
Oakland City, Indiana 47660

Phone Number:  (800) 737-5125
Website: http://www.oak.edu

**Oatmeal Studios**
PO Box 138
Town Rd. 35
Rochester, VT 05767

This company buys art form prisoners. Send a SASE and ask for Writer's Guidelines. They will send you instructions and samples of what they want to buy.

**Occasion Gallerie**
Blue Mountain Arts
P.O. Box 1007
Boulder, CO 80306

Notecard poetry is welcome. Send with SASE.

**Oceana Press**
75 Main St.
Dobbs Ferry, NY 10522

They sell legal manuals. Write/Send SASE for more information.

**OCSlocal.com**

This is a discount phone service.

Phone Number: (888) 813-0000.

**The Office**
PO Box 30003
Tucson, AZ 85751

This is a typing service. Write/Send SASE for more information.

**Office of Correctional Education**
US Dept. of Education
400 Maryland Ave. SW
Washington, DC 20202

Write for information about education grants and federal and state prisoners.

**Office of the Public Defender**
Carvel State Office Building
820 N. French St.
3rd Floor
Wilmington, Delaware 19801

Phone Number: (302) 577-5200

**Off Our Backs Magazine**
2337B 18th St NW
Washington, DC 20009

A radical feminist news journal **FREE** to women in prison.

**Ohio University College Program for the Incarcerated**
Haning Hall 222
Ohio University
Athens, OH 45701

They offer correspondence courses. Write for more information and cost.

**Ohio University Correctional Education**
102 Haning Hall
1 Ohio University
Athens, OH 45701

Provides college-level courses and certificate and degree programs acceptable in most prisons. FREE info packet on admission, course offerings and cost. Ask if their program is authorized in your state.

**Oklahoma Innocence Project**

2501 N. Blackwelder
Oklahoma City, OK 73106

Phone Number: 405-208-6161
Website: innocence@okcu.edu

## On Demand Inmate Services
PO Box 81
Cheltenham, PA 19012

"Best photo catalog magazines ever printed –
guaranteed! Our catalogs are full color, non-nude and
have thousands of options. They are $5 each or 11 flat
stamps each (30 stamps for vol. 6).

Catalogs...

Bad Broads: 12 pages. Features porn stars in various
positions, non-nude. Also features fine amateur broads
(over 300 shots).

Bad Broads Vol. 2, Battle of the Camel Toe: This
catalog has 16 pages and over 450 shots. The shots
include, but are not limited to camel toe, porn stars,
entertainers and random big booty broads.

Bad Broads Vol. 3, Sticky Booty Bounce: This catalog
has 16 pages and features 400 shots of porn stars, camel
toe, juicy huge booty, action shots, celebs and much
more.

Bad Broads Vol. 4, Extreme Freak Edition: This catalog
features but is not limited to approximately 400 shots of
the finest and nastiest porn stars and strippers of all
races, celebs, extreme big bootys, camel toe, extreme
sex faces and money shots.

Bad Broads Vol. 5, Huge Booty Drip and Wet: Glory
hole, camel toe, huge wet booty, big and beautiful,
celebs, cum shots, extreme sex faces and more. Over
580 shots!

Bad Broads Vol. 6, Naughty Celebs (Special Edition):
This catalog features over 1000 shots and is 20 pages!
Features the widest selection of camel toe, hugs tits,
huge booties, the baddest porn stars in action, the
nastiest glory hole shots, etc. This catalog also features
the hottest celebs in action and the wildest erotic poses.
Nude versions are also available on select celeb photos.
$12 or 30 flat stamps. **FREE** shipping.

Bulk photo packages: Buy 50, get 15 **FREE**. Buy 100-
199 photos, get them for 65¢ each. Buy 200 or more, get
them for 50¢ each. Include s/h on all bulk packs. Offers
cannot be combined.

Grab bag: 25 photos for $9, while supplies last. We will
pick from our overstock flow. Let us know what you
can't get. No returns or exchanges for grab bags.

Erotic stories, $19.00: 178 pages of hot and steamy
mouthwatering erotic stories. Topics include, but are not
limited to, group sex, control/domination, cheating wife,
swinger's sex parties, lust, gang bang, freaky horny
sluts, anal and much more.

U.S. Female Pen Pal list 3 with contact info: 60 female
pals, ages 19-50; $22, shipping included. 21 pages.

U.S. Female Pen Pal list 4 with contact info: 69 female
pals, ages 23-50; $25, shipping included. 22 pages.

Please send an institutional check, money order or
stamps to On Demand Inmate Services. We will ONLY
accept stamps for photo catalog purchases."

## Open Inc.
(Offender Preparation and Education Network)
Po Box 472223
Garland, TX 75047

They sell prison and transition publications for $9.95
and up. Write for a catalog.

## Operation Outward Reach, Inc.
227 South Sixth Street
Youngwood, PA 15697

They offer skill development and vocational training for
resident offenders of five state penal institutions:
Greensburg, Huntingdon, Mercer, Cresson, and
Somerset. They take trainees into the community to
teach carpentry and masonry by providing low-cost
construction to senior citizens, other economically
disadvantaged and non-profit agencies. Juvenile Day
Treatment is provided in the Westmoreland County area
for out-of-school young men ages 15 through 21.
Purpose of this training is to provide on-the-job
construction learning, G.E.D., drug & alcohol
education, life skills, job skills, and adolescent
fatherhood components.

Phone Number: (724) 925-2419
Website: operationoutwardreach.org

## The Order of the Earth
21431 Marlin Circle

Shade Gap, PA 17255

This newspaper costs $25 for a 1-year subscription, 10-12 issues per year.

Phone Number: (814) 259-3680
Website: theorderoftheearth.com.

## Oregon CURE (Citizens United for the Rehabilitation of Errands)
1631 NE Broadway #460
Portland, OR 97232

Website: oregoncure.org.

## Oregonians for Alternatives to the Death Penalty
OADP
PO Box 361
Portland, OR 97207

Website: oadp.org

## The Osborne Association
Attn: Keenan Pace
809 Westchester Ave.
Bronx, NY 10455

They sell publications. Write for a list and prices.

## Our Bodies, Ourselves

This book about women's health and sexuality, produced by a nonprofit organization, has been called "America's best-selling book on all aspects of women's health" by the New York Times and is an essential resource for women of all ages. This book is 944 pages, $26.00, and it can be bought from Prison Legal News.

## Our Daily Bread
RBC Ministries
PO Box 2222
Grand Rapids, MI 49501

They offer **FREE** monthly devotionals.

## Our Enemies in Blue
c/o AK Press
674-A 23rd street
Oakland, CA 94612

Let's begin with the basics: violence is an inherent part of policing. The police represent the most direct means by which the state imposes its will on the citizenry. They are armed, trained, and authorized to use force.

Like the possibility of arrest, the threat of violence is implicit in ever police encounter. Violence, as well as the law, is what they represent. Using media reports alone, the Cato Institute's last annual study listed nearly seven thousand victims of police "misconduct" in the United States. But such stories of police brutality only scratch the surface of a national epidemic. Every year, tens of thousands are framed, blackmailed, beaten, sexually assaulted, or killed by cops. Hundreds of millions of dollars are spent on civil judgments and settlements annually. Individual lives, families, and communities are destroyed. In this extensively revised and updated edition of his seminal study of policing in the United States, Kristian Williams shows that police brutality isn't an anomaly, but is built into the very meaning of law enforcement in the United States. From antebellum slave patrols to today's unarmed youth being gunned down in the streets, "peace keepers" have always used force to shape behavior, repress dissent, and defend the powerful. Our Enemies in Blue' is a well-researched page-turner that both makes historical sense of this legalized social pathology and maps out possible alternatives.

This book, by Kristian Williams, is 420 pages, and $16.50 plus $3 s/h.

## Outlaw Bikers
820 Hamilton St., #C-6
Charlotte, NC 28206

This is a biker magazine. It's $16 for l-year subscription; 4 issues per year.

## OutlawsOnline.com

Post your profile immediately, just like any other dating website, and edit it any time day or night. Friends and family can register, pay for your ad with PayPal, and upload your photo, address description and bio.

Website: outlawsonline.com.

## Outlook on Justice
Publication of Criminal Justice Program of the AFSC
2161 Massachusetts Ave
Cambridge, MA 02140

A newsletter of the American Friends Services Committee (Quakers). $2/year for prisoners.

Phone Number: (617) 661-6130 x120

**Out of Control Lesbian Committee to Support Women Political Prisoners**
3543 - 18th Street, Box 30
San Francisco, CA 94110

Website: prisonactivist.org/ooc/

**Oxford University Press Inc.**
198 Madison Ave.
New York, NY 10016

They publish "Prisoner's Self-Help Litigation Manual" ($35), "Brief Writing and Oral Arguments" ($40), "Introduction to the Legal system of the United States" ($25), & more.

# P

**Pace Post Conviction Project**
Barbara Salken Criminal Justice Clinic
78 North Broadway
White Plains, NY 10603

Phone Number: 914-422-4230

**PA Lifers Association**
Attn: Gary Jones AY 7024 SCI- Huntingdon
1100 Pike Street
Huntingdon, PA 16654

**PA Lifers Association**
Staff Liaison Charles Bradley CAS
Attn: Tyrone Wets AF 6337 SCI Graterford
PO Box 244
Graterford, PA 19426

**PA Lifers Association**
Staff Liaison Attn: Gary Mobley #AM 4256 SCI
Rockview
PO Box A
Bellefonte, PA 16823

**PA Prison Directory Action**
c/o Book 'Em
PO Box 71357
Pittsburgh, PA 15213

7 lists of PA and national resources: LGBTQI; Women and Parents; Legal, Pro Bono and Advocacy on the Inside; Prison Justice and Advocacy Groups, PA Prison,

Jails and Court Info; Education on the Inside; Tips for Survivors of Abuse. Send SASE if possible.

**Pack Central Music**
PO Box 8448
Van Nuys, CA 91409

They sell CDs and cassettes. Send $2 for their catalog.

Phone Number: (818) 760-2828.

**Package Trust**
370 W. Pleasantview Avenue, Suite 0303
Hackensack, NJ 07601

Package Trust is powered by Don Diva.

"Send $7.00 for our full-color catalog of services and over 500 available sexy, non-nude photos. We sell our photos for $1.00 each.

Photo Duplication: 4x6 prints are $1 each, 4x7 prints are $5 each, 8x10 prints are $10 each.

People Search! Are you looking for a person or information on a business? We can do the research for you for $5.00.

Background Search: Need a background check on someone? We will search criminal records in 43 states for $40.00.

Internet Research: For $20.00 an hour, we will provide you with thorough research from credible and relevant sources. We will research any subject you request and send you printouts of all information found.

If you would like a return response from Package Trust, you MUST send a SASE."

Phone Number: 347-815-3229
E-mail: packagetrust@dondivamag.com

**Pagan Educational Network**
P.O. Box 24072
Indianapolis, IN 46224

Member's eligible for *Water* after receipt of $4 (stamps okay).

**Palmetto Innocence Project**
P.O. Box 11623
Columbia, SC 29211

**PARfessionals**
PO Box 155601
Fort Worth, TX 76155

National certified peer addiction recovery coach training program for inmates, family and others working with inmate/ex-offender population. Internationally approved. Send SASE.

**The Paralegal Institute**
18275 N 59th Ave. Suite 186 Building N.
Glendale, AZ 85308

Associate degree program. Accredited by distance education training council. Registered with the National Association of Legal Assistants. Write for more information.

**Partnership for Safety and Justice**
825 NE 20th Avenue, #250
Portland, OR 97232

Phone Number: (503) 335-8449

**PASS Program**
P.O. Box 2009
San Francisco, CA 94126

Phone Number: 1-888-670-7277
Website: passprogram.org

Prisoner Assistance Scholastic Service provides educational materials (national) to prisoners in state and federal prisons and jails. Prisoners who successfully complete the PASS program earn a degree in Personal Psychological Development which can be used as evidence of rehabilitation before parole boards and with prison officials. $500 for the entire course and study degree.

**Penn Foster Career School**
925 Oak Street
Scranton, PA 18515

This is a career school with various programs of study.

**Comment:** They offer a ton of programs to choose from a very reasonable rates. If career training is your objective, and finances are taught, Penn Foster Career School is a great option. - - Mike

**Pathfinders of Oregon**
PO Box 3257

Gresham, OR 97030

Pathfinders are a cognitive restructuring/skills building process. It was designed to transform criminally deviant behavior into responsible conduct. FOR OREGON PRISONERS ONLY.

Phone Number: (503) 286-0600

**Pathfinders Press**
P.O. Box 162767
Atlanta, GA 30321-2767

50% prisoner discount. Write for a catalog. Books on the works of revolutionary and working class leaders. There is a flat shipping and handling fee of $2.75. Books in English, Spanish, French, Farsi, Arabic, Swedish, Greek, Chinese, Russian, and Indonesian.

**PB&J Family Services, Inc.**
1101 Lopez SW
Albuquerque, NM 87105

Provides transportation, enhanced visiting, parent education, information, referrals, case management, child care, and more at 4 New Mexico prisons.

Phone Number: (505) 877-7060

**Pelipost.com**

Don't miss another special moment. Pelipost is the easiest and most convenient way to share photos from home!

How it works: 1) Upload favorite photos on Pelipost.com; 2) Enter recipient's information; 3) Photos are processed and shipped the next day! FREE shipping!

Tell friends and family to visit pelipost.com to join FREE!

**Penal Law Project**
Chico State University 25 Main Street, Suite 102
Chico, CA 95929

Penal Law Project assists incarcerated individuals. The program's primary purpose is to provide legal information and research for those held in California state prisons.

Phone Number: 530-898-4354

Website:aschico.com/clic/programsandadvocacy

## PEN American Center
588 Broadway, Suite 303
New York, NY 10012

The PEN's Prison Writing Program has three basic areas of concentration:
1. The Handbook For Writers In Prison. This handbook teaches elements of writing fiction, non-fiction, and poetry. It also provides resources for inmates in terms so next steps for their completed works. The Handbook is FREE for all prisoners who write us a letter requesting one.
2. Our annual Prison Writing Program awards contest. PEN awards cash prizes in five categories of writing from prisoners (fiction, essay, memoir, poetry, and drama/screenplay). We receive 1500 entries a year; the contest ends September 1st. We encourage inmates of all writing levels to enter the contest. To enter, simply mail the entry to the address above. No application or form is necessary, though most inmates do send us a short letter telling us a little bit about themselves. Winners lists are available upon request.
3. Our Mentor Program. The Prison Writing Mentorship Program pairs up established writer mentors with incarcerated mentees. Our program requires at least three exchanges of writing between mentees and mentors (that is, three submissions from mentees and three observations/commentaries to the submissions from mentors). To become eligible
for the program, an inmate must first enter the annual contest. Winners are offered the opportunity to participate in the mentorship program and, in some instances, writers who do not win an award but show promise are also offered a mentor.

## Penn Foster
14300 N. Northwest Blvd., Suite 111
Scottsdale, AZ 85260

They provide correspondence courses. Write for a **FREE** catalog.

Phone Number (800) 572-1685

## Pennsylvania Innocence Project
Temple University Beasley School of Law
1719 North Broad Street
Philadelphia, PA 19122

Phone Number: 215-204-4255
Website: innocenceprojectpa@temple.edu

## Pennsylvania Prison Society
245 N Broad Street suite 300
Philadelphia, PA19107-1518

Does advocacy work, including prison visits, and publishes "Graterfriends," a monthly newsletter for people in prison which is primarily inmate guided.

Phone Number: (215) 564-6005.

## Pen Pal Project
PO Box 9867
Marian Del Ray, CA 90295

## People's Law Office
1180 North Milwaukee Ave
Chicago, IL 60642-4019

Phone Number: 773-235-0070
Website: peopleslawoffice.com

## PETA
501 Front St.
Norfolk, VA 23510

Write for a **FREE** "Animals Belong in the Jungle" coloring book.

Phone Number: (757) 622-PETA

## Phantom Prisoner
Po Box 114379
Centerdale, RI 02911

This is a newsletter. It's $5 for a 1-year subscription; 6 issues per year.

## Philadelphia Brotherhood Rescue Mission
401 East Girard Avenue
Philadelphia, PA 19125

The Recovery Through Faith program provides a community-oriented environment for PBRM program participants to gain the skills, stability and self-esteem necessary to become productive, self-sufficient members of society. This program provides long term rehabilitation by integrating spiritual and emotional counseling, life skills, education, Bible Study and work therapy.

Phone: 267-284-0405
Website: pbrm.org

## Philadelphia FIGHT/Institute for Community Justice
1233 Locust Street, 5th Floor
Philadelphia, PA 19107

Locally, they support inmates living with HIV within the Philadelphia Prison System, providing advocacy, linkages to services, education and expedited access to their HIV primary care clinic upon release. Prison Health News is a quarterly newsletter written by and for people who have been in prison or are currently living behind the walls.

Phone Number: (215) 985-4448 x.162
Website: fight.org

## The Philadelphia Trumpet
PO Box 3700
Edmond, OK 73083

Christian magazine.

**Comment:** This is a mag for serious Christians, but it's not a normal religious mag. This mag covers conspiracy theory - type shit. It somehow finds ways to tie in any and every single story in the bible. It's very informative. They also send inmates FREE booklets. I have a subscription and recommend it, yet every time I read an issue I get the feeling that I'm reading a mag produced by a cult. - - GURU

## Photo Tryst
PO Box 10756
Jacksonville, FL 32247

"All catalogs have 450 color pics. Summer 2013 catalog is **FREE** with SASE. All other catalogs are $4.00 or 10 Forever stamps, and it's shipped with a coupon for 5 **FREE** pics with your minimum order of 10. We offer catalogs Winter 2014, Spring 2014, Summer 2014, Asian/Hispanic #1, Topless #1 (contains frontal nudity), and All Nude #1 (see it all).

Our next general (season) catalog is **FREE** with each order. You can deposit funds with us and order your pics 'on account'. We accept checks and money orders. Stamp orders are only with stamp coupons obtained with regular orders.

Oregon, Utah and Virginia consistently deny our catalogs so we cannot do business there. Sorry."

## Photoworld
PO Box 401016
Las Vegas, NV 89140

Celebrity photos for sale.

## PictureDonkey.com

Get pictures mailed to you from friends and family on the outside! Our picture printing service is EASY. Friends and family can send us pictures from their smart phone, tablet, or a computer and we will print them on high quality photo paper and mail them to you on the next mail day! All you loved one needs is: your inmate ID; your mailing address; their email address; a smart phone tablet or computer!

As low as $0.40 each! Our prices are all flat rate! No hidden fees, shipping and handling included! Don't be fooled by low cost prints "plus shipping and handling" where a single picture can cost $2! Our service also allows you to add captions, FREE!
You cannot sign up directly yourself. Our service is for your loved ones on the outside. Tell them to sign up at PictureDonkey.com. There is more information on the website, including frequently asked questions and information on pricing and discounts.

## Picture Entertainment
PO Box 54806
Los Angeles, CA 90054

"We sell our photos for $1 or 3 stamps each. 25 photos for $17 or 54 stamps. Order our catalog for $2.75 or 9 stamps. Add $2 or 6 stamps for shipping on photo orders. We are not responsible for rejected photos and there are no refunds."

**Comment:** These guys offer some nice shots. - Mike

## Picmate.net
UVP, Dept. XA
P.O. Box 110620
Jamaica, NY 11411

Send SASE for **FREE** catalog of sexy non-nude photos of models and dancers.

## Pleasures Limited
PO Box 870
New York, NY 10013

100 pages of erotica for only $19.95. **FREE** shipping and handling. Sexy stories, no nude photos, safe for inmates!

Phone Number: (212) 334-0227

## PLN Cumulative Index

Provides detailed information about all PLN articles, including title, author, issue, page number, topics covered, citations, and if it is state, Jail, or BOP specific. Can be searched on over 500 subjects such as medical neglect or sexual assault. Notify them of the index(es) you are ordering: 1990495, 1996-98, 1999-01, 2002-04. $22.50 each. Order directly from Prison Legal News.

## PMI Center for Biblical Studies
POB 177
Battle Creek, MI 49016-0177

Bible correspondence courses available FREE to inmates.

## PM Press
PO Box 23912
Oakland, CA 94623

Zines, Prisoner-based pubs.

Website: http://www.pmpress.org

## The Poetry Wall; Cathedral of St. John the Divine
1047 Amsterdam Ave.
New York, NY 10025

They accept poetry of all kinds for display, and invites people to correspond with inmates whose poetry is on display.

## Poets and Writers, INC
90 Broad St., Suite 2100
New York, NY 10004

An organization that publishes many books on writing, as well as a bi-monthly magazine. Write to receive a catalog.

## The Poet's Workshop
C/O Sarah Lindahl
St Louis County Jail
4334 Haines Rd
Duluth, MN 55811

Publishes monthly magazine including poetry by prisoners. **FREE** to prisoners who submit poetry that is published.

## Poetry Society of America
15 Gramercy Park
New York, New York 10003

Writer's competition.

Phone Number: (212) 254-9628

## Popular Enterprise
215 W. Troy St. #2004
Ferndale, MI 48220

They sell sexy photos. 20 photos for $14, plus you get an extra 20 photos **FREE!**

## The Portia Project
PO Box 3567
Eugene, OR 97403

They provide legal and other assistance to women incarcerated at Coffee Creek Correctional Facility, and women who are under post-prison supervision throughout the state.

Phone Number: (541) 255-9988
Website: theportiaproject.com

## Portland Books To Prisoners
P.O. Box 11222
Portland, OR 97211

Sends **FREE** books to prisoners nationwide.

## Positively Aware, National Magazine On HIV/AIDS
5537 N. Broadway
Chicago, IL 60640

Covers treatment, medical, and social issues. **FREE** subscription for prisoners. Annual Drug Guide available in Spanish, not the magazine.

## Power Inside
P.O. Box 4796
Baltimore, MD 21211

Provides women centered services to women including trans women and trans men. Offers support and advocacy for those who are incarcerated, homeless, addicted, or in the sex trade.

**PREP**
PO Box 77850
Los Angeles, CA 90007

Basic self-help; gang awareness and recovery, parenting, domestic violence and more. Sends certificates upon completion. Great for board. Send for info and first module FREE.

**Prism Optical, Inc.**
10954 N.W. 7th Ave.
North Miami, FL 33186

They sell a nice variety of eye glasses/frames. Write and request their **FREE** catalog.

Phone Number: (800) 637-4104
Website: prisoptical.com.

**Prison Activist Resource Center**
P.O. Box 70447
Oakland, CA 94612

PARC is a prison abolitionist group committed to exposing and challenging all forms of institutionalized racism, sexism, able-ism, heterosexism and classism, specifically within the Prison Industrial Complex.

Phone Number: 510-893-4648
Website: prisonactivist.org

**Prison AIDS Resources Center**
926 J St. #801
Sacramento, CA 95814

They offer HIV/AIDS information.

Phone Number: (800) 221-7044

**Prison AIDS Resources Center**
PO Box 2155
Vacaville, CA 95696

**Prison Ashram Project**
**Human Kindness Foundation**
PO Box 61619
Durham, NC 27715

Website: http://www.humankindness.org/prison-ashram-project

Phone Number: (919) 383-5160

**Prison Bay**

PO Box 2606
Red Oak, TX 75154

They do internet searches, photo duplications, etc. Write/Send SASE for more information.

**Prison Book Program**
c/o Lucy Parsons Bookstore
1306 Hancock St Ste 100
Quincy, MA 02169

Does not send books to CA, MA, MD, MI, PA, KY, LA, NV or TX. Offers a **FREE** 40-page "We the People" legal primer. Allows two book shipments per year. Takes 3 to 6 months.

Phone Number: (617) 423-3298

**Prison Book Project**
Open Books Bookstore
1040 N Guillemard Street
Pensacola, FL 32501

Open Books is a non-profit, volunteer-run bookstore. Proceeds from the sale of books support the Prison Book Project, which sends thousands of books each year to indigent inmates in Florida prisons.

Phone Number: 850-453-6774
Website: openbookspcola.org

**Prison Books Collective**
PO Box 625
Carrboro, NC 27510

The Prison Books Collective is a North Carolina-based anti-prison group that sends books to prisoners in Southern states (primarily MS, AL and central and eastern NC) each month, and maintains an extensive radical 'zine catalog, widely distributes a monthly poster promoting political prisoner support, and publishes prisoners' art and writing.

**Prison Connection**
PO Box 18489
Cleveland Heights, OH 44118

This is a pen pal service. Special - $20 for 2 years. Send SASE for more information.

**Prison Creative Arts Project**
University of Michigan
Ann Arbor, MI 48109

This is an art exhibit that serves Michigan prisoners. Write for information.

## Prison Dharma Network
11 South Angell St. #303
Providence, RI 02906

Mission is to provide prisoners, and those who work with them, with the most effective contemplative tools for self-transformation and rehabilitation. Provides books and educational materials.

Phone Number: (401) 941-0791

## Prison Fellowship
PO Box 11550
Merrifield, VA 22116-1550

Prison Fellowship partners with local churches across the country to minister to prisoners, ex-prisoners, and their families. Publishes a variety of prisoner support literature including the Prison Survival Guide.

Phone Number: (877) 478-0100

## Prison Fellowship Ministry
44180 Riverside Parkway
Lansdowne, VA 20176

"Prison Fellowship is a Christ-centered ministry which seeks the transformation and reconciliation of prisoners to God, family and community through Jesus Christ. We train 26 volunteers from local churches to execute their ministry. Re-entry is a focus area as well. Prison Fellowship is facilitating re-entry conferences around the United States in order to build coalitions in local communities so that each service organization, non-profit organization, church and local government agencies are able to contribute to the successful return of offenders."

Phone Number: 610-255-3926
Website: prisonfellowship.org

## Prison Grievances

This book, written and published by Dr. Terri LeClercq, is an easy to understand guide on "when to write, how to write" prison grievances. Dr. LeClercq has published Expert Legal Writing, Guide to Legal Writing Style, and more than a hundred articles on rhetoric. She and her husband live in Austin, Texas where they both teach at the School of Law, University of Texas. Learn more about Dr. LeClercq and her work at prison grievances.com. Her book (ISBN 9780615739755) is $9.

**Comment:** Prison Grievances is an easy-to-understand, step-by-step guide on how to navigate through the very frustrating prison grievance system. It's an invaluable resource that should be read by every inmate. -- Mike

## Prison Health News
1233 Locust Street, 3rd Floor
c/o Philadelphia FIGHT
Philadelphia, PA 19107

Quarterly newsletter published by former prisoners about prisoners' health.

Phone Number: 215-985-4448.

## Prison Inmates Online
8033 W. Sunset Blvd. #7000
Los Angeles, CA 90046

"Prison Inmates Online is much more than a pen pal service. It's your link to the free world during your incarceration! A lot of inmates lose touch with family and friends after being incarcerated. With a PIO profile, friends and family can always find you, see what's going on in your life, and send you a message. Keep your profile updated and never be forgotten. If you find love, don't pull your profile down, just change your relationship status to 'In a Relationship' in your bio and keep your profile going!

**Best value for your money**: PIO is the best value for your online profile. Why pay more on other websites that only provide less? See how we compare to our competitors with better prices/service.

**Profile price and renewals**: PIO charges $50 for a profile that includes up to 300 words. Plus, every time you make a PAID update, your profile is extended for 1 year from the date of the update. Compare that to other websites who charge $40 for a profile that only contains 250 words and renewal rates up to $30 per year.

**More photos than anyone else**: PIO allows you to submit 5 photos with your profile. Compare that with the 1-2 photos most other services allow you to submit. Additional photos, art and tattoos are 5 for $10. Compare that to other websites that charge you $10 for EACH photo.

**Featured Inmate**: Our Featured Inmate panel is shown on nearly every page of PIO website and includes a courtesy in the 'ad' space section of the website. Compare that to other services who only show only show featured inmates on the homepage. Become a Featured Inmate for just $30 per month or $180 for the whole year!

**Blogs and poems**: List a blog or poem on PIO up to 300 words for just $10. Compare that to the $15 other websites charge. Other services like videos, tattoos and documents aren't even provided by other websites.

**Documents section**: Share documents (legal, stories, journals, diaries) for others to view or download. A great way to inform people who are following you or your case! It's also a rest place to store digital copies of your records in one place. Only $10 for each document title, up to 50 pages.

**Tattoo section**: Many men and women are drawn to people with tattoos. Why not show off yours in the tattoo section? The photos of your tattoos are linked to your profile page so it's another way to get more visitors to your page. $10 for up to 5 photos.

**Videos:** YouTube is the Internet's largest video sharing website and is integrated into this site. You can post any video that is listed on YouTube directly to your profile page. Your favorite music video, comedian, or even your own videos if they are posted on YouTube! Only $5 per video!"

Website: prisoninmates.com
Corrlinks: infoprisoninmates.com

**Comment:** This may very well be the best profile service I've seen. You can practically have everything a real, personal/company website can have. – Mike

## The Prison Journal
6041 Watch Chain Way
Columbia, MD 21044

"The Journal is a publication of poems, short essays, and artwork from inmates all over the country. All works should be original. As we seek to publish items that are relevant to the prisoner community, we encourage submissions that reflect your own experiences, although we welcome inspirational work of all subjects. We receive many spiritual items.

We are particularly interested in receiving artwork/drawings. The Journal is printed in black and white, so (if you submit a color item) please keep this in mind.

We are blessed to receive so many high-quality submissions, and continued to be inspired by the voices of incarcerated men and women. We hope you will stay enthusiastic about being creative, and submit some of your own items.

God bless,
John and Ann Worley"

## Prison Law Clinic
UC Davis School of Law
One Shields Avenue, TB30
Davis CA 95616

Their students provide legal services to clients incarcerated in state prison.

Phone Number: 530 752-6942

Website:.law.ucdavis.edu/Faculty/Murphy

## Prison Law Office
General Delivery
San Quentin, CA 94964

Litigates and monitors class action law suits regarding medical care, mental health care, and disabled access for prisoners in CA only. Also distributes self-help legal material on a number of topics. Write with your concerns.

Phone Number: 510-280-2621
Website: prisonlaw.com.

## Prison Legal News
PO Box 1151
Lake Worth, FL 33460

PLN reports on legal cases and news stories related to prisoner rights and prison conditions of confinement. PLN welcomes all news clippings, legal summaries and leads on people to contact related to those issues. Article submissions should be sent to -- The Editor -- at the above address. We cannot return submissions without an SASE. Check our website or send an SASE for writer guidelines.

PLN is a monthly publication and a one year subscription is $30 for prisoners, $35 for individuals, and $90 for lawyers and Institutions. Prisoner donations of less than $30 will be pro-rated at $3.00/issue. Do not send less than $18.00 at a time. All foreign subscriptions are $100 sent via airmail. PLN accepts Visa and MasterCard orders by phone. New subscribers please allow four to six weeks for the delivery of your first issue. Confirmation of receipt of donations cannot be made without an SASE. PIN is a section 501 (c)(3) non-profit organization. Donations are tax deductible.

## IMPORTANT NOTICE!!

Are phone companies taking money from you and your loved ones?

HRDC and PLN are gathering information about the business practices of telephone companies that connect prisoners with their friends and family members on the outside. Does the phone company at a Jail or prison at which you have been incarcerated overcharge by disconnecting calls? Do they charge excessive fees to fund accounts? Do they take money left over in the account if it is not used within a certain period of time?

## IMPORTANT NOTICE!!

Prison Legal News is collecting information about the ways people get cheated by the high cost of sending money into your account?

Is someone skimming money or otherwise charging you and your loved ones high fees to deposit money to fund prisoners' accounts.

Please write to PLN and/or have the person on the outside contact us to let us know specific details about the way that the system is ripping them off. We are interested in all business practices that result in money being diverted away from prisoners' accounts. Please direct all correspondence to:
Ptsolkasprisonlegalnews.org or Prison Legal News;
Attn: Panagioti Tsolkas;
P0 Box 1151; Lake Worth, FL 33460.

We want details on the ways in which prison and jail phone companies take money from customers. Please contact us, or have the person whose money was taken contact us, by e- mail or postal mail:
cwilkinsonhumanrightsdefensecenter.org or Prison Legal News; Attn: Carrie Wilkenson; PO Box 1151; Lake Worth, FL 33460.

## Prison Legal Services of Michigan

209 E Washington Ave.
Jackson, MI 49201

Phone Number: (517) 780-6639
Website: http://www.prisoneradvocacy.org/

## Prison Letters 4 Our Struggling Youth
603 B East University Dr. #219
Carson, CA 90746

"We are a youth gang prevention program operating with the assistance of prisons inmates. We are a program under Brothers Against Banging Youths -- a non-profit. Our mission is to dismantle the cradle to the prison pipeline for our children. We believe whole heartedly that we need to eradicate the violence in children's lives and to save as many youth from entering the prison system. We believe our youth are not really aware of the dangers of gang life. One wrong decision will land them in prison for the rest of their lives. We believe that inmates that feel the same way as we do can help deter youth from the lifestyle that these inmates took on and landed them in prison. We believe that these inmates contributing to our mission lost their youth because of gang life and they now possess a commitment to ensuring that we continue the work of writing and educating youth as to the real dangers of gang life. WE believe that youth will make the right decisions for themselves and their families when they are exposed to the letters from inmates explaining the consequences of gang life. We believe that it has an entirely different effect on the youth when they hear directly from the inmates verses Just being told about consequences. We believe rehabilitated inmates possess an understanding and familiarity with 'Youth At Risk' and sensitivity to the cultural and ethnic needs of 'Youth At Risk'."

If you participate by sending letters, this organization will send letters to the Board of Prison Terms and let them know you are working towards keeping the youth out of prison. Write them for their guidelines, details and suggested topics.

## Prison Library Project
915C W. Foothill Blvd, PMB-128
Claremont, CA 91711

**FREE** books: self-help, personal and spiritual growth, wellness, and metaphysical books.

## Prison Literature Project
c/o Bound Together Books
1369 Haight St.

San Francisco, CA 94117

They'll send you 2 **FREE** books. You may request them every 4 months. Orders take a while to be filled, so please be patient. Do not ask for specific books. Give a subject, as well as alternative subjects, and then wait for them to arrive. Topics include: Black studies, Chicano history, basic math/writing/science, books in Spanish, novels, politics, history, and more.

## Prison Mindfulness Institute
11 S. Angell St. #303
Providence, RI 02906

Website: http://www.prisonmindfulness.org/

## Prison Nation: The Wherehousing of America's Poor

PLN's second anthology exposes the dark side of the 'lock-em-up' political-agenda and legal climate in the U.S. This book is 287 pages, $22.95, and can be bought from Prison Legal News.

## Prison Outreach Worldwide
13610 North Scottsdale Road, Suite 10-291
Scottsdale, AZ 85254

The Jailhouse Journal is a quarterly magazine of the incarcerated Christian community. Inmates receive 4 issues per year.

Phone Number: 480-443-2511
Website: www.thepownetwork.com

## Prison Pen Pals
PO Box 235
East Berlin, PA 17316

Connecting prisoners with pen pals since 1996.

"Our award-winning web site has been seen in 100's of newspapers, dozens of magazines and many TV shows all around the world --Cosmopolitan, The New York Times, The Ricci Lake Show, MSNBC's Homepage and more! We are the most visited, largest and longest running site of its kind on the Internet!

Economy Ad: 1 photo with your name, # and address for a FULL year on the site -- $9.95

Basic Ad: Up to 200 words and 1 photo with your name, # and address for a FULL year on the site -- $19.95

Gold Star Ad: Up to 300 words and 2 photos with your name, # and address, highlighted with a GOLD STAR and placed on a special list for a FULL year on the site - - $39.95

Platinum Ad: Up to 500 words and 5 photos or artwork with your name, # and address, highlighted with LARGE BOLD TEXT and a flashing arrow, placed on the highest traffic area on our site for a FULL year, plus 4 week processing time or 2 **FREE** months -- $79.95

Gallery Ad: Up to 500 words and 20 photos or artwork in a fully animated slide show with up to 5 personalized words captioned on each photo, BACKGROUND MUSIC, your name, if and address, highlighted with LARGE BOLD TEXT and a flashing camera, placed on the highest traffic area of our site for a FULL year, plus 4 week processing time or 2 **FREE** months -- $99.95

We accept stamps for payment! For a **FREE** brochure/application, send us a SASE today!"

Website: prisonpenpals.com

## Prison Performing Arts
3547 Olive St Ste 250
 St. Louis, MO 63130

A nonprofit multi-discipline, literacy and performing arts program that serves incarcerated adults and children at St. Louis City Juvenile Detention Center, City Workhouse, City Justice Center, County Jail, Hogan Street Regional Youth Center, Northeastern Correctional Center (NECC) in Bowling Green, MO and Women's Eastern Reception, Diagnostic and Correctional Center (WERDCC) in Vandalia, MO.

Phone Number: (314) 727-5355
Website: prisonartsstl.org.

## Prison Place

Started by an ex-prisoner, this website is a place for friends and families of those on the inside to communicate and support each other.

Website: prisonplace.com

## Prison Professor
3333 Michelson Drive, Suite 500
Irvine, CA 92612

Michael G. Santos offers 4 books:

• Earning Freedom: Conquering a 45-Year Term, $25.00
• Success After Prison: How I Built Assets Worth $1,000,000 Within Two Years of Release, $15.00
• Prison! My 8,344th Day: A Typical Day in an Ongoing Journey, $15.00
• Triumph! Conquering Imprisonment and Preparing for Reentry, $15.00

Package deal: Get all 4 books for $60.00!

Website: MichaelSantos.com/Order
Phone: 949-334-9119
Email: Michael@MichaelSantos.com

## Prison Profiteers

This is the third and latest book in series of Prison Legal News anthologies that examines the reality of mass imprisonment in America. Prison Profiteers is unique from other books because it exposes and discusses who profits and benefits from mass imprisonment, rather than who is harmed by it and how. This book is 323 pages, $24.95, and can be bought from Prison Legal News.

## Prison Publications, Inc.
PO Box 174
Thompson, CT 06260

"Our available photo catalogs include 'Spring/Summer 2011, Spring/Summer 2012, Fail 2012, May 2013, November 2013, Summer 2014 and Winter 2015. We also sell books and mags."

**Comment:** I've seen the May 2013 catalog. It was good; lots of celebs and other fine girls — Next Door Nikki, etc. I ordered a few photos, too, and the prints were good quality. I think you can get their black and white catalog FREE, and a color version for $8.00. Clarify whether you want nude or non-nude.

## Prison Rape Elimination Act Oregon (PREA)

The DOC has an Inspector General Hotline that is toll free.

Inmate: (503) 555-1234
Public: (877) 678-4222

## Prison Rape Elimination Act (PREA)
320 First St. N.W.
Washington, D.C. 20543

 Phone Number: (800) 995.6423

## Prison University Project
PO Box 492
San Quentin, CA 94964

They provide higher education programs to people incarcerated at San Quentin State Prison.

Phone Number: 415-455-8088
Website: www.prisonuniversityproject.org

## Prison Yoga Project
PO Box 415
Bolinas, CA 94924

Two yoga manuals written especially for people in prison. A Path for Healing and Recovery offers physical practices (asana), breathing practices (pranayama) and meditation (dyhana) to improve mental, emotional and physical well-being. The book also serves as a powerful resource for anyone trying to break free of negative behavioral patterns. A Women's Practice: Healing from the Heart offers a simple and clear guide for women, whether free or behind bars who wish to use yoga to help heal themselves from trauma, stress or addiction. Write for a FREE copy of either book.

## Prisonworld Magazine
c/o Dawah International
PO Box 380
Powder Springs, GA 30127

"We have published Prisonworld Magazine bi-monthly since 2007 In order to communicate with those behind the wall. It is back in print but sold as single issues only. Past issues of the magazine can be read online for **FREE**. We also have Prisonworld BlogTalk, Prisonworld Radio Hour, which broadcasts in PODCAST and streams LIVE on Thursdays @ 2pm EST and MYPRISONWORLD. For more Information about any of our products, send SASE for latest brochure."

facebook.com/prisonworld
dawahinc.com
prisonworldblogtalk.com
prisonworldradiohour.com
prisonworldmagazine.com

## Prisoner Correspondence Project

QPIRG Concordia
C/O Concordia University
1455 de Maisonneuve O
Montreal, QC H3G 1M8

The Prisoner Correspondence Project is a collectively-run initiative based out of Montreal, Quebec. It coordinates a direct-correspondence program for gay, lesbian, transsexual, transgender, gender variant, two-spirit, intersex, bisexual and queer inmates in Canada and the United States, linking these inmates with people a part of these same communities outside of prison.

Phone Number: (514) 848 7583.

## Prisoner Diabetes Handbook

Living with diabetes in prison is very difficult. Order your **FREE** copy of this handbook and start managing your diabetes and health. Order from PLN.

## Prisoner Express

127 Anabel Taylor Hall Cornell University
Ithaca, NY 14853

Prisoner Express promotes rehabilitation by offering inmates information, education and the opportunity for creative self-expression in a public forum. Our semi-annual newsletter contains a description of our projects including poetry, essay writing, art, math, history, book club and chess programs. The newsletter is full of writings and art from the participants. Send a note for your **FREE** copy.

Phone Number: 607-255-6486
Website: prisonerexpress.org

## Prisoner Information Network (PIN)

980 S 700 W.
Salt Lake City, UT.

Phone Number: (801) 359-3589

## Prisoner Legal Services

1540 Market St Ste 490
San Francisco, CA 94102

Legal services for prisoners.

Phone Number: (415) 255-7036

## PrisonerPal.com

PO Box 19689
Houston, TX 77224

Pen Pals for prisoners. Your ad on the Internet, worldwide, only $9.95 for one year. Mail name and address for **FREE** order form.

## PrisonPath.com

A new and **FREE** search engine, www.PrisonPath.com. provides information for the public. The site helps users in clarifying confusion and fear of the unknown when a loved one is charged and arrested, or sentenced to Imprisonment in the United States. PrisonPath provides Information Including the ability to find a person Incarcerated, visitation rules, contact numbers, and more about every American prisons or jails. It also allows family and friends of inmates to communicate with each other on a specific page.

## Prisoner Promotions

2355 Fairview Avenue #214
Roseville, MN 55113

"With our service, we connect you to the best and most popular social networking sites on the Internet today. Our plan includes a Facebook profile. Your photo and personal ad will be posted for all to see, thus allowing more people to contact you. Up to 20 other networking sites are also available to you, ranging from religion, beliefs, culture, friendship, and dating/romance. Our service allows you to have a voice and gives you the opportunity to become a part of the outside world. Site options: Craigslist Personal Ad; Lost Vault Pen Pal Profile; OK Cupid; Hot or Not; Elove Dates; Zoosk; Ourtime; Matchmaker; Jdate; Single Parent Meet; Jumpdates; Date Hookup; True Love; Six Singles; Oceans of People; Fdating; Smooch; Real Christian Singles; Black Christian Dating; Christian Fishing; Green Singles. $20.00 for 10 sites, $30.00 for 20.

Pick your 10/20 web sites; write a short bio (300 words or less); include up to 3 photos; enclose payment; send away and let the networking begin!"

For a **FREE** brochure/application, send SASE.

## Prisoner Rights Information System of Maryland INC.

PO Box 929
Chestertown, MD 21620

## Prisoners For Christ
PO Box 1530
Woodinville, WA 98072

Bible correspondence courses available to inmates for **FREE**!

## Prisoner Solidarity
PO Box 4337
Canton, OH 44705

They publish research and educational material from writers and activists.

## Prisoners Resource
17503 La Cantera Parkway, Suite 104 #415
San Antonio, TX 78257

Need a better way to stay connected? Tired of not getting any responses? Try our solutions FREE for 5 days. Add us on corrlinks: info@prisonersresource.com.

Phone: 888-700-2511

## Prisoner Visitation and Support
1501 Cherry Street
Philadelphia, PA 19102

PVS is a nationwide visitation that has 300 volunteers across the U.S. who visits federal and military prisoners. Their goal is to visit any federal or military prisoner who wishes to receive a visit with special priority paid to prisoners on death row, in solitary confinement, or those who are serving long sentences. The PVS volunteers visit once a month, with limited visiting services for Spanish-speaking prisoners.

Phone Number: 215-241-7117
Website: prisonervisitation.org

## Prisoner/Inmate Family Service
PO Box 1852
Pismo Beach, CA 93448

This company will buy stamps, order books from online retailers , copy photos and artwork, etc., and much, much more. Send SASE for a **FREE** catalog.

Comment: This service is run by one guy named George Madison. I used him before and when I had someone email him because I thought he was taking too long, he responded that he is only one person

with over 4,000 clients. I had him do some gifts for X-mas and they landed separately from each other and sporadically over the course of a week. Worse still, the gifts came as from "George Mason" and my girl thought it was some creep so she threw them in the garbage. Eventually I stopped getting mailed responses from him, and likewise when I had someone email him.so I think he gave up the game. Not recommended. -- CW Carney

## PrisonerPal.com
PO Box 19689
Houston, TX 77224

Your ad on the internet, worldwide, for one year -- $9.95. Mail name and address for **FREE** order form.

## Prisoninmate.com
PO Box 6560
Pahrump, NV 89041

They offer to set up a MySpace/Facebook for you, as well as connect you with your family and friends. Write for details.

## Prisonnewsnetwork.us

Search this site for criminal records, warrants, inmate locations, prison headlines, gangs, news links and more.

## PrisonPenPalMingle.com
**B.F.I.A.**
P.O. Box 5618
Chicago, IL 60680

Get your photo and a 300 word bio posted on their website and facebook for only $25 a year.

## Prisoners for Christ Outreach Ministry
PO Box 1530
Woodinville, WA 98072

They offer bible college courses. Write for more details.

## Prisoners' Guerilla Handbook
C/O Prison Legal News
PO Box 1151
Lake Worth, FL 33460

Handbook to Correspondence Programs in the US & Canada by Jon Marc Taylor. 212 program profiles, listing tuition rates, time limits, courses offered degree programs, accreditation, and much more. "Any prisoner seeking to begin or continue their education behind bars

will find this to be an invaluable road map."- Paul
Wright. PLN, $49.95 + $2 S&H.

## Prisoners' Legal Services of New York
41 State Street, Suite M112
Albany, NY 12207

Phone Number: 518-445-6053
Website: http://plsny.org/

## Prisoners' Legal Services (formerly Massachusetts Correctional Legal Services)
Ten Winthrop Square, 3d Floor
Boston, MA 02110

The mission of the Massachusetts Legal Aid Websites
Project is to improve access to justice for low-income
and disadvantaged persons in Massachusetts through
innovative use of the web and other technologies.

Phone Number: 617-482-2773
Website: http://www.plsma.org

## Prisoners' Rights Office
6 Baldwin Street, 4th Floor
Montpelier, VT 05633-3301

Phone Number: 802-828-3194

## Prisoner's Rights Research Project
504 E Pennsylvania Ave
Champaign, IL 61820

Phone Number: (217) 333-0931
Website: law.illinois.edu/faculty/profile/judithrowan

## Prisoners' Rights Union
PO Box 161321
Sacramento, CA 95816

They publish self-help legal manuals based on
California law, for $7.50 each. They also publish PRU
News Review, quarterly; $6 per year for prisoners. Send
SASE for catalog of publications and more information.

Phone Number: (916) 442-2240.

## Prisoner's Self-Help Litigation Manual, 4th edition

The premiere, must-have "Bible" of prison litigation for
current and aspiring Jailhouse lawyers. If you plan to
litigate a prison or jail civil lawsuit, this book is a must-
have. 1500 pages, $39.95, and can be bought from
Prison Legal News.

## Prisoners with AIDS Rights Advocacy Group
P.O. Box 2161
Jonesboro, GA 30237

Provides practical and political support for prisoners
with HIV/AIDS.

## PrisonVoice.com
PO Box 6560
Pahrump, NV 89041

Penpal website. Write/Send SASE for more
information.

## Professional Press
P.O. Box 4371
Chapel Hill, NC 27515

This company provides you with an opportunity to
publish your book(s) at an affordable price. Send a
SASE for their **FREE** brochure containing details.

Phone Number: 800-277-8960
Website: profpres.com

## Project AVARY
385 Bel Marin Keys, Suite G
Novato, CA 94949

Project AVARY offers long-term support and
enrichment for children and youth in the San Francisco
Bay Area with a parent in prison or jail. Our program
services include a summer camp, monthly outings,
leadership training, and family support. Write for
further details.

Phone Number: 415-382-8799
Website: projectavary.org

## Project Blanket

Helps male and female prisoners with history of
substance abuse make the transition from prison to the
community.

Phone Number: 412-244-0329 (Pittsburgh)

## Project for Older Prisoners
George Washington University Law School
2000 H Street NW
Washington, DC 20052

Law students interview and evaluate older and geriatric inmates in obtaining parole or other forms of release from incarceration. Operates in six states: LA, MD, MI, NC, VA and DC.

Phone Number: (202) 994-7001

## Project Rebound
Associated Students Inc.
Cesar Chavez Student Center
1650 Holloway Avenue, T-138
San Francisco, CA 94132-1722

They support the formerly incarcerated on their journey through successful reintegration in a college setting.

Phone Number: (415) 405-0954
E-mail: projectrebound@asi.sfsu.edu

Website:
asi.sfsu.edu/asi/programs/proj_rebound/about.html

## Project Return
806 4th Avenue South
Nashville, TN 37210

Phone: 615-327-9654
Email: pri@projectreturninc.org

## Protecting Your Health and Safety

This book explains basic rights that prisoners have in a Jail or prison in the U.S. It deals mainly with rights related to health and safety, such as communicable diseases and abuse by prison officials; it also explains how you can enforce your rights within the facility and, if necessary, In court through litigation. This book is 325 pages, $10.00, and it can be bought from Prison Legal News.

## Providence Books Through Bars
c/o Paper Nautilus Books
5 Angell Street
Providence, RI 02906

Requests are received for reading materials from inmates nationwide. Be sure to include mailing address with Prisoner ID# as well as subject matter preferences.

Phone Number: 401-356-0388
Website: providencebtb.org

## PSI Publishing
413-B 19th St., #168

Lynden, WA 98264

They publish "The Prisoner's Guide to Survival." A comprehensive legal assistance manual for post conviction relief and prisoners' civil rights actions. It's a 750-page paperback. It costs $49.95 for prisoners', plus $5 shipping and handling; allow 3-4 weeks for delivery.

Phone Number: (800) 557-8868.

## PSSC/Parallax Press
46 Development Rd.
Fitchburg, MA 01420

## Public Interest Law Firm
152 N. Third St. 3rd Floor
San Jose, CA 95112

This is a small litigation firm specializing in high-quality representation for class action and impact suits. They serve Santa Clara and San Mateo counties only. No cases re the CDC.

Phone Number: 9408) 293-5790.

## Purdue University North Central at Westville Correctional Facility

Contacts: David Crum
Director, Correctional Education Programs
Phone Number: (219) 785-5440

## Rambles to the (Libertarian) Connection
James N. Dawson
PO Box 292
Malden, WA 99149
.

Debates, discussions, and diatribes on libertarianism, anarchism, religion, ethics, philosophy, and more. Write/send SASE for more information.

## Ramsey Media Group
9328 Elk Grove Blvd. Suite 105-238

Elk Grove, CA 95624

Ramsey Media is a small press and production company of books, music, and film. This Bay Area one-stop of a creative venture was developed to further assist artists of written and musical works, develop their crafts, and display arts to the public.

Services of this district branch of RMG include the publishing and distribution of raw and uncut urban novels, true crime sagas, controversial autobiographies, and ghost writing for the incarcerated along with other stories of interest. Music production services include distribution, vocal recording, and management of artists, video production and beat-making services.

Interested in being published? We are now accepting manuscripts!

Order our new novel Yadadamean: Bay Bizness today. By Stone Ramsey, Keak Da Sneak, and Big Tray Deee!

Email: bluntmuzic@gmail.com

### Randy Radic
200 Van Dyken Way
Ripon, CA 95366

Randall Radic aka John Lee Brook has written several books...

"Blood In Blood Out: The Violent Empire of the Aryan Brotherhood" (Headpress, 2012), a genre bestseller.

"Blood + Death: The Secret History of Santa Muerte and the Mexican Drug Cartels (Headpress, June, 11,2015).

"United Blood Nation: The Untold Story of the East Coast Bloods" (Headpress 2016).

"Killing God's Enemies: The Crazy War Against Jews, African Americans and the U.S. Government" (Trine Day 2016); co-authored by Anthony Tinsman.

Mr. Radic is a contributor to Crime Magazine, HuffPo, BlogCritics, AND Magazine, ArtSlamMag and PopMatters. He now offers a new publishing service for prisoners at the following prices.

*Editing, formatting and publishing on Kindle and CreateSpace (print books): $500. Manuscripts must be typed and you have to provide cover artwork. He will provide general editing, but developmental editing and/or extensive rewriting will cost more.

*Book Review Published on Premium Outlet: $199. Prisoner-authors who provide a **FREE** T-shirt to the reviewer will receive a 50% discount $99.

*Author's Website on SquareSpace 7: $200. Includes custom site, bio and 'pushes' to Facebook and Twitter pages). Does not include hosting or custom domain name. Author must pay for hosting -- $144 per year for personal site; $240 per year for business site. Author also pays for custom domain name, if desired -- $15 to $20 per year, depending upon availability.
*Book Trailer -- 1 to 2 minute trailer, posted on YouTube: $250.

*Ghostwriting: Contact about pricing.

*Typing: $2.00 per page -- handwriting must be legible. Email/CorrLinks: doctorradic@msn.com

**Comment:** If you're an inmate author looking to hire someone to help you get your book(s) published, Dr. Randy Radic is the best you can get. Simply put, he does it better and cheaper than anyone else. Tell him Mike, The Cell Block, said hi. - - Mike

### Reaching Beyond The Walls
P.O. Box 6905
Rutland, VT 05702

### Read Between The Bars
c/o Daily Planet Publishing
PO Box 1589
Tucson, AZ 85702

Will fill requests from AZ prisoners only.

Website: readbetweenthebars.com.

### Real Artist Tattoo Art Gallery

This company sells 24x30 paintings for $35. Have your people check out the website for more details.

Phone Number: (205) 545-3656
Website: kdsartworld.com.

### Real Cost of Prisons Project
5 Warfield Place
Northampton, MA 01060

100

RCPP works to expand the organizing capacity of people and communities struggling to end mass incarceration. They'll send the comic books "Prisoners of the War on Drugs," "Prison Town," and "Prisoners of a Hard Life" to prisoners for **FREE**.

Website: realcostofprisons.org.

## RedBird Books to Prisoners
PO Box 10599
Columbus, OH 43201

RedBird Books-to-Prisoners is a volunteer group providing Ohio prisoners with **FREE** reading material. Please send requests by subject.

## Reentry Division Adult Probation Department City and County of San Francisco
Attn: Jennifer Scaife Director
880 Bryant Street, Room 200
San Francisco, CA 94103

The purpose of the Reentry Council of the City & County of San Francisco is to coordinate local efforts to support adults exiting San Francisco County Jail, San Francisco juvenile justice out-of-home placements, the California Department of Corrections and Rehabilitation facilities, and the United States Federal Bureau of Prison facilities.

Phone: (415) 553-1593
email reentry.council@sfgov.org
Website: http://sfreentry.com

## Re-Entry Services, Philadelphia Prison Society
The Pennsylvania Prison Society
245 North Broad St.
Philadelphia, Pennsylvania 19107

The mission of the Pennsylvania Prison Society is to advocate for a humane, just and restorative correctional system, and to promote a rational approach to criminal justice issues.

Phone Number: (800) 227-2307
Website: prisonsociety.org.

## Reinvestigation Project
Office of the Appellate Defender
11 Park Place, Suite 1601
New York, NY 10007

Phone: 212-402-4100

## Represent Yourself in Court: How to Prepare and Try a Winning Case

Breaks down the civil trial process in easy-to-understand steps so you can effectively represent yourself in court. The authors explain what to say in court, how to say it, etc. This book is 528 pages, $39.99, and can be bought from Prison Legal News.

## Resentencing Project
Center for Policy Research
2020 Pennsylvania Ave. NW, #465
Washington, DC 20006

They offer sentence reductions for assistance to federal agencies concerned with prison gang violence, homicide, and heroin trafficking, extortion, terrorism, and child exploitation. Prisoner advocacy through resentencing. Write for literature and application. (Please allow 6-8 weeks for a response).

## Restore Pell Grants for Prisoners!

Prison education is on the federal legislative agenda in a way not seen since the mid-1990s. For prisoners and their supporters that provides renewed hope. It is now time to act on that hope: contact members of Congress and urge them to co-sponsor or support the REAL Act, H.R. 2521. The bill has been referred to the House Committee on Education and the Workforce, which is chaired by Rep. John Kline. The ranking Democratic member of the committee is Rep. Robert Scott. Both can be contacted at: U.S. House of Representatives, Committee on Education and the Workforce; 2182 Rayburn House Office Building; Washington, D.C. 20515.

What else can you do?
- Contact your members of Congress and let them know you support the REAL Act and ask them to support the bill, too.
- Ask friends and family to use social media to spread the word and show your support for the REAL Act.
- Ask family and friends to contact their members of congress and ask them to contact their members of Congress and ask them to co-sponsor and support the bill. They can use this link to locate them online: www.congressmerge.com/onlinedb/

"The REAL Act is about restoring education opportunities for our nation's prisoners so they will have the opportunity to reintegrate as productive members of the community post-incarceration." -- Congresswoman Donna F. Edwards

**HUMAN RIGHTS DEFENSE CENTER SUPPORTS PASSING THE REAL ACT!!**

**Revolution or RCP Publications**
Box 3486, Merchandise Mart
Chicago, IL 60654

**FREE** bi-monthly, radical newspaper.

**Comment:** This paper is written from a revolutionary view point. Every time there's a police shooting these people are there protesting. They were in New York, Boston and Missouri every time the cops killed someone. It's a cool paper. -- GURU

**R. Hughson**

I DO NOT RECOMMEND DOING BUSINESS WITH THIS BUSINESS

**RJ Publications**
3375 Centerville HWY 392694
Snellville, GA 30039

This is an urban-book publishing company. Their books are $15 each or 4 for $45. Write/send SASE for catalog.

Phone Number: (718) 471-2926
Website: rjpublications.com.

**Robert Kennedy Publishing**
400 Matheson Blvd. West
Mississauga, Ontario, Canada L5R 3M1

This is a company that sells back issues of American Curves Magazine. This is only to purchase back issues. They do not sell subscriptions to American Curves. Write for more information.

**Robert's Company**
15412 Electronic Lane #101
Huntington Beach, CA 92649

Sells "Smith's Guide to Habeas Corpus Relief," which includes example pleadings from the initial habeas corpus petition to the final petition for a writ of certiorari. This book is 380 pages, $24.95.

**Rolling Stone --LETTERS**

1290 Avenue of the Americas
New York, NY 10104-0298

Letters become the property of Rolling Stone and may be edited for publication.

**Rock of Ages Prison Ministry**
C/O Prisoners Bible Institute
P.O. Box 2308
Cleveland, TN 37320

**FREE** King James Bible, correspondence course. Offers New Testament study course through the Discipleship Institute. Also available in Spanish.

**Rocky Mountain Innocence Center**
358 South 700 East, B235
Salt Lake City, UT 84102

Phone Number: 801-355-1888
Website: rminnocence.org

**Rodriquez, Stephen G. & Associates**
633 West 5th St., 26th Fl.
Los Angeles, CA 90071

Phone Number: (213) 223-2173
Website: lacriminaldefenseattorney.com.

**Ruiz De La Torre Law Firm**
1801 Rio Grande Blvd. NW, Suite C.
Albuquerque, NM 87104

We help law make sense!
Need post-conviction relief? We can help in State and Federal convictions concerning: direct appeals, habeas corpus petitions, extraordinary writs, sentence reduction and modification motions, petitions for rehearing, pardon and clemency applications.
We also help you challenge: conditions of supervised release, involuntary severance of parental rights, long term administrative segregation.
Feel free to write.

Phone: 505-544-5400

**S**

**The Safer Society Foundation**
P.O. Box 340
Brandon, VT 05733-0340

"Today we view sexual abuse as a public health issue, and work to engage survivors, treatment professionals, persons with sexual behavior problems, family members, friends, policy makers, researchers and educators in creating evidence-based strategies for preventing sexual abuse, supporting those who have been abused, and managing those who have abused."

Phone Number: (802) 247-3132

## Safe Streets Arts Foundation
2512 Virginia Ave. NW #58043
Washington, DC 20037

The Safe Streets Arts Foundation exhibits prisoners' art at major art fairs and festivals. In addition to selling prison art in their retail outlets, they provide the names and addresses of imprisoned artists to anyone who wishes to use their artistic service. They exhibit and sell the art of imprisoned artists, with the proceeds of art sales used for inmate art supplies and restitution requirements, if any. Prisoners receive support to use the arts to develop their self-esteem and a positive attitude vital for successful reentry.

Phone Number: 202-393-1511
Website: safestreetsarts.org

## Sagewriters
Box215
Swarthmore, PA 19081

SageWriters is a community of free and imprisoned writers, artists, musicians, filmmakers, playwrights and activists working together to give an artistic voice to movements for justice, healing, reawakening compassion in our elected officials, creating a community love ethic, supporting effective re-entry programs, ending prisons as we know them and developing community-based Houses of Healing.

Phone Number: 610-328-6101
Website: SAGEWRITERS.com.

## The Salvation Army
615 Slaters Lane
Alexandra, VA 22313

They offer residential programs in some cities.

## Samizdat-Socialist Prisoners Project
PO Box 1253
Fond Du Lac, WI 54936

This is a revolutionary group for prisoners that sends Marxist and radical literature as well as sells and donates the "Socialist Action" newspaper. The cost of the Socialist action is $1.

## San Francisco AIDS Foundation
1035 Market St. #400
San Francisco, CA 94103

HIV/AIDS hotline at 800- 367-AIDS for CA prisoners only. Publishes "BETA," available in Spanish and English.

Phone Number: (415) 487-3000

## San Francisco Bay View
Willie Ratcliff, Publisher
4917 Third St.
San Francisco, CA 94124-2309

Bay View is an independent newspaper of liberation journalism. Subscribe for $24 per year, $12 for six months, or $2 per month. Make checks payable to Bay View. You may also pay in postage stamps.

To our readers behind enemy lines: A resource list is circulating that tells you subscriptions to the Bay View are "free to prisoners." This is only half true. The Bay View is not funded by anyone. Subscriptions, advertising and donations are our only income. If you have no funds or stamps, your subscription request can be paid from the Prisoners Subscription Fund when donations are sufficient. Pen Pal ads are **FREE** to prisoners!

However, many who have submitted pen-pal ads are distressed not to see them in the paper. Be assured your ad is posted on our website within a month after we receive it, but because of the volume, it will take longer to appear in print.

Web Site: sfbayview.com

**Comment:** This is a fantastic newspaper that every prisoner should have, regardless of ethnicity or geographical location. This is the real deal. Support by subscribing or sending a donation today. - Mike

## San Francisco Children of Incarcerated Parents Partnership.
P.O. Box 293

1563 Solano Ave.
Berkeley, CA 94707

2.4 million U.S. children have a parent behind bars today. The partnership formed to improve the lives of incarcerated children and to demand a "Bill of Rights" for them, downloadable from the website in English and Spanish.

**San Francisco Forty Niners Limited**
4949 Centennial Blvd.
Santa Clara, CA 95054

Write for **FREE** fan information on the team.

**San Francisco Zen Center**
c/o Jeffrey Schnieder
300 Page Street
S.F., CA 94102

This spot provides Buddhist inmates with free-world pen pals.

**Comment:** The key word is Buddhist. Their "gatekeeper" is Jeffrey Schnider. He's cool, but when I originally wrote he asked me to write an introduction letter, and when he got back at me he told me that I wasn't a real Buddhist so he wasn't going to hook me up, but he would write me a provide me with resources. I had to respect his gangsta. - - GURU

**Sanders, Ms Julia A.**
Tightwad Magazines Inc.
PO Box 1941
Buford, GA 30515

She provides discount magazine subscriptions and even sells some gifts, such as roses, teddy bears, etc. She accepts stamps as payment for subscriptions of magazines.

**Sanders, Louise S**
PO Box 361402
Decatur, GA 30036

They type manuscripts and papers. They also format paragraphs and chapters, edit grammar, punctuation, etc. Send SASE for **FREE** price list.

**San Quentin News**
1 Main St.

San Quentin, CA 94964

San Quentin News is a 16-page monthly newspaper written, edited, and produced by prisoners incarcerated at San Quentin State Prison. The SQ News encourages prisoners, staff, and others outside the institution to submit articles, poems, artwork and letters to the editor for possible inclusion. To receive a mailed copy of the SQ News, send $1.32 in postage. This process should be repeated every month for each new edition.

Please use the following criteria when submitting:

- Limit your articles to no more than 350 words.
- Know that articles will be edited for content and length.
- The newspaper is not a medium to file grievances. (For that, use the prison appeals process.) We encourage submitting articles that are newsworthy and encompass issues that will have an impact on the prison populace.
- Please do not use offensive language in your submissions.
- Poems and artwork (cartoons and drawings) are welcomed.
- Letters to the editor should be short and to the point.

Send submissions to: CSP - San Quentin; Education Dept. / SQ News; 1 Main Street; San Quentin, CA 94964

**Sandra Z. Thomas**
PO Box 4178
Winter Park, FL 32793

Typing services designed with special rates for the Incarcerated person. Send SASE for a **FREE** price list and more information.

Phone Number: 404-579-5563

**Santa Cruz Barrios Unidos**
817 Soquel Ave
Santa Cruz CA 95062

The Santa Cruz Barrios Unidos Prison Project is dedicated to providing cultural and spiritual education, support, and hope to incarcerated individuals. The Project advocates for prison policy reform and programs that reduce recidivism, support re-entry, and re-unifies families.

Phone: 831-457-8208
http://www.barriosunidos.net/prison-project.html

## Save on Prison Calls

This is a discount call service. Go to their website for details.

Website: saveonprisoncalls.com.

## Schatkin, Andrew Esq.
350 Jericho Turnpike
Jericho, NY 11753

This is an attorney that has 25 years' experience and specializes in prisoner rights, appeals, habeas corpus, etc. Write for details.

Phone Number: (516) 932-8120

## Schmidt, William Esq.
791 Price St., #170
Pismo Beach, CA 93449

This is an attorney that specializes in helping lifers parole.

## Second Chance Act
68 Betts St.
Winder, GA 30680

Halfway house for federal prisoners. Write for details.

## Second Chance Books
PO Box 4149
Philadelphia, PA 19144

"Second Chance Books is geared towards helping to give individuals who are or were incarcerated that second chance they need in life. Second Chance Books is a non-profit organization, which was founded by Abdul J. Fowler, an inmate in the Pennsylvania State Department of Corrections. The purpose of Second Chance Books is to help inmates/ex-offenders utilize their time and talents to do something constructive/productive with themselves as well as give back to their communities. Each inmate/ex-offender who becomes productive not only benefits themselves and their families, but their communities as well as society as a whole. In order for things to charge we must first make the necessary changes within ourselves. The only way for those who haven't been is for those who

have been to teach them. Knowledge is the key, and like they say on G.I. Joe, 'Knowing is half the battle.'

The more inmates we help become better, the more families we can help become better. Which will in turn help better their neighborhoods, communities, and ultimately society. Not to mention the fact that it will reduce the amount of tax dollars which are going into the prison systems, and increase the amount of tax dollars for schools and educating our youth. It's a win for everyone as a whole. Therefore I ask you to support/help us by purchasing our books and/or sending us at donation. You can do it through mail, or gofundme.com/secondchancebooks.

I ask you to please look at the big picture. In order to make a difference and change things we have to play our part and at least try. Nothing beats a try but a failure. I'm trying extremely hard, and in all honesty I seriously doubt that you'd leave me hanging because this can truly be a game changer!

For more info, please contact our Administrative Assistant Sheena Nicole "Essence" through one of the contacts below:

Phone Number: 267-601-6956 or 267-815-2349
Email: duladym.secondchancebooks@gmail.com
Twitter: @SecondChanceBks
Instagram: @SecongChanceBooks
Facebook: /SecondChanceBooks

Send SASE for our current newsletter containing news and our available books now!

## Secrets to Prison Pen Pal Success: How to Post FREE Ads on the Internet

This book is by Dupreme Washington and it's $14.95. The ISBN is 978-0-615-36993-8

**Comment:** I read most of this book and it was really good. My celly has put some of its lessons to use and has received success. - - Mike

## Sentel, Sentel
9550 S. Eastern Ave Ste 253
Las Vegas, NV 89123

Phone Number: 702-430-9445

Cheap local federal calls. Get a local number and save up to 85% on prison calls.

**Sentencing and Justice Reform Advocacy**
PO Box 71
Olivehurst, CA 95961

Barbara Brooks publishes SJRA Advocate Monthly. The publication lists case summaries that she will mail to prisoners. To receive a copy of the monthly publication, send a SASE plus 1 loose stamp.

**The Sentencing Project**
1705 DeSales Street NW 8th FL
Washington, DC 20036

The Sentencing Project is a 501(c)(3) non-profit organization which promotes reduced reliance on incarceration and increased use of more effective and humane alternatives to deal with crime. It is a nationally recognized source of criminal justice policy analysis, data, and program information. Its reports, publications, and staff are relied upon by the public, policymakers and the media.

Phone Number: 202-628-0871
Website: sentencingproject.org.

**Sentinel Writing Competitions**
Sentinel Poetry Movement
Unit 136
113 - 115 George Lane
South Woodford, London E18 1AB; United Kingdom

Writer's competition.

**The Senza Collection**
PO Box 5840
Baltimore, MD 21282

"Senza specializes in providing you several choices -- all-nude 4X6 prints in startling vivid color imagery, or non-nude 4X6 prints in startling vivid color imagery.

We have divided our catalogs into these categories: Caucasian, African-American, Hispanic, Asian, and Mixed Hotties. Each page of our catalogs has 99 gloriously seductive ladies posing just for your enjoyment. There are over 250 catalogs to collect at just $2.50 per catalog. You can order a **FREE** "99 Hotties" sample catalog by sending 2 US Forever stamps and a SASE.

For those that just cannot wait, take advantage of our introductory special -- Dirty Dozen. $19.99 gets you all of this, plus **FREE** s/h: 12 eye-popping catalogs, each

with 99 pics to choose from, and 12 4X6 random prints from our Mixed Hotties selection to show off our 4X6 print quality. All for just $19.99!

Remember, you must specify nude or non-nude, as well as your institution's restrictions as to the number of prints allowed in one envelope.

Please review our policies carefully: All Senza images are sold at a flat rate of $.35 each. Anyone wishing to purchase 1000+ prints at one time will be given a flat rate of $.30 per image. We have a minimum requirement of $15, which doesn't include s/h charges.

S/H charges are as follows:
1-5 4X6 prints: $1 per envelope
6-15 4X6 prints: $1.50 per envelope
16-25 4X6 prints: $2.00 per envelope

You must notify us on the order form the amount of prints your institution will allow in each envelope. We will accept brand-new US first-class postage stamps at the rate of $5.00 per book of 20. You are required to know your institution's policies regarding what images are acceptable into your facility. There are no exceptions to this policy. Returned/rejected mail: You will have 15 business days to send us a SASE (3 stamps per 25 rejected photos) with a street address in which to mail your returned/rejected photos. After 15 days the prints will return to our inventory. All sales are final, no refunds or exchanges.

**Services to Elder Prisoners, Pennsylvania Prison Society**
245 North Broad Street, Suite 300
Philadelphia, PA 19107-1518

**Set My Way Free Ministries, INC.**
221 North Hogan St, No 141
Jacksonville, FL 32202

Not attorneys, but provide legal research, attorney searches, manuscript proofreading, and revise pro se pleadings for a fee.

**Sex Abuse Treatment Alliance**
P.O. Box 1022
Norman, OK 73070-1022

Phone Number: (517) 482-2085
Website: www.satasort.org

**SexyPrisoners.com**
T. Ison (X)

P.O. Box 1445
Flushing, NY 11354

Pen pal site and sexy photo seller. Send SASE for Info.

**Shotcaller Press**
8316 N. Lombard #317
Portland, OR 97203

They have an art and writing contest. Writes/send SASE for more information.

**Shots That Rock**
9668 Westheimer Rd., Suite 200-303
Houston, TX 77063

Color catalogs - $5 per catalog page (70 images per page). Small b/w catalogs -- $.50 each
Big b/w catalogs -- 1.80 each

Picture prices (10 photo minimum):

10-19: $1 each, **FREE** s/h
20-49: 80 each **FREE** s/h
50-99: .75 each, **FREE** s/h
100-149: .65 each, **FREE** s/h
150-299: .50 each, **FREE** s/h
300+: .45 each, **FREE** s/h

Order at your own risk! No guarantees or refunds!

Email: ShotsThatRock@yahoo.com

**Slingshot Magazine**
3124 Shattuck Avenue
Berkeley, CA 94705

Slingshot is a quarterly, independent, radical newspaper published in the East Bay since 1988 by the Slingshot Collective. Subscriptions are **FREE** to USA prisoners. Back issues are $1.

Phone Number: 510-540-0751 x3
Website: slingshot

**Sinister Wisdom, INC.**
P.O. Box 3252
Berkeley, CA 94703

Publishes work by lesbians only – prose, poetry, essays, graphics, and book reviews. **FREE** to women in prison.

**Sisyphean Tasks, LLC**
PO Box 7956

Woodbridge, VA 22195

Publishes the Book "Black American in the Desert Kingdom," $19.95 plus shipping and handling.

**SJM Family Foundation, Inc.**
PO Box 167365
Irving, TX 75016

Publishes "Getting Ahead: An Ex-Con's Guide to Getting Ahead in today's Society." Each book is $10, they accept postage stamps. Also, they offer a new correspondence course on grant writing and non-profit management. Send 4 stamps for brochure and application.

Website: sjmfamilyfoundation.org.

**Skin&Ink Letters**
219 Route 4 East, Suite 211
Paramus, NJ 07652

Send letters, photos, drawings, etc., to this tattoo magazine. Must include return postage if you want you shit back.

**Skye Services**
Attn: Brochure Dept.
PO Box 1768
Maricopa, AZ 85139

Variety of services at low. prices! Social media, typing, CL, photos, booklets, letters, Wiki, email and more. Send SASE.

**Slammer Books**

I DO NOT RECOMMEND DOING BUSINESS WITH THIS COMPANY!

**Slipstream Poetry Contest**
Dept. W-1
PO Box 2071
Niagara Falls, New York 14301

Writer's competition. The annual Slipstream poetry contest offers a $1,000 prize plus 50 professionally-printed copies of your book.

**Guidelines:**
Send up to 40 pages of poetry: any style, format, or theme (or no theme), and a $20 check, bank draft, or money order for reading fee. Due to recent increases in

the cost of mail, manuscripts will no longer be returned. Send only copies of your poems, not originals.

## Slingshot Magazine
3124 Shattuck Avenue
Berkeley, CA 94705

Slingshot is a quarterly, independent, radical newspaper published in the East Bay since 1988 by the Slingshot Collective. Subscriptions are **FREE** to USA prisoners. Back issues are $1.

## Smith's Guide to Chapter 7 Bankruptcy for Prisoners

Get immediate freedom from liens against offender account by filing chapter 7 bankruptcies. Includes required bankruptcy forms and detailed filing instructions. This book is $31.90 ($34.08 in CA), and can be ordered from Roberts Company and online retailers.

## Smith's Guide to Executive Clemency for State and Federal Prisoners

For those who have exhausted all legal remedies or have sentences that are too long to serve, this book lays out every aspect of the clemency process. Its 288 pages, $31.90 ($34.08 in CA), and can be ordered from Roberts Company and online retailers.

## Smith's Guide to Habeas Corpus

See Robert's Company

## SMOOTH Fiction, c/o SMOOTH
P.O. Box 809
New York, NY 10013

Website: fiction@smoothmag.com

SMOOTH magazine accepts short fiction submissions to be published in their magazine.

## SMOOTH Magazine
P.O. Box 809
New York, NY 10013

SMOOTH is an "urban-style" magazine with beautiful women and interesting articles.

## SMOOTH-Talk
P.O. Box 809
New York, NY 10013

Feeling like nobody cares? Here's your chance to speak your mind and let your voice be heard -- even if nobody's listening. Send your letters, photos, drawings, x-rays, etc.

## Snow Lion Publications
605 W State St.
Ithaca, NY 14850

Phone Number: (607) 273-8506
Website: snowlionpub.com.

## Socialism and Democracy
411A Highland Ave., #321
Somerville, MA 02144

The Roots of Mass Incarceration in the US: Locking Up Black Dissidents and Punishing the Poor. Edited and Introduced by Mumia Abu-Jamal and Johanna Fernandez. Scholars' and activists, including former and current political prisoners, explore criminalization, police terror, and the abuse of prisoners, in their political context.

Copies @ $10+ p&h ($5 in US; $10 elsewhere; no extra postage charge for larger orders).

Phone Number: 617-776-9505
Email: info@sdonline.org

## Socialist Worker
PO Box 16085
Chicago, IL 60616

Prisoners can request a **FREE** subscription to this newsletter.

## Soiled Doves
PO Box 2588
Fernley, NV 89408

"Out with the old and in with the new. Soiled Doves is a new high resolution photo company that utilizes the latest technology to provide you the best quality intimate photos for your viewing pleasure. New standards of erotica designed to give you the greatest experience possible within your institutions rules by offering a selection from non-nude to non-nude penetration, fully nude softcore scenes.

The following catalogs are $3.00 each, plus $1.00 s/h:

Sexy Selfies Volume 1

Bang Them Up (action shots) Volume 1
Latinas Volume 1
MILFs Volume 1
Snow Bunnies Volume 1
Hip-Hop Honeys Volume 1
 Big Booty Babes Volume I
Heavy Hitters Volume 1
Asian Cuties Volume 1
Famous Sweethearts Volume 1
Prison Friendly (non-nude) Volume 1
Amateurs Volume 1
G-Male Volume 1

Each photo order must be a minimum of 10 photos. Photos are $1.00 each, and for every 10 photos you will receive 2 additional photos of your choice **FREE**. $1.00 s/h per envelope, which means... $1.00 per envelope for shipping and handling! All photos are 4X6 unless special requests are made. We also offer a special search service where you can request your particular interests and we'll do our best to find the images you seek. Please include 3 choices as some images might not be readily available. So don't hesitate! Order your catalog now! Or send a SASE for your **FREE** brochure. A SASE must be sent if you want a reply to special requests or questions. All special requests must be within your institution's rules and start at $1.50 per picture plus $1.00 s/h per envelope. We look forward to doing business with you."

**Soledad Brother: The Prison Letters of George Jackson**

Lucid explanation of the politics of prison by well-known prison activist. More relevant now than when it first appeared 40 years ago. This book is 339 pages, $18.95, and can be bought from Prison Legal News.

**Solitary Watch**
c/o James Ridgeway
PO Box 11374
Washington, DS 20008

Website: solitarywatch.com

**SOON**
Wilmington; Derby DE65 6BN; England

SOON contains the answers to many of life's problems such as worry, fear, and loneliness. Write or email for a **FREE** copy.

**South Beach Singles, Inc**
PO Box 1656

Miami, FL 33238

All photos are $1.00 each with a minimum order of 10 photos per brochure, plus a flat rate of $3.00 s/h. They offer a special -- 30 photos for $20.00. You can get 10 photos for 40 stamps (flat books only).

Brochure lists, non-nude, $2 each:

NBA Vol. 9: White, everyday women, amateurs, open logs and backshots.

NBA Vol. 10-13: Black women, strippers, amateurs, open legs, backshots. Some White girls here -- Sasha Cream, Cubana Lust (Cubana), and Amber (Vol. 12).

NBA Vol. 14-17: Mix of Black, White, action shots and adult stars.

Brochure lists, XXX, $5 each:

Tripple XXX Vol. 1: Pinky, Cherokee, Luscious Lopez, Olivia, Sky and Mason.

Triple XXX Vol. 2: Montana Fishburne, Next Door Nikki, Flower, Phoenix, Jada Isis, Angel, Kapri, more Pinky and Cherokee.

Triple XXX Vol. 3: Lacey, Misty, Mika, Kelly, Pleasure, Pinky and Cherokee.

Custom orders are 25 photos for $40 (s/h included): "I will allow you to choose from your favorite model, adult star, or celebrity of your choice. Send $40 along with your feature and I will send you 25 of the hottest photos I can find. The custom will also apply to fetishes. Also Instagram and Facebook photos you want me to find. You must have the specific Instagram or Facebook username they are using. I will not search for it. Please keep in mind this is a VIP service; you are getting photos that no one else has. Most celebs and models will NOT have action shots, but I will get you the best high-quality photos no company can match. (Sorry, no transgender.) Please allow 10 days for delivery." Karen Leblanc, CEO

Email/Corrlinks: RD@SOUTHBEACHSINGLES.ORG
Website: southbeachsingles.org

**South Dakota Prisoner Support Group**
PO Box 3285
Rapid City, SD 57709-3285

Their purpose is to provide support to inmates in jails and prisons and their families of those in the South Dakota prison system.

**South End Press**
PO Box 283132
Cambridge, MA 02238

They sell books to prisoners. Write/Send SASE for more information.

Website: southendpress.org.

**Special Needs X-Press, Inc.**
PO. Box 268
Bronx, NY 10468

**Southern Poverty Law Center**
400 Washington Ave.
Montgomery, AL 36104

Phone Number: (334) 956-8200
Website: http://splcenter.org.

**Southland Prison News**
955 Massachusetts Ave., PMB 339
Cambridge, MA 02139

This is a newsletter that covers prisoner news on East and Southern States. It's $15 per year.

**Special Litigation Section**
US Dept of Justice Civil Rights Division
950 Pennsylvania Ave. NE
Washington, DC 20530

They enforce federal civil rights statues regarding conditions of institutional confinement, law enforcement misconduct, and protection of institutionalized persons' religious exercise rights.

Website: usdoj.gov/crt/split

**Special Miracles, LLC**
PO Box 46884
Cincinnati, OH 45246

"Our mission at Special Miracles is and always will be to help inmates during and after released from prison. If it's help buying a gift for a loved one or even yourself to photos or custom work, contact us. We are here for you!

Gift Catalog: Do you want to send something different for birthdays, anniversaries, or just because? Send some jewelry to a spouse, parent, pen-pal, significant other, children, etc. to thank them for being in your life while doing your time. All jewelry has a lifetime guarantee. It's trendy, good quality and affordable. We even offer an ongoing sale of buying 2 pieces of jewelry and receive up to 4 pieces half off. Put a smile on your family and loved one's faces with something different. Request a catalog today!

Social Site Printouts: If you have your password and login to your Facebook or other social sites and want your friends list printed and sent, we will do that for you; $3 per page color print, or $2 per page black and white print. S/h is $2. Please contact us before you order so we can quote you the total cost of your printout.

Special Beauty Non-Nude Photos: We offer the best quality and cheapest photos in the system. To get our photos as low as .40 each, you must become a V.I.P. member. We offer a 1-year "Photo V.I.P. Membership" for as low as $15. All V.I.P. members will receive a membership card with a personal V.I.P. number to use to receive our new color catalogs, FREE shipping on all orders, exclusive sales throughout the year and much more. Also V.I.P. members will receive discounted prices on all bulk photos ordered. 100 glossy waterproof photos for $40.00, s/h included. Non-V.I.P. member's photos are .59 each and s/h is $2 per 10-25 photos ordered.

Photo Copying: Copies of your prison and personal photos (10), 4x6 copies is $6.99 plus $2 shipping per 25 ordered. Additional copies are .69 each.

Book Orders: Take advantage of ordering books directly from major book suppliers. Our staff will gladly search for new releases, used books, hard-to-find books, educational and vocational books for programs, comics, etc. Send us the information on the books you are looking for and we will send you a personalized price quote for the item(s).

Hot Erotic Stories: Steamy, hot, toe-curling erotic stories. BOP and state facility friendly. Get your catalog today. Stories are $3 each or 2 for $5 plus s/h.

Special Backgrounds: 4x6s are $3 each, 5x7s are $5 each, s/h handling included. We have a variety a backgrounds to choose from. Send $5 plus $2 s/h for five-catalog bundle.

Personal Email & Photo Service: Tired of trying to connect with family and friends and hearing, "I tried to set up CorrLinks," and either "the code doesn't work, I can't figure it out," or "we'll set it up later"? Or waiting and waiting for photos from family, friends, or that special someone and they are always telling you they are busy and haven't had the time to send them? Well, wait no more. Simply have your family and friends send their emails or photos to your very own personal email. We will send you emails and responses directly to you without the hassle of having your friends and family dealing with CorrLinks. We also will print and send any photos** directly to you that come to your inbox. Eliminate the headache of all the excuses and make it easy for them with the push of a button by pressing send! Email service is $10 a month or 6 months for $50 (must purchase 6-month service in one transaction for $50 special).

**Price of photos are not included in email price. Any photos printed are .49 each, plus $2 for s/h. Photo printing is a pre-paid service. You must have funds in your account to cover cost of photos before they are printed and sent.

Flowers, Teddy Bears, Balloons and Candy: We now offer a variety of roses, flowers, teddy bears, balloons and candy that you can send to your family and friends for any occasion. Request a flower catalog today!

Please send 3 loose stamps to address listed to receive catalogs and/or applications for service. Emails will now be answered within 72 hours once received. We kindly ask our custom8rs to limit their questions to services and important matters only. We answer email ONLY Mon-Fri. No holidays or weekends! At this time, we are not accepting custom photo orders or custom catalog requests.

Be advised all services must be pain in advance before we complete customer's orders. We accept facility checks, money orders and Western Union. Customers can also have their family and friends send payments using their credit/debit cards through our website."

Website: specialmiraclesllc.com

**Comment:** They have a lot going on and some cool shit. However, even with a SASE their response rate has been wishy-washy. I don't like that. - - Mike

**Spinister Wisdom, Inc.**

PO Box 3252
Berkeley, CA 94703

Spletter

FREE app to send letters and photos!
• Use a phone to write a letter, add photos - we print the letter and photos and mail it for you!
• Includes reply envelope -- Spletter instantly notifies your loved one on the phone.
• Earn Spletter Dollars by referring friends.
• Write letters anywhere anytime.
• Photos quality 4x6 prints.
• Available in every prison, same day shipping.

Get it now on Google Play!

**Sports Illustrated**
PO Box 61290
Tampa, FL 33661

Sports magazine.

**Sports Weekly**
PO Box 50146
McLean, VA 22102

A sports magazine that provides stats on the NFL and MLB.

Phone Number: (800) USA-1415
Website: mysportsweekly.com.

**Spring Grass Book 'Em**
PO Box 71357
Pittsburgh, PA 15213

Spring Grass Book 'Em is a **FREE** books-to-prisoners program that mails books to inmates nationwide (except for PA which is served by Book 'Em same address). Request books and magazines by subject or title and or author, or just request any. No catalog is available and some books may be substituted for those requested due to scarcity Please let Spring Grass Book 'Em know of any book restrictions (or changes to any restrictions), or upon transfer to a different institution.

Phone Number: 412-251-7302
Website: springgrassbookem.org

**SP Telecom**
1220 Broadway - # 801-A
New York, NY 10001

Guaranteed savings of up to 90% on your long distance, out-of-state, and international calls from Federal prisons, county Jails and State prisons. Call, write or have your loved ones check out their website for more information.

Phone Number: 845-326-5300
Website: inmatefone.com

**Spanish For Prisoners**
1094 DeHaven Street, Suite 100
West Conshohocken, PA 19428

This book by Ronald Bilbrey is $18.95. It's available through Infinity Publishing Book Sales.

**St. Dismas Guild**
PO Box 2129
Escondido, CA 92033

They offer **FREE** bible study, bibles, rosaries, pamphlets, etc.

**St. Mark's School of Legal Studies**
1840 Coral Way, Room 4-754
Miami, FL 33145

Become a financial mediator and earn over $185,000 a year! In its annual list of best careers, "U.S. News" and "World Report" names mediator as a top choice for 2011. Law degrees not required, no restrictions for ex-felons to practice in any state. Write for **FREE** brochure and application.

**St. Patrick Friary**
102 Seymore St.
Buffalo, NY 14210

Counseling provided at Attica, Wyoming, Collins, Orleans, Albion, Groveland, Gowanda, & Rochester prisons. Post release services include housing, and job training. Also assist with educational and job training opportunities.

Phone Number: (716) 856-6131

**Stanford Law School**
Crown Quadrangle
559 Nathan Abbott Way
Stanford, CA 94305-8610

The Stanford Three Strikes Project is the only legal organization in the country devoted to addressing excessive sentences imposed under California's Three Strikes sentencing law.

Phone: 650 723.2465

Website:www.law.stanford.edu/organizations/programs-and-centers/stanford-three-strikes-project

**Stanley Tookie Williams Legacy Network**
C/O Neighborhood House of North Richmond
820 – 23rd Street
Richmond, CA 94804

Stan Tookie Williams was the co-founder of the Los Angeles Crips. In 1981 he was convicted of murdering four people and sentenced to death row at San Quentin State Prison. He was executed on 12/13/05. He became a famous activist struggling against the death penalty and to overcome gang violence, and fought up to his death bed. He drafted the Tookie Protocol for Peace, a national street peace initiative. This is a framework for peace between gangs. This Legacy network was founded to achieve Tookie's last wishes, including violence prevention education, literacy projects, and work for social justice, including abolishing the death penalty. Go online and read the Protocol for Peace! Sign it and pass it along!

Phone Number: (510) 235-9780
Website: www.tookie.com

**State Public Defender; San Francisco**
221 Main St., 10th Fl.
San Francisco, CA 94105

This office handles capital and non-capital appeals only for indigent convicted felons. Contact Michael Hersek.

Phone Number: (415) 904-5600.

**Stop Prison Profiteering!**
Prison Legal News
Attn: CFPB Comments
PO Box 1151
Lake Worth, FL 33460

Take action on prison money transfer services!!

For many years, corporations that provide money transfer services in prisons and jails have profited from price gouging prisoners and their families by charging excessive fees for putting money on prisoners' institutional trust accounts.

The time to take action against these practices is now!

You can submit a complaint to the Consumer Finance Protection Bureau (CFPB) regarding your experience with prison or jail money transfer services. Please send your complaint or comments as soon as possible, addressing any of these topics:

- Excessive Fees For Money Transfer Services: Let the CFPB know what service charges are required to transfer funds, as well as any limitations on the amount that can be transferred in one transaction.
- Ancillary Fees: In addition to transaction fees, do you or your family have to pay extra (ancillary) fees to set up money transfer accounts or talk with a company customer service representative?
- Customer Service: Does the company that provides money transfer services provide a toll-free number that connects you to a live person who can assist you? Are you able to access the information you need through the company's website? Do you have any choice in which money transfer service you use?

Send us your comments by mail, and we'll file them with the CFPB for you!

Please speak from your own personal experience, and note your comments will become a public record. People with Internet access can send their comments via email tocwilkinson@prisonlegalnews.org, or submit them through our website: www.stopprisonprofiteering.org

## Stop Prisoner Rape
3325 Wilshire Blvd., Ste. 340
Los Angeles, CA 90010

Seeks to end sexual violence committed against men, women, and youth in all forms of detention.

Phone Number: (510) 235-9780
Phone Number: (213) 384-1400
Website: www.spr.org

## Stopmax Campaign
American Friends Service Committee
1501 Cherry St.
Philadelphia, PA 19102

Phone Number: 215-241-7000.

## Stratford Career Institute
Po Box 1560
St. Albans, VT 05478

They offer correspondence courses in 52 career fields.

Phone Number: (612) 788-4197
Website: scitraining.com.

## Strawberry Dragon Zendo
1800 Robertson Blvd. #197
Los Angeles, CA 90035

Website: www.strawberrydragon.org.

## Street Life Publishers
PO Box 2112
Minneapolis, MN 55402

This company publishes urban books such as Murda Squad, A Real Goon's Bible, Omerta, Supply and Demand, Street Kingz and more. Each book is $15, plus $3.99 shipping for first book and $1.99 each additional book. Money order or institutional check only. For a 10% promotional discount, write code #3733 on all orders.

## Subscription Services
PO Box 2107
San Marcos, CA 92079

They offer magazine subscriptions at a discount. Write/Send SASE for more information.

## Sue the Doctor and Win! Victim's Guide to Secrets of Malpractice Lawsuits

Written for victims of medical malpractice and neglect, to prepare for litigation. Note that this book addresses medical malpractice claims and issues in general, not specifically for prisoners. Its 336 pages, $39.95, and can be bought from Prison Legal News.

## Sullivan Productions, LLC
2020 West Pensacola St Unit 20323
Tallahassee, Florida 32316

"Sullivan Productions brings you the very best in Urban literature with National Best Selling authors and their books. Our company is unlike any other publishing company. We cater specifically to inmates on and up close and personal level. You get to communicate with the power house authors in the game today and our team of fantastic staff members that will personally assist you. Request an order form to see all of our books. Each book is $15 plus $3.95 s/h for first book and $1.50 for each additional book. BUY 3 BOOKS, GET 1 **FREE**!

We accept Institutional Checks, Money Orders, and Postage Stamps as payment."

**Comment:** Sullivan Productions ain't playin'. They're really trying to be a major force in the urban-book game. They offer over 80 books and have more coming soon. -- Mike

Phone Number: 850-368-5185
E-mail: leosullivan25@yahoo.com

## SummerBunnies.com
Po Box 741145
Houston, TX 77272

They sell sexy, non-nude photos. Send $3 and a SASE for their latest catalog.

## The Sun Magazine
Attn: Molly Herboth, Circulation Manager
107 North Roberson Street
Chapel Hill, NC 27516

Independent, ad-free monthly magazine that publishes personal essays, short stories, interviews, poetry, and photographs by emerging and established artists. **FREE** subscription offered to prisoners. Also accepts submissions.

## Supreme Design
PO Box 10887
Atlanta, GA 30310

Supreme Design is a publishing company operated by Supreme Understanding. Supreme Understanding is a community activist, educator, and expert on the socioeconomically and psychological struggles of oppressed people. His extensive research and life experience helped him design a system of success for even the most disadvantaged. The following books are available...

- How to Hustle and Win, Part 1: A Survival Guide for the Ghetto, by Supreme Understanding (Forward by the Real Rick Ross)

This is the book that started it all. Now an international bestseller, this book has revolutionized the way people think of "urban literature." It offers a street-based analysis of social problems, plus practical solutions that anyone can put to use. 336 pages, $14.90 (ISBN: 978-9816170-0-8)

- How to Hustle and Win, Part 2: Rap, Race, and Revolution; by Supreme Understanding (Forward by Sticamn of Dead Prez)

The controversial follow up to How to Hustle and Win digs even deeper into the problems we face, and how we can solve them. Part 1 focused on personal change, and Part 2 explores the biggest picture of changing the entire hood. 384 pages, $14.95 (ISBN: 978-9816170-9-1)

- La Brega: Como Sobrevivir En El Barrio, by Supreme Understanding

Thanks to a strong demand from Spanish-speaking countries, we translated our groundbreaking "How to Hustle and Win" into Spanish, and added new content specific to Latin America. Because this book's language is easy to follow, it can also be used to brush up on your Spanish. 336 pages, $14.95 (ISBN: 978-0981617-08-4)

- Locked Up But Not Locked Down: A Guide to Surviving the American Prison System, by Ahmariah Jackson and IAtomic Allah (Forward by Mumia Abu Jamal)

This book covers what it's like on the inside, how to make the most out of your time, what to do once you're out, and how to stay out. Features contributions from over 50 insiders, covering city jails, state and federal prisons, women's prisons, juvenile detention, and international prisons. 288 pages, $14.95 (ISBN: 978-1935721-00-0)

- Knowledge of Self: A Collection of Wisdom on the Science of Everything in Life; edited by Sumpreme Understanding, C'BS Alife Allah, and Sunez Allah (Forward by Lord Jamar of Brand Nubian)

Who are the Five Percent? Why are they here? In this book, over 50 Five Percenters from around the world speak for themselves, providing a comprehensive introduction to the esoteric teaching of the Nation of Gods and Earths. 256 pages, $14.95 (ISBN: 978-1935721-67-3)

- The Science of Self: Man, God, and the Mathematical Language of Nature, by Supreme Understanding and C'BS Alife Allah (Forward by Dick Gregory)

How did the universe begin? Is there a pattern to everything that happens? What's the meaning of life? What does science tell us about the depths of our SELF? Who and what is God? This may be one of the deepest books you can read. 360 pages, $19.95 (ISBN: 978-1935721-67-3)

- The Hood Health Handbook, Volume 1 (Physical Health). Ed. by Supreme Understanding and C'BS Alife Allah (Forward by Dick Gregory)

Want to know why Black and Brown people are so sick? This book cover the many "unnatural causes" behind poor health, and offers hundreds of affordable and easy-to-implement solutions. 480 pages, $19.95 (ISBN: 978-1-936721-32-1)

- The Hood Health Handbook, Volume 2 (Mental Health), Ed. by Supreme Understanding and C'BS Alife Allah

This volume covers mental health, how to keep a healthy home, raising healthy children, environmental issues, and dozens of other issues, all from the same down-to-earth perspective as Volume 1. 480 pages, $19.95 (ISBN: 978-1-935721-33-8)

## Sunshine Artist
4075 L.B. McLead Rd., Suite E
Orlando, FL 32811

This magazine has articles on marketing crafts and selling your art. It's $34.95 for a 1-year subscription, 12 issues per year.

## Support for Kids with Incarcerated Parents, Philadelphia Prison Society

They help children with incarcerated parents build their self-esteem and cope with their parents' incarceration.

Phone Number: (215) 564-4775 x123 Contact: Ted Enoch

## Support Housing and Innovative  Partnerships
PO Box 8803
Boise, ID 83707

Phone Number: (208) 331-0900

## SureShot Books Publishing LLC
PO Box 924
Nyack, NY 10924

"SureShot Books is a publishing company and bookstore. Our products range from law books, Bibles, urban books, self-help, sobriety, education, etc. We also have a large selection of Spanish books and magazines. Our primary objective at SureShot Books, is to assist in the process of both socializing and improving the overall education level of prison inmates, helping provide you a greater opportunity at succeeding in life. We ensure you that we clearly understand your needs and that we will fully leverage our resources to fulfill them. Please forward us any ideas that you have to help us serve you better. Send $12.95 for our current 2017 catalog."

Website: sureshotbooks.com
Email/Corrlinks: Info@sureshotbooks.com

**Comment:** Write these guys and request books by Mike Enemigo and thecellblock.net. I need them to start carrying ALL TCB books. - - Mike

## Surrogate Sisters

I DO NOT RECOMMEND DOING BUSINESS WITH THIS COPMPANY!

## Suthern Cumforts
PO Box 920098
Norcross, GA 30010

"Some play the picture game... We run it! We are the ULTIMATE picture catalog!

All photos are $1.00 each, with a minimum of 10 photos per order. Shipping and handling is $2.00 per envelope needed. Please include any specific requirements when ordering. Only checks and Money Orders are accepted forms of payment for pictures. However, we will accept stamps for our catalogs, which are 5 Forever stamps for each addition. You can order from any edition at any time. All pics are 4X6, high-gloss!

**Comment:** I've seen several catalogs from SC. Most the pics/images they offer look like still shots from porn movies. Bad bitches, just how we like them. My penis has never once been angry at me for inspecting the catalogs of SC! Fuck with them. - Mike

## Surviving the System, Inc.
P.O. Box 1860
Ridgeland, MS 39158

## Susan L. Burke
Law Offices of Susan L. Burke

1611 Park Avenue
Baltimore, MD 21217

"Please contact me if you want to join the nationwide class actions against telephone companies who have been overcharging inmates and their families for phone calls."

Website: burkepllc.com
Phone Number: (410) 733-5444

### Susman, Eli
PO Box 961896
Boston, MA 02196

Write for **FREE** sample essays and book information about living congenially forever in a spirit world.

### The Sutra Translation Committee of the U.S. and Canada

To request books (**FREE** of charge) from the Sutra Translation Committee, please send a message to ymba@ymba.org. Please include your mailing address in the message. They will inform you by e-mail if the books are available.

### SYDA Foundation Prison Project
PO Box 99140
Emeryville, CA 94662

They will mail a correspondence course titled "In Search of Self" to prisoners for **FREE**. Their mission is to improve the state of individuals through the teaching of Siddha Yoga Meditation practices.

Email: PrisonProject@siddhayoga.org
Website: www.siddhayoga.org/SYDA-foundation/prison-project
Phone Number (510) 898-2700 ext 4113

### Sylvan Clarke
PO Box 160486
Brooklyn, NY 11216-0486

Lonely? Need a partner? Looking for marriage, friendship, someone to correspond with? This is a worldwide club with members across the world waiting to hear from you. Send $1.00 U.S. or 2 IRC's for application. Join today, be a member for life!

### Sylvia Rivera Law Project
147 West 24th St. 5th Floor
NY, NY 10001

Provides **FREE** legal services to transgender and gender nonconforming low-income people and people of color. Only available in NY and surrounding areas.

Phone Number: (212) 337-8550

### Tarantula
818 SW 3rd Ave PMB 1237
Portland, OR 97204

Website: www.socialwar.net/tarantula

### Task Force on Prisoner Re-Entry
C/O Dept. of Public Safety and Correctional Services
Hampton Plaza, Suite 1000
300 East Joppa Rd.
Towson, MD 21286

Phone Number: (410) 585-3727

### Tattoo Review
5 Marine View Plazas, Suite 207
Hoboken, NJ 07030

This magazine interviews tattoo artists, discusses their art and lifestyle. Its $21 for a 1-year subscription; issues per year.

### Tattoo Flash
Box 3000
Agoura Hills, CA 91376

If you have a pattern that has what it takes, Tattoo Mag would like to see it! Designs can be black and white or color, you decide, but original art only please. Every full page design pays $75, and the smaller designs pay $25. Send your drawings.

### Teachers and Writers Corroborative
520 8th Ave., suite 2020
New York, NY 10018

This organization publishes a number of books on writing, which are filled with ideas and exercises. Write to request a catalog.

Website: twc.org.

### Tele-pal.com

Tired of waiting on pen pals? Talk to a phone pal! Why write when you can call? We have a phone pal for you and it's more affordable than ever.

Phone Number: (719) 297-1909

## Tenacious V. Law
PO Box 20388
New York, NY 10009

A zine (2-3 issues/year) of writings and art formally and currently incarcerated women. **FREE** to women (including trans women) in prison. Men in prison are asked to send 2 stamps (or $1 check or money order made out to V. Law).

## Ten Men Dead

Relies on secret IRA documents and letters smuggled out from IRA political prisoners during their 1981 hunger strike at the Infamous Long Kesh prison in Belfast, where 10 men starved themselves to death. Written by David Beresford.

## Texas Civil Rights Project
AUSTIN
1405 Montopolis Drive
Austin, TX 78741-3438

Phone: (512) 474-5073
tcrp.questions@gmail.com

## Texas Innocence Network
University of Houston Law Center
100 Law Center
Houston, TX 77204

## Texas Prisoners Network Support
3005 S. Lamar Blvd.; Suite D 109-224
Austin, TX 78704

They offer **FREE** internet listing for Texas prisoners. You must have served 2 years, have at least 2 years to go, and have a sentence of at least 10 years-life.

## T.F.L.
I DO NOT RECOMMEND DOING BUSINESS WITH THIS COMPANY!

## The Action Committee For Women In Prison
769 Northwestern Drive
Claremont, CA 91711

Advocates for humane treatment of incarcerated women.

Phone Number: (626)-710-7543
Website: www.acwip.net.

## The Other Death Penalty Project
PO Box 1486
Lancaster, CA 93584

They provide materials to assist you and your imprisoned loved ones in your advocacy efforts to urge elected officials and others in positions of power to end life without parole sentences.

Website: info@theotherdeathpenalty.org

## The Prison Mirror
c/o Pat Pawlak
970 Pickett Street North
Bayport, MN 55003-1490

The Prison Mirror is published monthly by and for the men of the Minnesota Stillwater Correctional Facility. Subscriptions are $12. The Prison Mirror was founded in 1887 and is the oldest continuously published prison newspaper in the United States.

Phone Number: 651-779-2700

## The Last Resort Innocence Project
Seton Hall University School of Law
One Newark Center
1109 Raymond Boulevard
Newark, New Jersey 07102

Phone Number: 973-642-8500

## Third Coast Gifts and Books
9668 Westheimer Rd, Suite 200-303
Houston, TX 77063

## Thomas M. Cooley Innocence Project
300 S. Capitol Ave. P.O. Box 13038
Lansing, MI 48901

Phone: 517-371-5140

## Thomas Merton Center
5129 Penn Avenue
Pittsburgh, PA 15224

They are people from diverse philosophies and faiths who find common ground in the nonviolent struggle to bring about a more peaceful and just world.

Phone Number: 412-361-3022
Website: www.thomasmertoncenter.org 28.

## Thomson Reuter's
610 Opperman Dr.
Eagan, MN 55123

They sell books on legal topics. Write for a list.

## Thousand Kites
91 Madison Avenue
Whitesburg, KY 41858

Cooperative storytelling project. Send your story to them and they will incorporate it into a performance. Ongoing Project!

Phone Number: 606-633-0108
Website: www.thousandkites.org

## Thurgood Marshall School of Law Innocence Project
3100 Cleburne Street
Houston, TX 77004

Phone Number: 713-313-1139

## Tightwad Magazines
PO Box 1941
Buford, GA 30515

They have discount magazine subscriptions. Write/Send SASE for a mini catalog.

**Comment:** This is my favorite place to order mags from. They are super inexpensive and they accept stamps. The lady who runs it, Julie, is fast and her business is official. - - Mike

## Timberwolf Litigation and Research Services, LLC
402 North Wayne Street, Suite B
Angola, Indiana 46703

"You don't have to do it alone!... Run with the pack! Attorneys, paralegals, researchers and consultants dedicated to serving your legal needs. For more info, call 1-855-712-5276 or (260) 243-5649."

## Time Magazine
Time & Life Building

Rockefeller Center
New York, NY 10020

## TimeZone Gifts, L.L.C.
P.O. Box 41093
Houston, TX 77241

For a **FREE** catalog with over 150 gifts ranging from $2 $12.95 (greeting cards, toys, T-shirts, stuffed animals, Jewelry and more), write them.

## Timothy C. Chiang-Lin, PLLC
2155 112th Ave NE
Bellevue, WA 98004

This law office represents all individuals who suffers childhood sex abuse in Washington and Oregon.

Website:chiang-lin.com

## Tim's Inmate Mail Service
3301-R Coors Rd NW #247
Albuquerque, NM 87120-1292

"Cheap in-state phone # for 1-time $50 set-up fee. Send SASE.

## T.I.P. Journal
## Gender Identity Center of Colorado, Inc.,
1151 S Huron St
Denver, CO 80223

Newsletter for transgender prisoners. Write for details.

## Total Access Services
Po Box 31764
Capitol Heights, MD 20731

All photos are $1 each and there is a 5-photo minimum per order. 30 photos for $20, 10 photos for 40 stamps (flat books only). Tell us how many photos your facility will allow per envelope. We are not responsible for rejected photos, but will replace up to 5.

**Comment:** The quality of the catalog is ratchet, but the images they offer are cool. - - Mike

## Transformative Justice Law Project of Illinois
4707 North Broadway, Suite 307
Chicago, IL 60640

Provides legal services to transgender and gender non-conforming people targeted by the criminal legal system; will send resources and provides trainings to outside agencies.

Phone Number: (773) 272-1822

**Transgender, Gender Variant, and Intersex Justice Project**
TGIJP
1201 46th Avenue
Oakland, CA 94601

Phone Number: 510-533-3809
Website: www.tgijp.org.

**Transition of Prisoners, INC.**
PO Box 02938
Detroit, MI 48202

They offer resources and support.

**Transitional Housing for Georgia**
Po Box 35305
Charlotte, NW 28235

Website: socialserve.com.

**Tranzmission Prison Books**
P.O. Box 1874
Asheville, NC 28801

Offers **FREE** books and resources. (Queer/Trans. related)

**The Threepenny Review**
PO Box 9131
Berkeley, CA 94709

1. At present The Threepenny Review is paying $400 per story or article, $200 per poem or Table Talk piece. This payment buys first serial rights in our print and digital editions, and the copyright then reverts to the author immediately upon publication.

2. We do not consider submissions that arrive via email. Everything must be sent either through the regular mail or via our designated online upload system (see www.threepennyreview.com). All mailed manuscripts must include an SASE; those that arrive without as SASE will not receive a reply. Mailed submissions should be sent to 'The Editor's at the above address.

3. We do not print material that has previously been published elsewhere, and we do NOT consider simultaneous submissions. We do our best to offer a

quick turnaround time, so please allow us the privilege of sole consideration during that relatively brief period; writers who do not honor this request will not be published in the magazine.

4. Response time for unsolicited manuscripts ranges from one week to two months. Please do not submit more than a single story of article, or more than five poems, until you have heard back from us about your previous submission.

5. All articles should be double-spaced (except poetry, which can be single-spaced or double-spaced)! Critical articles should be about 1500 to 3000words, stories and memoirs 4000 words or less, and poetry 100 lines or less. Exceptions are possible.

6. Critical articles that deal with books, films, theater performances, art exhibits, etc. should cite these occasions at the front of the article, using the following format:

Book Title
by Author's Name.
Publisher, Year Published, Price (cloth) (paper).

Remember that The Threepenny Review is a quarterly and national (and in some respects international); therefore, each 'review' should actually be an essay, broader than the specific event it covers and of interest to people who cannot see the event.

7. Writers will be consulted on all significant editing done on their articles, and will have the opportunity to proofread galleys for typographical errors.

8. It is recommended that those submitting work for the first time to The Threepenny Review take a look at a sample copy beforehand. Sample copies are available from the publisher for $12.00.

9. We do not read manuscripts in the second half of the year (July through December), so please do not submit work during those six months. Anything sent them will be discarded unread. The only two ways to submit work to us are through the mail and via our online system."

**TR&R**
16625 Redmond Way, Suite M PMB 20
Redmond, WA 98052

"Have a civil rights claim against state or prison officials? We can help! If you have a claim, write us and we will provide you information by return mail." SASE required.

**Tricycle Magazine: The Buddhist Review**
1115 Broadway, Suite 1113
New York, NY 10010

**Tri-State Legal Journal**
355 Fifth Ave. #618
Pittsburgh, PA 15222

"Serving jail inmates across the globe. Tri-State Legal Journal is a monthly publication. The TLJ is the official legal journal for inmates to keep updated on current legal issues, House and Senate Bills, major legal cases affecting individual rights, world news and headline news stories covering local regions. The journal is your official resource guide to outside resources that will help you help yourself. The journal also provides family members the opportunity to reach out to inmates through ad announcements. Help us tell your story! If you have an interesting life story and would like your voice to be heard, submit your story to us and we will see how we can help or even publish your story in the next issue **FREE!** Family and friends can go to tristatelegaljournal.com to submit announcements to be published for loved ones. Subscriptions are $5 per issue, $12 for three months, $55 per year (12 issues), or $28 for six months/issues. Payment must be enclosed with subscription form to receive first issue and to have any writings reviewed for publication. Your family can pay for your subscription online."

Website: tristatelegaljournal.com

**Triune Arts**
1804 Bedell Road RR #5
Kemptville, Ontario
Canada K0G 1J0

Educational resource for restorative justice programs; intended to raise public awareness of an alternative to the existing justice system's approach, to provide training and to encourage citizens to participate in community justice programs.

Triune Arts, a non-profit, charitable institution established in 1981, has developed award-winning educational programs on a variety of subjects including: conflict resolution, anti-bullying, restorative justice, cross-cultural communication and inter-cultural conflict, workplace violence prevention, employment training for youth, preventive intervention with preschoolers and international development.

**Truman State University Press**
100 East Normal Avenue
Kirksville, MO 63501-4221

Reviews literary works.

**Trump, President Donald**
1600 Pennsylvania Ave. NW
Washington, DC 20500

Phone Number: (202) 456-1111

**Turning the Tide: Journal of Anti-Racist Action**
Research and Education; ARA-LA/PART
PO Box1055
Culver City, CA 90232

This covers the analysis and perspectives of the oppressed in the struggle for liberation and it's **FREE** to prisoners.

U

**Unchained Books**
PO Box 784
Fort Collins, CO 80522

Unchained Books is a small group in Fort Collins, Colorado committed to prisoner support. Our primary focus is collecting donated books and making them available **FREE** to people imprisoned in Colorado

**Un-Common Law**
220 4th St., Suite 201
Oakland, CA 94607

They offer prisoner rights services.

Phone Number: (510) 271-0310.

**Under Lock & Key**
MIM (Prisons) PO Box 40799
San Francisco, CA 94140

This is a communist-type newsletter for prisoners. It's **FREE**.

**Comment:** If you're a conscious prisoner and you want to be up on prison politics across the country, this is for you. These are serious comrades. Real talk. -- GURU

## Union Supply Direct
Dept. 100, P.O. Box 9018
Rancho Dominguez, CA 90220

This is a package company that sells just about everything -- food, electronics, clothes, CDs, religious items and more.

Comment: In our survey, Union Supply did well with their promo items, timeliness, and did not seem to charge for missing items. They were doing well in the price category until they published their recent catalog in which they seemed to raise their prices across the table. Now they fail in the price category. They also seem to delete or substitute excessively. --Voices.con Newsletter

**Comment:** Let me tell you about these grimy muthafuckas. First, last year they advertised all kinds of cheap mixtapes, so everyone rushed to order packages from them just to get new music. Then, when their packages came, nobody got any of the CDs because Union claimed that our prison doesn't allow explicit CDs. Straight bullshit! Then, in their catalog they advertise a layaway program so I had my people put a big-ass package on layaway. They ended up paying around a hundred dollars on it, then they skipped a month. When they went to pay the remainder, Union Supply told them that the package was forfeited because they didn't pay the monthly minimum -- a detail that they don't advertise. I won't fuck wit' 'em again unless I got a stolen credit card or something. Fuck 'em! -- GURU

## United Prison Ministries International
890 County Rd 93
P.O. Box 8
Verbena, AL 36091

Prisoners can order two at a time: What the Bible Says, The Desire of Ages, Bible Answers, Bible Questions Answered, God Still answers Prayers and Keys to Happiness.

## United Shuttle

California inmate visitors' transportation services.

Phone Number: (818) 504- 0839

## University Beyond Bars
PO Box 31525
Seattle, WA 98103

Website: http://universitybeyondbars.org/

## University of Baltimore Innocence Project Clinic
1401 N. Charles St.
Baltimore, MD 21201

Phone Number: 410.837.4468

## University of North Carolina
The Friday Center
Center for Continuation Education
Chapel Hill, NC 27599

Highly recommended college.

## University of Texas Center for Actual Innocence
University of Texas School of Law
727 East Dean Keeton St.
Austin, TX 78705

## Upaya Prison Outreach Project
1404 Cerro Gordo Rd.
Santa Fe, NM 87501

## Upper Iowa University
External Degree Program
P.O. Box 1861
Fayette, IA 52142-1861

Highly recommended college.

## Uptown People's Law Center
4413 N. Sheridan
Chicago, IL 60640

No criminal law cases or appeals, post-conviction or habeas petitions. Works to protect the civil rights of people in state, federal and county facilities in IL. They help find pro bono (**FREE**) lawyers for people challenging denial of medical care, excessive force, denial of religious rights, and access to the courts, discrimination, and cruel and unusual punishment: Unless they get your permission in writing, they can't discuss your case with family members.

### Urbana-Champagne Books to Prisoners Project
PO Box 515
Urbana, IL 61803

Sends various books to state & federal prisoners in Illinois. Has large selection of novels.

Phone Number: (217) 344-8820.
Website: books2prisoners.org

### USA TODAY
7950 Jones Branch Dr.
McLean, VA 22108

This is one of the best newspapers you can get. Subscription rates: 13 wks, $65; 26 wks, $130; 52 wks, $260.

### U.S. Dept. of Justice
950 Pennsylvania Ave., NW
Washington, DC 20530

The attorney general is Eric Holder.

Phone Number: (202) 353-1555.

### U.S. Small Business Association
409 3rd St, SW
Washington, DC 20416

Write for **FREE** information.

### USA Song Writing Contest
2881 E. Oakland Park Blvd., Suite 414
Ft. Lauderdale, FL 33306

Song writers, write for **FREE** details.

Website: songwriting.net.

### UVP
PO Box 110620
Jamaica, NY 11411-0620

"UVP is your source for non-nude photo sets of beautiful Black and Latina girls. We have exclusive photos of models, strippers, and your regular girl next door. All photos are only available in high quality 4X6 prints. All photo sets contain 10 photos of the model shown in various non-nude poses. The price for each photo set of 10 photos is $12.00 which includes **FREE** shipping. Each photo set is mailed in a separate envelope. Mall orders with checks or money orders are payable to the above company/address. If photos are being shipped to correctional facilities, please be advised we are not responsible for merchandise that is rejected by correctional institutions. Order at your own risk. In the event merchandise has to be reshipped, you will be required to pay an additional $5 s/h charge. There are no refunds. Please allow 1-3 weeks for delivery. Your friends and family can order photos for you quickly from our website."

We also offer "grab bags" of sexy random girls (sorry, you cannot pick models) at the following prices:

Set GB10 (10 photos) $12
Set GB 20 (20 photos) $20
Set GB 30 (30 photos) $28
Set GB 40 (40 photos) $36

Website: picmate.net

**Comment:** Fine bitches in stripper outfits. Reminds me of the hoes I was around before coming to prison. Ah... The good ol' days. ~ Mike

# V

### Valley Bible Fellowship
PO Box 6266
Bakersfield, CA 93217

This is a church.

**Comment:** They'll send you a FREE bible, Daily Bread and a correspondence course. If you send for their correspondence course they'll send you 2 stamped envelopes for each time you complete an assignment, thus paying you to participate. -- GURU

### VFC (Voice Freedom Calls)
2442 NW Market Street #612
Seattle, WA 98107

"VFC is a voice message system just like ones you have used on the outside. When you sign up, you get your own personal phone number In any US area code you choose. Friends and family call your personal number and leave voice messages and listen to voice messages from you. Inmates call their personal number and listen to messages, send messages, and place return calls to anyone that has left a message. When you send voice messages, we send a text with your phone number. It's easy for friends to tell when you have called. You use your regular prison phones to call into the system --that part cannot be avoided. But once you have called into your number, you can send multiple voice messages and place multiple return calls from a single connect -- you are not limited to calling a single person. VFC works with all major prison and Jail telecom providers: GTL, Securus, and others. VFC is available in State, County, and local jail facilities. VFC cannot be used in federal institutions. The charge for using VFC is $4.95/month, plus $2.50 per message and $1.50 per minute. These charges are in addition to what you pay the institution for making an outgoing call. Send SASE for more info, or get your own personal message number now, in less than 5 minutes by calling (603) 821-9535."

## Villa Entertainment Company, Inc
14173 NW Freeway, Ste. 203
Houston, TX 77040

"Like the beautiful women on the pages of StreetSeen Magazine and the car shows we attend? Order 4X6 glossy Photos of them! $12 for 10 photos of random 4X6 glossy premium non-nude photos of car show hotties. Add $1 for each additional photo you want. Add $2 s/h for each envelope you need to have your pictures sent in. We are not responsible for rejected pictures!

product...

Car show hotties photo catalog now available. Filled with over 800 photos of the sexiest REAL girls in the car show scene. LOTS of back shots! Only $7.99 + $3 s/h! We will add 10 sexy sample photos for an extra $5!

Corrlinks: StreetSeen@ymail.com
Phone: 713-465-9599

## Voices.con Newsletter
PO Box 361
King City, CA 93930

The Voices.Con Newsletter is written exclusively by term-to-life prisoners, unless otherwise noted, focusing on issues of primary concern to those serving a long-tern incarceration: The newsletter is published monthly at the VoicesDotCon.org website. This information has been designed to be of potential benefit in any jurisdiction having term-to-life prisoners and is made available to any other supportive family and friends as well. No persons affiliated with the Voices.Con newsletter are lawyers. Information provided herein is not intended as a substitute for proper legal advice. All questions or comments on information contained herein should be directed to Janet@VoicesDotCon.org.

Suggested Guidelines for Submissions:

1. We have only one agenda; advocating on behalf of the term-to-life prisoner and distributing information that will further this cause, enabling the term-to-life prisoner to effectively advocate on his or her own behalf.
2. You may write an essay/article on any related subject or issue of concern to the term-to-life prisoner population.
3. We prefer that all submissions be between 250 and 500 words. Please clearly print or type all submitted material.
4. We also accept and encourage all submissions of topical artwork. Please include a SASE with any submissions of artwork or written material where a return has been requested.

Website: VoicesDotCon.org
Email: Publisher@VoicesDotCon.org

## Wahida Clark Presents Publishing
134 Evergreen Place; Suite 305, Dept. DD
East Orange, NJ 07018

Wahida Clark, the Queen of "Thug Love" fiction, writes, sells, and publishes urban books.

Phone Number: (973) 678-9982
Website: wclarkpublishing.com.

## WaitingPenPals.com
PO Box 24592
Fort Lauderdale, FL 33307

Send a SASE for information on their pen pal service.

## Walkenhorst's
540 Technology Way
Napa, CA 94558

This prison package company sells tons of items; food, clothing, shoes, electronics, cosmetics, CDs, and more. Write and ask for their **FREE** color catalog.

Phone Number: (800) 660-9255
Website walkenhorsts.com.

**Wall Periodicals**
PO Box 2584
Plainfield, NJ 07060-0584

"Largest urban wholesaler in the USA."

Magazines: Don Diva, Bottles & Modelz, Bully Girl,
FEDS, Assets, AS IS, Phat Puffs, Body, Hip-Hop
Weekly, Urban ink, IAdore, Repect, Street Elements,
UHM and many more!

Books: Dynasty series; Dipped Up; 100 Years of
Lynching; Thug Lovin'; Thug Matrimony; Trust No
Man; Trust No Bitch; The Cartel series; Murderville;
Murda Mamas; and many, many more!

Send SASE for a **FREE** catalog. For easy ordering and
more titles visit their website.

Phone Number: 718-819-1693 or 866-756-1370
Website: wallperiodicalsonline.com

**Comment:** Write these guys and request books by
Mike Enemigo and thecellblock.net. I need
them to start carrying my books. - - Mike

**Watchtower**
25 Columbia Heights
Brooklyn, NY 11201

This is the Jehovah Witness Headquarters. They'll send
you **FREE** biblical material.

**Wesleyan Innocence Project**
1515 Commerce St.
Fort Worth, TX 76102

**West**
PO Box 64833
St. Paul, MN 55164

They publish many legal books. Write for a full list.

Phone Number: (800) 328-9352.

**West Virginia Innocence Project**
West Virginia University
College of Law
P.O. Box 6130
Morgantown, WV 26506

Phone: 304-293-7249

**Why Islam**
PO Box 1054
Piscataway, NJ 08855

This is a non-profit organization that provides Islamic
literature.

**William L. Schmidt**
Attorney at Law
P.O. Box 25001
Fresno, CA 93729

Civil rights; Section 1983; federal and state appeals and
writs; transfer, discipline, visiting and classification;
parole hearings and more! Please submit a single page
summary of your case. Due to the volume, they cannot
return documents or respond to all inquiries. They are
not a low cost or pro bono law firm, but if you want
results, contact them.

Phone Number: 559-261-2222

**Windham School District**
Mailing: P.O. Box 40
Physical: 804 Bldg. B, FM 2821 West
Huntsville, TX 77320

Phone: (936) 291-5300
Website: http://www.windhamschooldistrict.org

**Winning Habeas Corpus and Post-Conviction Relief,
4th edition**

Cases cited through 638 F.3d. Claims to be the best
book for prisoners who are researching post-conviction
relief and Ineffective Assistance of Counsel. Includes a
virtual law library in a single book, actual case quotes;
habeas procedures and prac. 2254, 2255 &rule 60(b);
sixth amendment & IAC, pretrial duty to investigate;
recognized defenses; over 1500 cited cases and more!
This book is over 620 pages, $58.50, and available from
Fast Law Publishing Associates.

**Winning Writ Writers**
PO Box 848
Richmond Hill, GA 31324

A writ writing team with a record of wins against the
U.S. Send SASE for details and other services offered.

Phone Number: (229) 344-3838

## Wisconsin Books To Prisoners Project
c/o Rainbow Bookstore
426 W. Gilman St.
Madison, WI 53703

No religious or legal books. LGBT for all states.

## Wisconsin Innocence Project- Shaken Baby Syndrome
University of Wisconsin Madison
Attn: Lindsey Smith
975 Bascom Mall
Madison, WI 53706-1399

## Wistful Expressions
P.O. Box 1284
Campbell, CA 95009

Phone Number: 888-748-9333
Website: wistfulexpressions.com

This is a greeting card company that is always open to art and poetry suggestions.

## With Liberty for Some: 500 Years of Imprisonment in America

The best overall history of the American prison system from 1492 through the 20th Century. Well written and fact filled. A must-read for understanding how little things have changed as far as prisons go in the U.S. over hundreds of years. This book is 372 pages, $18.95, and can be bought from Prison Legal News.

## Women and Prison: A Site for Resistance

The Women and Prison project is a website, installation and zine created entirely from the work and lives of America's incarcerated women.

Website: http://womenandprison.org

## Women in Prison Project
Correctional Association of NY
2090 Adam Clayton Powell Jr. Blvd., #200
New York, NY 10027
Serves women in NY but has info and brochures (many by incarcerated women) for those in any state. Write for "My Sister's Keeper" and a list of other pamphlets.

## Women's Prison Association
110 Second Avenue
New York, NY 10003

## Women's Prison Book Project
c/o Boneshaker Books
2002 23rd Ave South
Minneapolis, MN 55404

This program is for women prisoners only.

## Word of Life Christian Ministry
PO Box 2164
Rockwall, TX 75087

This is a **FREE** Christian newsletter. They also send puzzles and bible verses to study.

## Worker's Vanguard
PO Box 1377 GPO
NY, NY 10116

This is a communist newspaper.

**Comment**: Straight up, they real about they work. They even have a fund dedicated to class - struggle prisoners like Mumia and others and they put money on their books. This is a good publication for the conscious - minded prisoner. - - GURU

## Write4Life
613 Bryden Ave. Ste C #226
Lewiston, ID 83501

"Guaranteed pen pal with write4life! Tell us your interests and we will match you with a pen pal immediately. What are your favorite things to do? What makes you happy? What kind of people intrigue you? We want to know! Write to us and we'll write back! Note: Write4Life provides a guaranteed fictional pen pal with a $10 per month subscription fee. "

Comment: This seems very pathetic and desperate, but maybe it's a PG way of advertising a "freaky letter Service" -- like a sexy phone service, but through letters. – Mike

## WriteAPrisoner.com
PO Box 10
Edgewater, FL 32132

"We understand the loneliness incarceration can bring... There are other who understand as well. Thousands of people from all walks of life come to our website every day in search of pen pals. They are looking for friendship; they are prepared to offer support; they want to provide encouragement; and they understand the loneliness. If outside companionship could improve your quality of life while incarcerated, join WriteAPrisoner.com. We're dedicated to reducing recidivism. The first step is connecting you with those who understand.

Thousands of people who are interested in corresponding with inmates visit our site each day. Our site is easily accessed from all Internet connected devices including cell phones and is translated into 51 languages to attract overseas visitors as well. We advertise non-stop on all major search engines and receive millions of page views monthly. We've been seen on MSNBC's Lockup, Dr. Phil, CNN, Women's Entertainment, The Ney York Times, Washington Post, Boston Globe, O Magazine, and many, many more places. Place your pen-pal profile today and start making new friends!"

A one year profile (250 words and 1 picture) is $40. You can add an additional photo or piece of artwork for

3. Stamps must be an acceptable form of payment from your institution. If your institution prohibits using stamps as currency, we cannot accept them from you.

4. Only Forever stamps can be used as payment.

5. Stamps will not be accepted if they are removed from their original sheets and placed on new ones.

Profile Price List in Stamps...

Standard one year profile: 115 Forever stamps.
Additional photo/artwork: 30 Forever stamps.
Additional words: 15 Forever stamps for each additional 50 words.
Text change: 30 Forever stamps.
Photo change: 30 Forever stamps for 1 photo.
Additional photo/artwork: 30 Forever stamps.
Additional words: 15 Forever stamps for each additional 50 words.
Standard profile renewal: 90 Forever stamps.
Blogs: 45 Forever stamps for 1 250 word blog.
Poetry: 45 Forever stamps for 250 words.

Send SASE and request 'Stamp Payment Guidelines' for further details."

## Writeaprisoner.com
P.O. Box 10
Edgewater, FL 32132

$10 each. Each additional 50 words is $5. You can add a bio entry for $15 (250 words). Each additional 50 words is $5. You can pay for your profile via institutional check, money order or credit card. If you'd like to pay with postage stamps, request their Stamp Payment Guidelines/Prices first by sending them a SASE. For a **FREE** copy of their brochure with all the profile details, send SASE.

## WriteAPrisoner.com Stamp Guidelines/Prices

"When we accept stamps as payment, it prohibits us from utilizing lower bulk mail rates; therefore, prices are slightly higher when paying with stamps. The prices and rules are as follows:

1. Stamps must be on sheets or rolls. No more than 10 individual stamps can be accepted.

2. Stamps must not be taped, stapled or adhered together.

This is one of the best pen-pal websites they also offer a **FREE** reintegration profile. Send SASE for **FREE** application.

## Writers' Digest
4700 E. Galbraith Rd
Cincinnati, OH 45236

This magazine covers everything in regards to helping you write and or get published. It's $19.96 for a 1-year subscription, 6 issues per year. To contact Writer's Digest editorial, please e-mail: writersdigest@fwmedia.com

(Note: Due to the high volume of e-mails received, we are unable to answer all questions or requests.)

For query submissions, please e-mail: wdsubmissions@fwmedia.com;( Note: Allow 8-12 weeks for a response.)

For questions regarding Writer's Digest Competitions, contact Writer's Digest Competitions at (715) 445-4612 x13430.

For questions about our monthly Your Story Contest, please email YourStoryContest@fwmedia.com.

Phone Number: (513) 531-2222
Website: writersdigest.com.

**Writer's Guild of America – East**
555 West 57th St., Suite 1230
New York, NY 10019

This is an organization of professional writers and agents.

Website: wgaeast.org.

**Writer's Guild of America – West**
7000 West 3rd St.
Los Angeles, CA 90048

This is an organization of professional writers and agents.

Website: wga.org.

**Writing to Win: The Legal Writer**

Explains the writing of effective complaints, responses, briefs, motions and other legal pleadings. This book is 283 pages, $19.95, and can be bought from Prison Legal News.

**Writesomeoneinprison.com; Nubian Princess Ent.**
POB 37
Timmonsville, SC 29161

This is a good pen pal service. They accept stamps. Send SASE for more information.

**Writetoinmates.com**
5729 Main St., # 362
Springfield, OR 97478

Pen pal website.

**Wrongful Conviction Clinic Indiana University School of Law**
530 W. New York Street, Rm. 111
Indianapolis, IN 46202-3225

Cases Accepted: cases of actual innocence in Indiana; DNA and non- DNA cases (preference for DNA cases); will consider arson, shaken baby syndrome, and child abuse cases.

Phone Number: 317-274-5551

**Wrongful Conviction Project**
Office of the Ohio Public Defender

250 East Broad Street, Suite 1400
Columbus, OH 43215

Phone Number: 614-466-5394
Website: opd.ohio.gov/DP_WrongfulConviction…

**The Wrongful Death Institute**

The Institute conducts research on a multitude of issues within each of its departments. It performs case analysis on wrongful death and forensic science issues, and aggressively pursues issues of prison medical malpractice and negligence nationwide. The common denominator of all divisions is accountability and responsibility of those individuals who perform duties that involve the public trust. The Institute implements the team approach. All of our efforts are directed toward factually and efficiently applying investigative and scientific evidence to law.

Phone Number: (816) 941-0087

**Wynword Press**
P.O. Box 557
Bonners Ferry, ID 83805

They offer the book "Battling the Administration: An Inmates Guide to a Successful Lawsuit."

Phone Number: 208-267-0817

# X

# Y

**Y.S.E. Administration Services**
2402 Harbor Landing
Roswell, GA 30076

They offer paralegal, typing, and research services. Write/Send SASE for more information.

# Z

# ATTENTION INMATES!

Have an experience with any of the listed companies? Good or bad, write and tell us all about it!

THE CELL BLOCK

Re: Comments/Reviews

PO Box 1025 Rancho Cordova, CA 95741

**BBB**

**FOR PRISONERS**

# PRO BONO ATTORNEYS

Find lawyers who are willing to work "for the public good" (the meaning of *pro bono*). These law firms or organizations
may be willing to work for free or for a reduced rate depending on the circumstances. Contact the closest office for more information.

## ALASKA

**Alaska Disability Law Center**
3330 Arctic Blvd., Suite 103
Anchorage, AK 99501

Phone Number: (907) 565-1002

**Alaska Network on Domestic Violence and Sexual Assault**
130 Seward Street, #214
Juneau, AK 99801

Phone Number: (888) 520-2666

**Alaska Immigration Justice Project**
431 West 7th Avenue, Suite 208
Anchorage, AK 99501

Phone Number: (907) 279-2457

**Alaska Pro Bono Program**
P.O. Box 140191
Anchorage, AK 99514-0191

## ALABAMA

**Legal Services Corporation of Alabama, Inc.
Tuscaloosa Regional Office**
1351 McFarland Blvd. E, 11th Floor
Tuscaloosa, AL 35404

Phone Number: (205) 758-7503

**Alabama State Bar Volunteer Lawyers Program**

415 Dexter Avenue
Montgomery, AL 36104
334-269-1515

**Alabama Equal Justice Initiative**

122 Commerce Street
Montgomery, AL 36104

Phone Number: (334) 269-1803

## ARKANSAS

**Ozark Legal Services Pro Bono Project**
4083 N. Shiloh Drive, Suite 3
Fayetteville, AR 72703

Phone Number: (501) 442-0600

**Arkansas Volunteer Lawyers for the Elderly**
2020 W 3rd Street, Suite 620
Little Rock, AR 72205

Phone Number (501) 376-9263

**Legal Services of Arkansas**
615 West Markham Street, Suite 200
Little Rock, AR 72201

Phone Number: (501) 376-8015

## ARIZONA

**Arizona Justice for Children**

P.O. Box 45500
Phoenix, AZ 85064

Phone Number: (602) 235-9300

**AIDS Project Arizona**
1427 N. 3rd Street
Phoenix, AZ 85004

Phone Number: (602) 253-2437

**HIV/AIDS Law Project**
303 E. Palm Lane
Phoenix, AZ 85004

Phone Number: (602) 258-3434

**Arizona Federal Public Defender's Office**
222 N Central Avenue, Suite 810
Phoenix, AZ 85004

Phone Number: (602) 379-3670

CALIFORNIA

**California Center for Capital Assistance**
529 Castro Street
San Francisco, CA 94114

Phone Number: (415) 621-8860

**Pro Bono Project**
480 N. First Street
San Jose, CA 95112

Phone Number: (408) 998-5298

**Bay Area Legal Aid**
1735 Telegraph Avenue
Oakland, CA 94612

Phone Number: (510) 663-4755

**Asian Pacific Islander Legal Outreach**
1121 Mission Street
San Francisco, CA 94103

Phone Number: (415) 567-6255

COLORADO

**Southern Colorado AIDS Project**
1301 S. 8th Street
Colorado Springs, CO 80903

Phone Number: (719) 578-9092

**Northwest Colorado Legal Services**
P.O. Box 1904
Leadville, CO 80461
719-486-3238

**Heart of the Rockies Bar Association Pro Bono Program**
1604 H Street
Salida, CO 81201

Phone Number: (719) 539-4251

**Colorado Office of the Public Defender**
110 16th Street, Suite 800
Denver, CO 80202

Phone Number: (303) 620-4888

CONNECTICUT

**Connecticut Statewide Legal Services**
425 Main Street, #2
Middletown, CT 06457-3371

Phone Number: (800) 453-3320

**Connecticut Trial Services Unit**
1 Hartford Square West
Hartford, CT 06106
203-566-5328

DELAWARE

**Delaware State Bar Association Lawyer Referral Service**
Wilmington, DE 19803

Phone Number: (800) 773-0606

**Delaware Legal Aid Society**
913 Washington Street
Wilmington, DE 19801

Phone Number: (302) 575-0660

## DISTRICT OF COLUMBIA

**Legal Information Help Line**
Washington, DC

Phone Number: (202) 626-3499

**National Association of Criminal Defense Attorneys**
1627 K Street , NW, Suite 1200
Washington, DC 20006

Phone Number: (202) 872-8688 Ext: 224

**American Bar Association, Death Penalty Representation Project**
740 15th Street NW, Suite 1060
Washington, DC 20005-1009

Phone Number: (202) 662-1995

**Domestic Violence Intake**
DC Superior Court, 500 Indiana Ave., NW, Room 4235
Washington, DC 20001

Phone Number: (202) 879-0152

## FLORIDA

## GEORGIA

**Georgia Volunteer Lawyers for the Arts**
675 Ponce De Leon Ave NE
Atlanta, GA 30308

Phone Number: (404) 873-3911

**Georgia Indigent Defense Council**
985 Ponce de Leon Avenue
Atlanta, GA 30306

Phone Number: (404) 894-2595

**Georgia Resource Center**
101 Marietta Tower, Suite 3310
Atlanta, GA 30303

Phone Number: (404) 614-2014

**National Association of Criminal Defense Attorneys**
83 Poplar Street, NW
Atlanta, GA 30303-2122

Phone Number: (404) 688-1202

**State Bar of Georgia Pro Bono Project**
104 Marietta Street NW, Suite 100
Atlanta, GA 30303

Phone Number: (404) 527-8700

## HAWAII

**Volunteer Legal Services Hawai'i**
545 Queen Street, Suite 100
Honolulu, HI 96813

Phone Number: (808) 528-7046

**Legal Aid Society of Hawaii**
1108 Nuuanu Avenue
Honolulu, HI 96817
808-536-4302

## IOWA

**Iowa Legal Aid**
1111 9th Street, Suite 230
Des Moines, IA 50314

Phone Number: (800) 532-1275

## IDAHO

**Idaho Legal Aid Services**
310 North 5th Street
Boise, ID 83701-0913

Phone Number: (208) 336-8980

**Idaho Volunteer Lawyers Program**
P.O. Box 895
Boise, ID 83701

Phone Number: (800) 221-3295

## ILLINOIS

**Center for Disability and Elder Law**
79 W. Monroe Street
Chicago, IL 60603

Phone Number: (312) 376-1880

**Cabrini Green Legal Aid Clinic**
740 N. Milwaukee Ave.
Chicago, IL 60642

Phone Number: (312) 738-2452

**Chicago Volunteer Legal Services**
100 N. LaSalle Street, Suite 900
Chicago, IL 60602

Phone Number: (312) 332-1624

**Chicago Legal Clinic**
2938 E. 91st Street
Chicago, IL 60617

Phone Number: (773) 731-1762

## INDIANA

**Heartland Pro Bono Council**
151 N. Delaware Street, Suite 1800
Indianapolis, IN 46204

Phone Number: (317) 614-5304

**Indianapolis Legal Aid Society, Inc.**
615 North Alabama Street
Indianapolis, IN 46204

Phone Number: (317) 635-9538

**Community Development Law Center**
1802 N. Illinois Street
Indianapolis, IN 46204

Phone Number: (317) 921-8806

**Indiana Legal Services Support**
151 North Delaware Street, 18th Floor
Indianapolis, IN 46204

Phone Number: (317) 631-9410

## KANSAS

**Kansas Legal Services Inc.**
712 South Kansas Avenue, Suite 200
Topeka, KS 66603

Phone Number: (913) 223-2068

## LOUISIANA

**The Pro Bono Project**
615 Baronne Street, Suite 203
New Orleans, LA 70113

Phone Number: (504) 581-4043

## MASSACHUSETTS

**Legal Advocacy and Resource Center**
Boston, MA

Phone Number: (800) 342-5297

**Neighborhood Legal Services**
170 Common Street, Suite 300
Lawrence, MA 01840

Phone Number: (978) 686-6900

**Neighborhood Legal Services**

37 Friend Street
Lynn, MA 01902
781-599-7730

**Victim Rights Law Center**
115 Broad Street, 3rd Floor
Boston, MA 02110

Phone Number: (617) 399-6720

## MARYLAND

**Bar Association of Baltimore City Legal Services to the Elderly Program**
111 North Calvert Street, Suite 631
Baltimore, MD 21202

Phone Number: (410) 396-1322

**Civil Justice, Inc.**
520 West Fayette Street
Baltimore, MD 21201

Phone Number: (410) 706-0174

**Women's Law Center**
305 W. Chesapeake Avenue, Suite 201
Towson, MD 21204

Phone Number: (410) 321-8761

**Maryland Volunteer Lawyers Service**
1 North Charles Street, Suite 222
Baltimore, MD 21201

Phone Number: (800) 510-0050

## MAINE

**Main Equal Justice Partners**
126 Sewall Street
Augusta, ME 04330

Phone Number: (866) 626-7059 (toll free)

**Main Volunteer Lawyers Project**
P.O. Box 547
Portland, ME 04112

Phone Number: (800) 442-4293

## MICHIGAN

**Michigan Legal Services**
220 Bagley Avenue, Suite 900
Detroit, MI 48226

Phone Number: (313) 964-4130

**Farmworker Legal Services**
420 N. Fourth Avenue
Ann Arbor, MI 48104

Phone Number: (734) 665-6181

**Family Law Project**
Hutchins Hall, University of Michigan Law School
Ann Arbor, MI 48109

Phone Number: (734) 998-9454

**Legal Services of South Central Michigan**
420 N. Fourth Avenue
Ann Arbor, MI 48104

Phone Number: (734) 665-6181

## MINNESOTA

**Volunteer Attorney Program**
314 West Superior Street, Suite 1000
Duluth, MN 55802

Phone Number: (218) 723-4005

**St. Cloud Area Legal Services**
830 W. St. Germain, Suite 300
St. Cloud, MN 56302

Phone Number: (888) 360-2889

**Western Minnesota Legal Services**
415 SW 7th Street
Willmar, MN 56201

Phone Number: (888) 360-3666

**Legal Aid Society of Minneapolis**

430 First Avenue North, Suite 300
Minneapolis, MN 55401-1780

Phone Number: (612) 334-5970

**MISSOURI**

**Legal Services of Southern Missouri**
1414 East State Route 72
Rolla, MO 65402

Phone Number: (800) 999-0249

**Legal Aid of Western Missouri**
1125 Gran Blvd., #1900
Kansas City, MO 64106, MO 64106

Phone Number: (816) 474-6750

**Legal Services of Eastern Missouri**
4232 Forest Park Avenue
St Louis, MO 63108
800-444-0514

**MISSISSIPPI**

**North Mississippi Rural Legal Services**
5 County Road 1014
Oxford, MS 38655

Phone Number: (800) 498-1804

**Mississippi Center for Justice**
5 Old River Place, Suite 203
Jackson, MS 39202

Phone Number: (601) 352-2269

**Mississippi Volunteer Lawyers Project**
P.O. Box 2168
Jackson, MS 39225-2168

Phone Number: (800) 682-6423

**Mississippi Legal Services Coalition**
775 North President Street, Suite 300
Jackson, MS 39205

Phone Number: (601) 944-0765

**North Mississippi Rural Legal Services**
5 County Road 1014
Oxford, MS 38655

Phone Number: (800498-1804

**Mississippi Center for Justice**
5 Old River Place, Suite 203
Jackson, MS 39202

Phone Number: (601) 352-2269

**Mississipi Volunteer Lawyers Project**
P.O. Box 2168
Jackson, MS 39225-2168

Phone Number: (800) 682-6423

**Mississippi Legal Services Coalition**
775 North President Street, Suite 300
Jackson, MS 39205

Phone Number: (601) 944-0765

**MONTANA**

**Montana Legal Services Help Line**
616 Helena Avenue, Suite 100
Helena, MT 59601

Phone Number: (800) 666-6899

**Montana Pro Bono Project**
P.O. Box 3093
Billings, MT 59103

Phone Number: (406) 248-7113

**NORTH CAROLINA**

**Legal Services of Southern Piedmont**
1431 Elizabeth Avenue
Charlotte, NC 28204

Phone Number: (800) 438-1254

**Pisgah Legal Services**

P.O. Box 2276
Asheville, NC 28802

Phone Number: (800) 489-6144

**Legal Aid of North Carolina**
224 South Dawson Street
Raleigh, NC 27601

Phone Number: (866) 219-5262 (toll free)

**North Carolina Legal Services**
224 South Dawson Street
Raleigh, NC 27611

Phone Number: (919) 856-2121

## NORTH DAKOTA

**North Dakota State Bar Association LRS**
515 1/2 E. Broadway
Bismarck, ND 58501-4407

Phone Number: (701) 255-1406

**Legal Services of North Dakota**
1025 North 3rd Street
Bismark, ND 58502-1893

Phone Number: (800) 634-5263

## NEW HAMPSHIRE

**New Hampshire Pro Bono Referral System**
112 Pleasant Street
Concord, NH 03301

Phone Number: (800) 639-5290

**New Hampshire Legal Assistance**
15 Green Street
Concord, NH 03301

Phone Number: (603) 225-4700

## NEW JERSEY

**Legal Services of New Jersey**
100 Metroplex Drive at Plainfield Avenue
Edison, NJ 08818

Phone Number: (888) 576-5529

**Volunteer Lawyers for Justice**
P.O. Box 32040
Newark, NJ 07102

Phone Number: (973) 645-1955

**Legal Services Of New Jersey**
100 Metroplex Drive, Plainfield Avenue, Suite 402
Edison, NJ 08818-1357

Phone Number: (908) 572-9100

## NEVADA

**Clark County Legal Services**
800 S. 8th Street
Las Vegas, NV 89101

Phone Number: (702) 386-1070

**Washoe Legal Services**
299 South Arlington Avenue
Reno, NV 89501

Phone Number: (775) 329-2727

**Volunteer Attorneys for Rural Nevadans**
904 N. Nevada Street
Carson City, NV 89703

Phone Number: (866) 448-8276 (toll free)

**Legal Aid Center of Southern Nevada**
800 S. Eighth Street
Las Vegas, NV 89101

Phone Number: (702) 386-1070

## NEW MEXICO

**Albuquerque Bar Association Courthouse
Booth Lawyer Referral Service**

540 Chama Street NE
Albuquerque, NM 87108-2017

Phone Number: (505) 256-0417

**State Bar of New Mexico Referral Program**
P.O. Box 92860
Albuquerque, NM 87199

Phone Number: (505) 797-6066

**New Mexico Legal Aid**
P.O. Box 25486
Albuquerque, NM 87104

Phone Number: (505) 243-7871

## NEW YORK

**The Legal Aid Society**
175 Remsen Street
Brooklyn, NY 11201

Phone Number: (718) 243-6473

**Kids in Need of Defense**
767 Fifth Avenue
New York, NY 10153-0119

Phone Number: (646) 728-4104

**Legal Services NYC**
350 Broadway, 6th Floor
New York, NY 10013

Phone Number: (646) 442-3600

**Urban Justice Center**
123 William Street 16th Floor
New York, NY 10038

Phone Number: (646) 602-4598

## OHIO

**Legal Aid Referral Project (Greater Columbus)**
1108 City Park Avenue
Columbus, OH 43206

Phone Number: (614) 224-8374

**Volunteer Lawyers Project (Greater Cincinnati)**
215 E. Ninth Street, Suite 200
Cincinnati, OH 45202-2122

Phone Number: (531) 241-6800

**Legal Aid Society of Cleveland -- Volunteer Lawyers Program**
1223 W. Sixth Street
Cleveland, OH 44113

Phone Number: (216) 687-1900

**Greater Dayton Volunteer Lawyers Project**
109 N. Main Street, Suite 610
Dayton, OH 45402

Phone Number: (937) 461-3857

## OKLAHOMA

**Tulsa Lawyers for Children, Inc.**
P.O. Box 2254
Tulsa, OK 74101-2254

Phone Number: (918) 425-5858

**The Senior Law Resource Center, Inc.**
P.O. Box 1408
Oklahoma City, OK 73101-1408

Phone Number: (405) 528-0858

**Legal Aid Services of Oklahoma, Inc.**
2915 North Classen Boulevard, Suite 500
Oklahoma, OK 73106

Phone Number: (405) 557-0020

**Oklahoma Alternative Resources**
3015 E. Skelly Dr., Suite 385
Tulsa, OK 74105

Phone Number: (918) 742-8883

## OREGON

**Marion-Polk Legal Aid**
1655 State Street
Salem, Oregon 97301

Phone Number: (503) 581-5265

**Lane County Law and Advocacy Center**
376 East 11th Avenue
Eugene, Oregon 97401

Phone Number: (541) 485-1017

**Center for Non-Profit Legal Services**
225 W. Main Street
Medford, Oregon 97501

Phone Number: (541) 779-7291

**Legal Aid Services of Oregon**
921 SW Washington Street, Suite 500
Portland, Oregon 97205

Phone Number: (888) 610-8764

## PENNSYLVANIA

**Neighborhood Legal Services Association**
928 Penn Avenue
Pittsburgh, PA 15222-3799

Phone Number: (412) 255-6700

**Lackawanna Pro Bono**
321 Spruce Street
Scranton, PA 18503

Phone Number: (570)961-2715

**Pennsylvania Legal Aid Network**
118 Locust Street
Harrisburg, PA 17101

Phone Number: (800) 322-7572

**Philadelphia VIP**
42 South 15th Street, 4th Floor
Philadelphia, PA 19102

Phone Number: (215) 523-9550

## RHODE ISLAND

**Rhode Island Bar Association Volunteer Lawyer Program**
115 Cedar Street
Providence, RI 02903-1082

Phone Number: (401) 421-7799

**Rhode Island Legal Services**
56 Pine Street, 4th Floor
Providence, RI 02903

Phone Number: (401) 274-2652

## SOUTH CAROLINA

**South Carolina Legal Services - Charleston**
2803 Carner Avenue
Charleston, SC 29405

Phone Number: (843) 720-70441

**Low Country Legal Aid, Inc.**
167-A Bluffton Road
Bluffton, SC 29910

**South Carolina Legal Services -- Beaufort**
69 Robert Smalls Parkway, Suite 3-A
Beaufort, SC 29902

Phone Number: (843) 521-0623

**South Carolina Legal Services - Columbia**
2109 Bull Street
Columbia, SC 29201

Phone Number: (803) 799-9668

## SOUTH DAKOTA

**Second Judicial Circuit Pro Bono Project**
335 N. Main Avenue
Sioux Falls, SD 57104

Phone Number: (605) 336-9230

**East River Legal Services**
335 North Main Avenue, Suite 300
Sioux Falls, SD 57102

Phone Number: (605) 336-9230

**TENNESSEE**

**Nashville Pro Bono Program**
300 Deaderick Street
Nashville, TN 37201

Phone Number: (615) 244-6610

**Tennessee Alliance for Legal Services**
50 Vantage Way, Suite 250
Nashville, TN 37228

Phone Number: (888) 395-9297

**TEXAS**

**Lone Star Legal Aid**
1415 Fannin Street
Houston, TX 77002

Phone Number: (800) 733-8394

**Texas RioGrande Legal Aid**
17 Sunny Glen
Alpine, TX 79830

Phone Number: (432) 837-1199

**Legal Aid of Northwest Texas**
Dallas, TX

Phone Number: (800) 529-5277

**UTAH**

**Disability Law Center**
205 North 4th West
Salt Lake City, UT 84103-1125

Phone Number: (801) 363-1347

**Legal Aid Society of Utah**

450 South State Street
Salt Lake City, UT 84111-3101

Phone Number: (801) 238-7170

**Utah Legal Services Inc.**
254 West 4th Street, 2nd Floor
Salt Lake City, UT 84101

Phone Number: (801) 328-8891

**VIRGINIA**

**Virginia Poverty Law Center**
201 West Broad Street, Suite 302
Richmond, VA 23220

Phone Number: (804) 782-9430

**Virginia Legal Aid Society, Inc.**
513 Church Street
Lynchburg, VA 24504

Phone Number: (866) 534-5243

**Southwest Virginia Legal Aid Society**
227 W. Cherry Street
Marion, VA 24354

Phone Number: (800) 277-6754

**Rappahannock Legal Services, Inc.**
618 Kenmore Avenue, Suite 1-A
Fredericksburg, VA 22401

Phone Number: (540) 371-1105

**VERMONT**

**Legal Services Law Line of Vermont Volunteer
  Lawyer's Project**
274 North Winooski Avenue
Burlington, VT 05401

Phone Number: (802) 863-7153

**Vermont Legal Aid Inc.**
PO Box 1367, 12 North Street
Burlington, VT 05401

Phone Number: (802) 863-5620

## WASHINGTON

**Jefferson-Clallam County Pro Bono Lawyers**
816 East 8th Street
Port Angeles, WA 98362

Phone Number: (360) 417-0818

**Evergreen Legal Services**
101 Yesler Way, Suite 300
Seattle, WA 98104

Phone Number: (206) 464-5933

## WISCONSIN

**Wisconsin Judicare, Inc.**
300 Third Street, Suite 210
Wausau, WI 54403

Phone Number: (800) 472-1638

**Legal Action of Wisconsin**
230 West Wells Street, Room 800
Milwaukee, WI 53203

Phone Number: (414) 278-7722

## WEST VIRGINIA

**Legal Aid of West Virginia - Charleston Office**
922 Quarrier Street, 4th Floor
Charleston, WV 25301

Phone Number: (866) 255-4370

**West Virginia Legal Service Plan**
1003 Quarrier Street, Suite 700
Charleston, WV 25301

Phone Number: (304) 342-6814

## WYOMING

**Legal Aid of Wyoming, Inc.**
211 West 19th Street, Suite 300
Cheyenne, WY 82001

Phone Number: (877) 432-9955 (toll free)

**Wind River Legal Services Inc. - Southeast Wyoming Branch**
1603 Capitol Avenue, Suite 405
Cheyenne, WY 82001

Phone Number: (307) 634-1566

# RAW  LAW
## FOR PRISONERS

Below are two underground reports that are must-haves for every prisoner. These reports contain the secrets "they" DON'T want YOU to know! Order them today and be enlightened!

- **How to Copyright Your Name and Use It To Ward Off Authorities!**
- **Incredible Legal Remedy To Get Any Case Dismissed in Court!**

Each report is ONLY $9.99 + $2.00 shipping and handling, or two NEW books of 20 Forever stamps! Send institutional check, money order, or stamps to the authorized dealer TODAY, and we will RUSH your order back to you immediately!

Authorized Dealer

The Cell Block; RE: RAW LAW; PO Box 1025; Rancho Cordova, CA 95741

# BOOK PUBLISHERS

Looking for a publisher to help you publish that book you worked so hard on and finally finished? Well, here's a list of some who may be interested in working with you. Remember, you always want to send a publisher a query letter asking their specific guidelines and instructions, along with a SASE, before you submit anything!

**Affluent Publishing Corporation**
1040 Avenues of the Americas, 24 Floor
New York, NY 10018

Contact JB Hamilton, editor
(Mainstream/Contemporary), or I. Smushkin, editor
(Suspense/ Mystery).

**Alondra Press, LLC**
4119 Wildacres Dr.
Houston, TX 77072

Contact Pennelope Leight, Fiction editor.

**Angoor Press, LLC**
2734 Bruchez Parkway, Unit 103
Denver, CO 80234

Contact Carolina Maine, founder and editor.

**Arkham Bridge Publishing**
PO Box 2346
Everett, WA 98213

Contact James Davis, senior editor.

**Arsenal Pulp Press**
#101-211 East Georgia Street
Vancouver, BC V6A 126,
Canada

Contact Editorial Board.

**Arte Publico Press**
University of Houston
452 Collen Proformance Hall
Houston, TX 77204;2004

Contact Nicolas Kanellos. Looking for works by "Hispanics."

**Backbeat Books**
Hal Leonard Publishing Group
33 Plymouth St., Suite 302
Montclair, NJ 07042

Contact Mike Edison, senior editor

**Bancroft Press**
PO Box 65360
Baltimore, MD 21209-9945

Contact Bruce Bortz, editor and publisher.

**Barricade Books, Inc.**
185 Bridge Plaza N. Suite 309
Fort Lee, NJ 07024

Contact Carole Stuart, publisher.

**Black Mountain Press**
109 Roberts
Ashville, NC 28801

Contact James Robiningski, editor.

**Black Rose Writing**
PO Box 1540
Castroville, TX 78009

Contact Reagan Rothe.

**Bluebridge, Imprint of United Tribes Media, Inc.**
PO Box 601
New York, NY 10536

Contact Jan-Erik Guerth, publisher.

**The Blumer Literary Agency**

Olivia ("Liv") Blumer
350 Seventh Avenue, Suite 2003
New York, NY 10001

This is a publishing agency. Write/Send SASE for more information. Ask for submission guidelines. Specify what kind of book you are interested in submitting – fiction, non-fiction, etc.

Phone Number: 212-947-3040,
Fax 212-947-0460

**Borealis Press, LTD.**
8 Mohawk Crescent
Napean, ON K2H 7G6
Canada

**Branden Publishing Co., Inc.**
PO Box 812094
Wellesley, MA 02482

Contact Adolph Caso, editor.

**Broken Jaw Press**
Box 596, STN A
Frederiction NB E3B 5A6
Canada

**By Light Unseen Media**
PO Box 1233
Pepperell, MA 01463

Contact Inanna Arthen, owner and editor in chief.

**Camino Books, Inc.**
PO Box 59026
Philadelphia, PA 19102

Contact E. Jutkowitz, publisher.

**Center One Publishing**
PO Box 651
Kingsley, MI 49649

Contact Ann Dine, acquisitions editor; Justin Dine, publisher.

**Coffee House Press**
79 13th NE, Suite 110
Minneapolis, MN 55413

Contact Chris Fischbach, associate publisher.

**Cricket Books**

Imprint of Carus Publishing
70 E. Lake St., Suite 300
Chicago, IL 60601

Contact Submissions Editor.

**Daniel & Daniel Publishers, Inc.**
PO Box 2790
McKinleyville, CA 95519

Contact John Daniel, Publisher.

**Daw Books, Inc.**
Penguin Group (USA)
375 Hudson St.
New York, NY 10014-3658

Contact Peter Stampfel, submissions editor.

**Diskus Publishing**
PO Box 43
Albany, IN 47320

Contact Holly Janey, Submissions Editor.

**Divertir**
PO Box 232
North Salem, NH 03073

Contact Dr. Kenneth Tupper, publisher

**The Ecco Press**
10 E. 53rd St.
New York, NY 10022

Contact Daniel Halpern, editor-in-chief

**Elohi Gadugi / The Habit of Rainy Night Press**
900 NE 81st Ave., #209
Portland, OR 97213

Contact Patricia McLean, nonficton editor; Duane Poncy, fiction editor.

**Faber & Faber LTD**
3 Queen Square
London WC1N
3AU United Kingdom

Contact Lee Brackstone, Hannah Griffiths, and/or Angus Cargill for fiction.

**Farrar, Straus & Giroux**
175 Fifth Ave.
New York, NY 10010

Contact Margaret Ferguson, editorial director.

**First Edition Design Publishing**
5202 Old Ashwood Drive
Saratosa, FL 34233

Contact Deborah E. Gordon, executive editor.

**Flying Pen Press, LLC**
1660 Niagara St.
Denver, CO 80228
Contact David A. Rozansky, publisher

**Gambit Publishing**
1725 W. Glenlake Ave. #1W
Chicago, IL 60660

Contact Gail Glaser, editor.

**Gauthier Publications, Inc.**
Frog Legs Ink
PO Box 806241
Saint Clair Shores, MI 48080

Contact Elizabeth Gauthier, creative director.

**Genesis Press, Inc.**
PO Box 101
Columbus, MS 39701

Contact "Editor."

**The Glencannon Press**
PO Box 1428
El Cerrito, CA 94530

Contact Bill Harris

**Grey Gecko Press**
565 S. Mason Rd., Suite 154
Katy, TX 77450

Contact Hilary Comfory, editor-in-chief.

**Hawk Publishing Group**
7107 S. Yale Ave., #345
Tulsa, OK 74136

Contact "Editor."

**Homa & Sekey Books**
PO Box 103
Dumont, NJ 07628

Contact Shawn Ye, editor.

**Ilium Press**
2407 S. Sonora Dr.
Spokane, WA 99037-9011

Contact John Lemon, owner and editor.

**Insomniac Press**
520 Princess Ave.
London ON N6B 2B8
Canada

Contact Mike O'Connor, publisher; Gillian Urbankiewicz, assistant editor.

**Interlink Publishing Group, Ink.**
46 Crosby St.
Northampton, MA 01060

Contact Michel Moushabeck, publisher; Pam Thompson, editor.

**Martin Sisters Publishing, LLC**
PO Box 1749
Barbourville, KY 40906-1499

Conatct Denise Melton, publisher and editor; Melissa Newman, publisher and editor.

**Mondial**
203 W. 107th St., Suite 6C
New York, NY 10025

Contact Andrew Moore, editor.

**Nortia Press**
27525 Puerta Real, Ste. 100-467
Mission Viejo, CA 92701

Contact "Editor."

**Oak Tree Press**
140 E. Palmer
Taylorvolle, IL 625n8

Contact Billie Johnson, publisher; Sarah Wasson, acquisitions editor.

**Obrake Books**
Obrake Canada, Inc.
3401 Dufferin Street
PO Box 27538
Toronto, ON M6A 3B8
Canada

Contact Echez Godoy, acquisitions editor.

**Ooligan Press**
PO Box 751
Portland, OR 97207

Contact "Editor."

**Outrider Press, Inc.**
2036 North Winds Dr.
Dyer, IN 46311

Contact Whitney Scott, editor.

**Palari Publishing**
PO Box 9288
Richmond, VA 23227

Contact David Smitherman, publisher and editor.

**Philomel Books**
Imprint of Penguin Group, Inc. (USA)
375 Hudson St.
New York, NY 10014

Contact Michael Green, president and publisher.

**Polychrome Publishing Corp.**
4509 N. Francisco
Chicago, IL 60625

Contact "Editor."

**Red Hen Press**
PO Box 3537
Granada Hills, CA 91394

Contact Mark E. Cull, publisher and editor.

**SoHo Press, Inc.**
853 Broadway
New York, NY 10003

Contact Bronwen Hruska, publisher; Katie Herman, editor; Mark Doten, editor.

**Spout Press**
PO Box 581067
Minneapolis, MN 55458

Contact Carrie Eidem, fiction editor.

**Sunburry Press, Inc.**
2200 Market Street
Camp Hill, PA 17011

Contact "Editor."

**Swan Isle Press**
PO Box 408790
Chicago, IL 60640

Contact "Editor."

**Third World Press**
c/o Tia Chucha's Centro Cultural
13197-A Gladstone Blvd.
Sylmar, CA 91342

Contact Luis Rodriguez, director.

**Tightrope Books**
602 Maskham Street
Toronto, ON M6G 2L8
Canada

Contact Shirarose Wilensky, editor.

**To Read Aloud Publishing, Inc.**
PO Box 632426
Nacogdoches, TX 75963

Contact Michael Powell, president.

**Tokyo Rose Records / Chapultepec Press**
4222 Chambers
Cincinnati, OH 45223

Contact David Garza.

**Unlimited Publishing, LLC**
PO Box 99
Nashville, IN 47448

Contact "Editor."

**War Child Publishing**
PO Box 4897
Culver City, CA 90231

Contact Marci Baun, editor-in-chief.

**Wrod Warriors Press**
930 Blackoaks Ln.
Anoka, MN 55303

Contact Gail Cerridwen, managing editor.

Contact Roland Pease, editor.

**Zoland Books, Steerforth Press**
45 Lyme Rd., Suite 208
Hanover, NH 03755

# LITERARY AGENTS

Don't want to approach a publisher yourself and would rather a literary agent negotiate a deal for you? Try your luck with one of the following. As always, I suggest sending a query letter to get specific instructions before sending your entire book.

## Alive Communications, Inc.
7680 Goddard Street, Suite 200
Colorado Springs, CO 80920

Contact Rick Christian. Represents fiction and nonfiction. Fiction areas: adventure, contemporary issues, crime, family saga, historical, inspirational, literary, mainstream, mystery, police, religious, satire, suspense, thriller.

## Betsy Amster Literary Enterprises
6312 SW Capitol Hwy #503
Portland, OR 97239

Contact Betsy Amster. Represents fiction and nonfiction. Fiction areas: ethnic, literary, women's issues, high quality.

## B.J. Robbins Literary Agency
5130 Bellaire Ave.
North Hollywood, CA 91607-2908

Contact B.J. Robbins or Amy Maldonado. Represents fiction and nonfiction. Fiction areas: crime, detective, ethnic, literary, mainstream, mystery, police, sports, suspense, thriller.

## Bookends, LLC
136 Long Hill Road
Gillette, NJ 07933

Contact Kim Lionetti, Jessica Alverez, Lauren Ruth. Represents fiction and nonfiction. Fiction areas: detective, cozies, mainstream, mystery, romance, thrillers, women's.

## Briar Cliff Review
3303 Rebecca St.
PO Box 2100
Sioux City, IA 51104

Write/Send SASE for more information

## Browne & Miller Literary Associates
410 S. Michigan Ave., Suite 460
Chicago, IL 60605-1465

Contact Danielle Egan-Miller. Represents nonfiction books, most genres of commercial adult fiction and nonfiction, and young adult projects. Fiction areas: contemporary issues, crime, detective, erotica, ethnic, family saga, glitz, historical, inspirational, literary, mainstream, mystery, police, religious, romance, sports, suspense, thriller, paranormal.

## Castiglia Literary Agency
1155 Camino Del Mar, Suite 510
Delmar, CA 92014

Contact Julie Castiglia or Winifren Golden. Represents fiction and nonfiction. Fiction areas: contemporary issues, ethnic, literary, mainstream, mystery, suspense, women's.

## Concho River Review
Angelo State University, ASU Station
PO Box 10894
San Angels, TX 76909.

Reviews literary works.

## Defiore & Co.
47 E. 19th Street, 3rd Floor
New York, NY 10003

Contact Lauren Gilchrist. Represents nonfiction books and novels. Fiction areas: ethnic, literary, mainstream, mystery, suspense, thriller.

## Diana Finch Literary Agency
116 W. 23rd Street, Suite 500
New York, NY 10011

Contact Diana Finch. Represents nonfiction books, novels and scholarly. Fiction areas: action, adventure, ethnic, historical, literary, mainstream, police, thriller, young adult.

## Dunham Literary, Inc.
156 Fifth Ave., Suite 625
New York, NY 10010-7002

## Dystel & Godrich Literary Management
1 Union Square W., Suite 904
New York, NY 10003

Contact Michael Bourret or Jim McCarth. Represents nonfiction books, novels and cookbooks. Fiction areas: action, adventure, crime, detective, ethnic, family saga, gay, lesbian, literary mainstream, mystery, suspense, thriller, police.

## The Evan Marshall Agency
6 Tristam Place
Pine Brook, NJ 07058-9445

Contact Evan Marshall. Fiction areas: action, adventure, erotica, ethnic, frontier, historical, horror, humor, inspirational, literary, mainstream, mystery, religious, satire, sci-fi, suspense, western, romance (contemporary, gothic, historical, regency).

## Fineprint Literary Management
240 West 35th St., Suite 500
New York, NY 10001

Contact Peter Rubie. Represents nonfiction books and novels. Fiction areas: crime, detective, want, women's,

## Jeany Naggar Literary Agency. Inc.
216 E. 75th Street, Suite lE
New York, NY 10021

Contact Jean Naggar. Represents nonfiction books and novels. Fiction areas: action, adventure, crime, detective, ethnic, family saga, feminist, historical, literary, mainstream, mystery, police, psychic, supernatural, suspense, thriller.

## Jodie Rhodes Literary Agency
8840 Villa La Jolla Dr., Suite 315
La Jolla, CA 92037-1957

Contact Jodie Rhodes. Represents nonfiction books and novels. Fiction areas: ethnic, family saga, historical, literary, mainstream, mystery, suspense, thriller, women's, young adult.

## The Joy Harris Literary Agency, Inc.
381 Park Avenue S., Suite 428
New York, NY 10016

Contact Joy Harris. Represents nonfiction books, novels and young adult. Fiction areas: ethnic, experimental, family saga, feminist, gay, glitz, hi-Io, historical, humor, lesbian, literary, mainstream, multicultural, multimedia, mystery, regional, satire, short story collections, spiritual, suspense, translation, women's, young adult.

## Loretta Barrett Books, Inc.
220 E. 23rd Street, 11th Floor
New York, NY 10010

Contact Loretta A. Barrett, Nick Mullendore and/or gabriel Davis.

Represents nonfiction books and novels. Fiction areas: contemporary, psychic, adventure, detective, ethnic, family, historical, literary, mainstream, mystery, thriller, young adult.

## Lowenstein Associates, Inc.
121 W. 27th Street, Suite 601
New York, NY 10001

Contact Barbara Lowenstein. Represents nonfiction books and novels. Fiction areas: crime, detective, erotica, ethnic, fantasy, feminist, historical, literary, mainstream, mystery, police, romance, suspense, thriller, young adult.

## Mendel Media Group, LLC
115 W. 30th Street, Suite 800
New York, NY 10001

Represents nonfiction books, novels, scholarly with potential for broad/popular appeal.

Fiction areas: action, adventure, contemporary issues, crime, detective, erotica, ethnic, feminist, gay, glitz, historical, humor, inspirational, juvenile, lesbian, literary, mainstream, mystery, picture books, police, religious, romance, satire, sports, thriller, young adults, Jewish, etc.

## Michael Larsen/Elizabeth Pomada, Literary Agents
1029 Jones Street
San Francisco, CA 94109-5023

Contact Mike Larsen and/or Elizabeth Pomada. Represents nonfiction books and novels. Fiction areas: action, adventure, contemporary issues, crime, detective, ethnic, experimental, family saga, feminist, gay, glitz, historical, humor, inspirational, lesbian, literary, mainstream, mystery, police, religious, romance, satire, suspense, chick lit.

## Philip G. Spitzer Literary Agency, Inc.
50 Talmage Farm Lane
East Hampton, NY 11937

Contact Luc Hunt. Represents nonfiction books and novels. Fiction areas: crime, detective, literary, mainstream, mystery, police, sports, suspense, thriller.

## Richard Henshaw Group
22 West 23rd Street, 5th Floor
New York, NY 10010

Contact Rich Henshaw. Represents nonfiction books and novels. Fiction areas: ethnic, experimental, family saga, feminist, gay, glitz, hi-lo, crime, detective, historical, humor, literary, mainstream, mystery, police, psychic, romance, satire, sci-fi, sports, supernatural, suspense, thriller.

## RLR Associates, LTD
Literary Department
7 W. 51st Street
New York, NY 10019

Contact Scott Gould. Represents nonfiction books, novels, short story collections and scholarly. Fiction areas: action, adventure, cartoon, comic books, crime, detective, ethnic, experimental, family saga, feminist, gay, historical, horror, humor, lesbian, literary, mainstream, multicultural, mystery, police, satire, sports, suspense.

## Robin Straus Agency, Inc.
229 E. 79th Street, Suite 5A
New York, NY 10075

Contact Ms. Robin Straus. Represents high-quality adult fiction and nonfiction, including literary and commercial fiction, narrative fiction, women's fiction, memoirs, history, bios, books on psychology, pop culture and current affairs, science, parenting and cookbooks.

## Rosalie Siegel
International Literary Agency, Inc.
1 Abey Drive
Pennington, NJ 08534

Contact Rosalie Siegel. Represents nonfiction books, novels and short story collections.

## Russell & Volkening
50 W. 29th Street, Suite 7E
New York, NY 10001

Contact Jessica Salky. Represents nonfiction books and novels. Fiction areas: action, adventure, crime, detective, ethnic, literary, mainstream, mystery, picture books, police, sports, suspense, thriller.

## Sandra Dijkstra Literary Agency
1155 Camino Del Mar
PMB 515
Del Mar, CA 92014

Contact Sandra Dijkstra. Represents nonfiction books and novels. Fiction areas: erotica, ethnic, fantasy, juvenile, literary, mainstream, mystery, picture books, sci-fi, suspense, thriller, graphic novel.

## Sanford J. Greenburger Associates, Inc.
55 Fifth Ave.
New York, NY 10003

Contact Heide Lange, Faith Hamlin and/or Dan Mandel. Represents nonfiction books and novels. Fiction areas: action, adventure, crime, detective, ethnic, family saga, feminist, gay, glitz, historical, humor, lesbian, literary, mainstream, mystery, police, psychic, regional, satire, sports, super national, suspense, thriller.

## Sheree Bykofsky Associates, Inc.
PO Box 706
Brigantine, NJ 08203

Contact Sheree Bykofsky. Represents nonfiction books and novels. Fiction areas: contemporary issues, literary, mainstream, mystery, suspense.

## Trident Media Group
41 Madison Ave., 36th Floor
New York, NY 10010
Contact Ellen Levine. Represents nonfiction books, novels, short story collections and juvenile. Fiction areas: crime, detective, humor, juvenile , literary, military, multicultural, mystery., police, short story collections, suspense, thriller, women's, young adult.

## Veritas Literary Agency
601 Van Ness Ave., Opera Plaza, Suite E.
San Francisco, CA 94102

Contact Katherine Boyle. Represents nonfiction books and novels. Fiction areas: commercial, fantasy, literary, mystery, sci-fi, young adult.

**Victoria Sanders & Associates**
241 Avenue of the Americas, Suite 11 H
New York, NY 10014

Contact Victoria Sanders and/or Diane Dickenshied. Represents nonfiction books and novels. Fiction areas: action, adventure, contemporary issues, ethnic, family saga, feminist, gay, lesbian, literary, thriller.

**The Wendy Weil Agency, Inc.**
232 Madison Ave., Suite 1300
New York, NY 10016

Contact Wendy Weil. Represents fiction and nonfiction: literary, commercial fiction, mystery, thriller, memoir, history, current affairs, pop culture.

**WM Clark Associates**

186 Fifth Ave., Second Floor
New York, NY 10010

Represents nonfiction and fiction. Fiction areas: contemporary issues, ethnic, historical, literary, mainstream, southern fiction.

**Writers House**
21 W. 26th Street
New York, NY 10010

Contact Michael Mejias. Represents nonfiction books, novels and juvenile. Fiction areas: adventure, cartoon, contemporary issues, crime, detective, erotica, ethnic, family saga, fantasy, feminist, frontier, gay, hi 10, historical, horror, humor, juvenile, literary, mainstream, military, multicultural, mystery, new age, occult, police, psychic, regional, romance, thriller, war, young adult.

# LITERARY PUBS/REVIEWS

If you are a writer/poet, you want to be published as much as possible in order to build your name. At first you may have to give it away, but there are many publications that offer to pay for your work.

Several of the following pubs/reviews offer to buy poetry and or prose. As always, before submitting anything to them, I suggest you send a query letter to specify exactly what they want. Good luck!

**African American Review**
Saint Louis University
Adorjan Hall 317
3800 Lindell Boulevard
St. Louis, MO 63108

As a quarterly journal, AAR promotes a lively exchange among writers and scholars in the arts and humanities who hold diverse perspectives on African American literature, art, and culture.

**AGNI Magazine**
Boston University
236 Bay State Road
Boston, MA 02215

Reviews literary work.

Website: agni@bu.edu

**Alaska Quarterly Review**
University of Alaska Anchorage
3211 Providence Drive
Anchorage, Alaska 99508

Reviews literary work.

**Alligator Juniper**
Prescott College
220 Grove Ave
Prescott, AZ 86301

Reviews literary work.

**American Literary Review**
P.O. Box 311307
University of North Texas
Denton, TX 76203-1307

Reviews literary work.

**The American Scholar**
1606 New Hampshire Avenue NW
Washington, D.C. 20009

Phone Number: (202) 265-3808
Website: scholar@pbk.org

**The Antioch Review**
P.O. Box 148
Yellow Springs, OH 45387
Reviews literary works.
Phone Number: 937-769-1365

**Apalachee Review**
P.O. Box 10469
Tallahassee, Florida 32302

Reviews literary works. The latest issue of Apalachee Review is available for $8.00. Back issues may be purchased for $5.00 each.

**Arc Poetry Magazine**
PO Box 81060
Ottawa, Ontario
Canada, K1P 1B1

**Arion**
621 Commonwealth Ave 4th Floor
Boston, MA 02215

A journal of humanities and the classics.

**Arkansas Review**
P.O. Box 1890
State University, AR 72467.

A year's subscription (three issues) costs $20. Make checks payable to "ASU Foundation" with "Arkansas Review" on the memo line.

**Ascent; English Dept.**
Concordia College
901 Eight St.
Moorhead, MN 56562

**The Awakening Review**
5 Forest Hill Dr. Suite 201
Glen Ellyn, IL 60137

Reviews literary works.

**Baffler**
PO Box 378293
Chicago, IL 60637

**The Bayou Review**
One Main St.
Houston, TX 77002

Reviews literary works.

**Bellevue Literary Review NYU Dept of Medicine**
550 First Avenue, OBV-A612
New York, New York 10016 US

Reviews literary works.

**Bellingham Review**
MS—9053
Western Washington University
Bellingham, WA 98225

Reviews literary works.

**Bellowing Ark**
PO Box 55564
Shoreline, WA 98155

**Beloit Poetry Journal**
PO Box 151
Farmington, ME 04938

**The Bitter Oleander**
4983 Tall Oaks Drive
Fayetteville, NY 13066

This is a magazine of contemporary international
poetry and short fiction.

**Blackbird**
Dept. of English Virginia Commonwealth University
PO Box 843082
Richmond, VA 23284

**Blue Mesa Review**
MCS 03-2170
1 University of New Mexico
Dept. Of English/Hum 217
Albuquerque, NM 87131

Reviews literary works.

**Boston Review**
Building E 53 Room 407 MIT
Cambridge, MA 02139

Reviews literary works.

**Brilliance Corners**
Lycoming College
700 College Place
Williamsport, PA 17707

A journal of Jazz and Literature.

**Callaloo**
Dept. of English Texas A&M University
MS 4212 TAMU'
College Straton, TX 77843

**Calyx**
PO Box B
Corvallis, OR 97339

**Capilano Review**
Capilano College
2055 Purcell Way
North Vancouver, British Columbia V7J 3H5, Canada

Reviews literary works.

**The Caribbean Writer**
University of Virgin Islands
RR01 Box 10,000
Kingshill
St. Croix, VI USA 00850

**Carolina Quarterly**
CB #3520 Greenlaw Hall
University of North Carolina
Chapel Hill, NC 27599

**The Chattahoochee Review**
Georgia Perimeter College
555 North Indian Creek Drive
Clarkston, GA 30021

*The Chattahoochee Review* is a literary journal sponsored by Georgia Perimeter College as part of The Southern Academy for Literary Arts and Scholarly Research. Reviews literary works. PAYMENT; they typically pay $50/poem and $25/page for prose. Payment for reviews, interviews, plays, and art is determined on an individual basis. All contributors receive two copies.

## Chicago Review
5801 South Kenwood Avenue
Chicago, IL 60637

Guidelines for submission:
All submissions must include a self-addressed, stamped envelope with sufficient postage or International Reply Coupons for notification (or return of manuscript if desired). Address submissions to the appropriate genre editor: Poetry, Fiction, or Book Review. Simultaneous submissions are strongly discouraged. Due to the increasing volume of unsolicited submissions, the average response time is three to six months; it is especially slow during the summer.

## Cimarron Review
205 Morrill Hall
Oklahoma State University
Stillwater, OK 74078

"Cimarron Review is now accepting both electronic and postal submissions. Please read these guidelines before submitting.

We accept submissions year-round in poetry, fiction and art. All postal submissions must be accompanied by an SASE. Please, regardless of whether you're submitting electronically or by the postal mail, include a cover letter with, your submission.

Please send 3-6 poems or one piece of fiction. Address all the work to the appropriate editor (fiction or poetry) and mail postal submissions to the above address.

Artists and photographers interested in having their work appear on an upcoming cover of the Cimarron Review should query by E-mail at cimarronreview@okstate.edu. If our editors are interested, we'll reply and request to see more work.

We do NOT accept the following:

• Previously published work (includes work published online).

• E-mailed submissions of any kind.

We no longer accept international reply coupons from writers living outside the United States.

We do not publish theme issues. We are interested in any strong writing of a literary variety, but are not especially partial to fiction in the modern realist tradition and poetry that engages the reader through a distinctive voice -- be it lyric, narrative, etc. When submitting fiction, please do not include a summary of your story in the cover letter. Allow the work to stand on its own. We have no set page lengths for any genre, but we seldom publish short-shots or pieces longer than 25 pages. There are, however, exceptions to every rule. Our guiding aesthetic is the quality of the work itself.

For fiction, please number each page.

When submitting electronically, poets should include all poems for submission in a single file.

We do not accept more than one story -- even if the stories are very short – in a single submission. Please send only one story at a time.

When sending postal submissions, do not staple the manuscript; paperclips are the preferred fastener. Electronic submissions should be doc, docx, pdf, or rtf files and should include your contact information in the upper left or right-hand corner of each page.

Response time varies, but we typically respond to submissions within 3-6 months, often much sooner. At times, however due to a backlog, and especially for work submitted in the summer, a response may take longer. If you have not heard from us after six months, please feel free to query by sending an E-mail to cimarronreview@okstate.edu. Please do not query before six months.

Simultaneous submissions are welcomed, but please contact us immediately through postal or E-mail (with the date and genre of your original submission) should your work be accepted elsewhere. Please also withdrawal electronically-submitted stories accepted elsewhere through the online submission manager system. Unless poets wish to withdraw all poems from a submission, they should withdraw individual poems by E-mail or postal mail only.

For publication, Cimarron Review acquires First North American Serial Rights. After publication, rights revert to the author. At this time, Cimarron

Review pays its contributors two copies of the issue in which their work appears.

You may contact us through postal nail or at cimarronreview@okstate.edu. Also, please do not submit again to the Cimarron Review until you have heard back from us. We reserve the right to send multiple submissions back to the author with no response."

**College Literature**
West Chester University
210 East Rosedale Ave.
West Chester, PA 19382

**Colorado Review**
9105 Campus Delivery
Colorado State University, Dept. of English
Fort Collins, Colorado 80523-9105

Reviews literary works.

**Columbia**
Columbia University
2960 Broadway
New York, NY 10027

**Commentary Magazine**
561 7th Avenue, 16th Floor
New York, NY 10018

COMMENTARY welcomes submissions of articles or reviews for publication consideration. They should be sent via e-mail to:
submissions@commentarymagazine.com

**The Comstock Review**
4956 St. John Drive
Syracuse, NY 13215

Reviews literary works.

**Conjunctions**
21 East 10th St.
New York, NY 10003

**Connecticut Review**
39 Woodland St.
Hartford, CT 06105

Reviews literary works.

**Court Green**
Columbia College Chicago, Dept of English

600 South Michigan Ave
Chicago, IL 60605

**Crab Orchard Review**
Dept of English Southern Illinois University
Carbondale
Faner Hall 2380, Mail code 4503
1000 Faner Dr.
Carbondale, IL 62901

Reviews literary works.

**Crazyhorse**
College of Charleston; Dept. of English
66 George St.
Charleston, SC 29424

**Creative Nonfiction**
5501 Walnut St. Suite 202
Pittsburg, PA 15232

**Daedalus**
136 Irving St Suite 100
Cambridge, MA 02138

**Denver Quarterly**
University of Denver; Dept. of English
2000 E Asbury
Denver, CO 80208

**Descant, TCU**
Box 297270
Fort Worth, TX 76129

**Eclipse; A Literary Journal**
1500 North Verdugo Rd
Glendale, CA 91208

This is a literary publication. Submit up to 6 poems or 1 piece of prose.

**Ecotone**
Dept of Creative Writing, UNCW
601 south College Rd
Wilmington, NC 28403

This is a literary publication. Submit up to 6 poems or 1 piece of prose.

**Epoch; Cornell University**
251 Goldwin Smith Hall
Ithaca, NY 14853

This is a literary publication, submit one manuscript only.

**Esquire**
300 W. 57<sup>th</sup> St. 21<sup>st</sup> Floor
New Your, New York 10019

Literary publication.

**Eureka Literary Magazine**
Eureka College
300 East College Ave
Eureka, IL 61530

Literary publication.

**Event; Douglas College**
PO Box 2503
New Westminster, British Columbia V3L 5B2,
Canada

This is a literary publication. Submit up to 3-8 poems
or short stories with a cover letter.

**Fantasy & Science Fiction**
PO Box 3447
Hoboken, NJ 07030

This is a literary publication. Submit up to 25,000
words of fiction in one manuscript only. Artwork also
accepted.

**Faultline**
University of CA, Irvine
Dept. of English and Comparative Literature
Irvine, CA 92697

This is a publication that accepts poetry, fiction,
nonfiction, translations, and art.

Website: humanities.uci.edu/faultline.shing

**Fiction; Mark J Mirksy, Editor**
The City College of New York; Dept. of English
138<sup>th</sup> St. and Convent Ave
New York, NY 10031

This is a literary publication that only accepts fiction.

**Fiction International**
Harold Jaffe, Editor
San Diego State University
Dept. of English and Comparative Literature
5500 Campanile Dr.
San Diego, CA 92182

This is a Literary publication. Submit up to 3-5 poems
or 4,000 words of fiction.

**Fiddlehead; Campus House**
11 Garland Court UNB
PO Box 4400
Fredericton, NB E3B 5A3, Canada

**Field**
50 N. Professor St.
Oberlin, OH 44074

This is a literary publication that only accepts poetry.
No simultaneous submissions.

**The First Line**
PO Box 250382
Plano, TX 75025

This is a literary publication that only accepts fiction
and non-fiction. However, the topic rotates, so query
for current topic.

**Florida Review**
University of Central Florida; Dept. of English
PO Box 161346
Orlando, FL 32816

Review literary works.

**Folio; Dept of Literature**
The American University
Washington, DC 20016

This is a literary publication that accepts between
Aug 15 – Mar 1. Submit up to 5 poems or 3,500 of
prose.

**Fourteen Hills**
The SFSU Review; Dept. of Creative Writing
San Francisco State University
1600 Holloway Ave.
San Francisco, CA 94132

This is a literary review.

**Fourth Genre; Editor**
Michigan state University; Dept. of English
201 Morrill Hall
East Lansing, MI 48823

This is a literary publication that accepts between
Aug. 15 – Nov. 30.

**Georgia Review**

University of Georgia
Athens, GA 30602

This is a literary publication that accepts between Aug 15- May 15.

**Gettysburg Review**
Gettysburg College
Gettysburg, PA 17325

This is a literary publication that accepts between, Sept. 1 – May 31.

**Grain**
PO Box 67
Saskatoon, Saskatchewan
S7K 3K1, Canada

Submit up to 12 poems or 2 stories. Submissions must be one-sided and typed.

**Green Hill Literary Lantern**
Truman State University; Dept. of English
Kirksville, MO 63501

Literary publication.

**Greensboro Review; Jim Clark, Editor**
MFA Writing Program
3302 HHRA Building; University of North Carolina
Greensboro, NC 27401

Literary publication.

**Gulf Coast**
University of Houston; Dept. of English
Houston, TX 77204

Literary publication that accepts between Aug. 15 – Mar. 15.

**Harper's Magazine**
666 Broadway, 11th Floor
New York, NY 10012

Literary publication.

**Harpur Palate**
Binghamton University; Dept. of English
PO Box 6000
Binghamton, NY 13902

Literary publication.

**Harvard Review**

Lamont Library Harvard University
Cambridge, MA 02138

Literary publication.

**Hawaii Pacific Review**
Hawaii Pacific University
1060 Bishop St.
Honolulu, HI 96713

Literary publication that accepts between Sept. 1 – Dec 31.

**Hayden's Ferry Review**
Arizona State University Center for Creative Writing
C/O Virginia G. Piper
PO Box 875002
Tempe, AZ 85287

Literary publication.

**The Healing Muse**
Center for Bioethics & Humanities
725 Irving Ave. Suite 406
Syracuse, NY 13210

Literary publication that accepts between Sept. 1 – May 1.

**Hiram Poetry Review**
PO Box 162
Hiram, OH 44234

**Hotel Amerika**
Columbia College English Dept.
600 S. Michigan Ave
Chicago, IL 60605

Literary publication.

**Hudson Review**
684 Park Ave
New York, NY 10021

Literary publication.

**Hunger Mountain**
Vermont College
36 College St.
Montpelier, VT 05602

Literary publication.

**Idaho Review**
Boise State University; Dept. of English

1910 University Dr
Boise, ID 83725

Literary publication.

**Iris, UVA Women's Center**
PO Box 800588
Charlottesville, VA 22908

Literary publication.

**Iron Horse Literary Review**
TTU Mail Stop 43091
Lubbock, TX 79409

Literary publication.

**Isotope; Utah State University**
3200 Old Main Hill
Logan, UT 84322

Literary publication.

**Italiana Americana, University of Rhode Island**
Providence Campus
80 Washington St.
Providence, RI 02903

Literary publication.

**Jabberwock Reviews**
Dept. of English, Drawer E
Mississippi State University
Mississippi State, MS 39762

Literary Publication that accepts between Aug. 15 –
Oct. 20 and Jan15 – Mar 15.

**Jewish Currents**
PO Box 111
Accord, NY 12404

Literary publication.

**The Journal: Ohio State University; Dept. Of English**
164 West 17th Ave.
Columbus, OH 43210

Literary publication.

**Karanu**
English Dept.; Eastern Illinois University
Charleston, IL 61920

This is a literary publication that accepts between
Sept. 1 – Feb. 15.

**Kenyon Review**
Finn House, Kenyon College
102 W. Wiggin St.
Gambier, OH 43022

This is a literary publication that accepts between
Sept. 15 – Jan. 15.

**The Laurel Review; Dept. of English**
Northwest Missouri State University
800 University Dr.
Maryville, MO 64468

Literary publication.

**Literal Latte**
200 E. 10th St. Suite 240
New York, NY 10003

Literary publication.

**The Long Story**
18 Eaton St.
Lawrence, MA 01843

Literary publication that only accepts fiction.

**Louisiana Literature**
SLU 10792
Southern Louisiana University
Hammond, LA 70402

Literary publication.

**Louisville Review**
Spalding University
851 South Fourth St.
Louisville, KY 40203

Literary publication.

**Malahat Review**
University of Victoria
PO Box 1700, STN CSC
Victoria, British Columbia V8W 2Y2; Canada

Literary publication.

**Massachusetts Review**
South College, University of Massachusetts
Amherst, MA 01003

Literary publication that accepts between Oct. 1 – May 1.

Seeking experiences and suggested policy changes from Massachusetts based transgender prisoners through the "Transgender Prisoner Questionnaire." Write for a copy. Referrals to transfer specific organizations and support.

**McSweeney's**
849 Valencia St.
San Francisco, CA 94410

Literary publication.

**Meridian, University of Virginia**
PO Box 400145
Charlottesville, VA 22904

Literary publication that accepts between Aug 16 – Apr. 14.

**Michigan Quarterly Review**
University of Michigan 0576 Rackham Building
915 East Washington St.
Ann Harbor, MI 48109

Literary publication. Submit up to 8-12 poems or 7,000 words of prose. No simultaneous submissions.

**Mid-American Review**
Bowling green State University, Dept. of English
Bowling green, OH 43403

Literary publication.

**Midstream**
633 third Ave, 21st Floor
New York, NY 10017

Literary publication. Focuses on Jewish life and culture.

**Missouri Review**
357 McReynolds Hall
University of Missouri
Columbia, MO 65211

Literary publication.

**Natural Bridge; Dept. Of English, University of Missouri**
One University Blvd.
St. Louis, MO 63121

Literary publication that accepts between July 1 – Aug 31 and Nov. 1 - Dec. 31.

**New Delta Review**
Dept. of English; 15 Allen Hall
Louisiana State University
Baton Rouge, LA 70803

Literary publication that accepts between Aug. 15 – Mar. 31.

**New England Review**
Middlebury College
Middlebury, VT 05753

Literary publication that accepts between Sept. 1 – May. 31.

**New Letter, University of Missouri**
1 University House
5101 Rockhill Rd.
Kansas City, MO 64110

Literary publication that accepts between Oct. 2 – Apr. 30.

**New Ohio Review; English Dept.**
360 Ellis Hall
Ohio University
Athens, OH 45701

Literary publication.

**New Orleans Review**
PO Box 195
Loyola University
New Orleans, LA 70188

Literary publication that accepts between Aug. 15 – May 15.

**The New York Quarterly**
PO Box 2015
Old Chelsea station
New York, NY 10113

Literary publication that accepts poetry only. Submit up to 3-5 poems.

**Nimrod International Journal**
University of Tulsa
800 S. Tucker Dr.
Tulsa, OK 74104

Literary publication that accepts between Jan. 1 – Nov. 30.

**Ninth Letter**
University of Illinois; Dept. of English
608 S. Wright St.
Urbana, IL 61801

Literary publication that accepts between Sept. 1 – Apr. 30.

**North Carolina Literary Review**
Dept. of English
East Carolina University
Greenville, NC 27858

Literary publication that specializes in North Carolina stories.

**North Dakota Quarterly**
Merrifield Hall Room 110
276 Centennial Dr, Stop 7209
Grands Forks, ND 58202

Literary publication.

**Northwest Review;The Editor, NWR**
5243 University of Oregon
Eugene, OR 97403

Literary publication that accepts nonfiction only.

**Notre Dame Review**
840 Flanner Hall
University of Norte Dame
Notre Dame, IN 46556

Literary publication that accepts poetry and fiction only between Sept. – Nov., and Jan. – Mar.

**Nylon**
110 Greene St., Suite 607
New York, NY 10012

Literary publication.

**Oklahoma Today**
POB 1468
Oklahoma, City 73101

Literary publication.

**Oxford American**
201 Donaghey Ave, 107
Conway, AR 72035

Literary publication interested in stories from the South.

**Painted Bride Quarterly**
Drexel University Dept. Of English and Philosophy
3141 Chestnut St.
Philadelphia, PA 19104

Literary publication.

**Pearl**
3030 East Second St.
Long Beach, CA 90803

Literary publication that accepts between Jan – June.

**Phoebe; George Mason University MSN 206**
4400 University Dr.
Fairfax, VA 22030

Literary publication that accepts between Sept. 1 – Apr. 15.

**The Pinch, Dept. of English**
University of Memphis
Memphis, TN 38153

Literary publication.

**Pleiades**
University of Central Missouri
Warrensburg, MO 64093

Literary publication that accepts between Sept. 1 – Apr. 30.

**Ploughshares, Emerson College**
120 Boylston St.
Boston, MA 02116

Literary publication.

**Poet Lore**
The Writers Center
4508 Walsh St.
Bethesda, Maryland 20815

Literary publication.

**Potomac Review**
Montgomery College
51 Mannakee St. MT/212
Rockville, MD 20850

Literary publication that accepts between Sept. 1 –
May 1. Submit single manuscript only.

**Pottersfield Portfolio**
9879 Kempt Head Rd.
Ross Ferry, Nova Scotia B1X 1N3; Canada

**Prairie Fire**
423-100 Arthur St.
Winnipeg, Manitoba R3B 1H3; Canada

Literary publication.

**Prairie Schooner**
201 Andrews Hall
PO Box 880334
Lincoln, NE 68588

Literary publication that accepts between Sept. 1 –
May 1.

**Prism International**
University of British Columbia
Buchanan E462
1866 Main Hall
Vancouver, BC V6T 1Z1, Canada

**Quarterly West**
200 S. Central Campus Dr.
University of Utah
Salt Lake City, UT 84112

Literary publication that accepts between Sept. 1 –
May 1. Submit up to 3-5 poems and 1 fiction piece.

**Raritan, Rutgers University**
31 Mine St.
New Brunswick, NJ 08903

Literary publication that accepts fiction and essays.
Submit 1 piece.

**Rattle**
12411 Ventura Blvd,
Studio City, CA 91604

Literary publication.

**Rattapallax**
217 Thompson St., Suite 353
New York, NY 10012

Literary publication.

**Redivider, Emerson College**

120 Boylston St.
Boston, MA 02116

Literary publication. Submit 1 piece every 6 months.

**RHINO**
PO Box 591
Evanston, IL 60204

Literary publication that accepts material between
April 1 – October 1. Submit up to 3-5 poems only.

**Room**
PO Box 46160, Station D
Vancouver, BC V6J 5G5, Canada

Literary publication for women only.

**The Saint Ann's Review**
129 Pierrepont St.
Brooklyn, NY 11201

Literary publication.

**Salmagundi; Skidmore College**
815 North Broadway
Saratoga Springs, NY 12866

Literary publication.

**Salt Hill; English Dept.**
Syracuse University
Syracuse, NY 13244

Literary publication.

**Santa Monica Review**
1900 Pico Boulevard
Santa Monica, CA 90405

Literary publication.

**Seattle Review**
University of Washington
Padelford Hall
Box 354330
Seattle, WA 98195

Literary publication.

**Seneca Review**
Hobart & William Smith Colleges
Geneva, New York 14456

Literary publication.

**Seven Days**
PO Box 1164
255 south Champlain St.
Burlington, VT. 05042

Literary publication.

**Sewanee Review; University of the South**
735 University Ave.
Sewanee, TN 37383

Literary publication.

**Shenandoah**
Troubador Theater, 2nd Floor
Washington & Lee University
Lexington, VA 24450

Literary publication.

**Sonora Review**
Dept. of English
University of Arizona
Tucson, AZ 85721

Literary publication.

**So-To-Speak**
George Mason University
4400 University Dr., MSN 2C5
Fairfax, VA 22030

Literary publication.

**The South Carolina Review**
Center for Electronic & Digital Publishing
Clemson University, Strode Town, Room 611
Box 340522
Clemson, SC 29634

Literary publication.

**South Dakota Review**
University of South Dakota; Dept. of English
University Exchange
414 E. Clark St.
Vermillion, SD 57069

Literary publication.

**Southeast Review, English Dept.**
Florida State University
Tallahassee, FL 32311

Literary publication.

**Southern Humanities Review**
9088 Haley Center
Auburn University, AL 36830

Literary publication.

**The Southern Review**
43 Allen Hall
Louisiana State University
Baton Rouge, LA 70803

Literary publication.

**Southwest Review**
Southern Methodist University
307 Fondren Library West
Dallas, TX 75275

Literary publication.

**Speakeasy; The loft Literary Center**
1011 Washington, Ave. South; Suite 200
Minneapolis, MN 55415

Literary publication.

**The Spoon River Poetry Review**
4240, Dept of English; Illinois State University
Normal, IL 61790

Literary publication.

**St. Anthony Messenger**
1615 Republic St.
Cincinnati, OH 45210

Literary publication.

**Sun**
107 North Roberson St.
Chapel Hill, NC 27516

Literary publication.

**Swivel**
PO Box 17958
Seattle, WA 98107

Literary publication.

**Sycamore Review**
Purdue University; Dept of English
500 Oval Dr.

West Lafayette, IN 47907

Literary publication that accepts between Aug. 1 – Mar. 31.

**Talking River Review**
Division of Literature and Languages; Lewis-Clark State College
500 Eighth Ave.
Lewiston, ID 83501

Literary publication that accepts between Aug.1 – Apr. 1.

**Tampa Review, The University of Tampa**
401 West Kennedy Blvd.
Tampa, FL 33606

Literary publication.

**The Texas Review; English Dept.**
Box 2146 Sam Houston State University
Huntsville, TX 77341

Literary publication.

**Thema**
PO Box 8747
Metairie, LA 70011

Literary publication.

**Threepenny Review**
PO Box 9131
Berkeley, CA 94709

Literary publication.

**Tikkun**
2342 Shattuck Ave., Suite 1200
Berkley, CA 94704

Literary publication.

**Tin House**
Po Box 10500
Portland, OR 97210

Literary publication.

**Transition Magazine**
104 Mt. Auburn St. 3R
Cambridge, MA 02138

Literary publication.

**Turnrow; English Dept**
The University of Louisiana at Monroe
700 University Ave.
Monroe, LA 71209

Literary publication.

**War, Literature & the Arts; English & Fine Arts Dept.**
United States Air Force Academy
2354 Fairchild Dr., Suite 6045
Colorado springs, CO 80840

Literary publications.

**Wascana Review**
English Dept.,University of Regina
Saskatchewan S4S 0A2; Canada

**Washington Square Creative Writing Program**
New York University
58 W. 10th St.
New York, NY 10011

Literary publication.

**Watchword**
2704 Wallace St.
Berkley, CA 94702

Literary publication.

**Witness**
Black Mountain Institute
University of Nevada
Las Vegas, NV 89154

Literary publication that accepts between Sept. 1 – May 1.

**Xavier University**
Box 110C
New Orleans, LA 70125

Literary publication.

**Yale Review**
PO Box 208243
New Haven, CT 06520

Literary publication.

**Zahir; Sheryl Tempchin**
315 South Coast HWY. 101; Suite U8

Encinitas, CA 92024

Literary publication.

**Zoetrope**
The Sentinel Building
916 Kearney St.
San Francisco, CA 94133

Literary publication.

**Zyzzyva**
PO Box 590069

San Francisco, CA 94159

Literary publication that accepts submissions from west-coast writers only.

# Freebird Publishers

## Professional Self-Publishing Services

# MIKE ENEMIGO PRESENTS...

# THE CELL BLOCK BOOKSHOP

**THE CELL BLOCK; PO BOX 1025; RANCHO CORDOVA, CA 95741**

**#1 PRISONER INFORMATION & ENTERTAINMENT COMPANY!**

The Cell Block is an independent multimedia company with the objective of accurately conveying the prison/street experience and culture, with the credibility and honesty that only one who has lived it can deliver, through literature and other arts, and entertain and enlighten while doing so.

Represent and support the company that represents and supports *you*. Represent and support the TCB movement!

**To order, simply write what you want clearly on a piece of paper and send with proper payment via institutional check, money order, or NEW books of Forever Stamps. All books are also on Amazon!**

THE CELL BLOCK
PRESENTS
MIKE ENEMIGO CERTIFIED
THE
MILLIONAIRE
PRISONER
SPECIAL TCB EDITION
JOSHUA KRUGER
FORWARD BY MIKE ENEMIGO

## THE MILLIONAIRE PRISONER SPECIAL TCB EDITION

Why wait until you get out of prison to achieve your dreams? Here's a blueprint that you can use to become successful!

The Millionaire Prisoner is your complete reference to overcoming any obstacles in prison. You won't be able to put it down! With this book you will discover the secrets to:

Making money from your cell!
Obtain FREE money for correspondence courses!
Become an expert on any topic!
Develop the habits of the rich!
Network with celebrities!
Set up your own website!
Market your products, ideas and services!
Successfully use prison pen pal websites!
How to get FREE pen pals!
All of this and much, much more! This book has enabled thousands of prisoners to succeed and it will show you the way also!

**PRICE: $19.99 + $7 S/H**

***STAMP PRICE: 4 BOOKS + 1 BOOK S/H.**
***ALL STAMPS MUST BE NEW BOOKS OF FORVER STAMPS.**

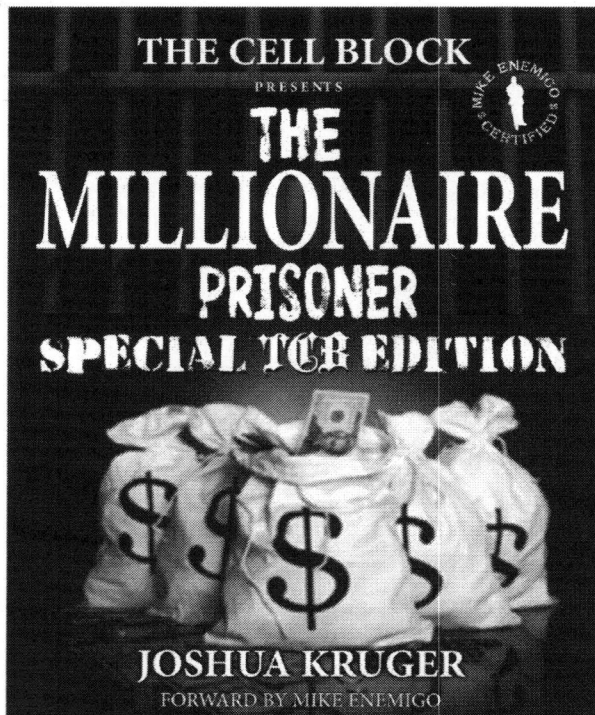

# CONSPIRACY THEORY

Kokain is an upcoming rapper trying to make a name for himself in the Sacramento, CA underground scene - home of rap stars Brother Lynch Hung, C-Bo, and Mozzy - and Nicki is his girlfriend .... One night, in October, Nicki's brother, along with her brother's best friend, go to rob a house of its $100,000 marijuana crop. It goes wrong; shots are fired and a man is killed .... Later, as investigators begin closing in on Nicki's brother and his friend, they, along with the help of a few others, create a way to make Kokain take the fall .... The conspiracy begins.

**PRICE: $15.00 + $5 S/H**

*STAMP PRICE: 2.5 BOOKS + 1 BOOK S/H. *ALL STAMPS MUST BE NEW BOOKS OF FORVER STAMPS.

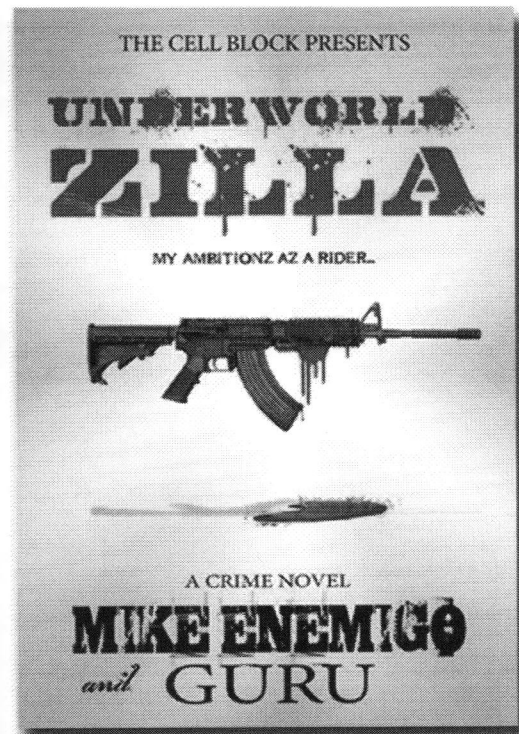

# UNDERWORLD ZILLA

When Talton leaves the West Coast to set up shop in Florida he meets the female version of himself: A drug dealing murderess with psychological issues. A whirlwind of sex, money and murder inevitably ensues and Talton finds himself on the run from the law with nowhere to turn to. When his team from home finds out he's in trouble, they get on a plane heading south...

**PRICE: $15.00 + $5 S/H**

*STAMP PRICE: 2.5 BOOKS + 1 BOOK S/H. *ALL STAMPS MUST BE NEW BOOKS OF FORVER STAMPS.

# LOYALTY AND BETRAYAL

Chunky was an associate of and soldier for the notorious Mexican Mafia -- La Eme. That is, of course, until he was betrayed by those he was most loyal to. Then he vowed to become their worst enemy. Though they've attempted to kill him numerous times, he still to this day is running around making a mockery of their organization . . .
This is the story of how it all began.

THE CELL BLOCK PRESENTS

LOYALTY AND BETRAYAL

TRUE CRIME STORY

MIKE ENEMIGO
and ARMANDO IBARRA

**PRICE: $12.00 + $4 S/H**

*STAMP PRICE: 2 BOOKS + 1 BOOK S/H. *ALL STAMPS MUST BE NEW BOOKS OF FORVER STAMPS.

---

THE CELL BLOCK
PRESENTS

ATTENTION: THIS BOOK IS A PRISONER MUST-HAVE!!

The Art & Power Of
LETTER WRITING
FOR PRISONERS

A COMPLETE GUIDE TO WRITING HIGH-QUALITY FORMAL (BUSINESS) & INFORMAL (PERSONAL) LETTERS!

FROM THE HIGHLY SUCCESSFUL PRISONER & CEO

MIKE ENEMIGO

# THE ART & POWER OF LETTER WRITING FOR PRISONERS

When locked inside a prison cell, being able to write well is the most powerful skill you can have! Learn how to increase your power by writing high-quality personal and formal letters! Includes letter templates, pen-pal website strategies, punctuation guide and more!

**PRICE: $9.99 + $4 S/H**

*STAMP PRICE: 1.5 BOOKS + 1 BOOK S/H. *ALL STAMPS MUST BE NEW BOOKS OF FORVER STAMPS.

# A GUIDE TO RELAPSE PREVENTION FOR PRISONERS

his book provides the information and guidance that can
nake a real difference in the preparation of a comprehensive
elapse prevention plan. Discover how to meet the parole
oard's expectation using these proven and practical princi-
les. Included is a blank template and sample relapse preven-
on plan to assist in your preparation.

**RICE: $15.00 + $4 S/H**

**TAMP PRICE: 2.5 BOOKS + 1 BOOK S/H. *ALL
TAMPS MUST BE NEW BOOKS OF FORVER STAMPS.**

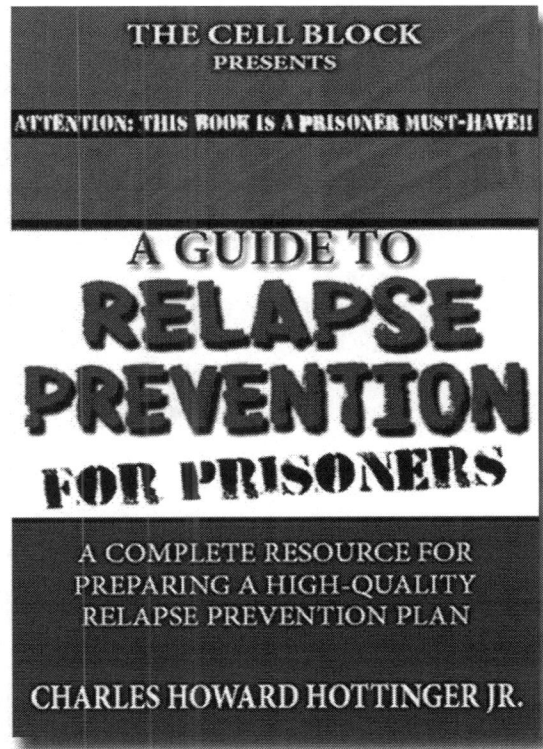

THE CELL BLOCK
PRESENTS

ATTENTION: THIS BOOK IS A PRISONER MUST-HAVE!!

A GUIDE TO
RELAPSE
PREVENTION
FOR PRISONERS

A COMPLETE RESOURCE FOR
PREPARING A HIGH-QUALITY
RELAPSE PREVENTION PLAN

CHARLES HOWARD HOTTINGER JR.

---

THE CELL BLOCK
PRESENTS

AT THIS POINT, IT BECOMES DEEPER THAN RAP...

MIKE ENEMIGO

THEE ENEMY OF THE STATE

SPECIAL EDITION

# THEE ENEMY OF THE STATE (SPECIAL EDITION)

Experience the inspirational journey of a kid who was introduced to the
art of rapping in 1993, struggled between his dream of becoming a professional rapper and the reality of the streets, and was finally offered a recording deal in 1999, only to be arrested minutes later and eventually sentenced to life in prison for murder... However, despite his harsh reality, he
dedicated himself to hip-hop once again, and with resilience and determination, he sets out to prove he may just be one of the dopest rhyme writ-
ers/spitters ever .... At this point, it becomes deeper than rap .... Welcome
to a preview of the greatest story you never heard.

**PRICE: $9.99 + $4 S/H**

**\*STAMP PRICE: 1.5 BOOKS + 1 BOOK S/H. \*ALL
STAMPS MUST BE NEW BOOKS OF FORVER STAMPS.**

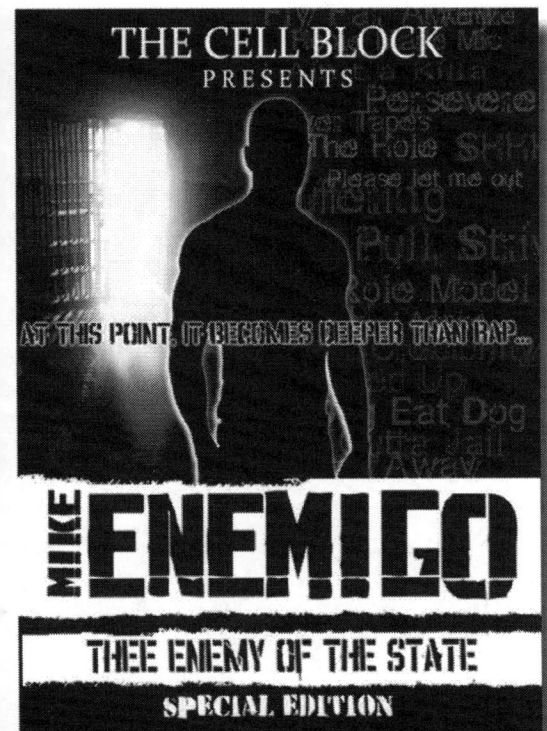

# HOW TO HUSTLE AND WIN: SEX, MONEY, MURDER

How To Hu$tle and Win: Sex, Money, Murder edition is the grittiest, underground self-help manual for the 21st century street entrepreneur in print. Never has there been such a book written for today's gangsters, goons and go-getters. This self-help handbook is an absolute must-have for anyone who is actively connected to the streets.

**PRICE: $15.00 + $5 S/H**

*STAMP PRICE: 2.5 BOOKS + 1 BOOK S/H. *ALL STAMPS MUST BE NEW BOOKS OF FORVER STAMPS.

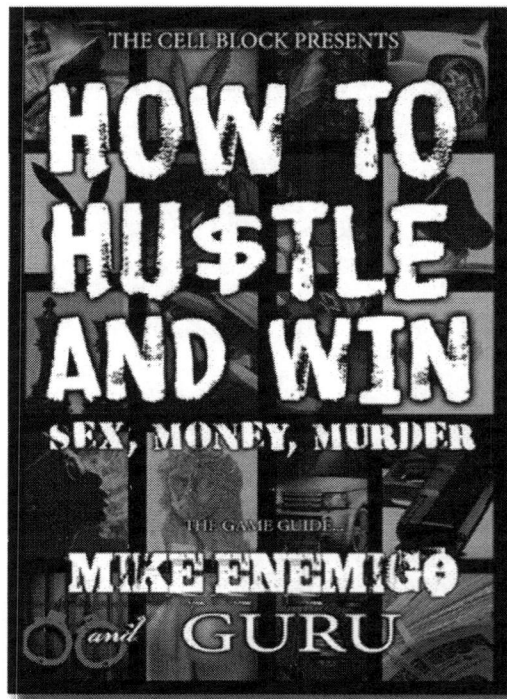

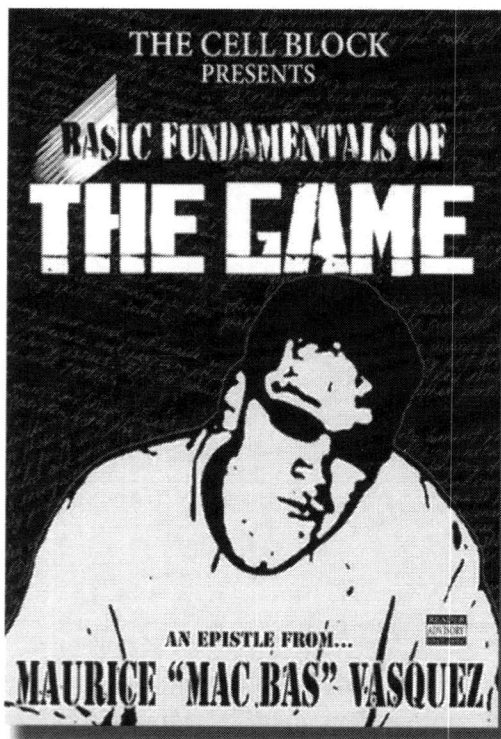

---

# BASIC FUNDATMENTALS OF THE GAME

Legendary Playboy, Mac BA$, gives essential clarification as to what actually constitutes a true player, and personally provides you with the BA$ic Fundamentals that are required to be an actual participant of the Life$tyle.

**PRICE: $12.00 + $4 S/H**

*STAMP PRICE: 2 BOOKS + 1 BOOK S/H.*ALL STAMPS MUST BE NEW BOOKS OF FORVER STAMPS.

# MONEY IZ THE MOTIVE

Like most kids growing up in the hood, Kano has a dream of going from rags to riches. But when his plan to get fast money by robbing the local "mom and pop" shop goes wrong, he quickly finds himself sentenced to serious prison time. Follow Kano as he is schooled to the ways of the game by some of the most respected OGs who ever did it; then is set free and given the resources to put his schooling into action and build the ultimate hood empire...

PRICE: $12.00 + $4 S/H

*STAMP PRICE: 2 BOOKS + 1 BOOK S/H. *ALL STAMPS MUST BE NEW BOOKS OF FORVER STAMPS.

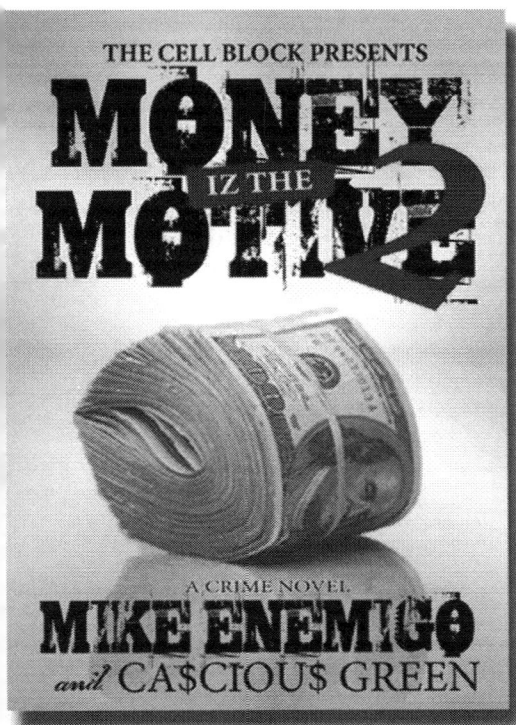

## MONEY IZ THE MOTIVE 2

After the murder of a narcotics agent. Kano is forced to shut down his D&C crew and leave Dayton, OH. With no one left to turn to, he calls Candy's West Coast Cuban connection who agrees to relocate him and a few of his goons to the 'City of Kings" -- Sacramento, CA, aka Mackramento, Killafornia! Once there, Kano is offered a new set of money-making opportunities and he takes his operation to a whole new level. It doesn't take long, however, for Kano to learn the game is grimy no matter where you go, as he soon experiences a fury of jealousy, hate, deception and greed. In a game where loyalty is scarce and one never truly knows who is friend and who is foe, Kano is faced with the ultimate life or death decisions. Of course, one should expect nothing less when...Money iz the Motive.

PRICE: $12.00 + $4 S/H

*STAMP PRICE: 2 BOOKS + 1 BOOK S/H. *ALL STAMPS MUST BE NEW BOOKS OF FORVER STAMPS.

# MOB$TAR MONEY

After Trey's mother is sent to prison for 75 years to life, he and his little brother are moved from their home in Sacramento, California, to his grandmother's house in Stockton, California where he is forced to find his way in life and become a man on his own in the city's grimy streets. One day, on his way home from the local corner store, Trey has a rough encounter with the neighborhood bully. Luckily, that's when Tyson, a member of the MOB$TAR$, a local "get money" gang comes to his aid. The two kids quickly become friends, and it doesn't take long before Trey is embraced into the notorious MOB$TAR money gang, which opens the door to an adventure full of sex, money, murder and mayhem that will change his life forever... You will never guess how this story ends!

PRICE: $12.00 + $4 S/H

*STAMP PRICE: 2 BOOKS + 1 BOOK S/H. *ALL STAMPS MUST BE NEW BOOKS OF FORVER STAMPS.

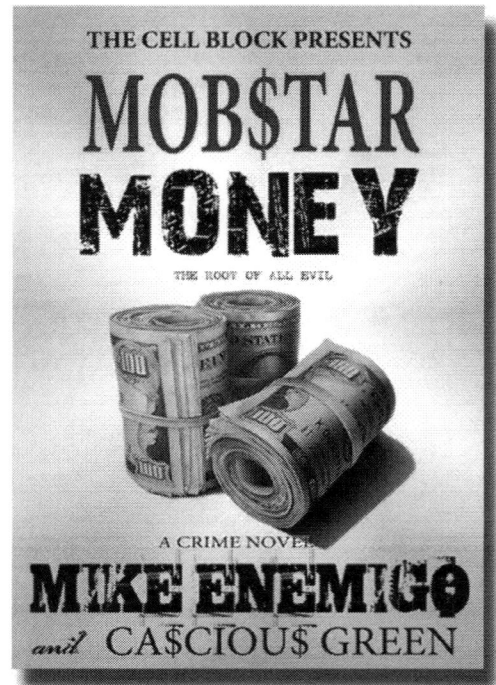

THE CELL BLOCK PRESENTS
MOB$TAR MONEY
THE ROOT OF ALL EVIL
A CRIME NOVEL
MIKE ENEMIGO and CA$CIOU$ GREEN

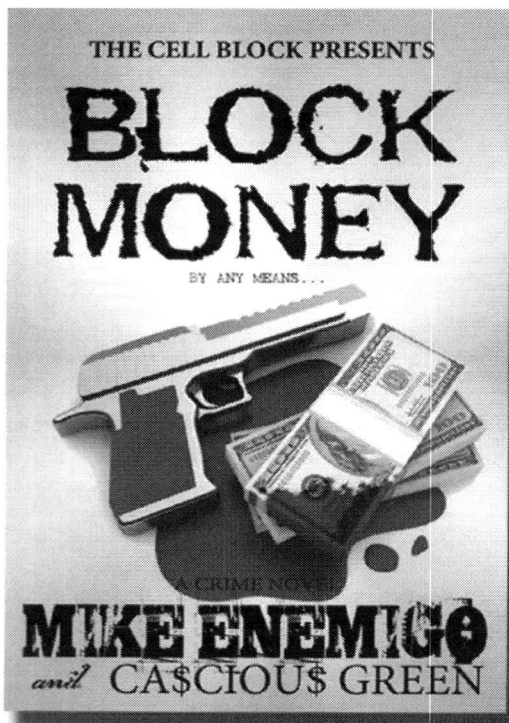

THE CELL BLOCK PRESENTS
BLOCK MONEY
BY ANY MEANS...
A CRIME NOVEL
MIKE ENEMIGO and CA$CIOU$ GREEN

## BLOCK MONEY

Beast, a young thug from the grimy streets of central Stockton, California lives The Block; breathes The Block; and has committed himself to bleed The Block for all it's worth until his very last breath. Then, one day, he meets Nadia; a stripper at the local club who piques his curiosity with her beauty, quick-witted intellect and rider qualities. The problem? She has a man -- Esco -- a local kingpin with money and power. It doesn't take long, however, before a devious plot is hatched to pull off a heist worth an indeterminable amount of money. Following the acts of treachery, deception and betrayal are twists and turns and a bloody war that will leave you speechless!

PRICE: $12.00 + $4 S/H

*STAMP PRICE: 2 BOOKS + 1 BOOK S/H. *ALL STAMPS MUST BE NEW BOOKS OF FORVER STAMPS.

# THE BEST RESOURCE DIRECTORY
## FOR PRISONERS

This book has over 1,450 resources for prisoners! Includes:
Pen-Pal Companies! Non-Nude Photo Sellers! Free Books and
Other Publications! Legal Assistance! Prisoner Advocates!
Prisoner Assistants! Correspondence Education! Money-Making Opportunities! Resources for Prison Writers, Poets, Artists, and much, much more! Anything you can think of doing
from your prison cell, this book contains the resources to do it!

**PRICE: $15.95 + $7 S/H**

*STAMP PRICE: 3 BOOKS + 1 BOOK S/H. *ALL STAMPS
MUST BE NEW BOOKS OF FORVER STAMPS.

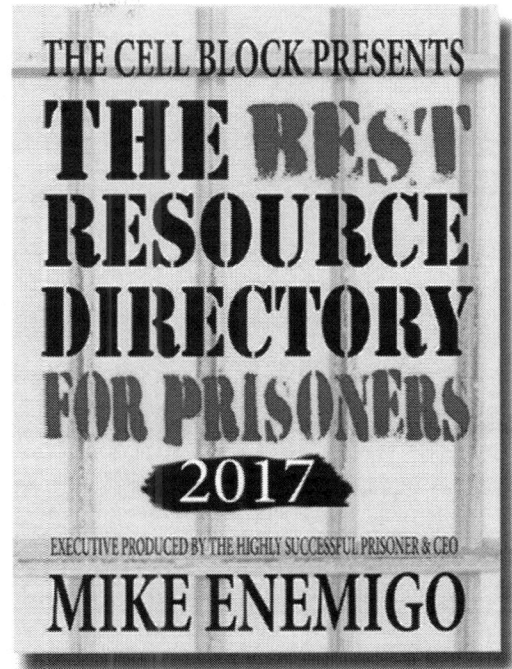

## THIS IS MY LIFE

Girls, gangbanging, murder, prison; love and hate.... Drake + NB
Ridaz + a little more thuggin' = Crow: This is My Life. And with a
co-sign by Mike Enemigo and forward by legendary Playboy and
boss Mac BAS, this book is certified.

**PRICE: $9.99 + $4 S/H**

*STAMP PRICE: 1.5 BOOKS + 1 BOOK S/H. *ALL STAMPS
MUST BE NEW BOOKS OF FORVER STAMPS.

# Freebird Publishers

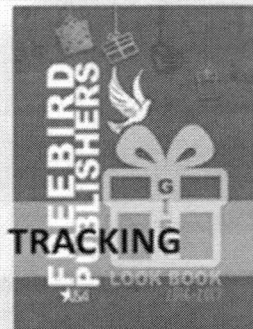

## LIFE WITH A RECORD: Reenter Society, Finish Supervision and Live Successfully   -NEW BOOK-

Information in this book help make sense of the major challenges facing ex-offenders today. Ten hard hitting chapters outline the purpose of making a Strategic Reentry Plan and making peace with supervisors, family, your community and your future, it packs an amazing amount of material into its pages and gives you a quick, easy to follow, full spectrum of instruction. explores the most commonly confronted issues and attitudes that sabotage reentry. It provides tools that cut across functions of discrimination, in corporations, political life and throughout society. It opens the door to empowerment, reminding ex-offenders that change and long term freedom begins with a commitment to daily growth. Addressing the whole reentry process. Softcover, 8x10", B&W, 360 pages $32.99 (25.99 plus $7. s/h)

## HOT GIRL SAFARI, Non Nude Photo Book          -NEW BOOK-

Full color gloss non nude photos. A different photo on every page. Over $100 worth of sexy photos in one book, for one low price. Non nude prison friendly. Softcover, 8.3x6", GLOSS COLOR, 128 pages... $31.99 ($24.99 plus $7 s/h)

## S.T.O.P. Start Thinking Outside Prison          -NEW BOOK-

Thinking is very critical to one's success, failure, and survival. Every decision requires thinking. If not, many actions will be done on impulse. And impulsive behavior tends to bring about situations from which one needs to be rescued. Think of a preteen, teenager, or young adult, all of whom can possess the impulsive behaviors of children. If the impulses aren't tamed or controlled, the behavior patterns will be present in each stage of life. Maybe this is the reason I see so many 40-year-olds that lack self-control or the ability to deal with some of life's simplest problems. They can't attack the situations from a professional, calm, and diplomatic standpoint. S.T.O.P. was written as a movement to help promote a greater thinking process - a thinking process believed to slow down the recidivism rate within our communities. Softcover, 6x9", B&W, 70 pages $18.99 ($13.99 plus $5. s/h)

## GIFT LOOK BOOK          -NEW BOOK-

**With Every Book Receive a $15.00 Voucher.** We carry hundreds of high quality gifts for every occasion to fit every budget. Our gifts are made in America! Gift Baskets, Flowers, Chocolates & Candies, Personalized Gifts and more. This color GIFT LOOK BOOK has hundreds of our high quality, beautifully handcrafted gifts to choose from, all made in U.S.A. We offer a complete line of gift baskets that have been custom designed. We have flowers that get delivered fresh in bud-form so they open up to full bloom in front of your loved ones. Our chocolates are of the finest quality, all made fresh. Animated singing plush gifts. All of our gifts are skillfully featured in detailed full color photographs. Softcover, 8x10", FULL COLOR, 110 pages $15.00 (Free s/h) With Every Book Receive a $15.00 Voucher, good towards a purchase of any gift order from our GIFT LOOK BOOK for $75.00 or more. (not including shipping & handling)

NO ORDER FORM NEEDED  CLEARLY WRITE ON PAPER & SEND PAYMENT TO:

**Freebird Publishers** Box 541, North Dighton, MA 02764

DIANE@FREEBIRDPUBLISHERS.COM WWW.FREEBIRDPUBLISHERS.COM

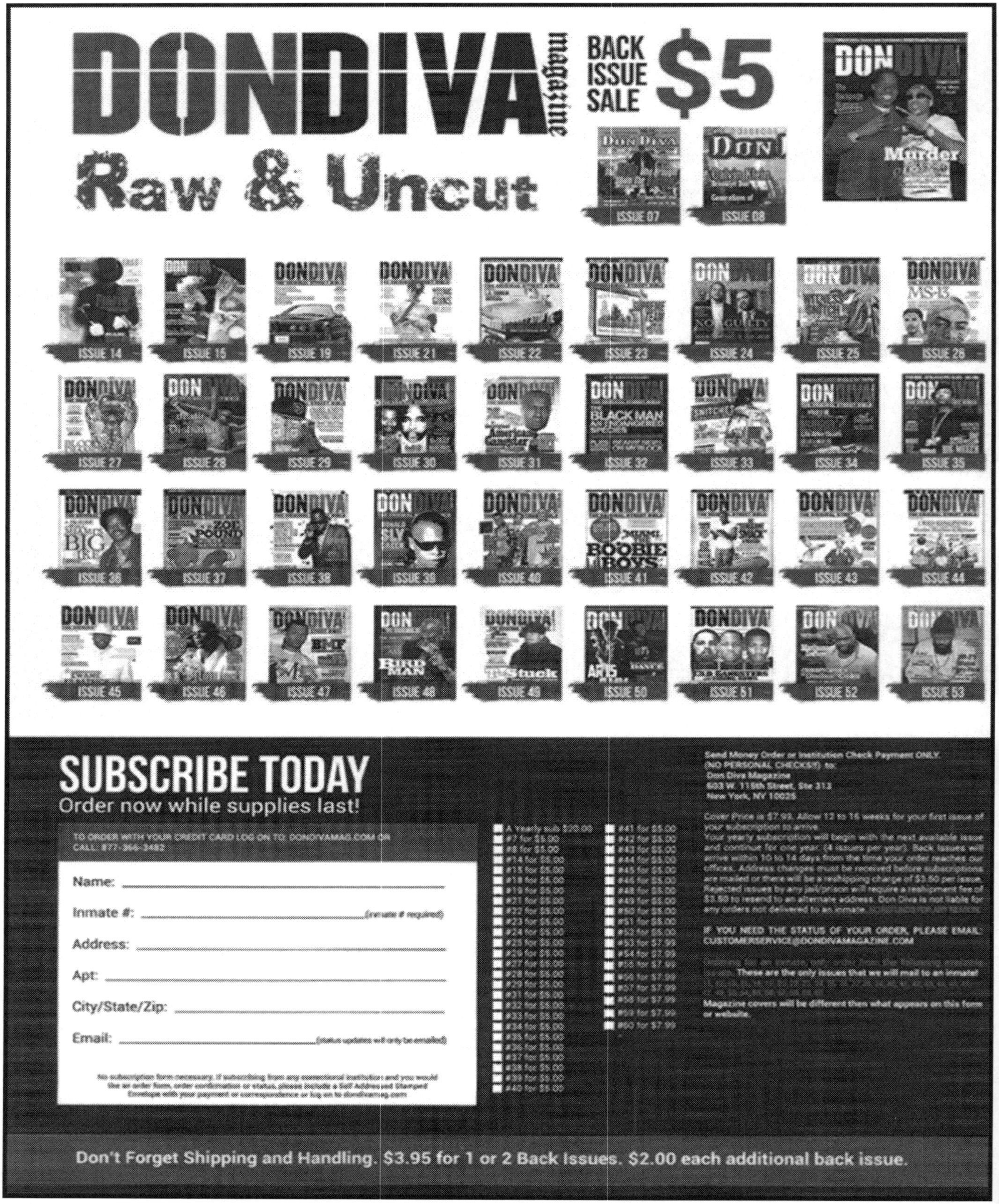
DONDIVA magazine
Raw & Uncut
BACK ISSUE SALE $5
ISSUE 07
ISSUE 08
ISSUE 14
ISSUE 15
ISSUE 19
ISSUE 21
ISSUE 22
ISSUE 23
ISSUE 24
ISSUE 25
ISSUE 26
ISSUE 27
ISSUE 28
ISSUE 29
ISSUE 30
ISSUE 31
ISSUE 32
ISSUE 33
ISSUE 34
ISSUE 35
ISSUE 36
ISSUE 37
ISSUE 38
ISSUE 39
ISSUE 40
ISSUE 41
ISSUE 42
ISSUE 43
ISSUE 44
ISSUE 45
ISSUE 46
ISSUE 47
ISSUE 48
ISSUE 49
ISSUE 50
ISSUE 51
ISSUE 52
ISSUE 53
SUBSCRIBE TODAY
Order now while supplies last!
TO ORDER WITH YOUR CREDIT CARD LOG ON TO: DONDIVAMAG.COM OR CALL: 877-366-3482
Name:
Inmate #: (inmate # required)
Address:
Apt:
City/State/Zip:
Email: (status updates will only be emailed)
A Yearly sub $20.00
Send Money Order or Institution Check Payment ONLY. (NO PERSONAL CHECKS!!) to:
Don Diva Magazine
603 W. 115th Street, Ste 313
New York, NY 10025
IF YOU NEED THE STATUS OF YOUR ORDER, PLEASE EMAIL: CUSTOMERSERVICE@DONDIVAMAGAZINE.COM
These are the only issues that we will mail to an inmate!
Magazine covers will be different than what appears on this form or website.
Don't Forget Shipping and Handling. $3.95 for 1 or 2 Back Issues. $2.00 each additional back issue.

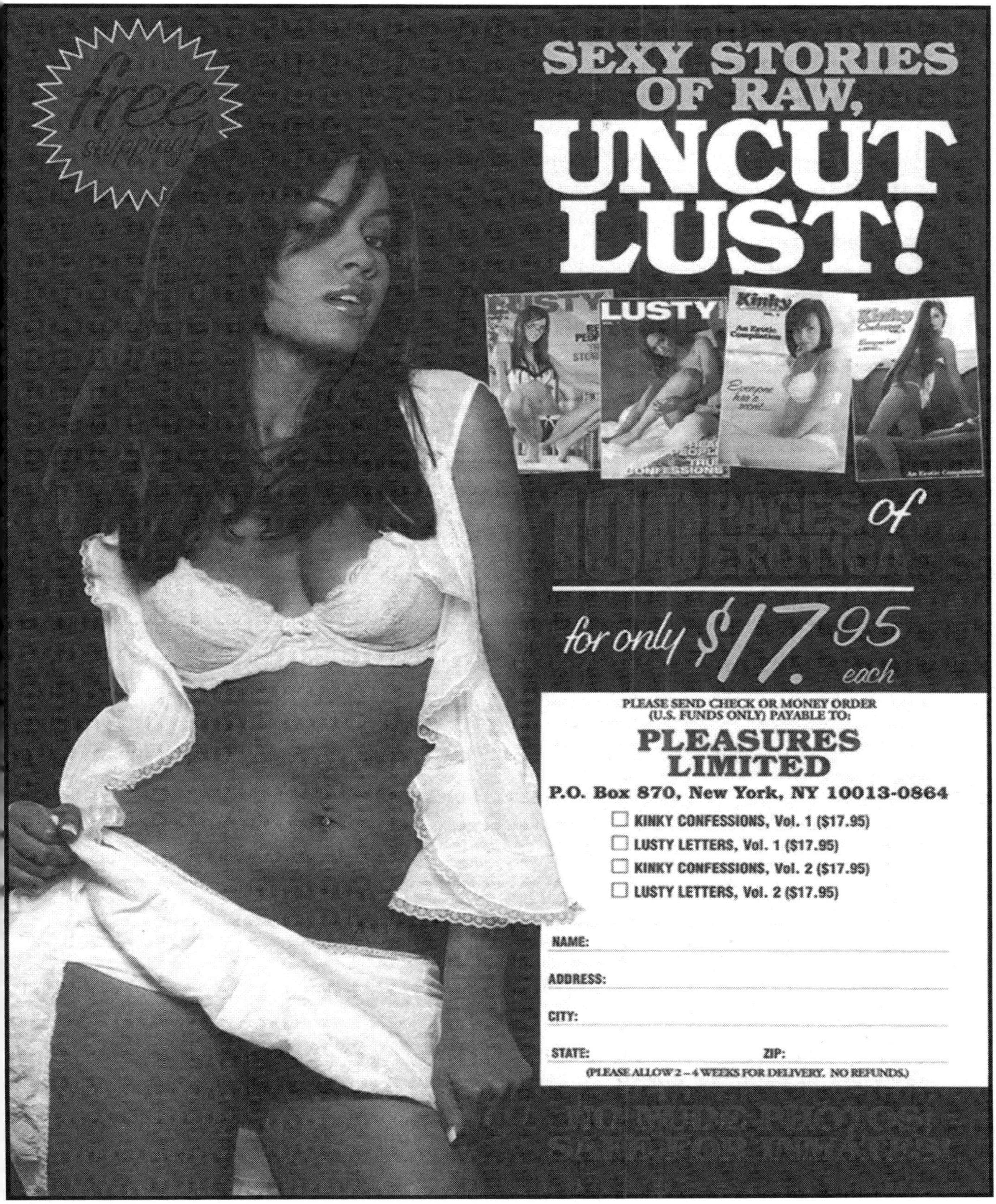

free shipping!
SEXY STORIES OF RAW,
UNCUT LUST!
LUSTY
Kinky
100 PAGES of EROTICA
for only $17.95 each
PLEASE SEND CHECK OR MONEY ORDER (U.S. FUNDS ONLY) PAYABLE TO:
PLEASURES LIMITED
P.O. Box 870, New York, NY 10013-0864
☐ KINKY CONFESSIONS, Vol. 1 ($17.95)
☐ LUSTY LETTERS, Vol. 1 ($17.95)
☐ KINKY CONFESSIONS, Vol. 2 ($17.95)
☐ LUSTY LETTERS, Vol. 2 ($17.95)
NAME:
ADDRESS:
CITY:
STATE:
ZIP:
(PLEASE ALLOW 2 – 4 WEEKS FOR DELIVERY. NO REFUNDS.)
NO NUDE PHOTOS! SAFE FOR INMATES!

WHERE ENTERTAINMENT MEETS SEXY!

# RHYMES & DIMES

BRANDS

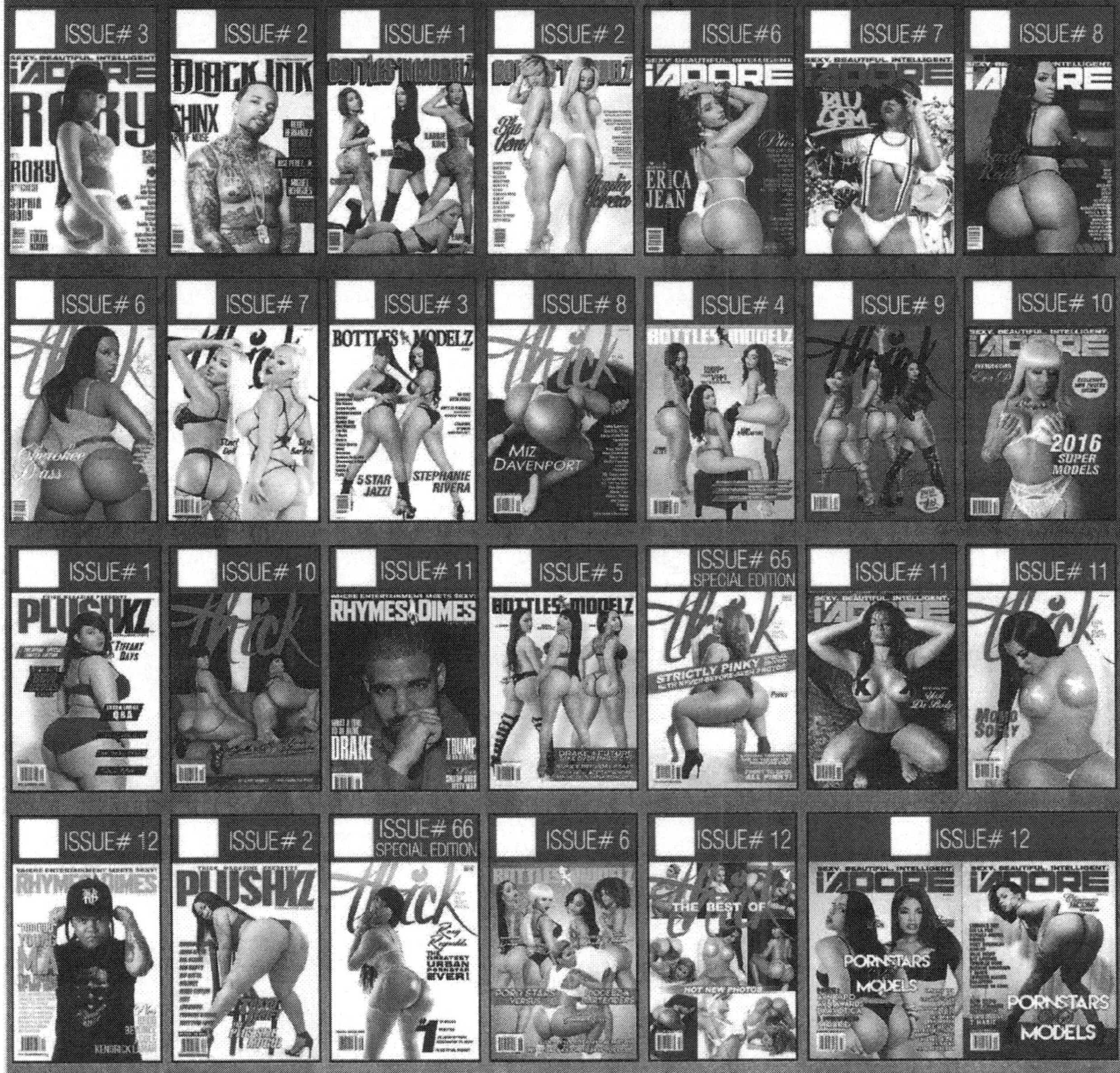
ISSUE# 3
ISSUE# 2
ISSUE# 1
ISSUE# 2
ISSUE#6
ISSUE# 7
ISSUE# 8
ISSUE# 6
ISSUE# 7
ISSUE# 3
ISSUE# 8
ISSUE# 4
ISSUE# 9
ISSUE# 10
ISSUE# 1
ISSUE# 10
ISSUE# 11
ISSUE# 5
ISSUE# 65 SPECIAL EDITION
ISSUE# 11
ISSUE# 11
ISSUE# 12
ISSUE# 2
ISSUE# 66 SPECIAL EDITION
ISSUE# 6
ISSUE# 12
ISSUE# 12

*ANY MAGAZINE COVER MAY CHANGE UPON DELIVERY*

## HOW TO ORDER

IF YOU WANT TO ORDER AN ISSUE THAT YOU DON'T HAVE OR YOU WANT AGAIN, MARK AN "X" IN THE SMALL WHITE BOX AS IT IS SHOWN HERE.

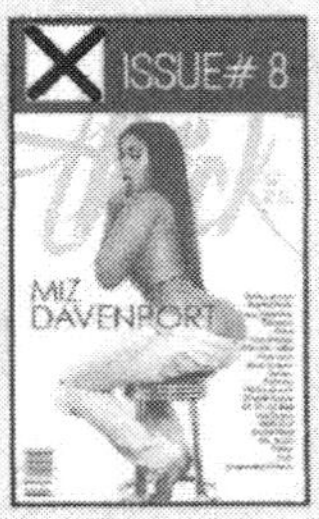
ISSUE# 8
MIZ DAVENPORT

IF YOU ALREADY OWN A PARTICULAR ISSUE AND YOU DO NOT WANT IT ORDERED FOR YOU AGAIN, MARK A BIG "X" OVER THE PICTURE OF THE MAGAZINE AS IT IS SHOWN HERE.

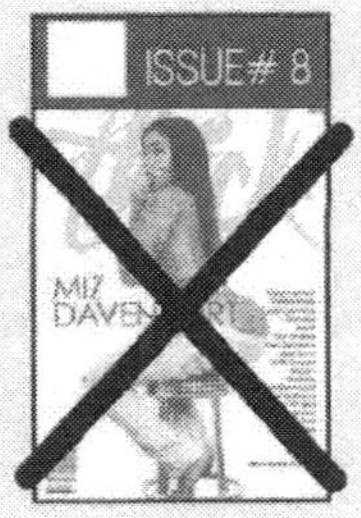
ISSUE# 8
MIZ DAVENPORT

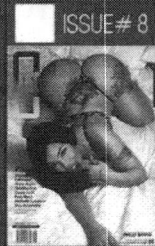

ROSA ACOSTA

KATHERINE

SOPHIA MARIE

YASMIN

JENNIFER SKYE

ESTELITA

KIMBERLY

ALANA MARIE

ANNETTE

NADIA

GIGI

CHARMAINE

DENISE

ORKIDIA

CAROL SELEME

JADE BRYCE

ELBA EVERLASTING

MARLENE

YEN

DIANA

MILEENA HAYES

BRITTANY

ALBA NITZA

VIVICA

SARAY

MELANIE

ELISHA JADE

SPICYMAGAZINE.COM

181

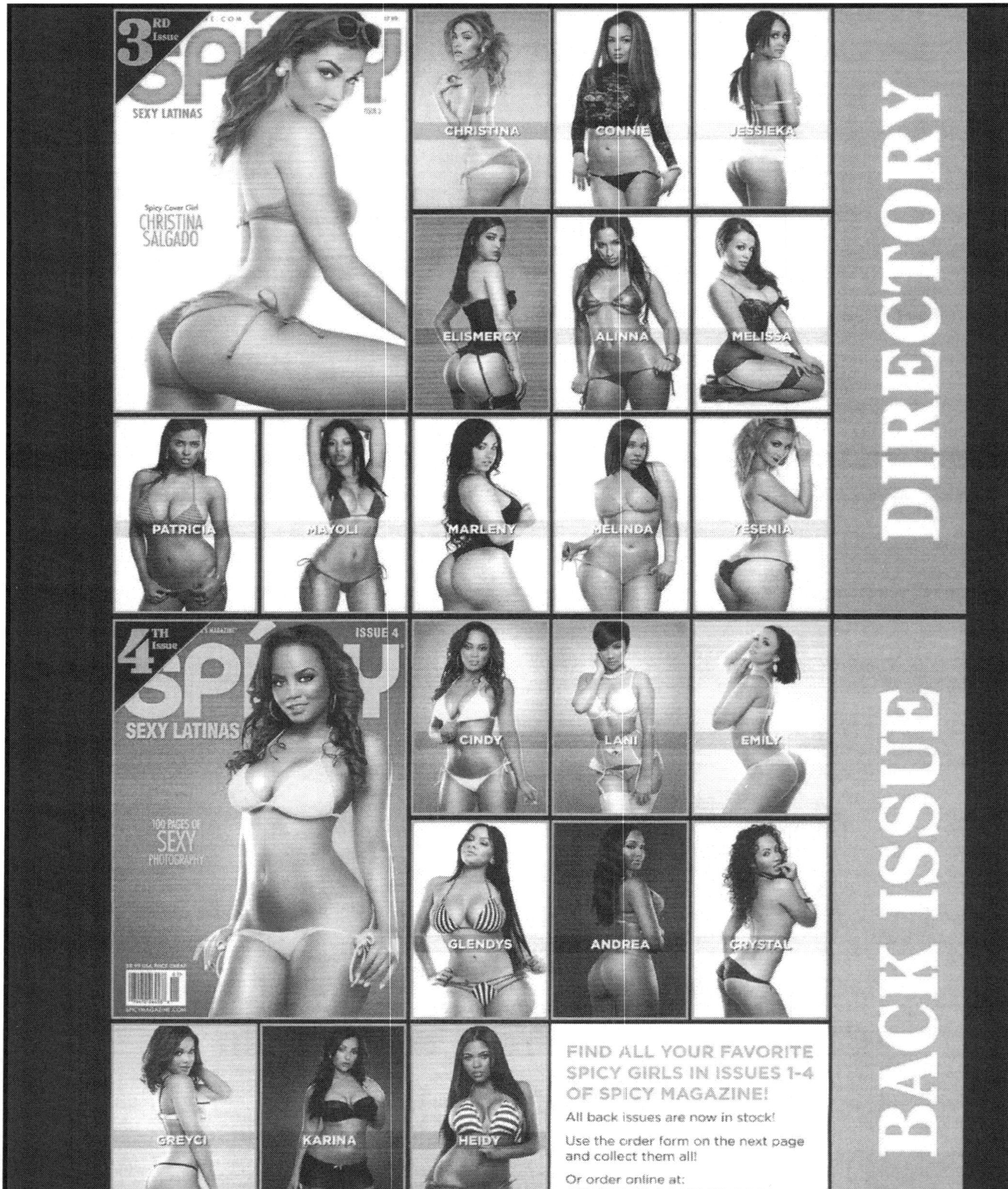
BACK ISSUE DIRECTORY
3RD Issue
SPICY
SEXY LATINAS
Spicy Cover Girl
CHRISTINA SALGADO
CHRISTINA
CONNIE
JESSIEKA
ELISMERCY
ALINNA
MELISSA
PATRICIA
MAYOLI
MARLENY
MELINDA
YESENIA
4TH Issue
ISSUE 4
SPICY
SEXY LATINAS
100 PAGES OF SEXY PHOTOGRAPHY
CINDY
LANI
EMILY
GLENDYS
ANDREA
CRYSTAL
GREYCI
KARINA
HEIDY
FIND ALL YOUR FAVORITE SPICY GIRLS IN ISSUES 1-4 OF SPICY MAGAZINE!
All back issues are now in stock!
Use the order form on the next page and collect them all!
Or order online at:
SPICYMAGAZINE.COM

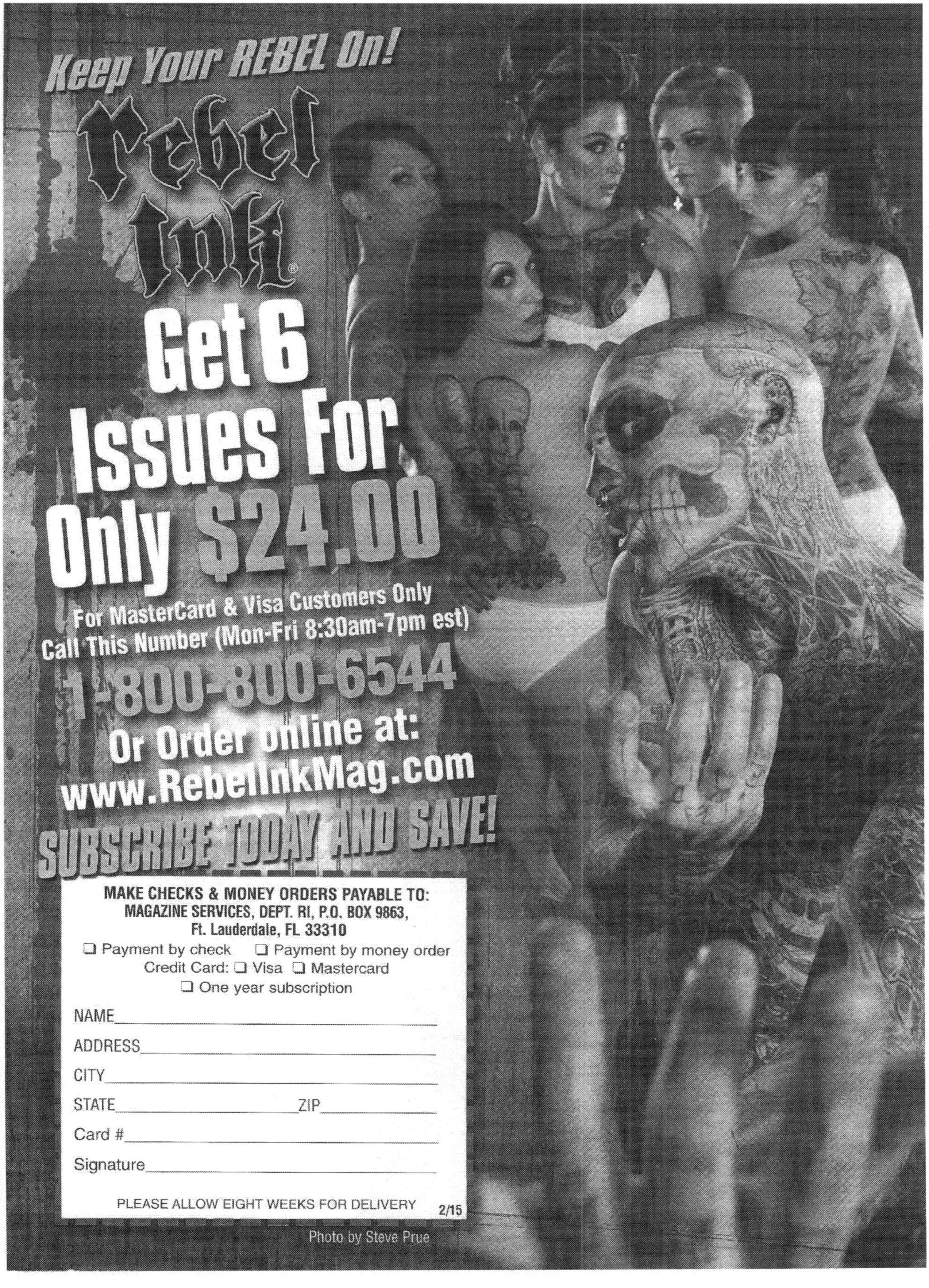
Keep Your REBEL On!
Rebel Ink®
Get 6 Issues For Only $24.00
For MasterCard & Visa Customers Only
Call This Number (Mon-Fri 8:30am-7pm est)
1-800-800-6544
Or Order online at:
www.RebelInkMag.com
SUBSCRIBE TODAY AND SAVE!
MAKE CHECKS & MONEY ORDERS PAYABLE TO:
MAGAZINE SERVICES, DEPT. RI, P.O. BOX 9863,
Ft. Lauderdale, FL 33310
❑ Payment by check ❑ Payment by money order
Credit Card: ❑ Visa ❑ Mastercard
❑ One year subscription
NAME
ADDRESS
CITY
STATE ZIP
Card #
Signature
PLEASE ALLOW EIGHT WEEKS FOR DELIVERY
2/15
Photo by Steve Prue

# A Case for Relapse Prevention for Prisoners
## By Charles Howard Hottinger Jr.

As with anything in life, preparation and planning is the key to success. It is vital to self-empowerment, and is a mechanism to reduce the rate of recidivism in the ex-offender population. The California Department of Corrections and Rehabilitation (CDCR), specifically the board of prison hearings (BPH), has taken notice of the importance in relapse prevention planning. Every prisoner who comes before the BPH is required to prevent a comprehensive "Relapse Prevention Plan"; one that addresses warning signs and triggers for maladaptive or problematic behaviors and demonstrates ways of successfully managing them in the community. What is a "Relapse Prevention Plan" exactly? How does one compose it?

Many California prisoners have fallen victim to the BPH's expectations in providing a comprehensive Relapse Prevention Plan, and subsequently have been faced with years of denials in obtaining a parole date. The BPH simply places the expectations on the prisoner without any instruction as to what a comprehensive Relapse Prevention Plan encompasses. This has left many prisoners ill-prepared or deficient in the plan they present to the BPH. First, prisoners must understand why the BPH is asking for this document. The reason is simple: a comprehensive Relapse Prevention Plan is a fortified plan for preventing a return to substance abuse before the prisoner is triggered to use again while on parole. The key is to plan ahead. The BPH wants to see that prisoners are prepared; that they have given real thought to how they are going to navigate parole and keep sobriety intact. If a prisoner's sobriety is constantly challenged, the regular obstacles of parole will be impossible to deal with; hence, the need for a Relapse Prevention Plan. During my research and learning process, I couldn't find anything directed a specifically addressing the issues of how to create a "relapse prevention plan." It took years of attending Narcotics and Alcoholics Anonymous, reading addiction literature and trying to understand my own reasons for using chemical substances before I began to understand what the word "comprehensive" meant as it relates to relapse prevention planning. The word "comprehensive" means "covering all the possibilities completely." When I began to understand addiction and relapse factors in such a broad term I was able to translate that insight into the development of my own personal relapse prevention plan, and subsequently a book titled A Guide to Relapse Prevention for Prisoners. I gained the awareness that success is a moving target that, in an ever-changing world, my life must actively be managed in a way that generates the high-quality results I desire. The benefits of a comprehensive Relapse Prevention Plan meant I had the proper stepping stones in life to remain abstinent. It inspired me with the goal of sharing what managing life is like when you have a consciously designed strategy that looks at maladaptive or problematic behaviors and shows you what life can be like when you effectively minimize or eliminate those problems. Understanding why something happens is helpful, but being able to predict that something is going to happen gives me more options. When I tried to stop using in the past, I tried to do it with self-control. I believed I was strong enough to do it on my own. It did not help because I failed to address any of the real issues that made me feel the need to start using drugs and, furthermore, those issues that triggered me to use drugs. The self-control method became a temporary band-aid to my addiction problem and only lasted a limited amount of time before my addiction would take control again. I remember feeling frustrated many times, and I thought I was a failure who would hopelessly use drugs to cope for the rest of my life. Everything changed, however, the moment I created my Relapse Prevention Plan And held it in my hands for the first time. For once, I felt like I had power over my addiction, and that I was in control of my life rather than out of control.

The information presented in A Guide to Relapse Prevention for Prisoners is a must-have for any prisoner, in any state, who wants the same control in their life and over their addiction. It is for any prisoner who finds themselves confronted with being the best candidate for parole before a Parole Board, and who believes in giving themselves every opportunity to succeed while on parole. Every prisoner will learn to identify and address issues that have caused them to become addicted, and move them towards responsibility and accountability by guiding the prisoner through the process of preparing and quality and comprehensive Relapse Prevention Plan.
With a Relapse Prevention in place, every prisoner will find themselves on a path to successfully re-enter into mainstream society where they can reunite with family and become productive citizens.

Author Charles Howard Hottinger Jr is a life-term prisoner and former addict who has dedicated his life to helping other prisoners change their way of thinking and remain abstinent.
To order "A Guide To Relapse Prevention for Prisoners" send $15.00 plus $5 for s/h to:
The Cell Block; PO Box 1025; Rancho Cordova, CA 95741

# PRISONER SERVICE ANNOUNCEMENT

## BY MIKE ENEMIGO

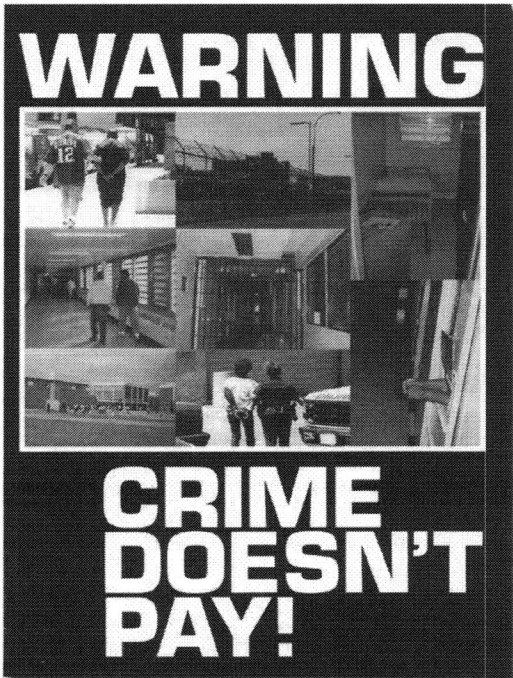

**WARNING**

**CRIME DOESN'T PAY!**

Crime is played out. Straight up. I don't say this to appeal to some moral compus; that is not my argument here. I say it's played out because it's simply not strategically intelligent under today's circumstances. Not only is the risk huge, as *you* know, and the loss almost 100% of the time outweighs the gain, but because with today's technology and resources, it's not even necessary. For example, I've been locked up since February 1999. When I was out, I was hustlin' and takin' chances to pay for studio time, which was hard to come by then. Now you can pretty much make your own studio with a computer, a mic, and a few programs, some of which you can get free on line. Last I was out, not a lot of folks had cell phones. Now, everyone, including kids, has them. The Internet? I had none of that. No social Media, nothin'. So for these reasons (lack of opportunity), I chose to invest my time and energy into illicit activity for cash. But now? All of the things I just mentioned (and more!) exist, and it's changed the game. Over the years I've learned many, many ways *anyone* can make money with what has become today's "basics" (Internet, social media, smartphone, etc.). Problem is, I think, is that most folks have come accustomed to having such resources that they are not able to see the tremendous advantages they provide. Not only do they take things for granted, they've gotten lazy. I, on the other hand, see clearly the opportunities that exist; and I must admit, a large part of this is probably due to my having to exercise certain muscles in my brain that build resourcefulness, as thinking outside the box in order to make something out of nothing has been necessary for my survival. I take nothing for granted. For these reasons and more, it has become my passion to learn how to hustle and win legally, to learn how I would *ball* if I were to ever be let out of prison, and without doing anything that would land me back in the devil's playground, and not only learn it, but to share it all through my new project called TCB University. TCBUniversity is where I provide educational information to prisoners and street hustlers to learn how to get REAL money, legally, in their quest for wealth, prosperity, and the lavish lifestyle. From A-Z, I can show you how to get A LOT of money, and LEGALLY, so you *remove* the risk from the risk/reward ratio when conducting your money motivated moves. From how to build your business to how to be a more effective boss; from how to get rich selling information to how a *teen* averages $2,800 in monthly profits; from how to get free money via cowdfunding and other ways, to how to get money in your mailbox 365 days a year; I can show you all of this, and much, *much* more. I believe in this *very* passionately. It is the future of hustlin'. And my methods are proven, as much of it, in some shape or form, with maybe just a few tweaks here and there, I am doing from my prison cell, even as I write this "Public Service Announcement". And for those of you who are wondering, I am doing very well. I'm making more now than I ever did off any illicit activity; *especially* when you consider the enormous costs I've paid for them. Need further evidence? Look around this book. I'm expanding TCB products and branch offices at a rapid pace. You can do it, too; **I can show you how.** In conclusion, if you're ready to start gettin' REAL money, *legally,* check out my Get Money! and Mailbox Money! packs available through TCB University, distributed exclusively through The Cell Block branch in MA at: The Cell Block; PO Box 595; Seekonk, MA 02771 and start gettin' *yours* TODAY!

# FREE MONEY

Need money for a lawyer, to publish your book, buy art supplies or any other legit project you have going on? Crowdfunding presents opportunities for prisoners!

Kickstarter and other crowdfunding websites provide an interesting option for prisoners with imagination and originality to explore career-expanding opportunities, raise money and gain access to a commodity often in short supply behind bars -- hope.

Basically, crowdfunding involves developing online campaigns for specific projects, charitable causes or services, or to develop certain products. People who want to support a campaign can donate funds, from as little as $1 to as much as they want. Hundreds, thousands or even tens of thousands of people may join together to support and fund a campaign, and once a project achieves its target funding amount the money is paid to the campaign organizer so they can make the project a reality.

Kickstarter, founded in 2009, is a popular crowdfunding site that specializes in entrepreneurial campaigns with an artistic focus, while other sites like GoFundMe, IndieGoGo, Fundly and RocketHub are more flexible. Some sites allow campaigns for legal defense expenses, bail money and prison ministries. Almost all of these services charge fees ranging from around 4 to 9 percent of the money collected during the campaign; some are all-or-nothing, meaning the entire amount of the project must be funded or the campaign is cancelled. Donors retain no equity interest in the funded projects but usually receive recognition or incentives for their contributions.

Modest crowdfunding projects that have been started by or on behalf of prisoners have included a $5,700 campaign to produce "Amazing Grace" by women in a New York prison, $582 to finance a creative writing class at the Garner Correctional Institution in Connecticut and a project to collect art supplies for incarcerated students. Individual prisoners have used crowdfunding to raise money to prove their innocence or to make bond. The success of such campaigns often depends on the ability to tap in to a large network of potential funders who might be interested in the project.

Since March 2014, the Cook County Jail has run a 10-week culinary program involving a small group of prisoners to help them learn marketable skills and obtain jobs in the food service industry upon their release. Chef Bruno Abate, an Italian native who runs the program, called "Recipe for Change," became inspired after learning about an award-winning bakery at the Due Palazzi prison in Padua, Italy. In May 2015, Abate wanted to take the culinary program to the next level.

"When you know how to make pizza well, you can find a job anywhere," he said. Abate joined forces with prominent businessman Ronald Gidwitz to buy a pizza oven for the program. They raised almost $5,000 through an IndieGoGo campaign and another $11,000 through Gadwitz's personal network, and were able to buy a top-of-the-line oven. They hope to eventually bake and sell pizzas to hungry customers outside the jail.

Innocence projects and prisoners' rights organizations have used crowdfunding for a variety of causes, too. The Human Rights Defense Center, PLN's parent non-profit organization, launched a successful campaign through IndieGoGo that raised around $15,000 for the Prison Ecology Project to fight toxic prisons.

Claudia Whitman with CURE's National Death Raw Assistance Network raised $2,600 through IndieGoGo to help fund a wrongful conviction investigation on behalf of Michigan prisoner Lacino Hamilton.

Many prisons and jails have institutional rules that make crowdfunding projects difficult if not impossible. Some have regulations that prevent prisoners from receiving funds from other prisoners, parolees or individuals not related to them. Others prohibit prisoners from having checking or savings accounts, and deduct expenses for the cost of incarceration from money placed in their prison trust accounts. Therefore, crowdfunding campaigns for prisoners and prison-related projects are usually organized and run by friends, family members of other contacts outside of prison.

While many prisoners have an entrepreneurial spirit, it generally goes unrewarded; creative outlets such as writing books, producing songs and creating artwork are not only discouraged but sometimes purposely impeded by corrections officials. Such Limitations, often justified by rote references to "institutional security," but in reality implemented by unimaginative and sometimes hostile guards and prison administrators, do little to assist with prisoners' rehabilitation.

The global economy is a digital economy that is ruled by computers, smart phones and Internet-savvy businesses, which are anathema to prison and jail officials who largely operate in the analog era. Although prisoners are increasingly being allowed to use secure, monitored email systems, such as Corrlinks in federal prisons, the vast majority do not have access to the Internet -- even though computer and online skills are a perquisite for most living wage jobs in the non-prison economy.

Projects such as those funded by Kickstarter and similar sites would be a welcome alternative to many prisoners, who would be encouraged to think in a positive, creative and thoughtful manner about how to successfully pursue funding campaigns for their projects, products and services -- a skill that would serve them well after they are released. Such endeavors should be encouraged, and prisoners with initiative should be given the resources and opportunities to either succeed or fail based upon their own originality, ideas and drive. Instead of fearing change our nation's corrections system needs to embrace it, taking advantage of all the Internet has to offer instead of viewing technology as an inherent threat. By devoting resources to online education, job training and business opportunities, including crowdfunding campaigns -- all available with a few keystrokes at often minimal cost -- prisoners could spend their time engaging in worthwhile and positive projects to help them prepare for their eventual release.

Sources: Derek Gilina for PLN, kickstarter.com, forbes.com, notimpossiblenow.com, rebelnews.com, dnainfo.com

**For more information on raising money for your idea or project, be sure to check out 8 Crowdfunding Secrets of the Successful, Understanding the Psychology of Investors and other fundraising reports available from TCB University!**

# PRI$ONER $UCCE$$ $TORY!

## Popular New Snack Born Behind Bars

In 2009, Seth Sundberg was sentenced to five years for a fraudulent $5 million tax refund. The former pro basketball player had managed a California mortgage office and went from a comfortable living in the real estate industry to earning $5.25 a month in a prison kitchen. While working in that position, Sundberg noticed a label on a box of frozen chicken that said "Not for Human Consumption."

That discovery led him to swear off prison poultry forever. He began to look for nutritious, protein-rich foods in the commissary to supplement the subpar institutional meals. He developed a recipe with another prisoner using trail mix, oatmeal, peanut butter and honey that merged to form a tasty, satisfying granola bar. Soon Sundberg and his partner were making about $200 a month selling the bars to other prisoners.

Upon his release, Sundberg sought help from a nonprofit whose motto is "transform your hustle." Defy Ventures offered him mentorship, business training and a small amount of funding; a year later, Sundberg launched a company called Prison Bars.

Prison Bars now uses organic, non-GMO and gluten-free ingredients in its "criminally delicious" snacks. The company markets and distributes the bars online and in the San Francisco area; it currently employees six people -- four of them formerly incarcerated. Sundberg is planning to expand into ten other cities with representatives who have left prison and face an adversarial job market. Prison Bars has also partnered with the grocery store chain Bi-Rite, which will start carrying the granola bars in September 2016.

"Everyone's made mistakes, and everyone's been given a second chance at some point," Sundberg said. "My vision was to see if people incarnated about this topic, to start having conversations that raise awareness. You never know what kind of ripple effect that can cause." According to the Prison Bars website (www.prison-bars.com), "Each purchase of criminally delicious Prison Bars supports our movement to provide redemption and second chances, reduce recidivism, and raise awareness of America's prison issues."

As a huge supporter of one turning his negative into a positive, cellpreneurship/entrepreneurship, and learning how to hustle and win legally, I respect what Mr. Sundberg has managed to accomplish and I find it inspiring. Not only did he create something that allowed him to make a few bucks while in prison, but he was able to take it to the next level when he was released from prison and turn it into an entire business. And it all started from an idea he had when doing something as common as working in the prison's kitchen! Many of you are creative. Keep your eyes and mind open at all times. Mr. Sundberg's accomplishment is the epitome of one turning his negative into a positive, what I often refer to as "pimping your time." You, too, can do it! Looking for money-making opportunities, ideas and hustles you can turn into the next big thing? Check out the courses and reports I offer from TCB University and get your creative juices flowing NOW! Mike

# THE CELL BLOCK Presents

# TCB UNIVERSITY

## SELF-EDUCATE. GET RICH. ENJOY LIFE.

TCB University provides educational information to prisoners and street hustlers to learn how to get money and win legally in their quest for wealth and prosperity.

## HOW TO GET MONEY & WIN LEGALLY...

### GET MONEY! PACK 1, $10

- 5 Steps to Starting your Own Business, Even from a Prison Cell!
- 5 Common Launch Errors you MUST Avoid!
- 6 Tips to Rev up your Company this Year!
- You MUST Read this to Improve your Business Success!
- How to Legally Protect your Assets Once and for All!
- Best Advice from 15 Self-Made Millionaires!
- The 6 Entrepreneurial Profiles: Which One Are You?!

### GET MONEY! PACK 2, $10

- BO$$ Status: A Guide to Entrepreneurial Leadership!
- BO$$ Status: How to Build your Team!
- BO$$ Status: How to Encourage your Team!
- BO$$ Status: How to be a Better Boss!
- BO$$ Status: 3 Easy Steps to Better Leadership!
- BO$$ Status: Focus on the Vision!

### GET MONEY! PACK 3, $10

- How one Guy Made $20 Million in Under a Year...and YOU Can, TOO!
- How a TEEN Averages $2,800 in Monthly Profits!
- How to Make Money Doing Internet Searches for Inmates!
- How to get Rich Selling Non-Nude Photos!
- How to Start an Independent Record Label in 9 Steps!

### GET MONEY! PACK 4, $10

- 7 Secrets of Book-Selling Success!
- How to get Rich Publishing Material you get FREE!
- How to Sell your Own Subscription Newsletter for HUGE Profits!

### GET MONEY! PACK 5, $10

- How to get Rich Selling Information!
- Get Rich Selling Real Estate ... that you don't Own!
- How a TEEN has Made OVER $80,000!

### GET MONEY! PACK 6, $10

- 10 EASY Ways to Build your Social Media Following!
- How to Find your Audience on Social Media!
- How to Build a Facebook Page for your Small Business!
- Twitter Tips for your Business!
- 12 Ways to Increase Sales with Social Media!
- Advanced Social Media Tips and Tricks!

### GET MONEY! PACK 7, $10

- Successful Promotional Letters and Marketing!
- How to Maximize Marketing Dollars!
- Change how you Think About Marketing: Go Inbound!
- The 7 Steps of Effective Product Development!
- How one Company Turned their Mission Statement into BIG Bucks!
- Your Brand IS your Story!

GET MONEY!

### GET MONEY! PACK 8, $10

- 5 Steps to Owning your Story!
- Scared Money Don't Make Money!
- Mind-Reading Marketing Secrets!
- How to Promote ANY Offer Successfully!
- Your Company Message: 4 Secrets to Help you Communicate with Clarity!

### GET MONEY! PACK 9, $10

- Self-Published Authors are Hitting it BIG with E-Books
- Writer Finds Runway Success with Self-Published E-Books!
- A Guide to Creative Writing!

### GET MONEY! PACK 10, $10

- Writing and Publishing from a Cell!
- New Tools Make Self-Publishing E-Books Easier!
- Direct Mail Book Selling Secrets!

### GET MONEY! PACK 11, $10

- Writing and Self-Publishing Successfully!
- 9 Author Marketing Tips for the Digital Age!
- How to get Started Writing your Urban Novel in just 10 Days

### GET MONEY! PACK 12, $20

- Online Goldmines: Turn your Smartphone or Computer into a Money Machine!
- 8 Crowdfunding Secrets of the Successful!
- Get Rich Click: Start your E-Business Right NOW!
- Downloadable Dollars: 5 SIMPLE Ways to Make Cash on your Computer!
- How to Drive Customers to your Website!
- 7 EASY Ways to Make Money from Home!
- Secrets of the Richest People!

### GET MONEY! PACK 13, $20

- How to Hustle from Home!
- How to Save $1,000 while Living Paycheck to Paycheck!
- FREE Money from the Bank!
- Where to get Money for your Start-Up Business!
- Understanding the Psychology of Investors!
- 5 Tips to Make your Business Fundable!

## HOW TO GET MAILBOX MONEY...

### MAILBOX MONEY! PACK 1, $7

- How to Get the Most from Your Reports!
- How to Make $1,000 Profit with 1,000-name Mailing List!
- The Amazing Power of Premium!
- How to get FREE Mailing Lists, Stamps, and Envelopes!
- Customer Service Tips for Mail Order!

### MAILBOX MONEY! PACK 2, $7

- The Big Money Secrets to Selling Books by Mail!
- How to Start a Mail Order Business on a Shoestring!
- How to get Orders in your Mailbox 365 Days a Year!
- Ad Designing Tips!
- Avoiding Mail Order Mistakes!
- How to Publish your Own Ad Sheet for Big, BIG Profits!

### MAILBOX MONEY! PACK 3, $7

- 5 Things you Must do to be Successful in Mail Order!
- Mail Order's Rule to Real Estate's "Location, Location, Location"!
- Why you SHOULD Publish your Own Newsletter!
- What REALLY Sells in Mail Order Magazines!

### MAILBOX MONEY: PACK 4, $7

- Make a Fortune Marketing Reports!
- 10 Crucial Steps to Mail Order Success!
- Advertising Secrets for Mail Order Selling!
- Start your Own Ad Sheet Business!

### MAILBOX MONEY: PACK 5, $7

- How to get LOTS of $2 Orders in your Mailbox!
- How to Write Classified Ads that get Orders!
- Marketing is the "Key" to Mail Order!
- 80 Tips to Improve your Direct Mail Response!

### MAILBOX MONEY: PACK 6, $7

- How to get Rich by Mail!
- Mail-Order Networking Secrets!
- How to get FREE Postage, Stamps and More!

## HOW TO SURVIVE PRISON...

Paroling from Prison (My 2¢), $3
Mental Health, $3
Surviving the Hole: The Secrets, $4
Surviving a Celly, $4
Social Game: The Strategies, $4
How to Benefit From your Prison Time, $4
Pen Pal Website: The Secrets, $5
Working Out: The Secrets, $5
Letter Writing Like A Pro!, $6

To order, simply send the name of the pack(s) you want written clearly on a piece of paper, enclose the proper payment in the form of a money order or institutional check, and send to:

**The Cell Block, Dept: TCBU;**
**PO Box 595, Seekonk, MA 02771**

# SOCIAL NETWORKING
## Start and Manage Your Social Media Site Today!

**ITEM #016 - Print Facebook Friend list pages!**
Color $ 1.50 per page / Black and White $1.00 per page (plus tax; shipping and handling) Have your entire Facebook friend list printed in color or black/white and mailed directly to you. Users of this service must first add info@inmatephotoprovider.com to your corrlinks.com account. An email must be sent providing the Facebook Username, Password, and if the order preference is color or black and white. Once I.P.P. is able to login; the total pages will be counted and an email will be provided detailing the total cost of the order. I.P.P. will not print any pages until payment has been received in full. It takes 2 to 3 business days for print receipts, based on institution location.

**Photo Prints:** Once the I.P.P. email address has been added to the corrlinks.com account and an email has been provided detailing the Username and password to access the Facebook page, photos of family/friends from your page and/or from photo album folders can be printed. In order to print photos nom photo albums, provide the individual s first/last name and/or the photo album name to print from. Include the total number of copies of each photo. All orders will be processed at the standard 4x6 size, price and shipping rate listed on the I.P .P. order form. Orders will be received within 2 to 3 business days, dependent on institution location. All Local or State inmates who do not have email access are required to physically write I.P.P. all appropriate information, listed above, in order to take advantage of this service.

**ITEM #017 - Set-up a Dating/Social Networking page................... $15 per account (Flat Fee)**
I.P.P. will set up a dating/social networking page on the most popular sites around. Examples include websites such as Facebook, Tagg, Instagram, POF (plenty of fish) or any FREE site. Provide I.P.P. with site(s) and your bio and photo(s) will be uploaded to the site(s). To take advantage of this service you must-first add info@inmatephotoprovider.com to your corrlinks.com account. Afterwards, mail I.P.P. (1) profile page photo, (3) additional pictures to have added to your page during the set-up phase and a typed or neatly handwritten Bio of up to 200 words. If a general profile description page is provided, I.P.P. will update the information within the space provided on each page. Accounts will be created within 24-hours
once payment is received in full. Please allow 2 to 3 business days for receipt of your profile page information, dependent on institution location. An email with the username and password will be provided. In addition, a copy of profile pages with original photos will be provided by mail. All Local and State inmates who do not have email access contact I.P.P. by mail in order to get connected to an online world of male/female singles.

**ITEM #018 - Add and Upload Photos to all social media pages $7.50 (Flat Fee)**
Email I.P.P. your user name and password or physically mail in your requests in order to take advantage of this service. (10-photo limit)

**ITEM #019 - Social Media Monitoring Service (prices vary)**
Accounts/pages must be previously created and ACTIVE in order for I.P.P. to manage/monitor each of the accounts. Four (4) monitoring options are offered at this time. With each option, provide the actual website(s) address, email user name and account password. Once I.P.P. is able to gain access and payment is received in full the monitoring service will begin. Socialmedia@inmatephotoprovider.com must be added directly to an inmates corrlinks email account. All State and Local inmates without email accounts can write I.P.P. at the company address to take advantage of this monitoring service.

**\*GENERAL SERVICE PACKAGE: $21 per month!**
From Monday-Sunday I.P.P. will monitor one (1) social media page. Tax and S/H is included. What better way to spend $.70 a day for 30 days? Quality service is guaranteed and $21 is all you pay! No 24/7 monitoring however messages will be received daily. Send UNLIMITED inbox messages to friends/family daily. Receive all responses sent from your friends/family daily. (No maximum number of messages) Print received friend's photos. (Use regular photo; copying rates.) Create new photo albums and upload additional .photos.to social media website page(s). (Use the regular advertised rate.) NO WALLPOST are allowed with this package. NO FRIEND search requests are allowed with this package. Friend list color print outs are not included with this package. Friend photos are not included with this package.

**BASIC SERVICE FEES:** Less than $35 per month!

For only $1.15 a day (30 day timeframe), I.P.P. will monitor one (1) social media page from Monday- Sunday. *Total price of $34.45, Tax and S/H included in total pricing.

- Receive around the clock page monitoring ALL DAY.
- Send unlimited inbox messages to friends/family daily.
- Receive inbox messages from friends/family daily.
- Search up to three (3) people per week. Full name, city and state MUST be provided.
- Update page status/wallpost once per week.

**GOLD SERVICE FEES:** Less than $60 per month!

30 days of quality guaranteed 24/7 service of one (1) social media page at only $1.86 a day! (Total price of $55.75. All fees included.)

- Receive one (1) color copy of the account's friends. (Mailed to address provided. Will not email.)
- Update page status/wall post daily.
- Send unlimited inbox messages to friends/family daily.
- Receive inbox messages from friends/family daily.
- Search up to five (5) people per week. Full name, city and state MUST be provided.

**PLATINUM SERVICE FEES:** Approximately $100 for a three (3) month package!

90 days of uninterrupted service for $109.00 (all fees included). Only $1.22 a day for three (3) months to have I.P.P. manage/monitor up to three (3) social media pages of your choice 24/7, seven days a week. Quality Service GUARANTEED!

- Receive one (1) color copy of your friend list from each website page.
- Receive messages 24/7, seven days a week as received on ALL SITES.
- Receive weekly wallpost responses and pictures of senders in the mail.
- Upload ten (10) new photos to each page per month.
- Send unlimited inbox messages to friends/family on all sites.
- Receive daily messages from all sites daily.
- Update page status/wallpost daily on all sites.
- Search up to ten (10) people a week. Full name, city and state MUST be provided.
- Change page profile pictures for FREE as desired.

**EXCLUSIVE VIP SERVICE FEES:** $163 for a six (6) month package!

For $.90 a day (6 month timeframe) I.P.P. will maintain, manage and monitor up to five (5) social media pages 24/7 for seven (7) days a week. That's 180 days of service for $162.25 with all fees included! Quality Service GUARANTEED!

- Receive one (1) color copy of your friend list once every two (2) months (ALL sites).
- Receive messages 24/7, seven (7) days a week as received on ALL sites.
- Print up to three (3) 4x6 size friend photos per month. Additional photo copies at standard rates.
- Upload fifteen (15) new photos to each page per month.
- Create new photo albums as desired.
- Send unlimited inbox messages to friends/family on all sites.
- Receive daily messages from all sites daily.
- Update page status/wall post daily on all sites.
- Search up to fifteen (15) people a week. Full name, city and state MUST be provided.
- Update bio, page profile information and change page profile pictures once a month.

Mail All Payments To:  Institutional Checks ; IPP Company
P.O. Box 2451
Forrest City AR, 72336

For Faster Service Send Money Gram Payments To:
Richardett Edwards
Email address:.Jonese531@yahoo.comj
P.O. Box 2451
Forrest City, AR 72336

When sending payment always click yes when it ask about the address you are sending funds to. Due to you sending funds to an unlisted street address your system will ask you if you're sure you would like to proceed. Clicks and we will load your account and start your service.

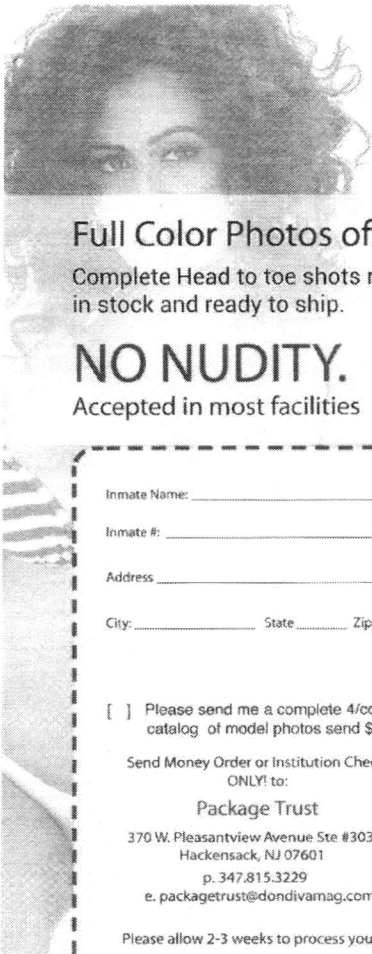

# PACKAGETRUST

POWERED BY DON DIVA

## Full Color Photos of Sexy Woman

Complete Head to toe shots real photo processing in stock and ready to ship.

## NO NUDITY. $1 PER PHOTO

Accepted in most facilities

### Photo Duplication

$1.00 | 4 x 6 print

$5.00 | 5 x 7 print

$10.00 | 8 x 10 print

### People Search

$5.00

Are you looking for a Person or information on a business? We can do the research for you.

- Full Name
- Aliases
- Address
- Age & DOB
- Aliases
- Phone Number
- Relatives
- Address History
- Social Network
- Email Address
- Property Owned
- Relatives
- Employer
- Education

### Background Search

$40.00 | Need a background check on someone? We will search criminal records in 43 states.

### Internet Research

$20.00 per hour | We will provide you with thorough research from credible and relevant sources. We will research any subject you request and send you print outs of all information found.

---

Inmate Name: _____

Inmate #: _____

Address _____

City: _____ State _____ Zip _____

[ ] Please send me a complete 4/color catalog of model photos send $7.00.

Send Money Order or Institution Check ONLY! to:

**Package Trust**

370 W. Pleasantview Avenue Ste #303
Hackensack, NJ 07601
p. 347.815.3229
e. packagetrust@dondivamag.com

Please allow 2-3 weeks to process your order

* Please label all photos clearly

* Photo specialist will provide minor color correction as a courtesy only

* Oddly sized photos will need to be resized at company discretion

USE ADDITIONAL PAPER IF NEEDED
NO ORDER FORM NECESSARY

### Photo Duplication

Photo 1

_____ 8 x 10 ($10 each) = _____
(Qty)                      (Total)

_____ 8 x 10 ($10 each) = _____
(Qty)                      (Total)

_____ 5 x 7 ($5 each) = _____
(Qty)                    (Total)

_____ 5 x 7 ($5 each) = _____
(Qty)                    (Total)

_____ 4 x 6 ($1 each) = _____
(Qty)                    (Total)

_____ 4 x 6 ($1 each) = _____
(Qty)                    (Total)

## NOTE

Please be sure any photo you purchase will be allowed in your facility. Packagetrust is not responsible for any photos that are rejected by any institution for any reason. We will not reship orders rejected by any institution.

## ORDER ANY BOOK OR MAGAZINE

Order our brochure to find out how to order any book or magazine you are looking for- including vintage and out-of-print.

## SEND $7.00 FOR A FULL COLOR CATALOG OF SERVICES AND OVER 500 AVAILABLE SEXY PHOTOS .

# GetSocial!

Finally... real Social Media for inmates and a forum for their loved ones.

Sign up for your own Blog Page!

More than a penpal service- Inmates and their loved ones can post photos, messages, updates and blogs as well as showcase their poetry, novels, and artwork.

### Inmate New Profile

Standard One Year Profile:     $50

Blog (Must have an active profile)     $10

* inmate doesn't need internet access

TO SIGN UP, VISIT DONDIVAMAG.COM OR ORDER OUR CATALOG FOR SIGN UP INSTRUCTIONS.

---

If you would like a return response from Packagetrust, you **MUST** include a **SASE** (self addressed stamped envelope.)

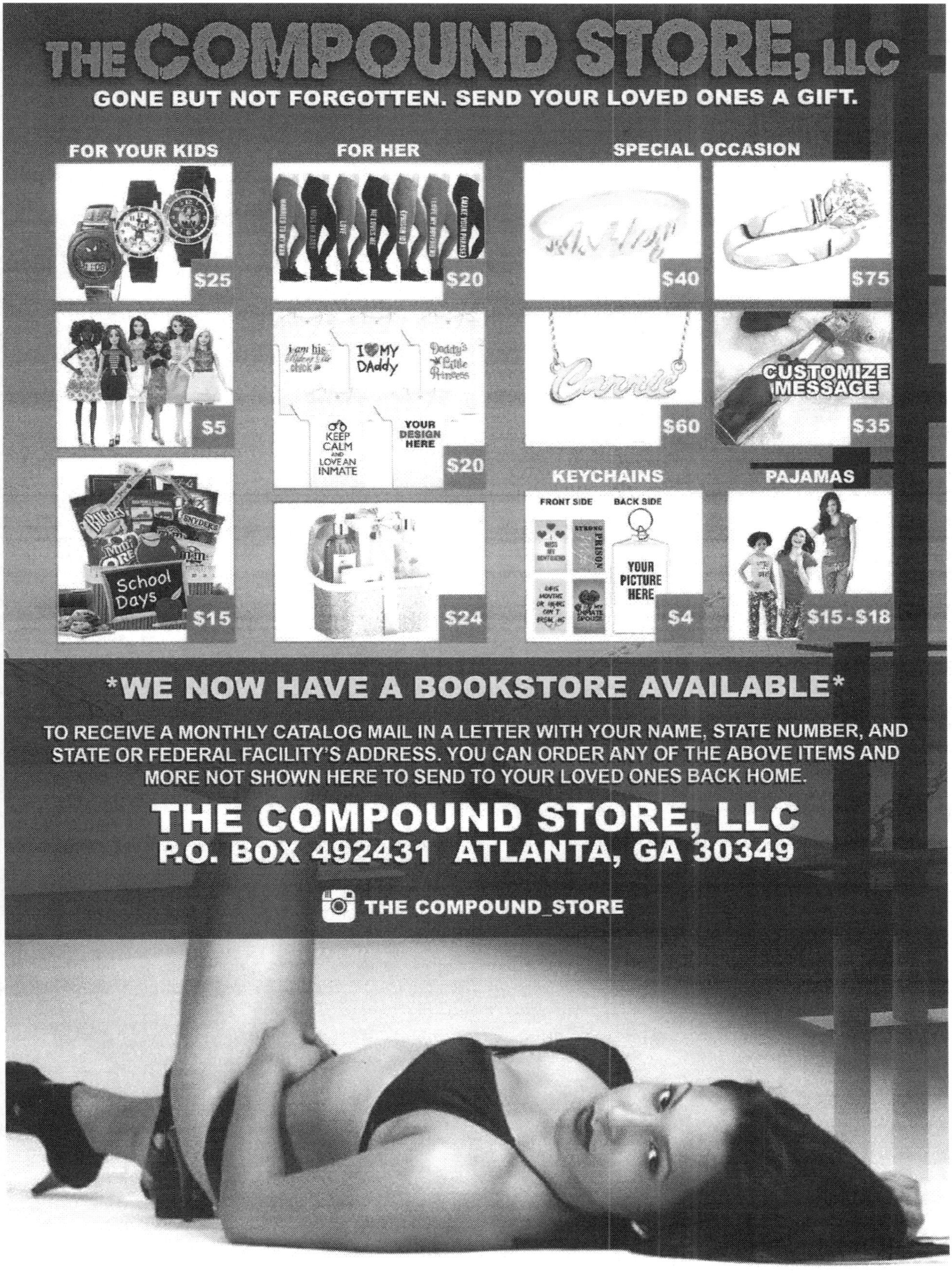
THE COMPOUND STORE, LLC
GONE BUT NOT FORGOTTEN. SEND YOUR LOVED ONES A GIFT.
FOR YOUR KIDS
FOR HER
SPECIAL OCCASION
$25
$20
$40
$75
$5
I ♥ MY DAddy
Daddy's Little Princess
KEEP CALM AND LOVE AN INMATE
YOUR DESIGN HERE
$20
$60
CUSTOMIZE MESSAGE
$35
School Days
$15
$24
KEYCHAINS
FRONT SIDE
BACK SIDE
YOUR PICTURE HERE
$4
PAJAMAS
$15 - $18
*WE NOW HAVE A BOOKSTORE AVAILABLE*
TO RECEIVE A MONTHLY CATALOG MAIL IN A LETTER WITH YOUR NAME, STATE NUMBER, AND STATE OR FEDERAL FACILITY'S ADDRESS. YOU CAN ORDER ANY OF THE ABOVE ITEMS AND MORE NOT SHOWN HERE TO SEND TO YOUR LOVED ONES BACK HOME.
THE COMPOUND STORE, LLC
P.O. BOX 492431 ATLANTA, GA 30349
THE COMPOUND_STORE

AS PAYMENT: WE ACCEPT MONEY ORDERS AND BUSINESS REMITS THAT YOUR INSTITUTION PROVIDES.

# PENACON

www.penacon.com

## Bringing Friendship and Romance to all.

Penacon.com dedicated to assisting the incarcerated community find connections of friendship and romance around the world. Your profile will be listed on our user-friendly website. We make sure your profile is seen at the highest visibility rate available by driving traffic to our site by consistent advertising and networking. We know how important it is to have your ad seen by as many people as possible in order to bring you the best service possible. Pen pals can now email their first message! We print and send these messages with return addresses every two weeks. We value your business and process profiles within two weeks.

**IN BUSINESS SINCE 2009**

### Please Send the Following Information:

1. AD. On a separate sheet of paper, in 250 words or less, describe yourself and the type of person(s) you are interested in.

2. Include the requested information below. DO NOT WRITE ON THIS PAGE.

Name, Address, DOC/Inmate #
Crime for Which Incarcerated: *Failure to submit crime will delay profile processing. Crime will not be posted on the same page as your profile.
Gender: Male OR Female
Ethnic Background: African-American/Black, Caucasian/White, Hispanic, Native American, Asian, Islands, Other
Date of Birth, Height, Weight, Hair Color and Eye Color
Death Row? Yes OR No , Release Date
Sexual Orientation: Straight, Gay, Bisexual
Willing to Write: Anyone, Male, Female, Gay, Straight, Bisexual

**NOW UNDER NEW OWNERSHIP!**
*Freebird Publishers*

3. PHOTO. You may include one photo of yourself at no extra charge. (Ads with photos get more attention). Photos become property of Penacon.com unless a SASE is received or Welcome Package is ordered.

4. PAYMENT. We accept Facility Checks, Money Orders, Personal Checks, E-Checks, Credit/Debit Card, PayPal Payments, MoneyGram and stamps with Pre-approval.

### Please Keep in Mind:

- Type or print your ad in English. If we are unable to read it, we cannot publish it.
- Sexual and explicit language is prohibited and no business may be conducted via your profile.
- Only YOU may be featured in the photo. If someone else is in the photo it cannot be used.
- When you refer a friend who purchases a profile, you will receive an additional two months added to the length of your profile and one month of listing on our featured profile section.
- A "New Member" banner will be displayed beside your profile for the first month of run time.

**Ad Tip:** Describe the type of person you would like to find. Be open about yourself in your ad; share enough information so the reader may connect with you and WANT to write to learn more

### Choose Your Package:
One Year $35
Until Release Date $95
Profile Renewal $25

**HAVE A LOVED ONE SUBMIT YOUR PROFILE ONLINE AND SAVE $5! USE CODE LOVE5**

### Options:
Welcome Package $5
Additional Text (250 words included)
$10/100 words over
Additional Photos (1 photo included)
$5/additional photo
Featured Profile - Prepaid Only
$10/month adds you to featured list

### Mail to:
# PENACON
Box 533
North Dighton, MA 02764
Penacon@freebirdpublishers.com
Corrlinks: diane@freebirdpublishers.com

197

# INCREASE YOUR POWER TODAY!

## ORDER NOW!

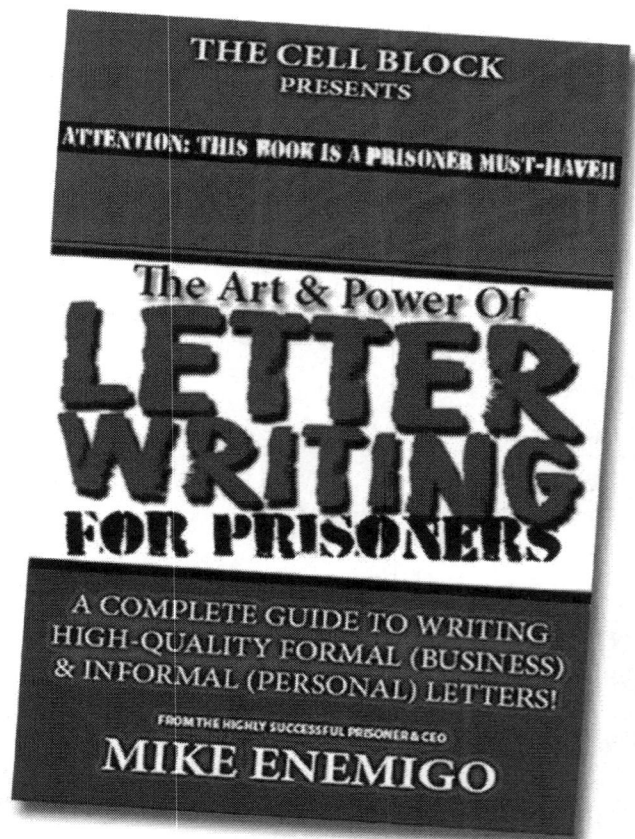

## ONLY $9.99!
### +$4.00 SHIPPING & HANDLING

When locked inside a prison cell, being able to write well is most powerful skill you can have! Learn how to increase your power by writing high-quality personal and formal letters! This book has the secrets, plus includes letter templates, pen-pal website strategies, punctuation guide and more!

*"Letter writing skills are EXTREMELY beneficial to have when doing time in prison, as it will probably be your main source of communication with the outside world. My ability to write well -- be it letters, instructions, etc. -- is how I pull off all that I do from a prison cell. However, I was not born a great writer; it is something I had to take the time out to learn to do. In my new book, The Art & Power of Letter Writing for Prisoners, I share all that I've learned with you so that you, too, may be successful. Take the time out to learn these proven methods. It is the best investment you can make as a prisoner."* -- Mike

**THE CELL BLOCK; PO BOX 1025; RANCHO CORDOVA, CA 95741**

# Postage Rates 2017

- ➢ First Class Letters (1 oz.) rates .49.
  - o Each additional ounce will cost an extra .21

- ➢ First Class Flats/Large Envelopes (1 oz.) rates .94.
  - o Each additional ounce will cost an extra .22
- ➢ Postcard rates $0.34.

First-Class Letters International - 1 oz. $1.15.
- ➢ Priority Mail Express - $40.95 up.
- ➢ Priority Mail - 1 lb. $6.45 and up.

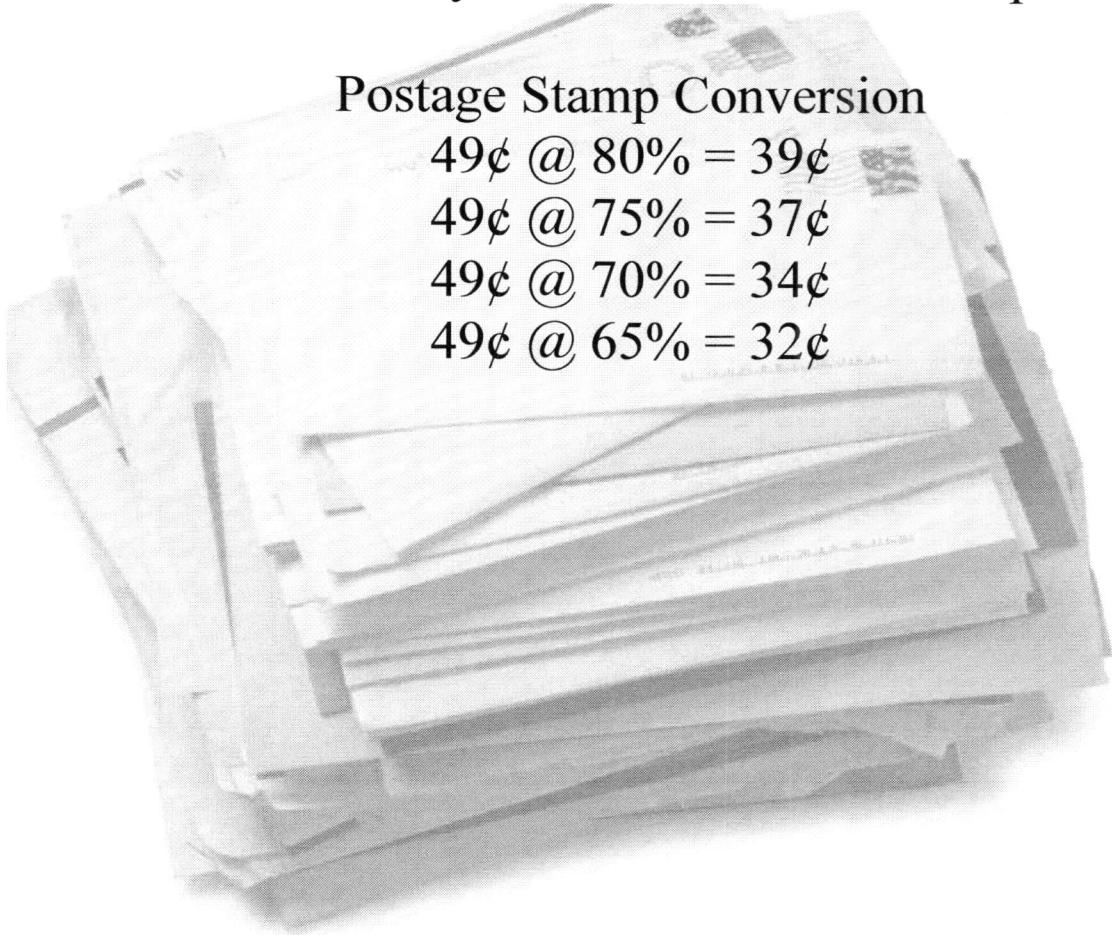

Postage Stamp Conversion
49¢ @ 80% = 39¢
49¢ @ 75% = 37¢
49¢ @ 70% = 34¢
49¢ @ 65% = 32¢

NAME: _____

STREET: _____

CITY: _____

ZIP: _____

PHONE: _____

EMAIL: _____

WEBSITE: _____


NAME: _____

STREET: _____

CITY: _____

ZIP: _____

PHONE: _____

EMAIL: _____

WEBSITE: _____


NAME: _____

STREET: _____

CITY: _____

ZIP: _____

PHONE: _____

EMAIL: _____

WEBSITE: _____


NAME: _____

STREET: _____

CITY: _____

ZIP: _____

PHONE: _____

EMAIL: _____

WEBSITE: _____


NAME: _____

STREET: _____

CITY: _____

ZIP: _____

PHONE: _____

EMAIL: _____

WEBSITE: _____


NAME: _____

STREET: _____

CITY: _____

ZIP: _____

PHONE: _____

EMAIL: _____

WEBSITE: _____


NAME: _____

CITY: _____

ZIP: _____

PHONE: _____

EMAIL: _____

WEBSITE: _____


NAME: _____

STREET: _____

CITY: _____

ZIP: _____

PHONE: _____

EMAIL: _____

WEBSITE: _____


NAME: _____

STREET: _____

CITY: _____

ZIP: _____

PHONE: _____

EMAIL: _____

WEBSITE: _____


NAME: _____

STREET: _____

CITY: _____

ZIP: _____

PHONE: _____

EMAIL: _____

WEBSITE: _____


NAME: _____

STREET: _____

CITY: _____

ZIP: _____

PHONE: _____

EMAIL: _____

WEBSITE: _____


NAME: _____

STREET: _____

CITY: _____

ZIP: _____

PHONE: _____

EMAIL: _____

WEBSITE: _____

NAME: _____
STREET: _____
CITY: _____
ZIP: _____
PHONE: _____
WEBSITE: _____
EMAIL: _____

NAME: _____
STREET: _____
CITY: _____
ZIP: _____
PHONE: _____
EMAIL: _____
WEBSITE: _____

NAME: _____
STREET: _____
CITY: _____
ZIP: _____
PHONE: _____
EMAIL: _____
WEBSITE: _____

NAME: _____
STREET: _____
CITY: _____
ZIP: _____
PHONE: _____
EMAIL: _____
WEBSITE: _____

NAME: _____
STREET: _____
CITY: _____
ZIP: _____
PHONE: _____
EMAIL: _____
WEBSITE: _____

NAME: _____
STREET: _____
CITY: _____
ZIP: _____
PHONE: _____
EMAIL: _____
WEBSITE: _____

NAME: _____
STREET: _____
CITY: _____
ZIP: _____
PHONE: _____
EMAIL: _____
WEBSITE: _____

NAME: _____
STREET: _____
CITY: _____
ZIP: _____
PHONE: _____
EMAIL: _____
WEBSITE: _____

NAME: _____
STREET: _____
CITY: _____
ZIP: _____
PHONE: _____
EMAIL: _____
WEBSITE: _____

NAME: _____
STREET: _____
CITY: _____
ZIP: _____
PHONE: _____
EMAIL: _____
WEBSITE: _____

NAME: _____
STREET: _____
CITY: _____
ZIP: _____
PHONE: _____
EMAIL: _____
WEBSITE: _____

NAME: _____
STREET: _____
CITY: _____
ZIP: _____
PHONE: _____
EMAIL: _____
WEBSITE: _____

NAME: _____     NAME: _____

STREET: _____     STREET: _____

CITY: _____     CITY: _____

ZIP: _____     ZIP: _____

PHONE: _____     PHONE: _____

EMAIL: _____     EMAIL: _____

WEBSITE: _____     WEBSITE: _____


NAME: _____     NAME: _____

STREET: _____     STREET: _____

CITY: _____     CITY: _____

ZIP: _____     ZIP: _____

PHONE: _____     PHONE: _____

EMAIL: _____     EMAIL: _____

WEBSITE: _____     WEBSITE: _____


NAME: _____     NAME: _____

STREET: _____     STREET: _____

CITY: _____     CITY: _____

ZIP: _____     ZIP: _____

PHONE: _____     PHONE: _____

EMAIL: _____     EMAIL: _____

WEBSITE: _____     WEBSITE: _____


NAME: _____     NAME: _____

STREET: _____     STREET: _____

CITY: _____     CITY: _____

ZIP: _____     ZIP: _____

PHONE: _____     PHONE: _____

EMAIL: _____     EMAIL: _____

WEBSITE: _____     WEBSITE: _____ _____


NAME: _____     NAME: _____

STREET: _____     STREET: _____

CITY: _____     CITY: _____

ZIP: _____     ZIP: _____

PHONE: _____     PHONE: _____

EMAIL: _____     EMAIL: _____

WEBSITE: _____     WEBSITE: _____


NAME: _____     NAME: _____

STREET: _____     STREET: _____

CITY: _____     CITY: _____

ZIP: _____     ZIP: _____

PHONE: _____     PHONE: _____

EMAIL: _____     EMAIL: _____

WEBSITE: _____     WEBSITE: _____

NAME: _____          NAME: _____

STREET: _____          STREET: _____

CITY: _____          CITY: _____

ZIP: _____          ZIP: _____

PHONE: _____          PHONE: _____

EMAIL: _____          EMAIL: _____

WEBSITE: _____          WEBSITE: _____


NAME: _____          NAME: _____

STREET: _____          STREET: _____

CITY: _____          CITY: _____

ZIP: _____          ZIP: _____

PHONE: _____          PHONE: _____

EMAIL: _____          EMAIL: _____

WEBSITE: _____          WEBSITE: _____


NAME: _____          NAME: _____

STREET: _____          STREET: _____

CITY: _____          CITY: _____

ZIP: _____          ZIP: _____

PHONE: _____          PHONE: _____

EMAIL: _____          EMAIL: _____

WEBSITE: _____          WEBSITE: _____


NAME: _____          NAME: _____

STREET: _____          STREET: _____

CITY: _____          CITY: _____

ZIP: _____          ZIP: _____

PHONE: _____          PHONE: _____

EMAIL: _____          EMAIL: _____

WEBSITE: _____          WEBSITE: _____


NAME: _____          NAME: _____

STREET: _____          STREET: _____

CITY: _____          CITY: _____

ZIP: _____          ZIP: _____

PHONE: _____          PHONE: _____

EMAIL: _____          EMAIL: _____

WEBSITE: _____          WEBSITE: _____


NAME: _____          NAME: _____

STREET: _____          STREET: _____

CITY: _____          CITY: _____

ZIP: _____          ZIP: _____

PHONE: _____          PHONE: _____

EMAIL: _____          EMAIL: _____

WEBSITE: _____          WEBSITE: _____

NAME: _____
STREET: _____
CITY: _____
ZIP: _____
PHONE: _____
EMAIL: _____
WEBSITE: _____

NAME: _____
STREET: _____
CITY: _____
ZIP: _____
PHONE: _____
EMAIL: _____
WEBSITE: _____

NAME: _____
STREET: _____
CITY: _____
ZIP: _____
PHONE: _____
EMAIL: _____
WEBSITE: _____

NAME: _____
STREET: _____
CITY: _____
ZIP: _____
PHONE: _____
EMAIL: _____
WEBSITE: _____

NAME: _____
STREET: _____
CITY: _____
ZIP: _____
PHONE: _____
EMAIL: _____
WEBSITE: _____

NAME: _____
STREET: _____
CITY: _____
ZIP: _____
PHONE: _____
EMAIL: _____
WEBSITE: _____

NAME: _____
STREET: _____

CITY: _____
ZIP: _____
PHONE: _____
EMAIL: _____
WEBSITE: _____

NAME: _____
STREET: _____
CITY: _____
ZIP: _____
PHONE: _____
EMAIL: _____
WEBSITE: _____

NAME: _____
STREET: _____
CITY: _____
ZIP: _____
PHONE: _____
EMAIL: _____
WEBSITE: _____

NAME: _____
STREET: _____
CITY: _____
ZIP: _____
PHONE: _____
EMAIL: _____
WEBSITE: _____

NAME: _____
STREET: _____
CITY: _____
ZIP: _____
PHONE: _____
EMAIL: _____
WEBSITE: _____

NAME: _____
STREET: _____
CITY: _____
ZIP: _____
PHONE: _____
EMAIL: _____
WEBSITE: _____

NAME: _____

STREET: _____

CITY: _____

ZIP: _____

PHONE: _____

EMAIL: _____

WEBSITE: _____


NAME: _____

STREET: _____

CITY: _____

ZIP: _____

PHONE: _____

EMAIL: _____

WEBSITE: _____


NAME: _____

STREET: _____

CITY: _____

ZIP: _____

PHONE: _____

EMAIL: _____

WEBSITE: _____


NAME: _____

STREET: _____

CITY: _____

ZIP: _____

PHONE: _____

EMAIL: _____

WEBSITE: _____

NAME: _____

STREET: _____

CITY: _____

ZIP: _____

PHONE: _____

EMAIL: _____

WEBSITE: _____


NAME: _____

STREET: _____

CITY: _____

ZIP: _____

PHONE: _____

EMAIL: _____

WEBSITE: _____

NAME: _____


STREET: _____

CITY: _____

ZIP: _____

PHONE: _____

EMAIL: _____

WEBSITE: _____


NAME: _____

STREET: _____

CITY: _____

ZIP: _____

PHONE: _____

EMAIL: _____

WEBSITE: _____


NAME: _____

STREET: _____

CITY: _____

ZIP: _____

PHONE: _____

EMAIL: _____

WEBSITE: _____


NAME: _____

STREET: _____

CITY: _____

ZIP: _____

PHONE: _____

EMAIL: _____

WEBSITE: _____

NAME: _____

STREET: _____

CITY: _____

ZIP: _____

PHONE: _____

EMAIL: _____

WEBSITE: _____


NAME: _____

NAME: _____

STREET: _____

CITY: _____

ZIP: _____

PHONE: _____

EMAIL: _____

WEBSITE: _____

# 2017

|  |  |
|---|---|
| **January** | 01: New Year's Day<br>16: M L King Day |
| **February** | 14: Valentine's Day<br>20: Presidents' Day |
| **March** | |
| **April** | 14: Good Friday<br>16: Easter Sunday |
| **May** | 14: Mother's Day<br>29: Memorial Day |
| **June** | 18: Father's Day |
| **July** | 04: Independence Day |
| **August** | |
| **September** | 04: Labor Day |
| **October** | 09: Columbus Day<br>31: Halloween |
| **November** | 11: Veterans Day<br>23: Thanksgiving Day |
| **December** | 25: Christmas Day |

## January

| S | M | T | W | T | F | S |
|---|---|---|---|---|---|---|
| 1 | 2 | 3 | 4 | 5 | 6 | 7 |
| 8 | 9 | 10 | 11 | 12 | 13 | 14 |
| 15 | 16 | 17 | 18 | 19 | 20 | 21 |
| 22 | 23 | 24 | 25 | 26 | 27 | 28 |
| 29 | 30 | 31 | | | | |

## February

| S | M | T | W | T | F | S |
|---|---|---|---|---|---|---|
| | | | 1 | 2 | 3 | 4 |
| 5 | 6 | 7 | 8 | 9 | 10 | 11 |
| 12 | 13 | 14 | 15 | 16 | 17 | 18 |
| 19 | 20 | 21 | 22 | 23 | 24 | 25 |
| 26 | 27 | 28 | | | | |

## March

| S | M | T | W | T | F | S |
|---|---|---|---|---|---|---|
| | | | 1 | 2 | 3 | 4 |
| 5 | 6 | 7 | 8 | 9 | 10 | 11 |
| 12 | 13 | 14 | 15 | 16 | 17 | 18 |
| 19 | 20 | 21 | 22 | 23 | 24 | 25 |
| 26 | 27 | 28 | 29 | 30 | 31 | |

## April

| S | M | T | W | T | F | S |
|---|---|---|---|---|---|---|
| | | | | | | 1 |
| 2 | 3 | 4 | 5 | 6 | 7 | 8 |
| 9 | 10 | 11 | 12 | 13 | 14 | 15 |
| 16 | 17 | 18 | 19 | 20 | 21 | 22 |
| 23 | 24 | 25 | 26 | 27 | 28 | 29 |
| 30 | | | | | | |

## May

| S | M | T | W | T | F | S |
|---|---|---|---|---|---|---|
| | 1 | 2 | 3 | 4 | 5 | 6 |
| 7 | 8 | 9 | 10 | 11 | 12 | 13 |
| 14 | 15 | 16 | 17 | 18 | 19 | 20 |
| 21 | 22 | 23 | 24 | 25 | 26 | 27 |
| 28 | 29 | 30 | 31 | | | |

## June

| S | M | T | W | T | F | S |
|---|---|---|---|---|---|---|
| | | | | 1 | 2 | 3 |
| 4 | 5 | 6 | 7 | 8 | 9 | 10 |
| 11 | 12 | 13 | 14 | 15 | 16 | 17 |
| 18 | 19 | 20 | 21 | 22 | 23 | 24 |
| 25 | 26 | 27 | 28 | 29 | 30 | |

## July

| S | M | T | W | T | F | S |
|---|---|---|---|---|---|---|
| | | | | | | 1 |
| 2 | 3 | 4 | 5 | 6 | 7 | 8 |
| 9 | 10 | 11 | 12 | 13 | 14 | 15 |
| 16 | 17 | 18 | 19 | 20 | 21 | 22 |
| 23 | 24 | 25 | 26 | 27 | 28 | 29 |
| 30 | 31 | | | | | |

## August

| S | M | T | W | T | F | S |
|---|---|---|---|---|---|---|
| | | 1 | 2 | 3 | 4 | 5 |
| 6 | 7 | 8 | 9 | 10 | 11 | 12 |
| 13 | 14 | 15 | 16 | 17 | 18 | 19 |
| 20 | 21 | 22 | 23 | 24 | 25 | 26 |
| 27 | 28 | 29 | 30 | 31 | | |

## September

| S | M | T | W | T | F | S |
|---|---|---|---|---|---|---|
| | | | | | 1 | 2 |
| 3 | 4 | 5 | 6 | 7 | 8 | 9 |
| 10 | 11 | 12 | 13 | 14 | 15 | 16 |
| 17 | 18 | 19 | 20 | 21 | 22 | 23 |
| 24 | 25 | 26 | 27 | 28 | 29 | 30 |

## October

| S | M | T | W | T | F | S |
|---|---|---|---|---|---|---|
| 1 | 2 | 3 | 4 | 5 | 6 | 7 |
| 8 | 9 | 10 | 11 | 12 | 13 | 14 |
| 15 | 16 | 17 | 18 | 19 | 20 | 21 |
| 22 | 23 | 24 | 25 | 26 | 27 | 28 |
| 29 | 30 | 31 | | | | |

## November

| S | M | T | W | T | F | S |
|---|---|---|---|---|---|---|
| | | | 1 | 2 | 3 | 4 |
| 5 | 6 | 7 | 8 | 9 | 10 | 11 |
| 12 | 13 | 14 | 15 | 16 | 17 | 18 |
| 19 | 20 | 21 | 22 | 23 | 24 | 25 |
| 26 | 27 | 28 | 29 | 30 | | |

## December

| S | M | T | W | T | F | S |
|---|---|---|---|---|---|---|
| | | | | | 1 | 2 |
| 3 | 4 | 5 | 6 | 7 | 8 | 9 |
| 10 | 11 | 12 | 13 | 14 | 15 | 16 |
| 17 | 18 | 19 | 20 | 21 | 22 | 23 |
| 24 | 25 | 26 | 27 | 28 | 29 | 30 |
| 31 | | | | | | |

# MIKE ENEMIGO

Mike Enemigo is the new prison/street art sensation who has written and published several books. He is inspired by emotion; hope, dreams and nightmares. He physically lives somewhere in a California prison cell where he works relentlessly creating his next piece. His mind and soul are elsewhere, seeing, studying, learning and drawing inspiration to tear down suppressive walls and inspire the culture by pushing artistic boundaries.

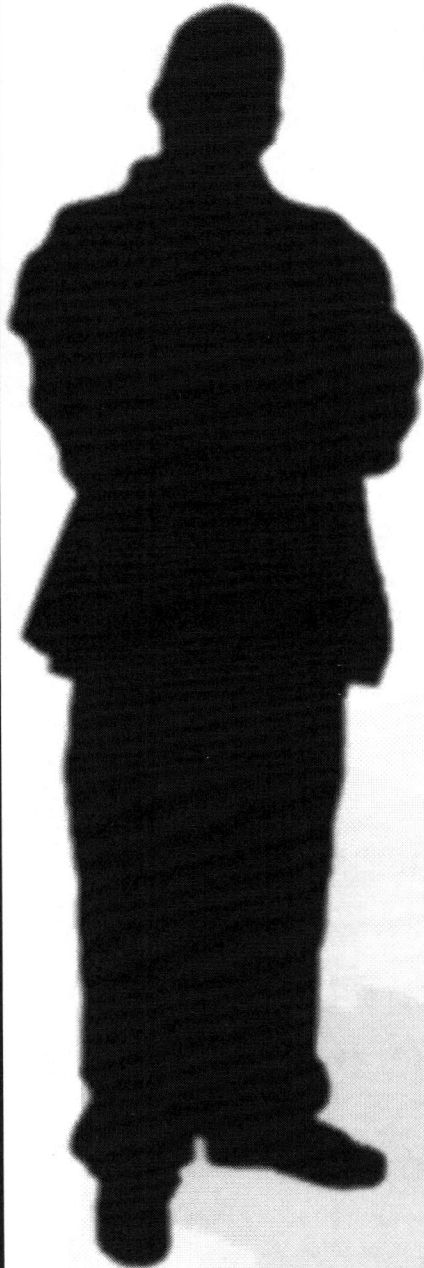

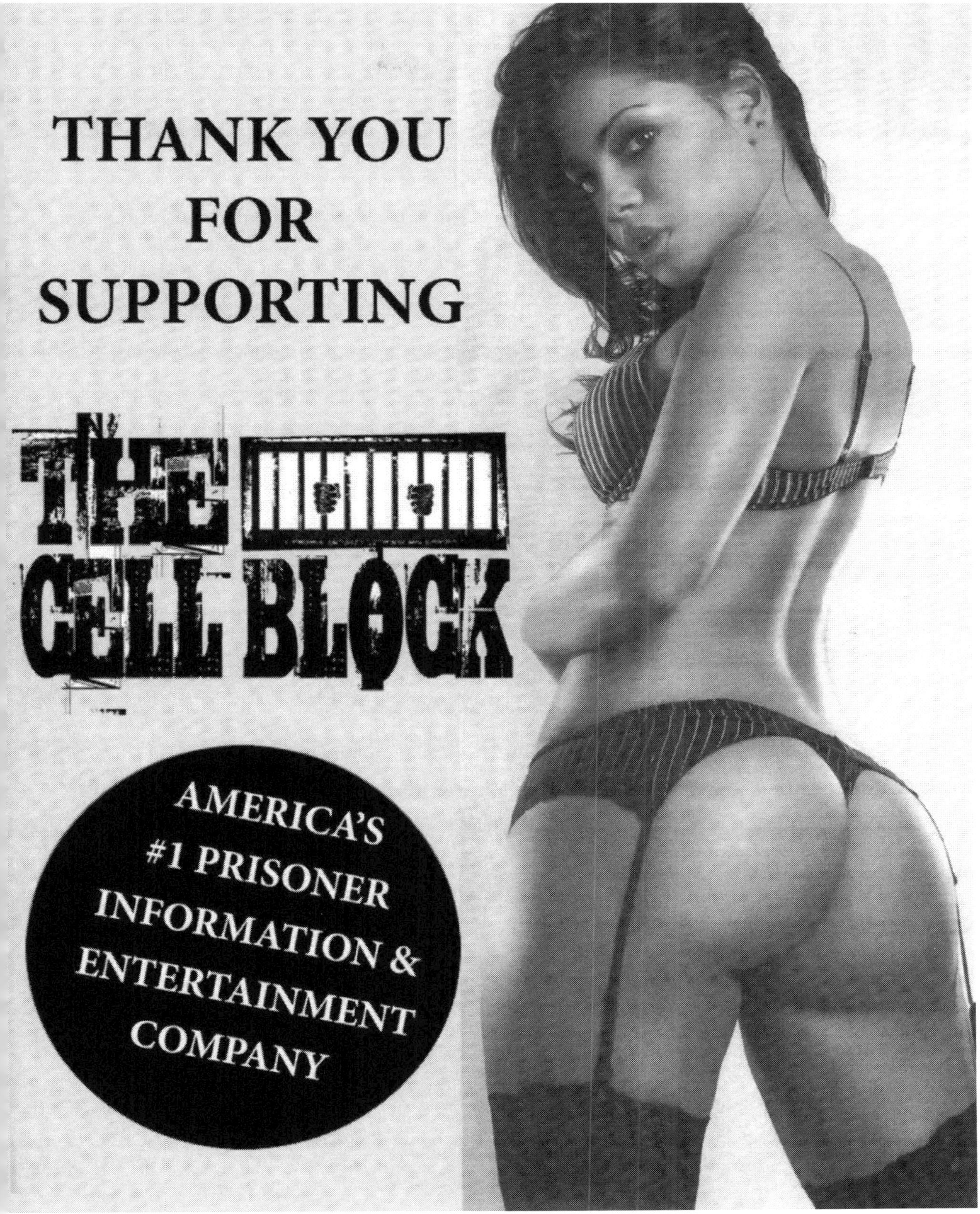
THANK YOU
FOR
SUPPORTING
THE CELL BLOCK
AMERICA'S
#1 PRISONER
INFORMATION &
ENTERTAINMENT
COMPANY

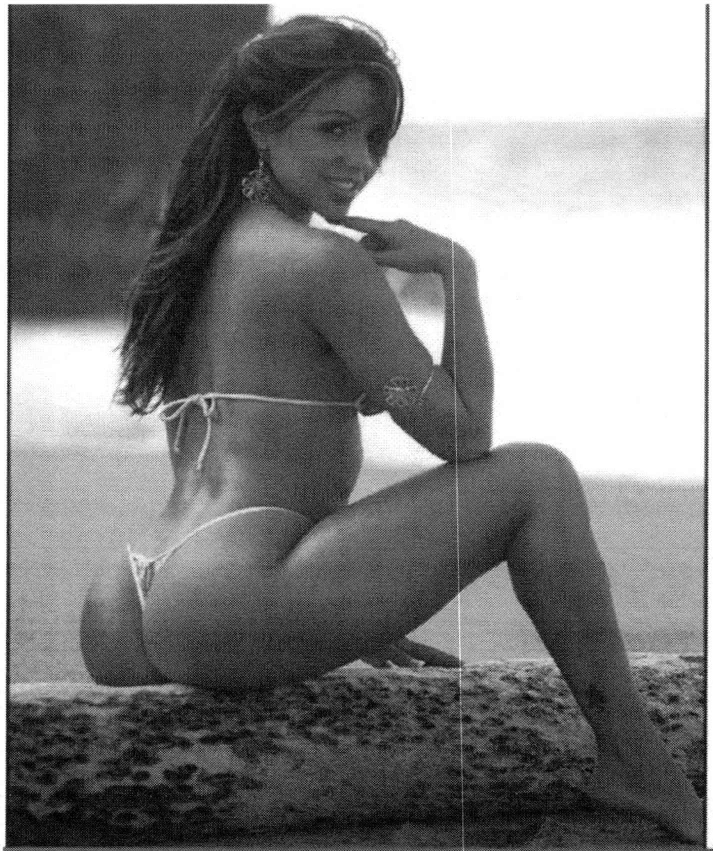
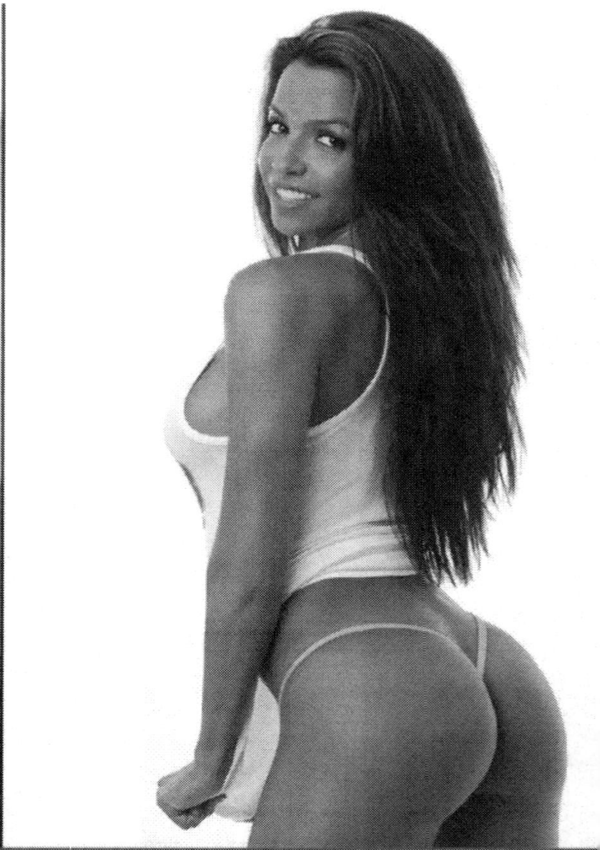
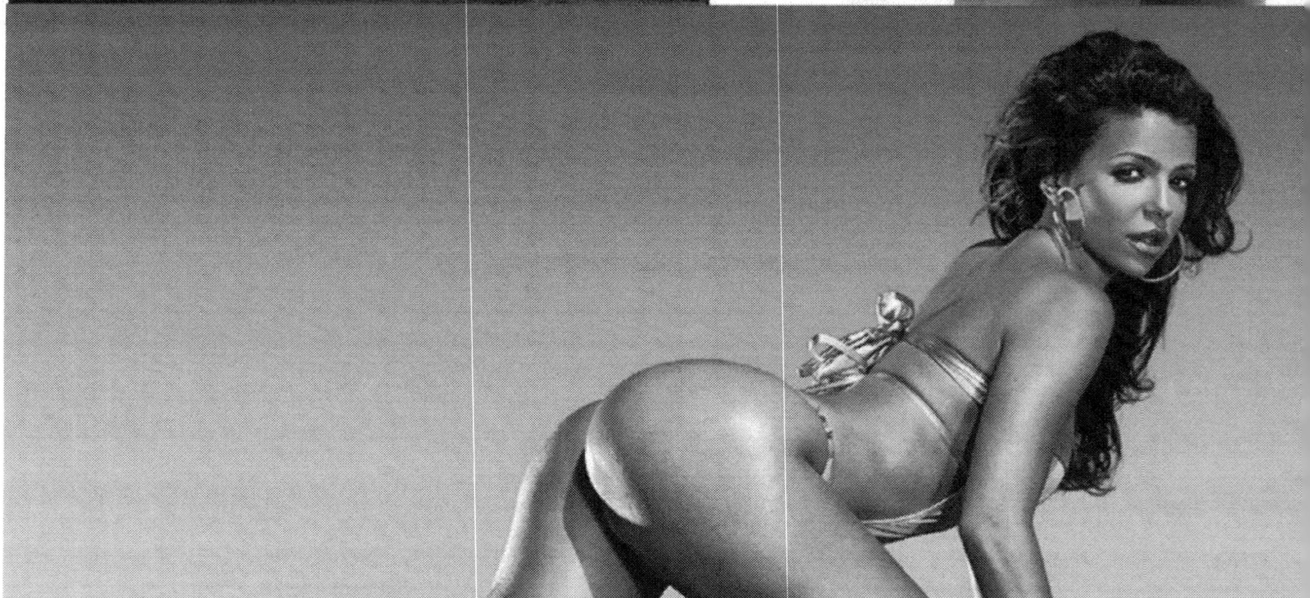

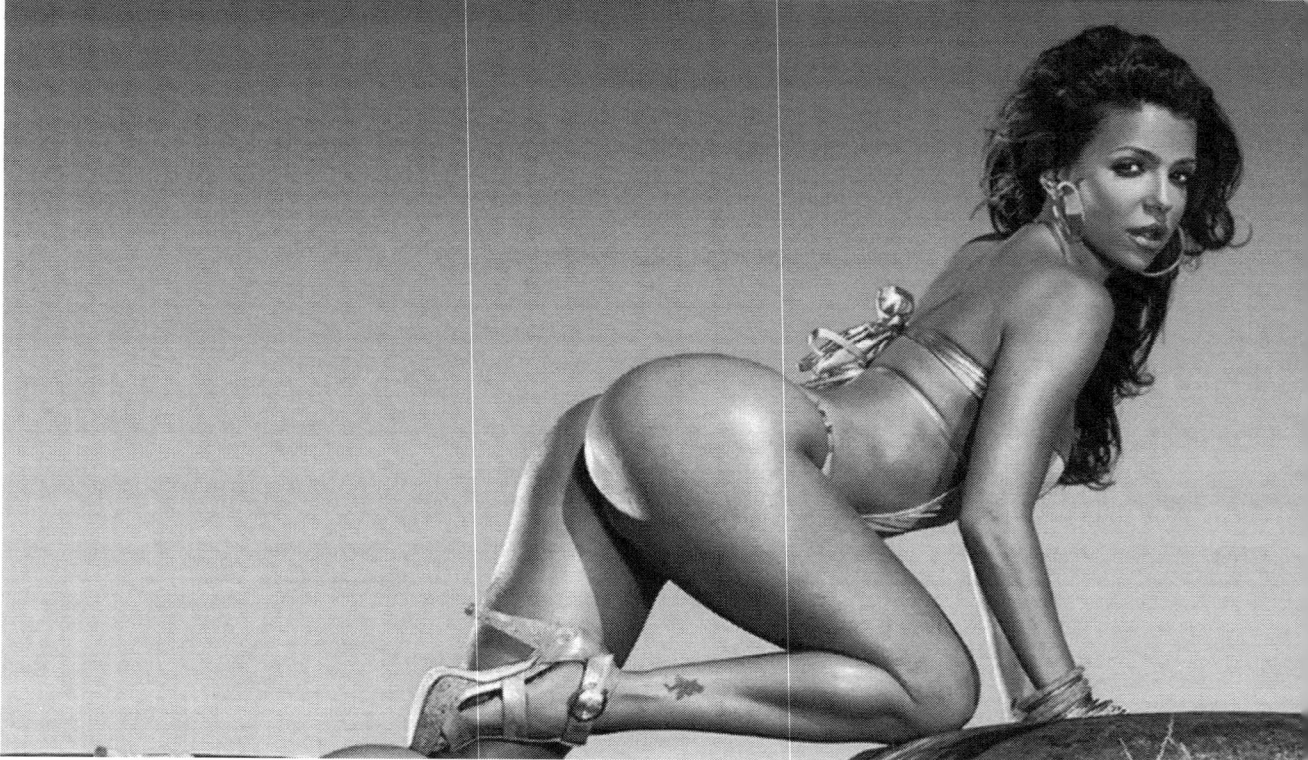

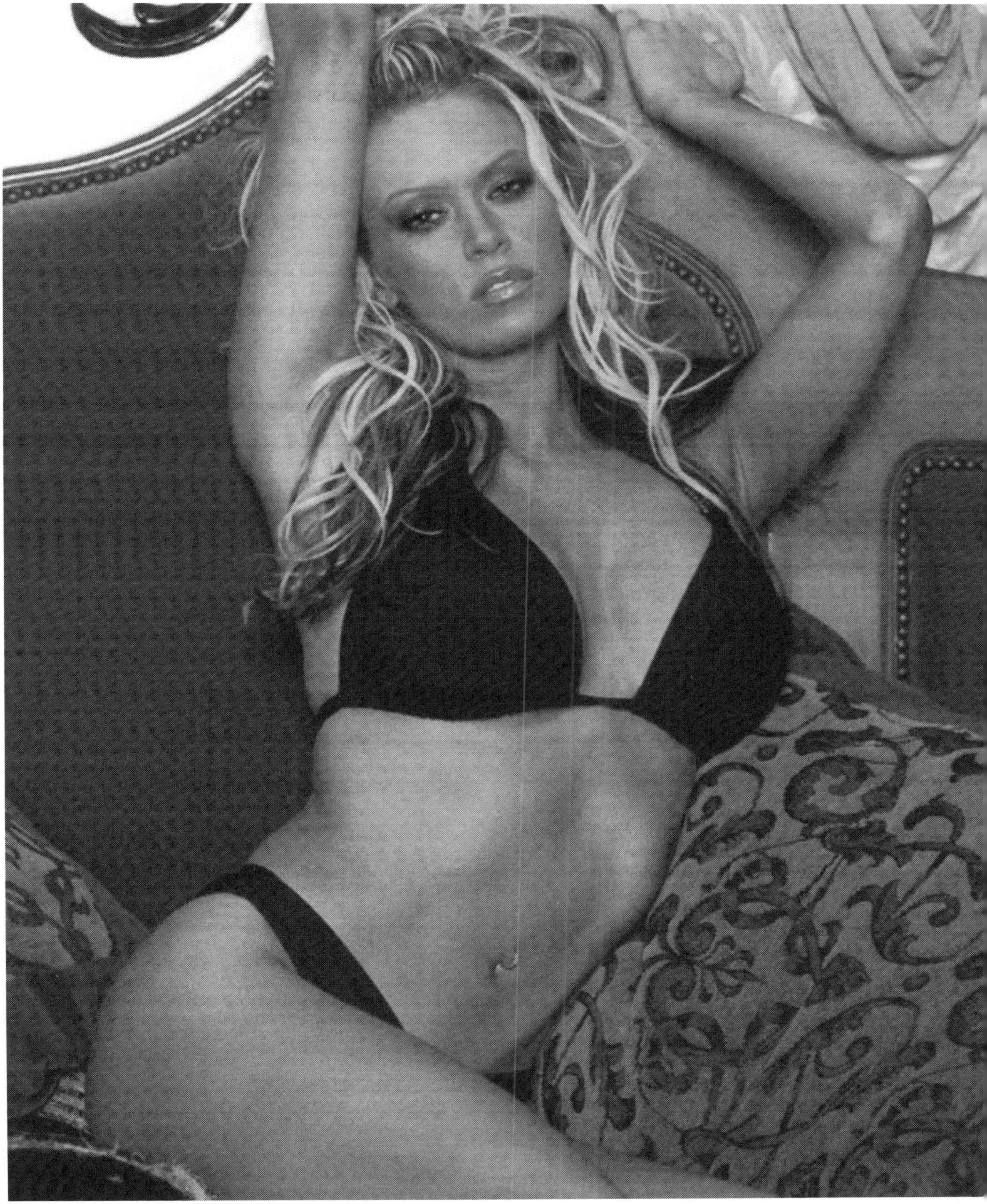

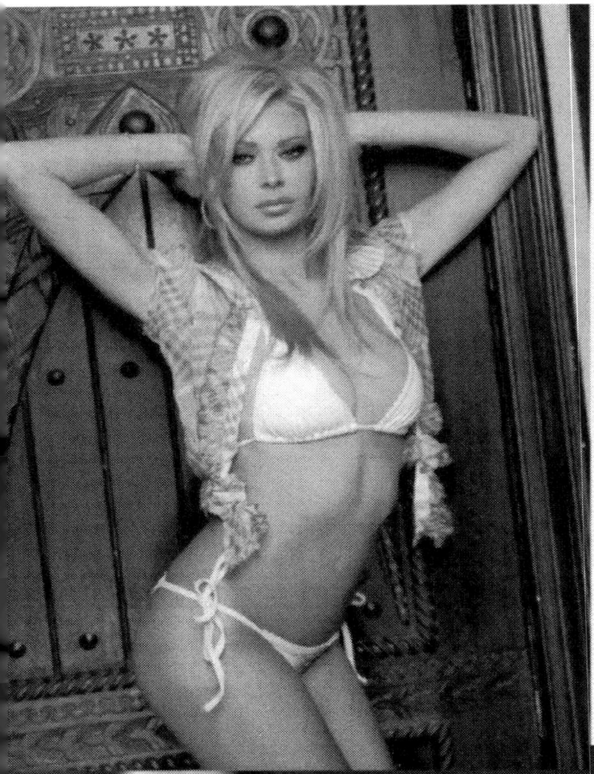

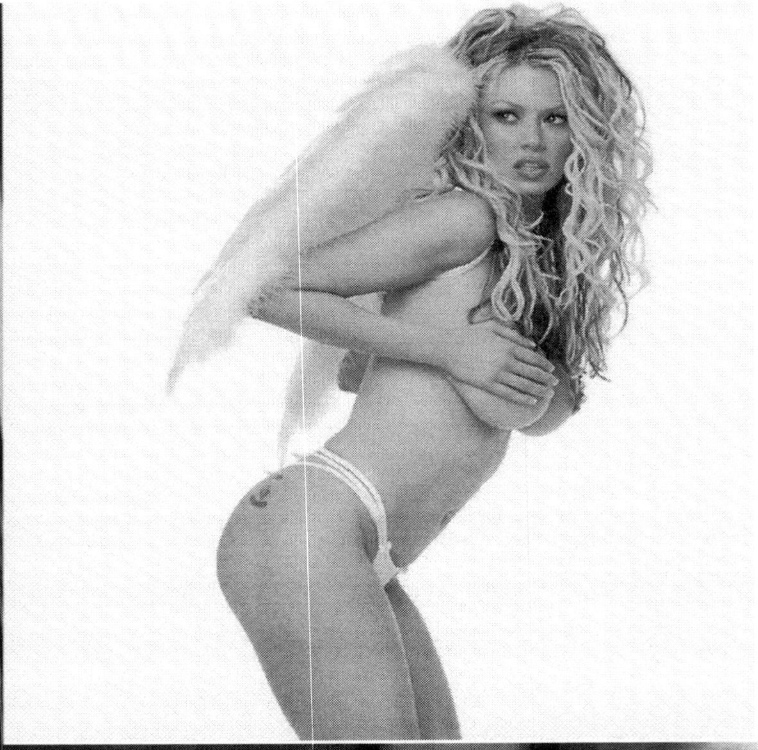

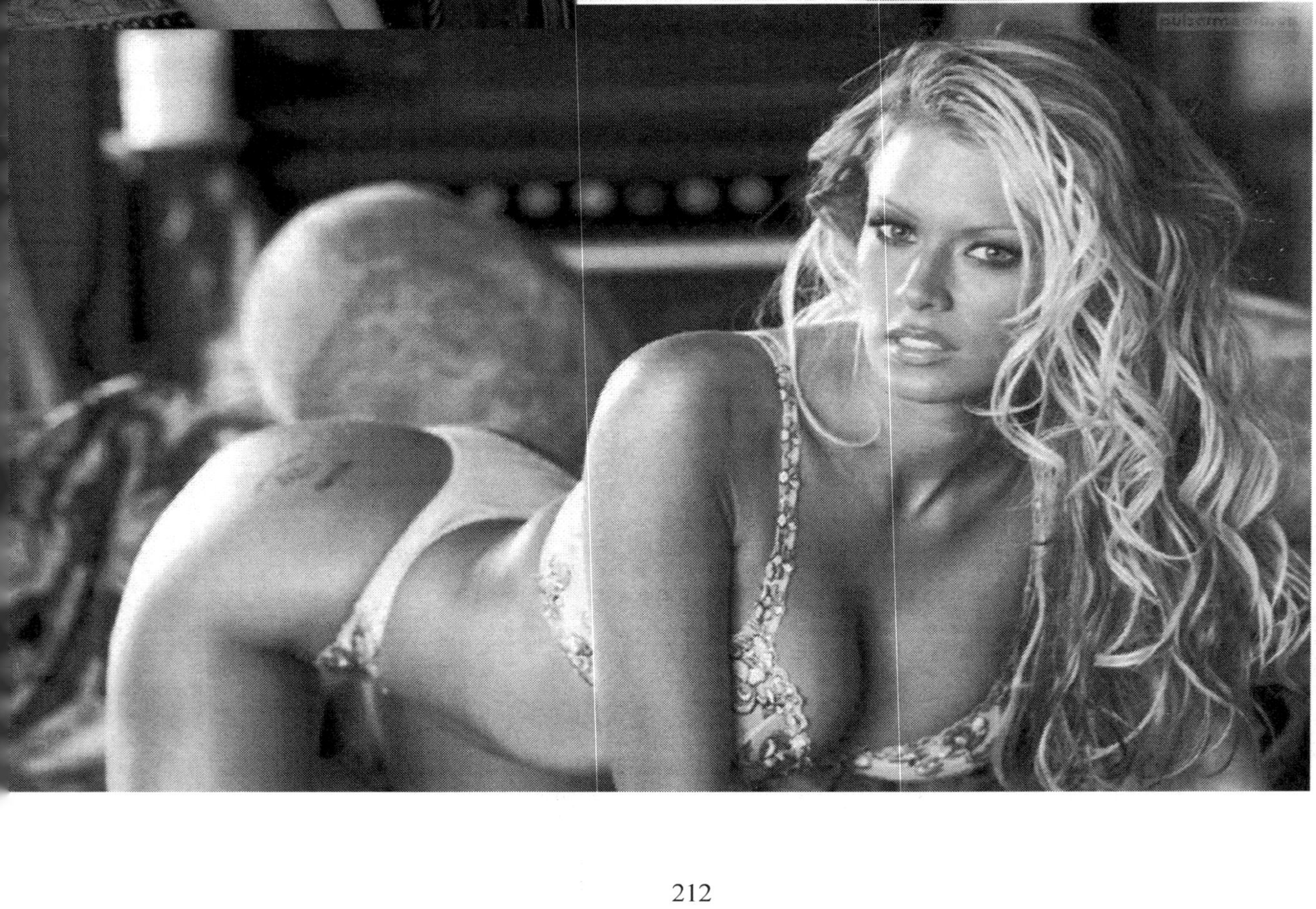

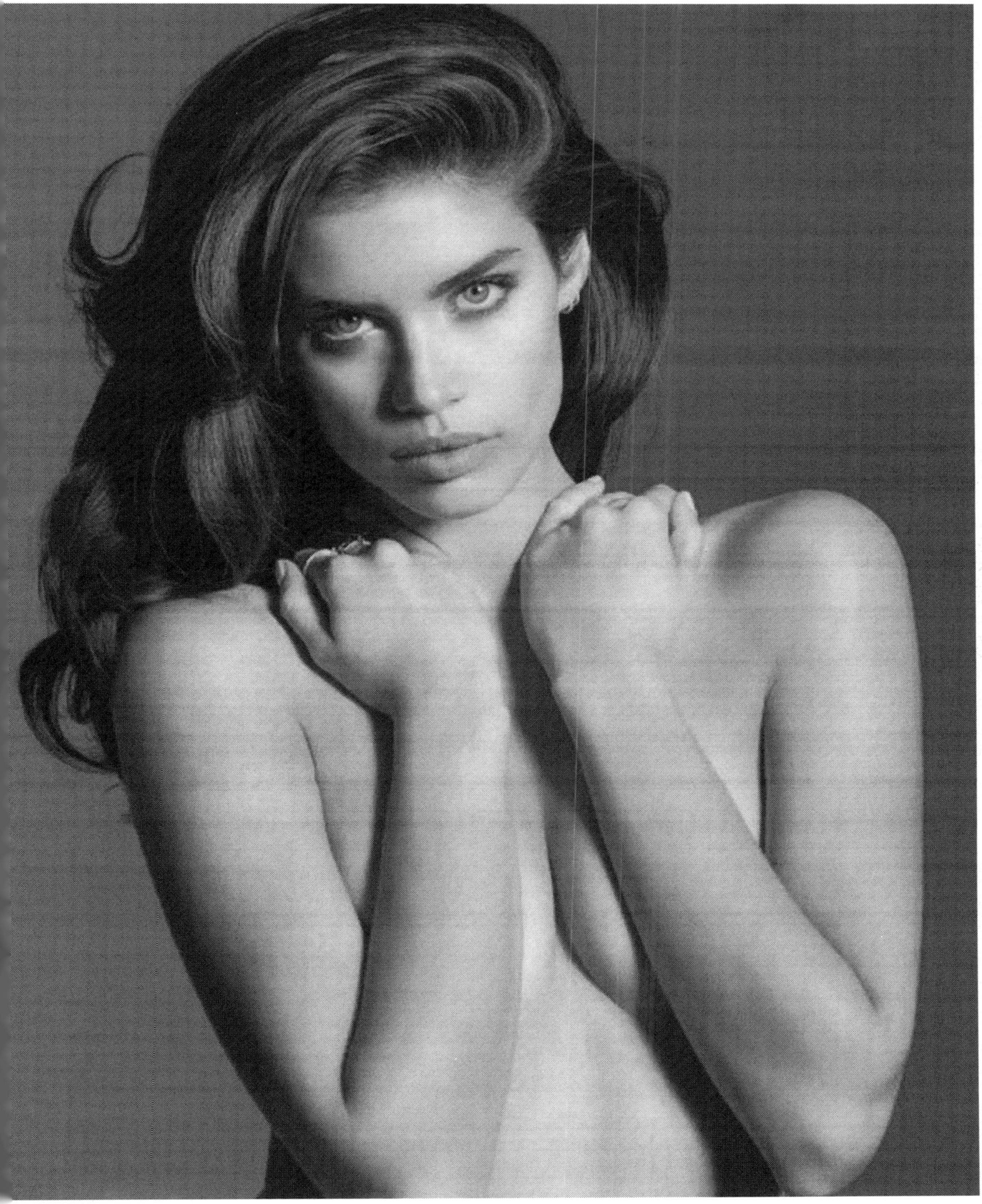

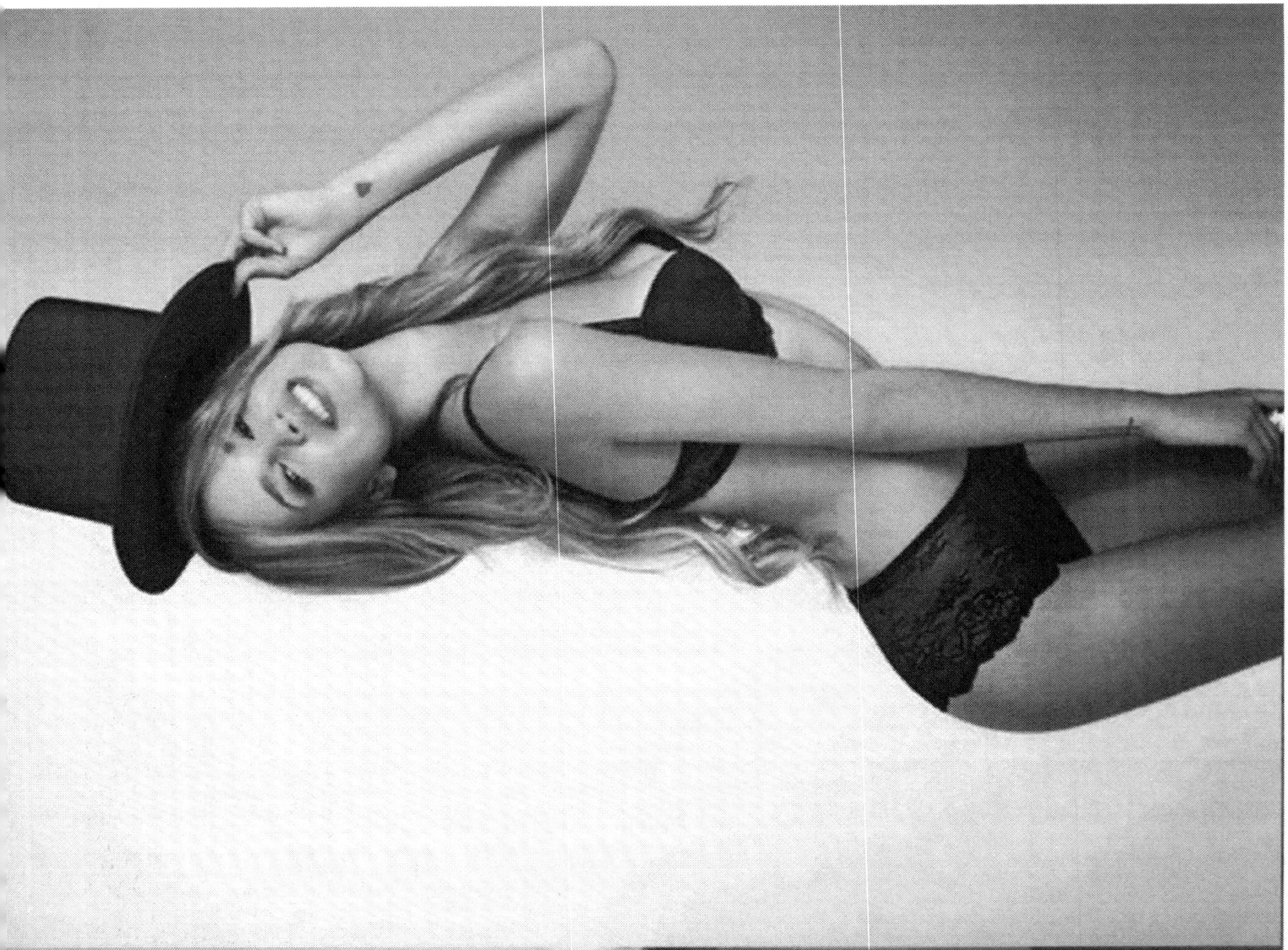

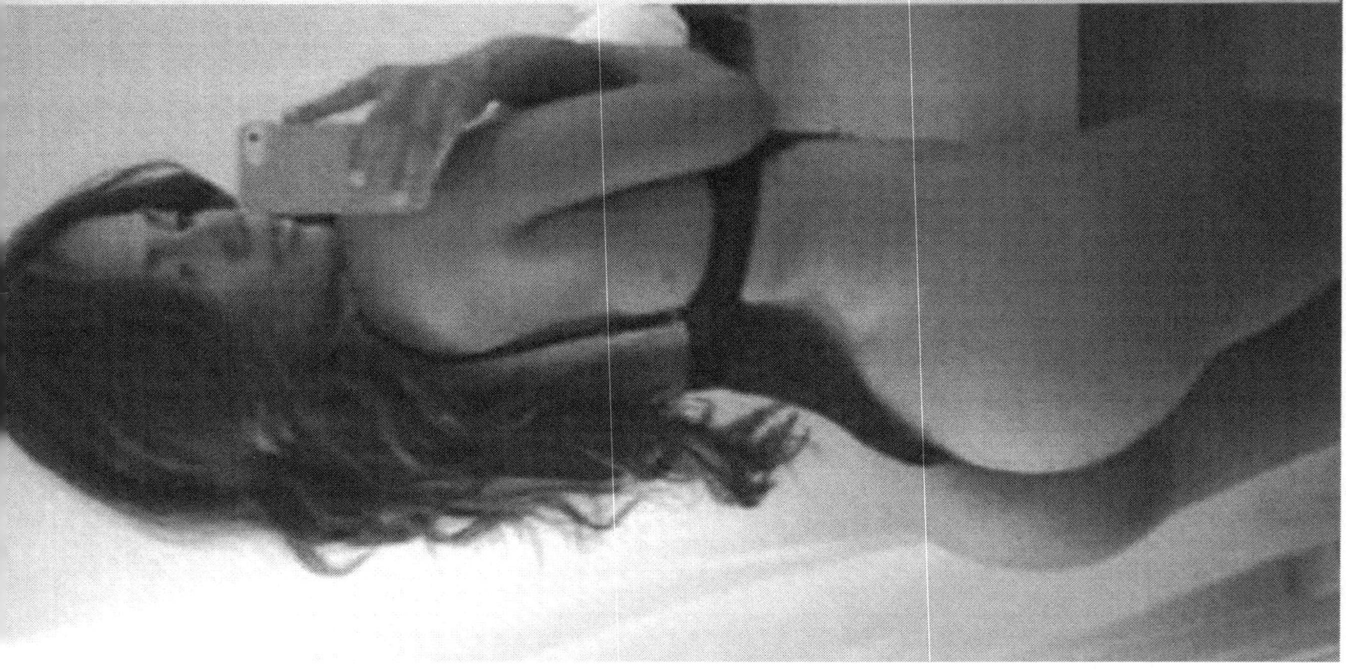

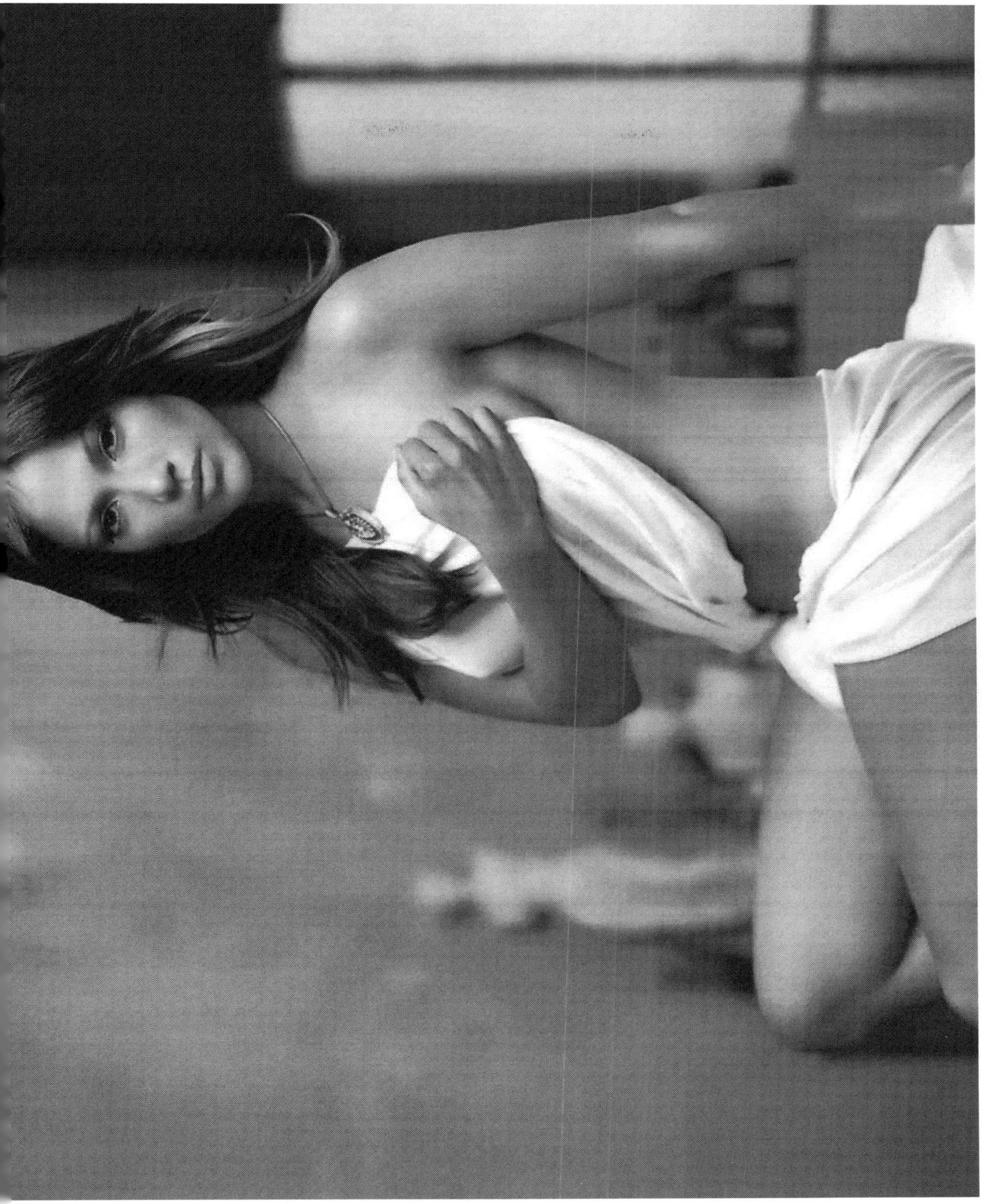

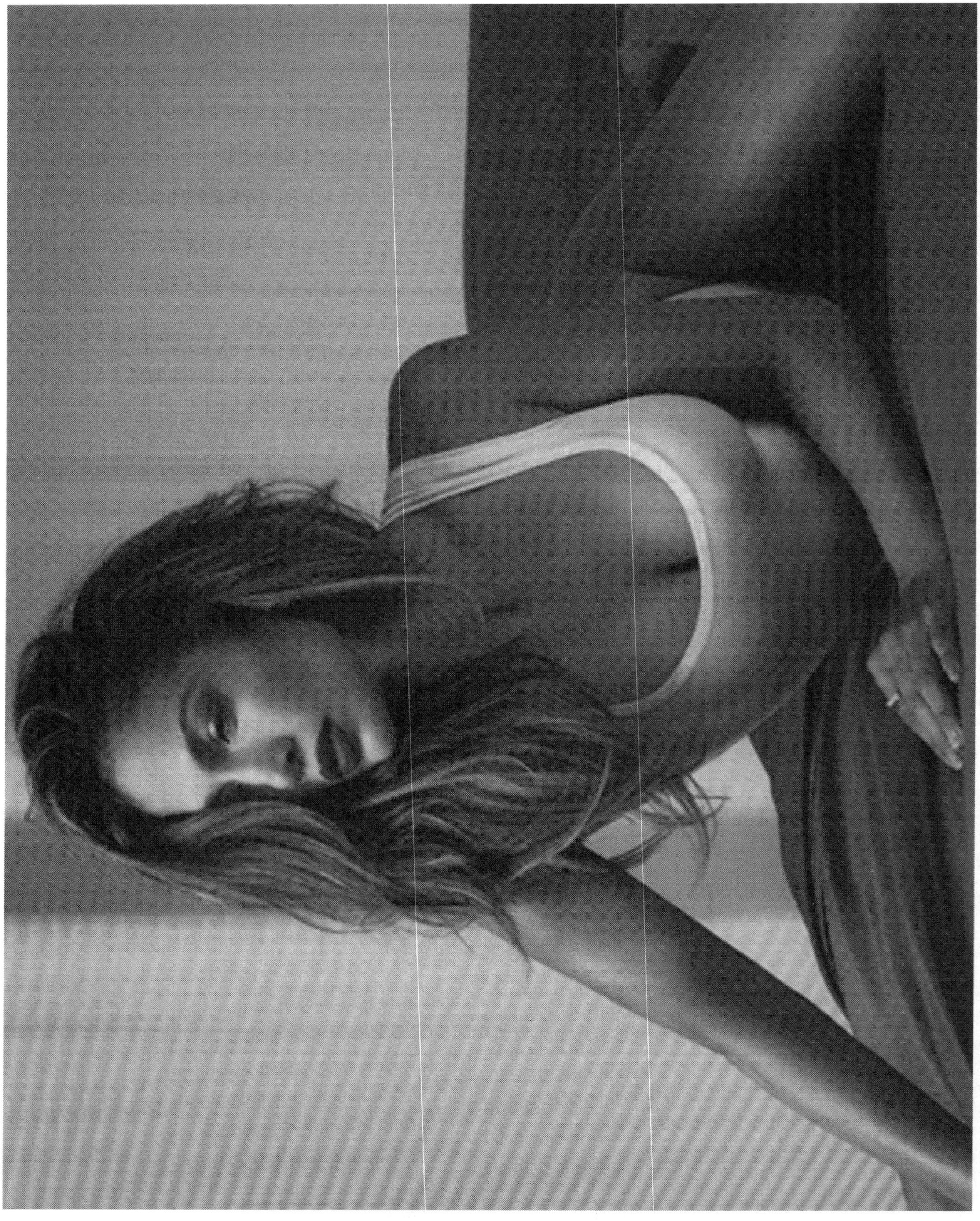

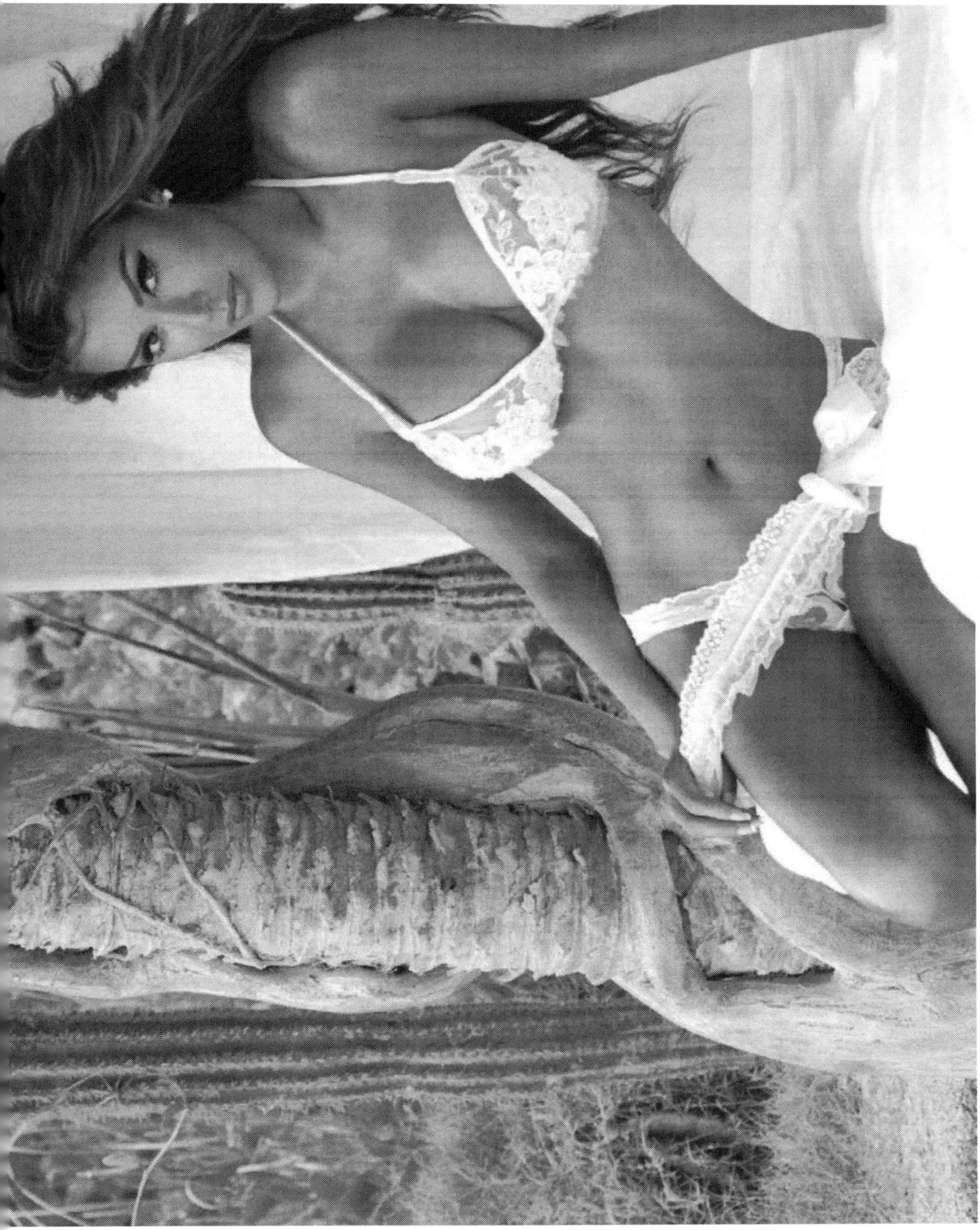

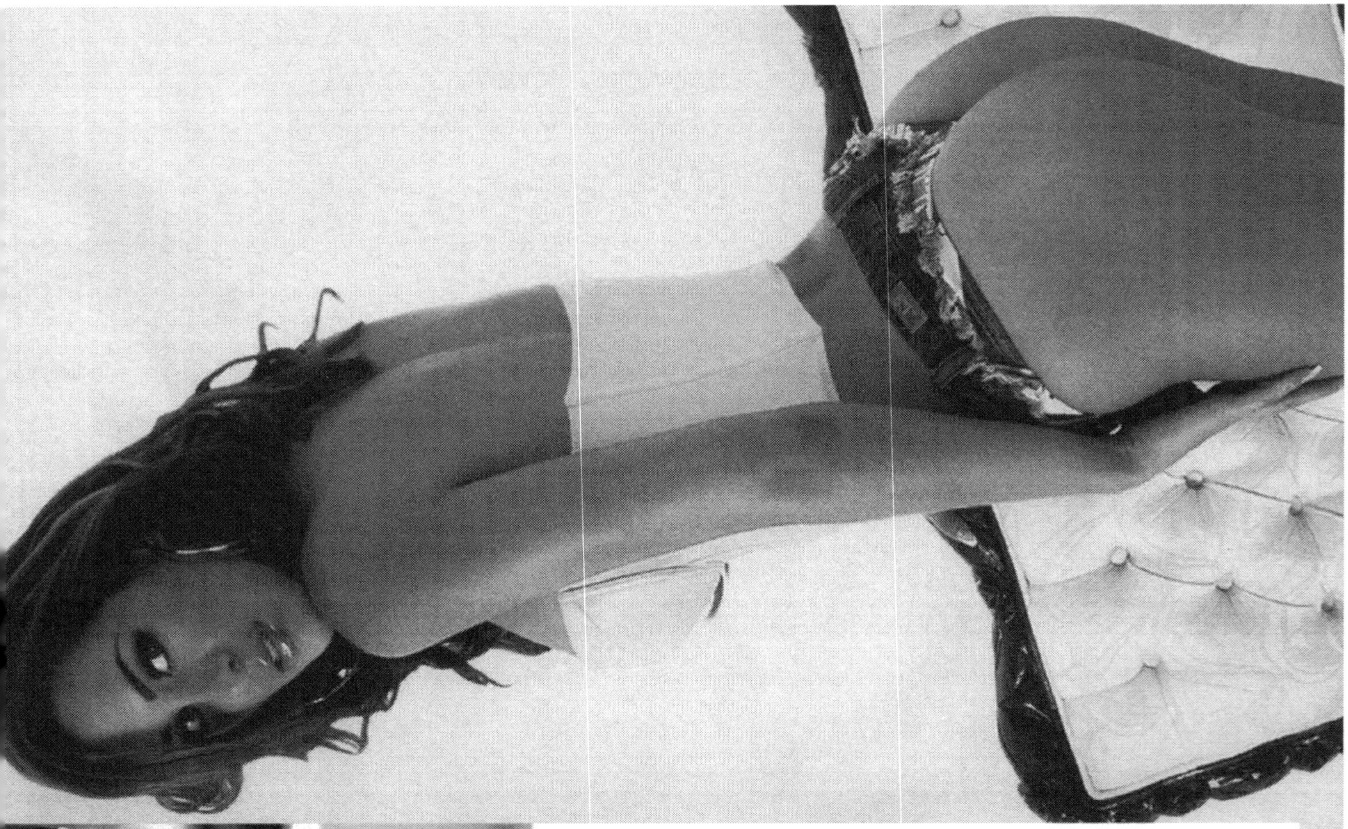

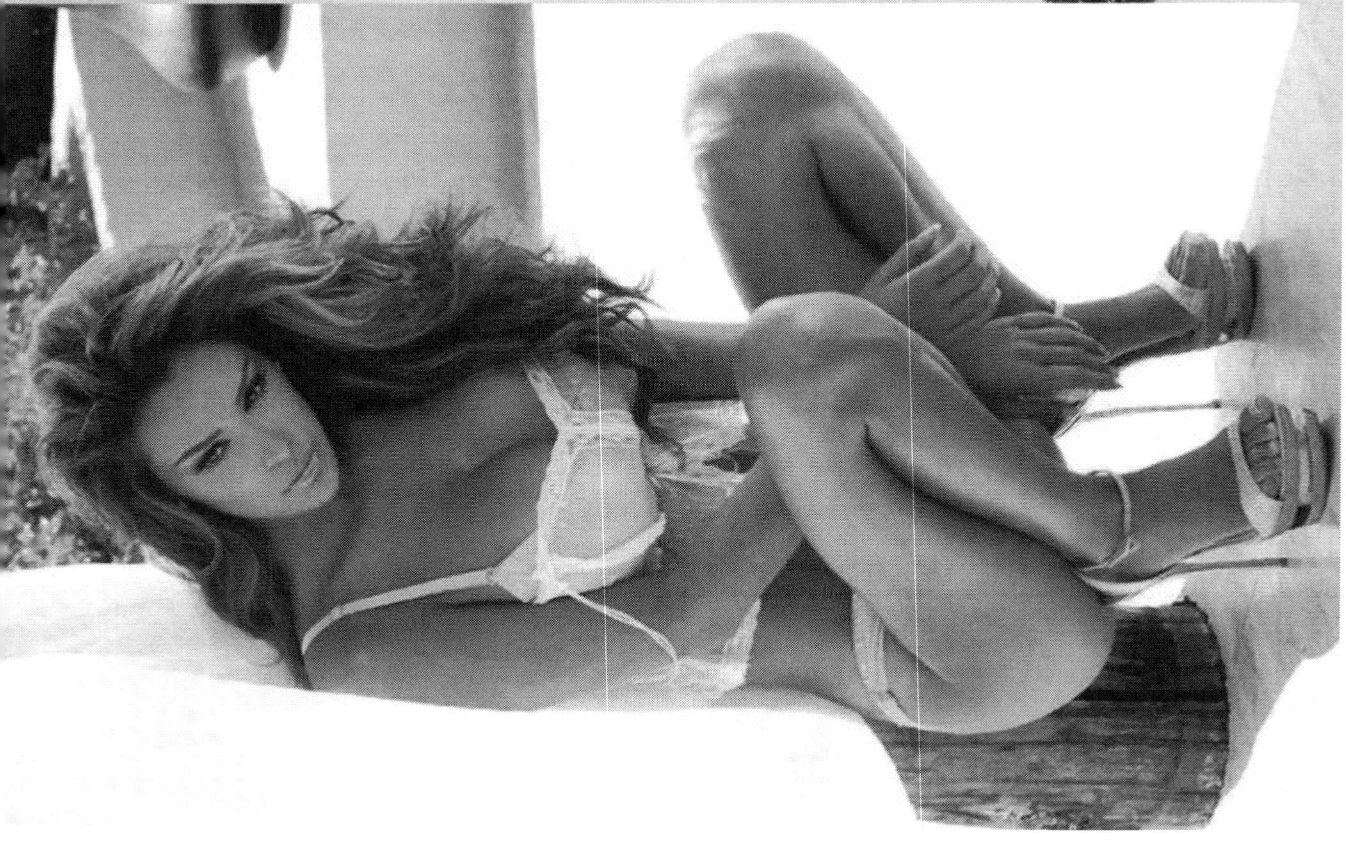

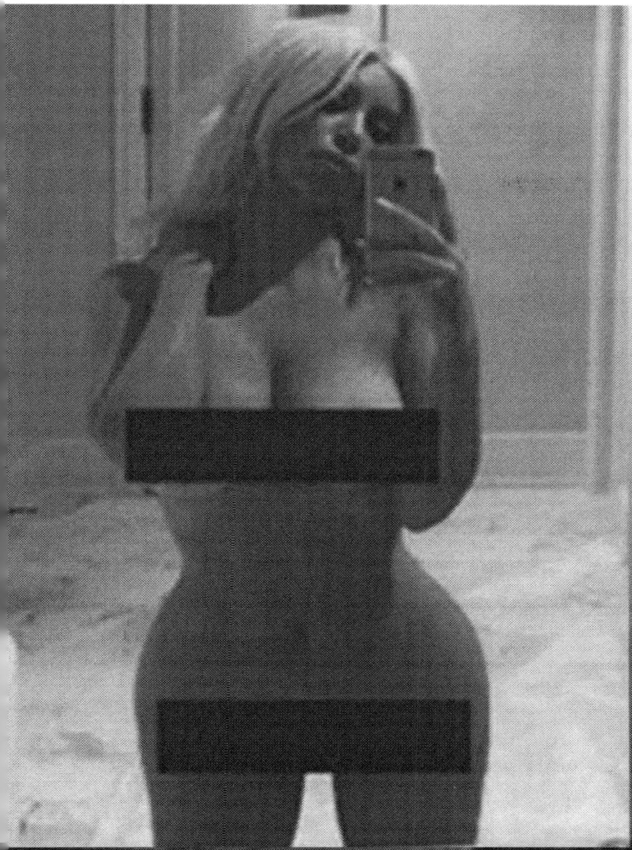

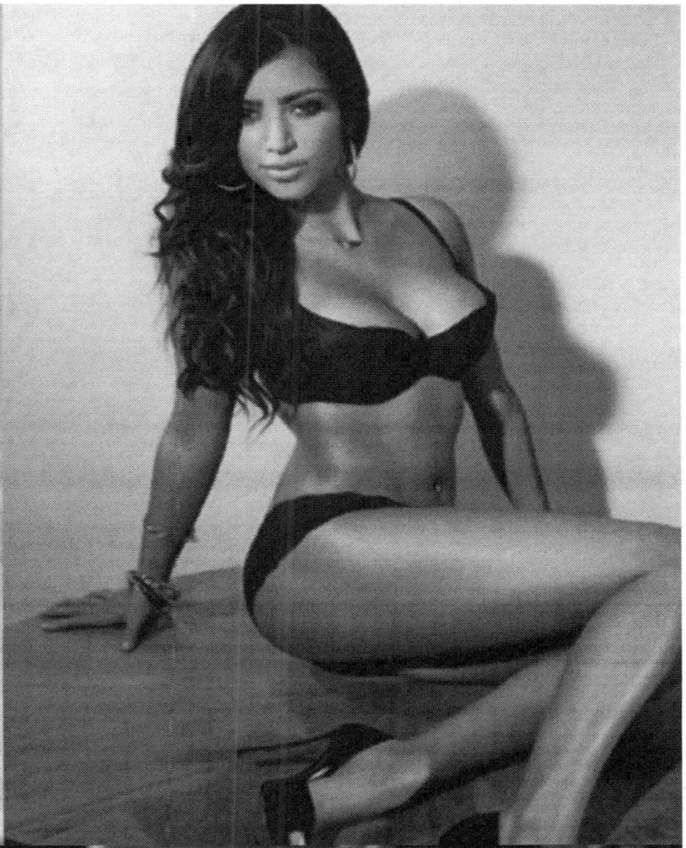

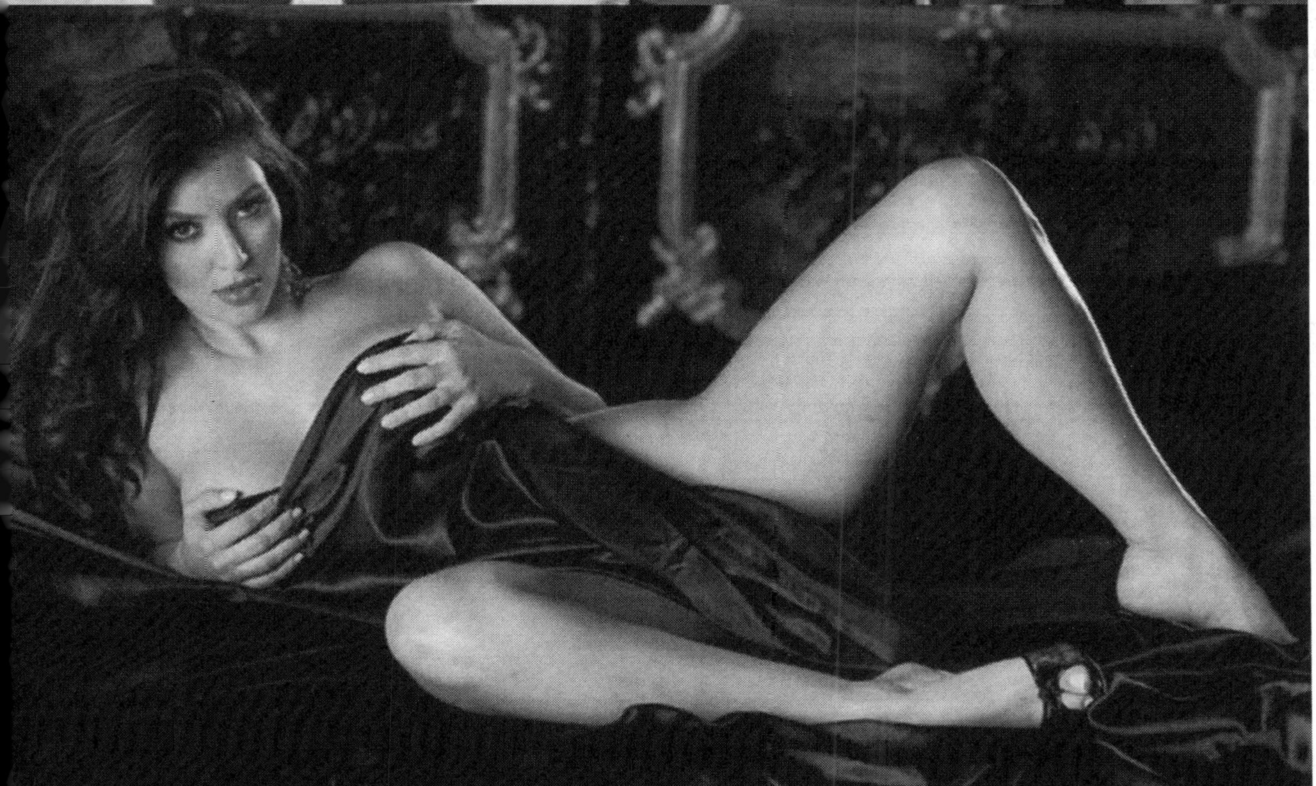

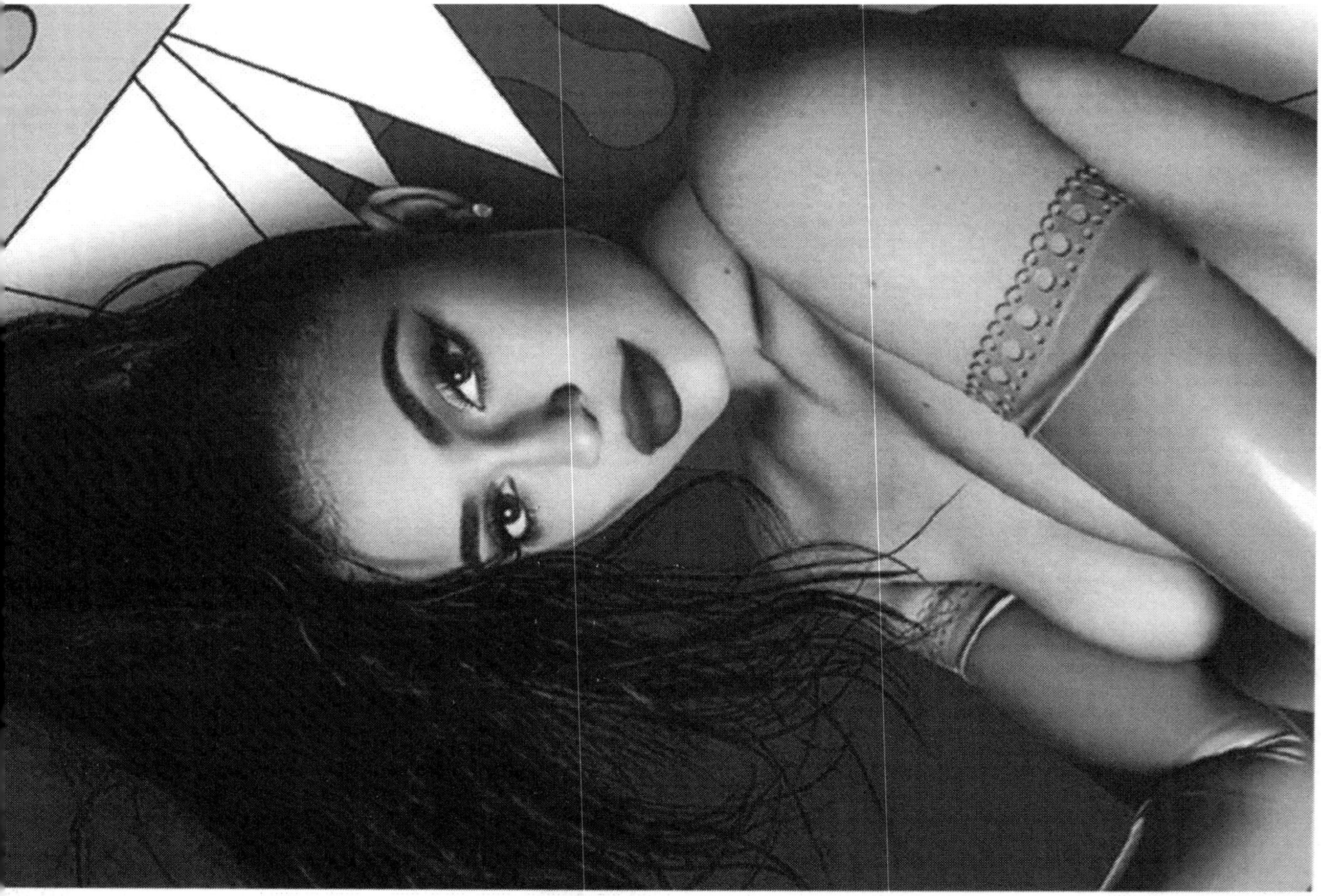

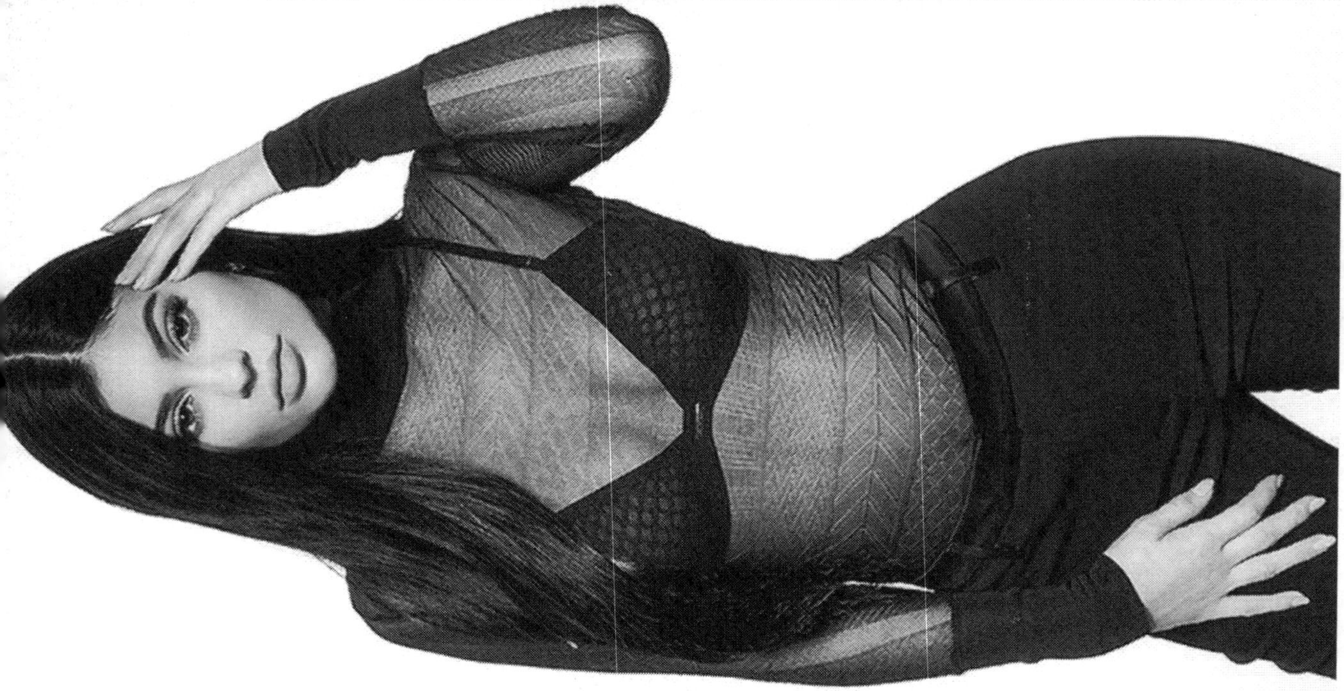

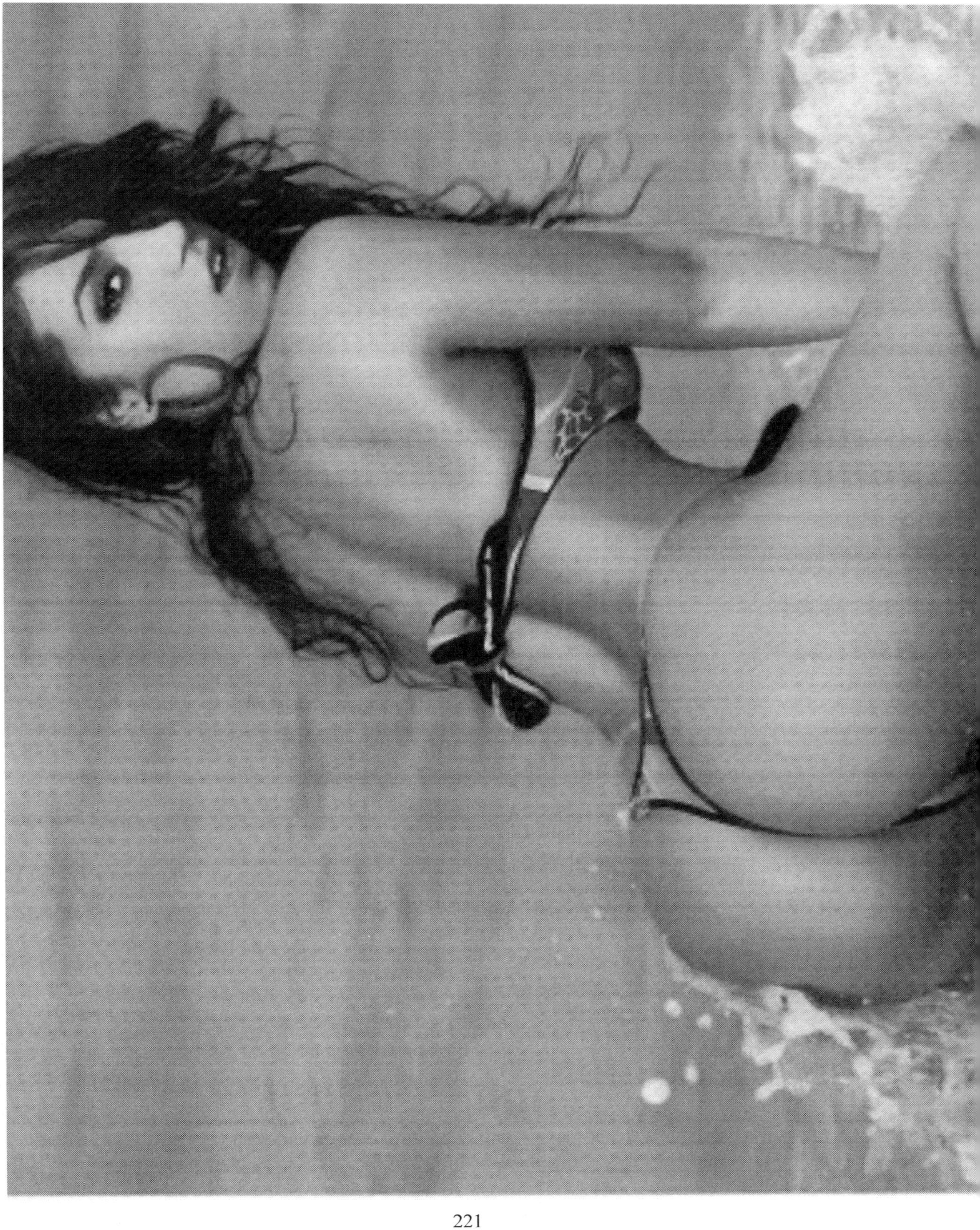

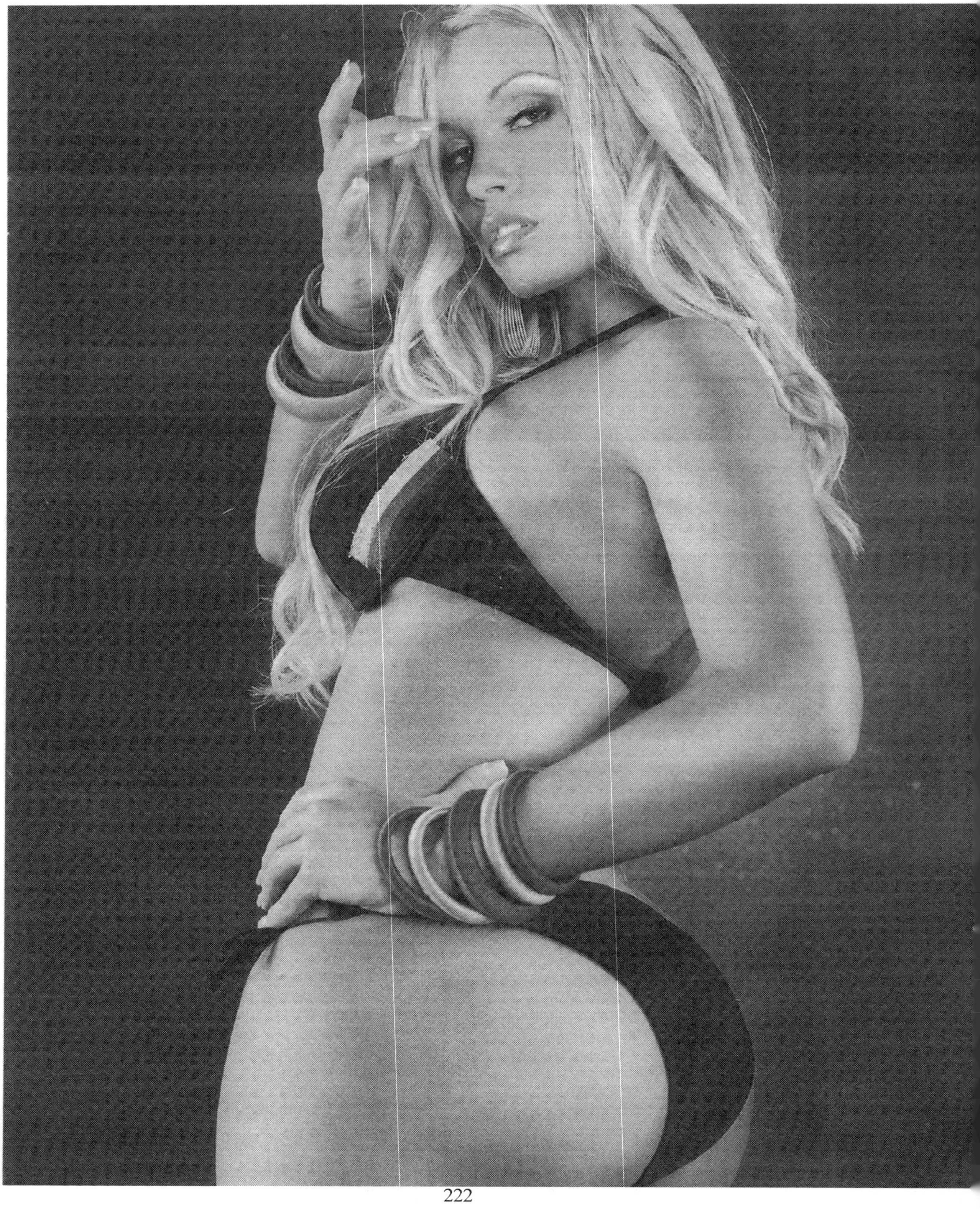

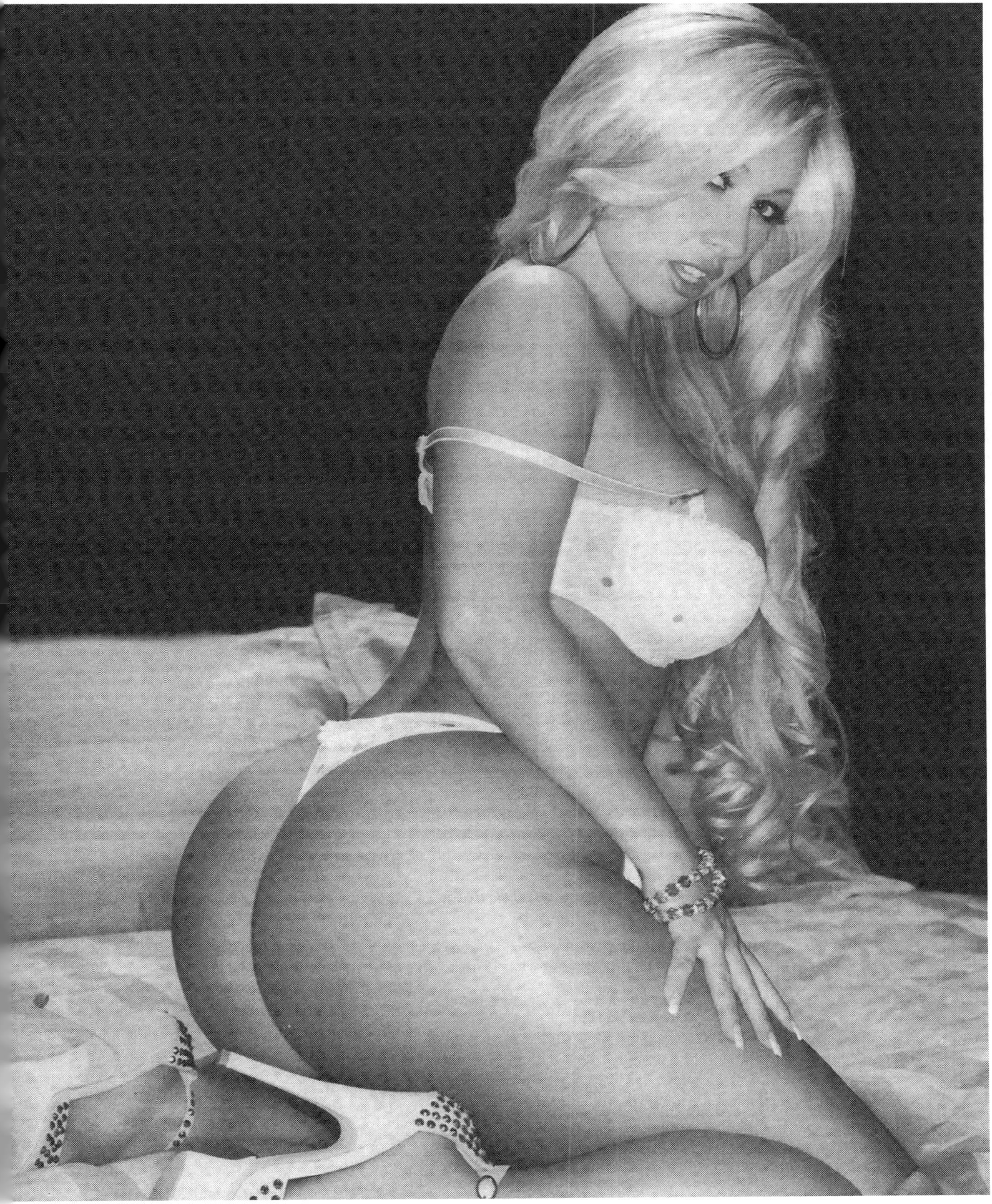

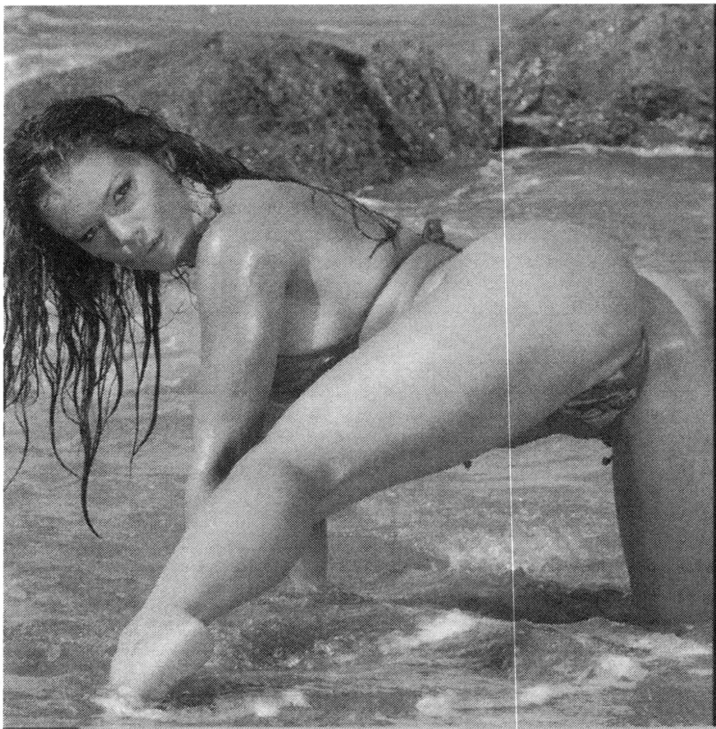
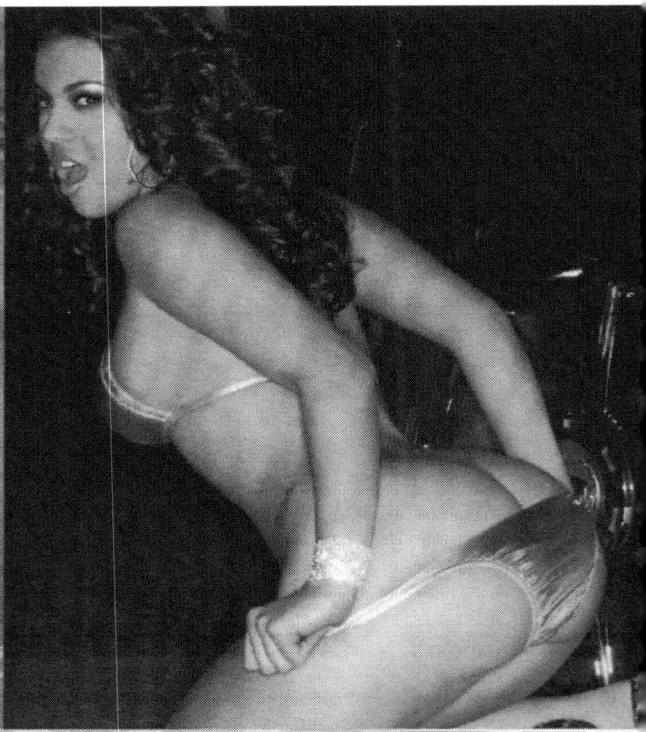
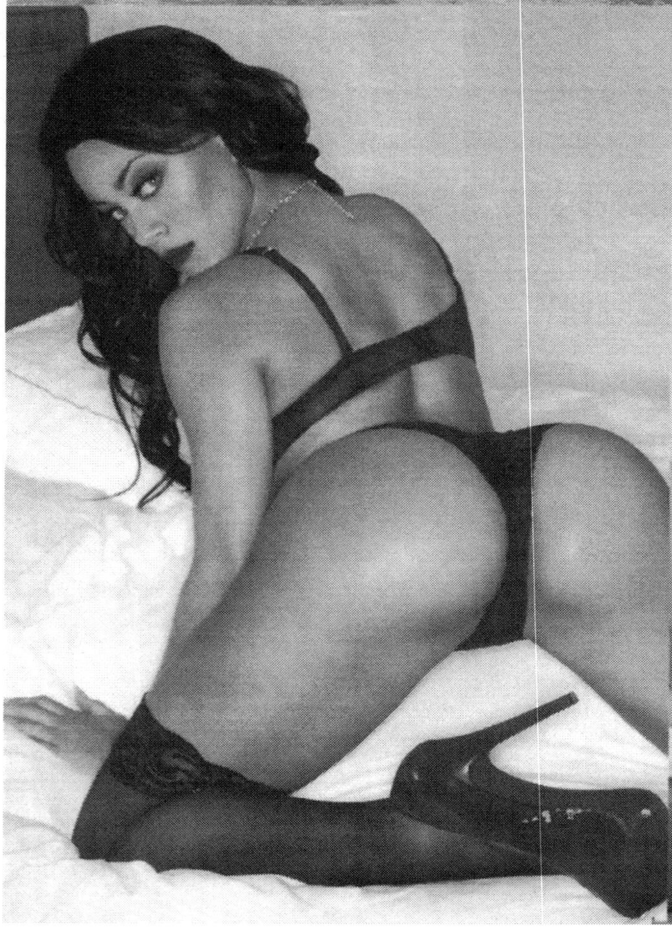
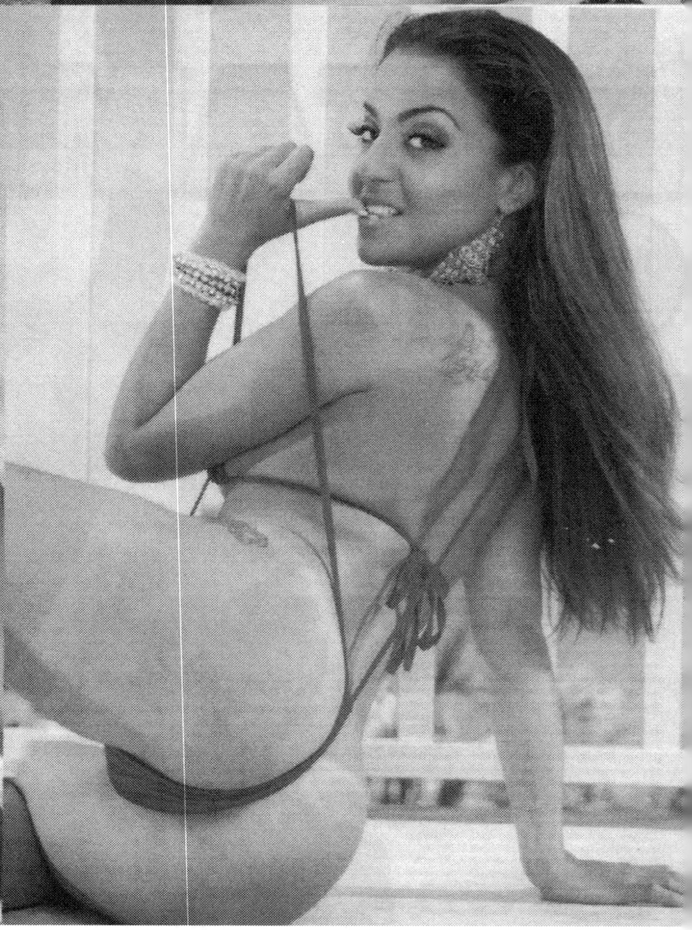

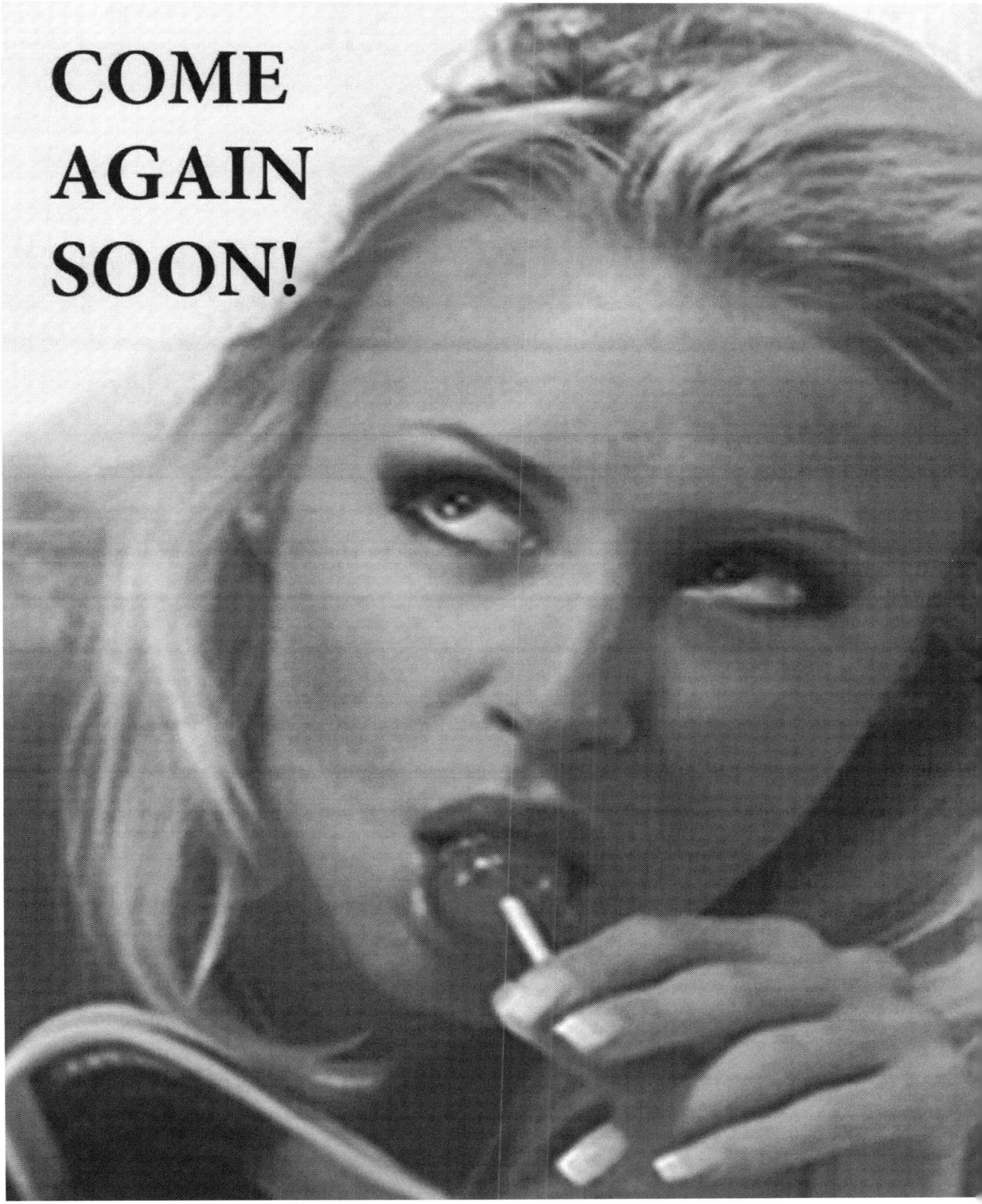
COME
AGAIN
SOON!

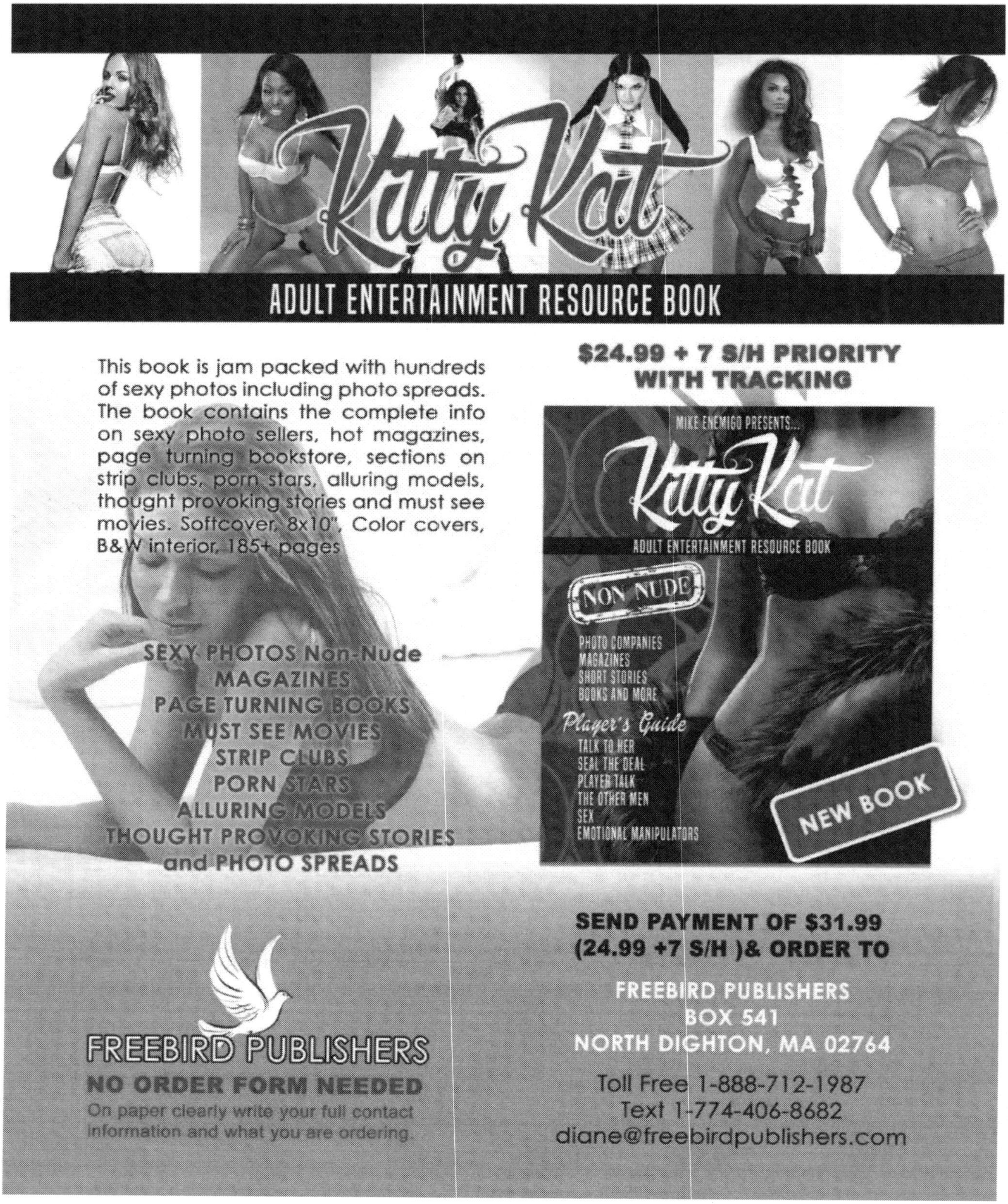
Kitty Kat
ADULT ENTERTAINMENT RESOURCE BOOK
This book is jam packed with hundreds of sexy photos including photo spreads. The book contains the complete info on sexy photo sellers, hot magazines, page turning bookstore, sections on strip clubs, porn stars, alluring models, thought provoking stories and must see movies. Softcover, 8x10", Color covers, B&W interior, 185+ pages
$24.99 + 7 S/H PRIORITY WITH TRACKING
MIKE ENEMIGO PRESENTS...
Kitty Kat
ADULT ENTERTAINMENT RESOURCE BOOK
NON NUDE
PHOTO COMPANIES
MAGAZINES
SHORT STORIES
BOOKS AND MORE
Player's Guide
TALK TO HER
SEAL THE DEAL
PLAYER TALK
THE OTHER MEN
SEX
EMOTIONAL MANIPULATORS
NEW BOOK
SEXY PHOTOS Non-Nude
MAGAZINES
PAGE TURNING BOOKS
MUST SEE MOVIES
STRIP CLUBS
PORN STARS
ALLURING MODELS
THOUGHT PROVOKING STORIES
and PHOTO SPREADS
SEND PAYMENT OF $31.99 (24.99 +7 S/H )& ORDER TO
FREEBIRD PUBLISHERS
BOX 541
NORTH DIGHTON, MA 02764
Toll Free 1-888-712-1987
Text 1-774-406-8682
diane@freebirdpublishers.com
FREEBIRD PUBLISHERS
NO ORDER FORM NEEDED
On paper clearly write your full contact information and what you are ordering.

# YOUR OPINION MATTERS!

The BEST Resource Directory For Prisoners begins and ends with YOU, THE PRISONER, which is why we would like to hear YOUR feedback! Please answer these questions, cut the page out and return it back to us. If you don't want to cut the page out, just write the answers on a blank sheet of paper!

How                old                are                you?

_____

What                is                your                nationality?

_____

What        kind        of        music        do        you        like?

_____

What        is        your        favorite        TV        show?

_____

How/where        did        you        first        hear        about        us?

_____

How    many    people    other    than    you    read    your    Directory    copy?

_____

Do  you  want  more  graphics  and  pictures  to  liven  up  the  book?  If  so,  what?

_____

Would        you        like        to        see        prison        artwork?

_____

Would        you        like        us        to        include        prison        recipes?

_____

Would        you        like        puzzles        and        other        games?

_____

What        subjects        would        you        like        to        see        more        of?

_____

What do you like best about our Directory?

_____

Is there anything you don't like about our Directory?

_____

Do you buy any other Directories? If so, which ones?

_____

If you buy other Directories, what do you like about them, and what don't you like?

_____

Do you want more "entertainment" articles?

_____

Anything else?

_____


Our Directory is made for YOU. Our objective is to provide you with the BEST Directory possible! Please tell us HOW you want us to do that. Your voice is HEARD! **Please send your opinion to: TCB, POB 1025, Rancho Cordova, CA 95741**

# THE CELL BLOCK
## PRESENTS

ATTENTION: THIS BOOK IS A PRISONER MUST-HAVE!!

# The Art & Power Of
# LETTER WRITING
# FOR PRISONERS

A COMPLETE GUIDE TO WRITING
HIGH-QUALITY FORMAL (BUSINESS)
& INFORMAL (PERSONAL) LETTERS!

FROM THE HIGHLY SUCCESSFUL PRISONER & CEO

## MIKE ENMEIGO

**ATTENTION!**
FOR ADDITIONAL COPIES OF THIS BOOKLET, SEND 1.5
NEW, COMPLETE BOOKS OF 20 FOREVER STAMPS, PER
COPY REQUESTED TO:

THE CELL BLOCK
RE: WRITING BOOKLET
PO BOX 1025
RANCHO CORDVA, CA 95741

Published by: The Cell Block™

The Cell Block
PO Box 1025
Rancho Cordova, CA 95741

www.thecellblock.net
Corrlinks: the cellblock.net@mail.com


Copyright © 2013 by The Cell Block

Cover Design: Mike Enemigo

Send comments, reviews, and sales/business inquiries to: thecellblock.net@mail.com

# THE ART & POWER OF LETTER WRITING

# WRITING

Writing (especially letter writing) skills are extremely beneficial to have when doing time in prison. After all, writing will probably be your main source of communication with the outside world. At times you may have access to a phone, or you may even get a visit, but both of those can easily be taken from you for various reasons. Letter writing, however, is pretty much something you'll always be able to do, even on lockdowns or from the hole.

Being able to write well is an extremely powerful tool; the better you learn to write, the more powerful you will become. Most of my communication, including the stuff pertaining to my business, is all accomplished through letter/instruction writing. My ability to write well is a major part of my ability to pull off the things I do, which is how I make money, and which is a big part of how I live as comfortable as possible while being in prison.

However, I was not born a great writer; it is something that I had to take the time out to learn to do. When strategizing how I was going to become successful from a prison cell, I quickly figured out that being a great writer was going to be a huge ingredient in my recipe for success. Whether it's articulating my ideas or convincing people to see things my way; whether it's writing out a long, detailed business plan or the instructions on how to pull off each part of my plan; it all starts with being able to not only write, but write well.

## A Bit Of Perspective:

Now, before we go on, let's think about what writing actually is and what it's used for.

Writing is a form of communication; it's used to communicate a message – information, thoughts, ideas, etc. With that in mind, if you wish to communicate your message clearly, you must be able to write it clearly and correctly.

If you do not learn how to write properly and convey your message clearly, the person/people you are communicating it to may *mis*understand the message rather than *understand* the message. Now, I understand that what I just wrote may seem like common sense, but what isn't common sense are all the rules to how to write (communicate) properly. And yes, the rules are important, because something as "minor" as a misplaced comma, the failure to put a comma, or the misspelling of a word can actually change the meaning of the sentence (statement, command, question, or exclamation).

If the meaning of your sentence is not what you intend it to be then your point might be missed. And when your point is missed, you've failed to communicate. And communication, my friend, is key.

So, since I am stressing the importance of writing for communication purposes, feel free to make the following word associations when reading this chapter.

| | | |
|---|---|---|
| Write | = | Communicate |
| Writing | = | Communicating |
| Written | = | Communicated |
| Writer | = | Communicator |

## Study & Learn:

Being able to write (communicate) well has increased my power immensely. However, as I mentioned earlier, it is something I had to teach myself to do.

A lot of prisoners have their own way of writing (typically a "prison" style), but I strongly recommend that you learn the *proper* way of constructing and punctuating sentences. The majority of people, even on the outside, don't actually write all that well. Learning how to construct and punctuate sentences properly – just these two things! – will put you on another level, so be sure to make it a *point* to learn and master these two aspects of writing.

There are many different ways you can improve your writing. If you have someone who will purchase you books, I suggest that you get/read/study "English Grammar for Dummies" by Geraldine Woods. I've read and studied "English Grammar for Dummies" and it really helped my dumb ass out a lot. In fact, it is one of the must-haves in my book collection; I keep a copy.

If you don't have someone who'll purchase books for you, you can get a *free* book from Pen American Center titled "Handbook for Writers in Prison." It's a writer's/resource handbook that will benefit you greatly. In fact, since it's free to prisoners anyway, I suggest you get this book even if you *do* have the ability to get other books. The more information, the better; all it can do is help you.

To request a free copy of "Handbook for Writers in Prison," write to:

Pen American Center
588 Broadway, Suite 303
New York, NY 10012

*Note:* There are many programs that send books to prisoners for free. They might not be able to get you a specific title, but if you tell them you'd like a book on English grammar, they will likely send you one.

Another way prisoners can learn to write well is by reading books (or magazines) and paying close attention to how they are written – how the writer constructs sentences, uses punctuation, etc. It's not a bad idea to pick up your favorite writers' books and study their style, their flow. Just make sure it's a writer whose books/articles are professionally edited.

There is no way I can teach you *all* the rules of grammar/punctuation in this booklet. However, to get you started towards becoming a great writer, study and learn the Basic Punctuation Guide. Once you do, you will already be a better writer than most of those around you. Then see what you can do about getting the other books that I mentioned (or similar ones), so that you can take your writing ability to an even higher level and learn how to write to the absolute best of your ability.

**Get And Use A Dictionary:**

A good dictionary is a must-have tool for anyone wishing to write well, as proper spelling/use of the word is critical when communicating.

There are many great dictionaries. However, I'd have to say that my favorite is the "MacMillan English Dictionary for Advanced Learners." Not only does it have a large selection of words (probably any-and-everything you'd ever want/need to use), but it also gives examples of how many of the words are used in a sentence, as well as common phrases, etc.

Get the best dictionary you have the ability to get – even if you have to pay a prisoner to steal you one from education, as they often have a bunch of collegiate dictionaries which are also very good – and *use* it. Do not be lazy! If you are unsure of how a word is to be spelled or exactly what it means, look it up so that what you end up writing is *absolutely* correct. Doing so will really improve the quality of your work and your communication.

**Letter-Writing Tips:**

OK, so we now know that writing is basically communicating, and that to write well (communicate well) we must learn how to write properly – learn proper grammar, use a dictionary, etc. Now let's get into a few other kinds of tips.

## The Art of Writing (a bit of perspective):

Think of writing as an art – because it is. When you write, imagine that you are writing a picture; you want your words to form a visual in your readers' minds.

## Sketch:

Just as an artist wishing to draw a picture will first grab a pencil and a piece of paper and sketch, erase, adjust, shade, etc., until the picture finally relays the message he/she wishes to express, and to his/her satisfaction, a writer (who is *also* an artist) must use his/her tools the same way: you grab your pen and paper and you write, edit, erase, adjust, etc., until you have expressed your message to *your* satisfaction.

*Note:* When writing an informal letter, if you have a lot to write about, I suggest you write a list of everything you want to touch on, put it in an order to where it makes the most sense, and then write your letter. When writing a formal letter (a business letter; long, detailed instructions; etc.), I suggest you always start with an outline and then write a rough draft. That way you can go back, reread it, make the necessary adjustments, and then rewrite it correctly, nice and neat. Sure, its extra work, but it will allow you to produce a better-quality letter.

## Stay on topic/theme:

A lot of people's – especially in this day and age – minds are going 100 miles a minute. Therefore, they often jump back and forth from topic to topic, and by doing so, it can confuse the reader.

When you write your letters, *stay on topic*. Write about one subject at a time until everything you want to communicate has been communicated. It will not only make the experience of reading one of your letters easier and much more enjoyable, but easier to understand, too.

## Paint a clear picture:

Never assume people know what you mean (intend to communicate). You need to be very thorough and paint a *clear* picture.

## Develop your own style:

Just as any great artist works towards developing his/her own drawing/painting style and perfecting it, you should do the same with your writing. Sure, it's OK to mimic someone else's style/flow while learning – just as an artist often learns how to draw/paint by drawing/painting others' works – but over time, as you get more comfortable, try to come into your own.

Now that we've went over a few basic tips that pertain to anything you write, let's get into a few *specific* categories of writing.

## Informal Letter Writing:

Informal letter writing is how you'd write a letter to your mom, dad, grandma, wife, sister, brother, pen pal, etc. Now, while it's best to use proper grammar no matter what you're writing or who you're writing to, as it will help you express your message clearly, it's OK to use a little bit of slang that the person you're writing to will understand. For example, if your sister or brother is from the internet/social networking/texting generation, it's OK to use abbreviations like LMAO, LOL, OMG, etc. Why? Because those are familiar terms to them, so your message will still clearly be conveyed. However, if your dad or grandma often complain that they are computer and technology illiterate, then you probably don't want to use those kinds of terms with them as they may not understand what you're trying to communicate.

The best thing for you to do in order to convey your message clearly is to write your message in a language that the person you're writing to uses – what *they* understand. This means that you should customize each letter you write to the specifications of each person you write to. And, of course, when in doubt, always use proper grammar.

**Informal Response:**

There is a proper way to respond to an informal letter that you have received; doing so will make your letter (communication) more thorough, detailed, and organized, which will make it easier to read and understand.

When responding to an informal letter, do so in these 3 steps:

1) The first thing you should do is give a brief, upbeat greeting: "Hello, how are you? Absolutely fantastic, I hope. I received your most-welcomed letter yesterday, so I've decided to spend today with you." Or, "I received your letter and I am extremely excited to hear from you. Thank you so much for taking the time out to write me." Stick to something like that; simple and basic.

Whatever you do, don't do the ol' cliché, half-page "prisoner-style" greeting: "Esteemed salutations. I send my upmost respects to you. Please excuse me for this brief interruption as I sprinkle these words upon you..." etc., etc., etc. That's 1970s shit – when the world/people was/were much slower. It's now Y2K+ and ain't nobody trying to read all that nonsense. Furthermore, it's corny.

2) The second thing you should do is respond to everything they wrote about in their letter; in the order it was written, one paragraph at a time. The only exception to this is if the person who wrote you is a bit scatter-brained and they jump back and forth between subjects in their letter. In that case, you will have to take control of the communication; you should put a mark be each "related" paragraph and respond to one *subject* at a time.

*Note*: Communicating via snail mail takes a while because you have to wait for it to go back and forth. With that said, sometimes people forget exactly what it was they wrote about (mentioned, asked, etc.) by the time they get your response. When this is the case, it is a good idea to write what your "pen pal" stated or asked first, then respond to it. For example: In your letter you asked me what I think about the pictures you recently sent me – the ones where you're in a white thong. Well, in my opinion, your body is absolutely beautiful; your booty is the definition of perfection...., etc.

3) The third and final thing you should do is write all of the things *you* want to write about – discuss, mention, etc.

**Formal Letter Writing:**

Sometimes while in prison you may need to write a more formal type of letter. In such a case, the rules are a bit different than when writing an informal letter.

When writing a formal letter or document – a letter in regards to business or something else you want to be taken seriously about – you *never* want to use slang, and you want to be as clear and to the point as possible. A lot of times, if you are writing a formal letter, the person you are writing to will be one who is often busy and pressed for time. You don't want to annoy them with a whole bunch of unnecessary script. Respect their time by choosing words that will convey your message clearly, without the possibility of confusion or misunderstanding, while still keeping it as short and simple as possible. Doing so is more likely to get you the results you're looking for.

**Instruction Writing Tips:**

In order to get anything even semi-major done from a prison cell, you are going to have to learn how to write very organized and detailed instructions. That way, whomever it is that's helping you on the outside knows exactly what it is they are to do, and with the *least* amount of chance for confusion/error as possible.

Writing very detailed and organized instructions is usually a bit of work. It usually always calls for you to:

1) Write an outline of the points you want to make and put them in an order they make the best sense.

2) Write a rough draft from your outline.

3) Edit your rough draft by reading and re-reading it over and over again until it clearly expresses all of your points.

4) Type your final draft; or, if you don't have access to a typewriter, print your instructions nice and neat and in an organized fashion.

Hopefully the information I have given you will help you improve your writing ability. However, you should remember that I have only given you the very basics, and it is in your best interest to take your writing studies much deeper. I cannot stress enough how important and powerful the ability to write great can be for a man in prison; although, as you improve on your ability, I expect that you will *see* how it will improve your lifestyle and make your stay in prison much more comfortable.

# PEN-PAL WEBSITES: THE STRATEGIES

There are many pen-pal services available on the internets that are specifically designed to connect prisoners with free-world pen-pals. Many of the services charge a fee; however, there are some free services as well.

Online prisoner-based pen-pal services are kind of like our version of Myspace and Facebook; they're our way of making friends and socially networking with people on the outside, all around the world. Sure, Myspace and Facebook are much bigger networks (and there are companies who build those for prisoners as well), but to utilize them properly they have to be maintained, and that's something that's hard to do if you don't have internet access yourself.

Some of the benefits of being on a pen-pal service that specializes in connecting prisoners with people on the outside, however, are:

1)   They are maintained, updated, adjusted, etc., by the service providers.

2)   The people on the outside who review these services are specifically looking to write, befriend, connect with, etc., a prisoner.

These services come in handy if you're looking to make friends on the other side of the wall. Whether your objective is to find romance, spiritual guidance, legal assistance, help with your projects, a drug runner, a sugar mama, or just get mail, if you use these sites correctly, you can usually find what you're looking for.

Contrary to what some may believe, there are many women (and even men; however, I'm going to write this from the perspective you're looking to write a woman) out there who go to these websites in order to befriend prisoners. In fact, some of these sites have hundreds of women a day reviewing them and searching for that special someone with whom they can share their time with for one reason or another. Some of the women are looking to minister, and some of the women are in school and want to learn about a prisoner's experience. Some of the women are looking for love, and some of the women simply want sex letters.

There are prisoners who try these websites and have no luck. However, there are also prisoners who use these websites and find exactly what they're looking for –*whatever* that may be. There is a way to use these services properly, and if you do, you will increase your chances of success. There is an art to pen-palling – a strategy, if you will.

Now, before I go on; I tend to look at things from a business perspective. So, with that said, I'm going to make a lot of comparisons between pen-palling and business to help explain the following strategies.

## Choosing Your Service(s):

The first thing you must do is decide what service(s) you'd like to use. The determining factor(s) in your decision may vary: Do you have money to pay for a service, or are you looking for a free service? What specifically are you looking for in a pen pal, and are there services or options that specifically target your objective(s)? What service has the most to offer? What service is said to provide the best results?

You can usually send a SASE (Self-Addressed Stamped Envelope) to these services and they will send you one of their brochures/applications, and if you have any specific questions that will not be covered in their brochure, they will usually answer those as well. Once you gather the necessary information, you can review each one and then decide which of them you think best suites your needs.

**Choosing A Photo (graphics for your ad):**

Choosing a photo to put on your profile is a critical part of the process. It will be your first impression. Your potential pen pal will first see your photo, then, if she likes what she sees, she will take the time out to read your intro.

   The best type of photo to use is a photo where you're smiling. You want to show that you are friendly and approachable. You don't want to look too menacing and scare off your potential pen pal(s). So even if you're a tough guy with tattoos all over, if you want to be successful with this, use a photo that doesn't make you look like an angry serial-killer.

**Intro (sales pitch/ad synopsis):**

The next thing you will need to do is write your intro. You will want to be sure that you do it within the allowed word count of your service, as going over the limit will usually cost an additional fee.

   Writing a proper intro is a very important part of this process. It is pretty much the second part of your first impression – the first part being your photo. The first thing a potential pen pal will do is see your picture. If she likes what she sees, she will read your intro. It is up to your intro to close the deal on getting you an initial response.

Now, when strategizing your intro, here's how you need to look at it:

*You are a product*; you're trying to sell *yourself*. Your intro is your sales pitch. You need to convince the women overlooking the site why they should write *you* verses somebody else. Remember, there are a lot of prisoners competing in this market. It's up to you to be the most attractive – colorful, creative, persuasive, inviting, etc.

   You also want to write your intro according to the type of pen pal you're looking for. If you're looking for a mature, professional woman, you will want to write a mature, professional into. If you're looking for a street-type girl, you should use a language that's more in *her* lane. Again, it is your ad. Just as companies create their ads to appeal to the market they are targeting, you need to create yours to appeal to the market (pen pal) *you* are targeting.

Show Qualities (sizzle):

Regardless of what type of girl you're aiming for, however, be sure to write an intro that's positive and upbeat, as well as one that showcases your qualities. If you have a sense of humor, show it. If you're creative, use creativity in your intro. You want to show your potential buyer (pen pal) that you are worth buying – that they will have a good experience with you. After all, that's what you're trying to sell – yourself; as an experience.

Note: Check out the intro-letter examples starting on page 36 so that you can get an idea of the kind of thing that works!

Extras (more sizzle):

Many of the pen pal services will allow you to add a piece of artwork and/or poem to your profile – usually for an additional fee, of course. If you can draw, it's an added bonus for your pen pal, as most women love getting drawings from prisoners. If your potential pen pal is trying to decide between you and another prisoner, the fact that you can draw and he can't might be the deciding factor.

When deciding on what kind of drawing to post, make sure you use one with an image that will appeal to the kind of pen pal you're targeting. Don't put a gangster-type drawing if that's not the kind of pen pal you're seeking. Instead, put something thematically relevant. For example, if you're looking for romance, put a romantic drawing.

Another thing that will better your chances is if you put a poem with your profile. Women love poetry, and if you can write or get a hold of the right poem, it, too, may just be the deciding factor of why a potential pen pal chooses you.

For an additional fee, there are services that will post you right on the front page of their website. From my experience, being posted on the front page where you are seen first is an extremely beneficial feature/option to take advantage of.

**Leave No Stone Unturned:**

You obviously want to maximize your chances of success, so do as many of the options as you can afford. You need to stand out from hundreds (or thousands, depending on the site(s) you use) of other businesses/products/experiences (prisoners), so make sure you leave no stone unturned. And if you can afford to be on more than one website, do so; be on as many as you can afford.

**Responding To A Pen-Pal Letter:**

If you do what I've explained thus far, it is very likely that you will start receiving mail from women who are interested in getting to know you. However, you aren't completely sold yet, as it is very likely those same women have each written to another prisoner or two, and are trying to decide which one of you will be the final purchase (choice).

At this point in the process, you will need to hit your pen pal with a response that will get you the final sale, so-to-speak. You do this by further showing your pen pal why an experience with you is the best one for her.

To show her why you're the best one, you do just that – you *show* her. You don't tell her. You show her by giving her the best letter – the best written, the most intelligent, the funniest, the most creative, etc. It will take some work, but if you want to be successful, you must go the extra mile.

There is a proper way to respond to an informal letter, no matter who it's from. And as we discussed in our writing section, it's to first start off with an upbeat greeting, and then to go over the letter you've received and respond to one paragraph at a time until you have responded to everything in the letter. The only exception to this is if the letter you've received jumps back and forth from subject to subject; in that case, you should mark each subject/paragraph separately, and respond to one *subject* at a time.

Once you've responded to what you were written about, then it's time to write what you'd like to talk about, ask, etc. Using this process will make your letters much more thorough, detailed, organized, and pleasant to read; which, of course, will make your pen pal that much more excited to receive your letters.

Hopefully the person receiving your letters notices the organization and process of how you answered her letters and responds to yours using the same method. Doing so will give you both the best pen-palling experience.

*Note:* Got a drifter? Yeah, it's fucking annoying, I know. It seems it's hard to make progress with a drifter because they always drift from subject to subject without ever coming to a point with one or the other. Unfortunately, for you, not many of your pen pals are going to read a how-to guide like you're doing now. Instead, they will just write you whatever comes to mind, when it comes to mind, without much consideration to the difficulty it creates for you who is undoubtedly trying to make some form of progress.

So, since your pen pal is probably not going to read a how-to guide, *you* will have to teach her how to write you the way you want to be written. There are several ways to teach your pen pal how to improve their responses to your letters. However, I've found it best to do so in a roundabout way by describing how *I* respond to *their* letters. For example: I really enjoy your letters. I find them very interesting; attention grabbing. I'm happy that you're my pen pal, and I take a lot of pride in how I respond to your letters. I like to try to make sure that I leave no stone unturned, so I found it best to just go down your letters and respond to one paragraph at a time. I value the communication that we have; I created the little method to ensure my side of the communication process is thorough. I've never been much of a pen-paller before, so if you see how I can improve my responding method, please feel free to let me know.

Doing this will let your pen pal realize that you are paying attention to things such as the quality of your response, which means it's likely you're paying attention to the quality of her response. This realization will make her question the quality of her own response, and if and how it can be improved. By telling her how you respond – which, of course, you already know is good, as does she – it will teach her a way to improve her own.

## The Elements (satisfaction guaranteed):

You want to make sure that you always provide a good experience for your pen pal so that they are always eager to receive mail from you. You must keep your customer (pen pal) satisfied at all times.

Here are a few key elements that you should try to include in each and every letter. If you do, the quality of your letters will be on point.

### Be positive:

Nobody wants to take time out of their busy life to write you (befriend you, help you, etc.), only to get a letter back that's negative and depressing. So, make sure that when you write your pen pal, you have a positive and uplifting attitude and energy. Your pen pal wants to feel happy when reading one of your letters, and you should want that, too. The better your letters make her feel, the more anxious she'll be to receive another one. And *that's* what it's all about – keeping her anxious to receive your letters.

### Be funny:

If you don't know how to be funny in a letter, you'd better learn quick. Women love to laugh, and even more than that, women love the men who make them laugh. You ever see a big fat guy with a super bad bitch and wonder how in the hell he pulled it off? That's how; he's a funny fat guy.

Look, you are in prison. As fucked up as prison is, funny-ass shit happens every day. Include in your letter a funny situation or experience. To you it might be everyday shit because you're used to the things that happen in prison, but to your pen pal, it's not only funny, but interesting, too.

### Be creative:

If you want to hook your pen pal, be creative. You need to provide your pen pal with an experience they won't get from anyone else. Furthermore, women love a creative man. You can impress a woman greatly with a little creativity....

## True Story:

I once got hooked up with a woman that I wanted rather badly. I knew she wasn't really the type to write someone in prison, so I really wanted to hit her with my best material in hopes I'd impress her enough to actually want/continue to write me.

Well, I'm a writer, and I'm super OCD when it comes to my writing. Whether it be books, blogs, letters, etc., I like everything to be nice, neat, and organized. One thing I don't like is making mistakes in my letters, and what I hate even more is to have my letters look messy with all kinds of scribbled-out words.

When I first began writing this woman, I wrote her very nice, long, and detailed letters that would literally take me an entire day or two. It was a ton of work and I barely had time to do anything else. Furthermore, every time I'd make a mistake, I'd start that page completely over. Yes; tons and tons of work.

After a while it just got to be ridiculous. All my other projects and responsibilities got put on the back burner, and it was all starting to pile up on me.

So, what I decided to do is come up with a way to use my mistakes to my benefit. And I did. Instead of writing one and a half pages and starting over because I made a small mistake, I started leaving my mistakes and making jokes out of them. For example, one time I was writing about getting out of prison, but when I wrote the word "out," I'd accidently spelled it "ot"; I got distracted and left out the "u." Stupid, right? Well, instead of starting over, I drew a real nice arrow from the side of the page (the margin), pointing in between the "o" and the "t." On the other side of the arrow (in the margin) I wrote, "Hey, u, get back in there!" accompanied by a little smiley face. Doing that allowed me to fix my mistake and let her know I was smart enough to spell the word "out"; I didn't have to start the page completely over to do it, I made her laugh, *and* I added character to my letter. She loved it, she mentioned it, she started doing it; it became part of my personal writing style.

Be intelligent:

Women are attracted to intelligent men. So, since you are doing time in prison, you should use some of this time to read a few books, articles, etc., and expand your mind a little bit so that you can stimulate hers with the things you write about. And one of the biggest things you can do to show intelligence to a woman you're writing to is to be a great writer; yes, like I've mentioned before, being a great writer is one of the *best* skills a prisoner can have... understand?

Now, please listen to me... What you don't want to do is try to sound more intelligent than you really are by using all kinds of big-ass words that probably neither you nor she really understands. For one, if she does know the word, you risk looking like a schmuck by using it in the wrong context (it's very easy to do). And for two, if she doesn't know/understand the word, you risk miscommunicating your point, and that's counterproductive. So, don't be a dumbass; show your true intelligence and be the authentic you.

Be charming:

You need to charm and flatter your pen pal – make her feel good about herself. There are a lot of women who are not properly complimented. Well, compliments feel good, right? We all like them. And if you're the one providing your pen pal with that good feeling, your letters will be like a drug to her and she will become addicted to them. The more you can get her to *need* your letters, the better of a position you will be in.

Look, let me explain something to you, playboy. It is not hard for a woman to get a man. Even if she's not the most attractive, she still has a mouth and a pussy, and as long as she does she has the ability to get *somebody*. So, with that said, not only are you competing with other people in prison whom she can be writing to, you are – at least to some extent – competing with guys on the outside, too. So what's the difference between you and a guy on the outside? He can give her dick whenever she wants it and you can't. Women like sex just as much as men, so the fact that he can give her dick creates some stiff competition for you (if you know what I mean).

Now, especially if she's not all that attractive, it's likely that the guy on the outside is *only* going to give her dick. Luckily for you, most women need more than just that. They need to be heard, romanced, loved, paid attention to, complimented, respected, etc. And that, my friend, is where *you* come in.

Like any smart businessman, when you want to start a business, you want to find out what *you* can supply (to your target market) that's *not* being supplied by competing businesses – in this case, other men. And since other businesses (men) are not providing an ear, romance, love, attention, compliments, respect, etc., you need to *specialize* in those areas....

Business 101: Supply the demand; understand?

## Be confident:

Ask any woman and she'll tell you she finds confidence in men to be sexy. I don't mean that you should be arrogant and obnoxious, but be confident in who you are and what you're doing. After all, you're a big, bad prisoner; you're supposed to be strong and tough. That is probably one of the reasons that your pen pal is attracted to you – because she likes a strong, confident man. If she was looking to befriend a weak, wimpy guy, she probably wouldn't have looked for a pen pal on a prisoner-pen-pal website; she would've found one from an online knitting club.

## Be interesting:

You need to keep the attention of your pen pal, and the way to do that is to consistently remain interesting. Something in every letter you send her should capture her attention – intrigue her.
There are many ways to appeal to a woman's interest, and some of those ways are all around you, and the things that you do daily without even thinking twice about. You may hate your prison experience, but to people who don't have to live here, the inner workings of our reality/society can be quite intriguing. I've had a couple of pen pals find the way I put my soups together to be interesting. To me it's nothing; a daily thing. But to my pen pals, putting beans and crushed-up chips in my Ramen soup is something they've never thought of. And when they find something so basic (to me) to be so interesting, imagine how impressed they are when I describe to them how I make tamales, wine, a tattoo gun, etc.

## The More You Put Into It, The More You'll Get Out Of It:

In regards to the music business, a guy once told me, "The more you put into it, the more you'll get out of it." I heard him, although I didn't fully understand what he was saying until years later when I learned more about the music business.

Anyway, that same concept applies to a lot of things in life; including other businesses, including the business of pen-paling. If you want to be successful at it, you're going to have to put in the work to be so.

The biggest misconception that many prisoners have is that, to keep a woman pen pal satisfied on a romantic level, they only have to write a two-page letter once every two weeks. Those are the same prisoners who're unsuccessful.

I learned a long time ago that the prisoners who are successful with women on the outside are the prisoners who write them letters almost daily, send cards and drawings, and who call as much as possible, too. Many prisoners who're successful put in 8-hour days, just like they would at a regular job. That's what women require, so that's what you have to do. Like I said, it's work. However, if you want full-time benefits, you have to work full-time; understand?

## An Even Exchange:

I know many prisoners who're what I consider professional pen pals, and they run their operation just like a business. They are the product, they promote/market their product/business online (pen pal service(s)), and they provide a product/service (letters) in exchange for something they want and/or need. I hate to put it so bluntly, but it is what it is.

You'd be surprised what letters from a prisoner can do for a woman. Think about how good a woman feels when she gets letters of support, compliments, encouragement or romance. Again, guys out there want sex; they're not too concerned with the woman's emotions. So there are a lot of women who get sex from a jerk on the streets, but then get romance and emotional support from a guy in prison.

A lot of prisoners become almost like therapists to their pen pals. As a prisoner pen pal, we devote a lot of time "listening" to the woman pour her emotions out on paper. And not only do we "listen," but we respond with words of support and encouragement.

Some people put a negative light on prisoner pen pals as if they're just using women on the outside. Well, sure, some prisoners do use women on the outside (just like some men on the outside use women on the outside), but there are many women on the outside who use prisoners. For example, many women turn to the comforting words of a prisoner when she is going through a time in her life where she needs the attention and support only a prisoner is willing to give, only to leave the prisoner hanging once that time in her life is fixed/fulfilled some other way. There are also women who love the love and romance they can get from a prisoner, including the letters discussing their sexual fantasies in the greatest of detail, only to leave the prisoner hanging once that part of her life is being fulfilled by somebody else; as if the prisoner has no feelings....

So, when you really look at the reality of the situation, who's using who? In my opinion, it's an even exchange; it's business.

## Looking For Love?

If you expect to find real, genuine love from a woman you've met from a prisoner pen pal site, you may be setting yourself up for disappointment. Don't get me wrong, I'm sure that real love can exist between a prisoner and a woman on the outside he's met via pen pal website; however, I'm also sure that it's *not* the norm.

When you and your pen pal first start "falling" for each other, it will probably feel like love. Your relationship will be new and exciting. However, you should be aware that a woman will usually stay on the team solid for about 18 months. After that you will probably notice things starting to fade. So, enjoy it while it lasts....

## Anything's Possible:

When it all boils down to it, anything is possible. And if you are in prison, you should be trying to do anything that will improve your lifestyle.

I've seen many successful romantic relationships between prisoners and their pen pals. I've also seen some marriages between prisoners and women they met by pen-palling first. If you have a release date, and if you can get family visits, your chances of success increase dramatically.

On the other hand, I've also seen many successful *business* relationships between prisoners and their pen pals. I've seen prisoners get thousands of dollars, lawyers, packages, weekly visits, you name it. In exchange, those guys pretty much devote their lives to the women who're providing such things for them. They spend their days writing, drawing, calling... *whatever* it takes.

# BASIC PUNCTUATION GUIDE

## APOSTROPHE'

1.   Indicates the possessive case of singular and plural nouns, indefinite pronouns, surnames with designations such as Jr. and Sr.:
The gangster's gun
My homie's car
Mike's bitch
2013's most valuable player
The Bloods' block

NOTE: When indicating possession for a plural noun, the apostrophe goes on the outside of the s

2.   Indicates the omission of letters in contractions:
He isn't the one.
I wouldn't've done that.
That's good shit.
I could've made a lot of money with that.

3.   Indicates that letters have intentionally been omitted from the spelling of a word in order to reproduce a perceived pronunciation, or to give an informal flavor to a of writing:
That beat is knockin'.
Tell 'im what I said.
Fuck all of 'em.
He knocked yo' ass out.

## BRACKETS [ ]

1.   Used to enclose words or passages in quotations to indicate the insertion of material written by someone other than the original writer/speaker:
I went to [the store on] the corner.
We smoked that [weed] right there and got high as fuck.
Fill the entire clip with [hallow point] bullets.

2.   Used to enclose material inserted within material already in parentheses:
I stopped by the house (in Sacramento [CA]) to drop off the guns.

## COLON :

1.   Introduces words, phrases, or clauses that explain, amplify, or summarize what has preceded:
Suddenly my reality hit me: I would die in prison.
In prison, a man has two things: his balls and his word.
I had what I needed to settle the score: my shank.

2.   Introduces a list:
I have everything we need for the job: 2 bulletproof vests, 2 handguns, 2 masks and 6 duffle bags.

3.   Follows the salutation in a business letter:

Dear Mr. Wright:
To whom it may concern:
Gentlemen:

## COMMA ,

1.   Separate's the clauses of a compound sentence connected by a  coordinated conjunction (for, yet, but, so, nor, and, or):
I like his drawings, but I wouldn't let him tattoo on me.
I used to love that girl, and I have no problem admitting it to the world.

NOTE: You can leave the comma out in short compound sentences in which the connection between the clauses are close:
I heard what he said and I didn't like it.
I got in my Chrysler 300 C and went home.

2.   Separates and/or from the final item in a series of 3 or more:
I got coke, weed, and meth for sale.
I love Nicki Minaj, Beyonce, Kate Upton, and about 999 other bad bitches.

3.   Separates two or more adjectives modifying the same noun and could be used between them without changing the meaning:
A cold, dark prison cell.
A beautiful, intelligent woman.

Sets off a nonrestrictive clause (one that if eliminated would not change the meaning of the sentence):
The Escalade that is sitting on 26-inch rims is cleaner than the Navigator, but the Escalade on 20-inch rims isn't.

NOTE: The comma should not be used when the clause is restrictive (essential to the meaning of the sentence): The Escalade that is sitting on 26-inch rims is grey with beige leather interior.

4.   Sets off transitional words and short expressions that require a pause in reading or speaking:
Unfortunately, I did not get a visit today.
It's painful, I know.
    Of course, I would love to get out of prison.

5.   Sets off a subordinate clause or a long phrase that precedes a principal clause:
If I ever get out of prison, I will never come back.
After I read the letter, I understood everything she meant.

6.   Sets off words used in direct address:
Thank you, mom, for all that you've done.
Nicki, please send me some pictures of you in a thong.

7.   Separates a tag question from the rest of the sentence:
Jessica Alba is a bad bitch, isn't she?

I think Drake's new CD is knockin', don't you?

8.   Follows the salutation in a personal letter, and the complimentary close in a business or personal letter:
Dear Ninel,
My dearest love,
Forever yours,
Sincerely,

## DASH —

1.   Sets apart an explanatory or defining phrase:
Some of the most beautiful women in the world – Beyonce, Alicia Keys, Rihanna, Ninel Conde, etc. – are also the wealthiest.
I immediately realized what prison is – hell.

2.   Sets apart parenthetical material –
My '68 Malibu – the candy blue one sitting on 22-inch rims – was my favorite car.

NOTE: If you use dashes to set apart an explanatory, defining phrase or parenthetical material, in the middle of a sentence, the sentence must also make sense if it were removed from it:
Some of the most beautiful women in the world are also the wealthiest.
My '68 Malibu was my favorite car.

## ELLIPSIS POINTS . . .

1.   Indicate, by 3spaced  points, the omission of words or sentences within quoted matter:
The Playboy Club was established in 1960 … It's now worth a fortune.

2.   Indicate, by 4 spaced points, the omission of words at the end of a sentence (one for the period, 3 for the ellipsis points):
Loyalty and respect is a must.... But you would never know it by the actions of these fools.

3.    Indicate, by 3 spaced points, a pause in the middle of a sentence for dramatic effect:
She turned around and saw ... nothing.

4.    Indicate, by 4 spaced points, a pause at the end of a sentence for dramatic effect:
In the end, he turned out to be what I suspected: a rat….

## EXCLAMATION POINT!

1.   Terminates an emphatic or exclamatory sentence:
I can't believe you!
Fuck you, bitch!

## HYPHEN -

1.   Indicates that part of a word of more than one syllable has been carried over from one line to the next:
When I go to the yard, I enjoy work-

ing out on the bars.
You could never fully understand how painful prison is unless you've been here.

2.    Joins the elements of compound modifiers preceding nouns:
That's a well-done tattoo.
It's a two-hour movie.
I hope you pick up game from my letter-writing book.

3.    Punctuates written-out compound numbers from 21 to 99:
I plan to be ballin' by the time I'm thirty-five.
I do twenty-five reps per set.

## PARENTHESES ( )

1.    Enclose material that is not an essential part of the sentence, and that if not included would not alter its meaning:
In about 3 hours (2 if we're lucky), the officers should pass out mail.
It was crazy (but justifiable) the way they stabbed that guy.

2.    Often enclose letters or figures to indicate subdivisions of a series:
Please go online and do the following: (A) e-mail Michelle and let her know it's a go; (B) Print me out the article about our new book; and (C) Find out how much Photo Doctor will charge me to do the graphics for the cover of my new book.

3.    Enclose figures following and confirming written-out numbers in legal and business documents:

I will have it done in fifteen (15) days.
I will pay you one thousand dollars ($1,000.00) per original beat.

4.    Enclose written-out words when the abbreviations are used for the first time and may be unfamiliar to the reader:
I am currently in Ad-Seg (Administrative Segregation).
I just came out of the SHU (Security Housing Unit).

## PERIOD .

1.    Terminates a complete declarative or mild imperative sentence:
I will write you tomorrow.
When you visit, bring money so we can eat.

## QUESTION MARK ?

1.    Terminates a direct question:
Are you going to pass out canteen tonight?
Is Nicki Minaj's ass bigger than Kim Kardashian's?

## QUOTATION MARKS (DOUBLE) " "

1.    Enclose direct quotations:

In the beginning of the movie the officer said, "Ain't no talkin' when I'm talkin', fellas, so shut the fuck up."

2.   Enclose words or phrases to clarify their meaning or use, or to indicate that they are being used in a special way:
"Playboy Business" represents a lifestyle.
I use the term "It's a new era" to express why I do what I do.
You got the "shit"?

## QUOTATION MARKS (SINGLE)

1.   Enclose quotations within quotations:
"In my opinion," he said, "the essence of the word 'beautiful' is Ninel Conde."
"Mike, your girl just called me and said, 'You better stop fuckin' with my man, bitch!' then hung up."

NOTE: Put commas and periods inside closing quotation marks; but put semicolons, colons, and dashes outside closing quotation marks. Other punctuation, such as exclamation points and question marks, should be put inside the closing quotation marks only if it is part of the matter quoted.

## SEMICOLON ;

1.   Separates the clauses of a compound sentence having no coordinating conjunction:
I'm the one who wrote the book; he's the one who typed it.
Chase money; once you catch it, everything you desire will chase you.

2.   Separates elements of a series in which items already contain commas:
Within my inner circle, there's Playboy, the mack; Stranger Gonzales, the hitter; Crow, the ladies' man; Cesar, the brute; and Johnny Boy, the young pit bull.

3.   Separates clauses of a compound sentence joined by a conjunction adverb, such as nonetheless, hence, or however:
Ol' girl's fine; however, she has a fucked up attitude.

4.   May be used instead of a comma to signal longer pauses for dramatic effect:
I'm about 3 things: money; power; and respect.

## SLASH /

1.   Means or and/or:
The drums and/or bassline are what made the beat pound so hard.
I'm looking for a Beyonce/Ciara/Rihanna type of girl.

**FORMAL-LETTER EXAMPLE:**

The Cell Block, Inc.
P.O. Box 1025
Rancho Cordova, CA 95741

www.thecellblock.net

Penitentiary Productions
P.O Box 76856
Atlanta, GA 30316

Date: December 22, 2012

Re: LYRIC SUBMISSION

Dear Mr. Lawson:

Enclosed are some of the lyrics to my song titled "Home-made Mic" (edited to fit submission criteria).

Also, I am not sure of exactly what your plans are for Penitentiary Productions; however, I have an e-file (on the outside) with the vocals to about 100 songs, as well as a "rough" mix of Home-made Mic and a few others. From what I have been able to see from Penitentiary Productions so far, I am led to believe that what I'm doing would fit perfectly with the "Penitentiary Productions" theme.

If you are interested in possibly doing something together, please send me a phone number or e-mail address and I will have you contacted with more information – actual vocals, a few rough mixes, etc., or whatever you request.

Thank you for your time and consideration.

Sincerely,

Michael Werth, pka Mike Enemigo; President
The Cell Block, Inc.

NOTE: This is an actual letter that I sent to a company requesting rap lyric submissions (the company name/address has been changed). Notice the order the contact information is in; my business address is at the very top (if you don't have a business address, this is where you'd put whatever address you do have – your prison/cell, etc.), followed by the address of the person/business I'm writing the letter to. Below that goes the date, then "Re:" — what the letter is regarding or in reference to. Below that is the name of the specific person the letter is to, followed by a colon; a colon is more appropriate than a comma for a formal letter.

The letter itself does not begin in a "personal" manner — "Hey, how are you? Fantastic, I hope," etc. Whoever you'd write/send a formal letter to is not interested in anything like that. They are interested in the point, and this letter gets straight to it; they requested lyric submissions, I'm submitting some. Only after that do I add an idea of my own; and I am clear and to the point when doing that, too.

Most formal letters have this same format. Use this as an example and your formal letters will look nice, neat, and professional, and you will be taken more seriously.

To give you an even clearer idea of how a formal letter should look, I will enclose a couple more examples. This next one is a letter of release and authorization"; rather than a big, complicated "contract," I opted to write it in the form of a formal letter.

**FORMAL-LEITER EXAMPLE:**

The Cell Block, Inc.
P.O. Box 1025
Rancho Cordova, CA 95741

www.thecellblock.net

Rider Records
P.O. Box 916
Sacramento, CA 95827

Date: May 5, 2010

Re: RELEASE & AUTHORIZATION

Dear Mr. Perez:

The purpose of this letter is to provide you with written authorization to use "Mike Enemigo Presents" on the below listed "Album"; additionally, you are authorized to use "Hosted by Mike Enemigo" on the below listed "Mixtape." Lastly, we hereby authorize the use of the below listed Mike Enemigo vocal performances and release them free of monetary compensation or any rights or claims outside of Mike Enemigo's continued ownership of lyrics, if ever we so choose to print or reproduce them. All Mike Enemigo performances are to be credited as, "Written By M. Werth for Murder Ink," and all art and/or linear notes are to identify, "Mike Enemigo appears courtesy of The Cell Block."

1  Album: A Day in the Life of a Rider
2. Mixtape: Rider Muzic

Vocal Performances:

1. Intro: "Thee Enemy of the State" skit on "Public Enemy"
2  Intro: "Respect thy Enemy" skit on "You don't wannit it wit me"
3  "Religous Sacrifice"
4  "Fire"

Sincerely,

X                                             X
Michael Werth, President                      Jacob Perez, President
The Cell Block, Inc.                          Rider Records

AGREED TO & ACCEPTED


Lastly, this third example is a "production agreement"; again, instead of a big, complicated contract, I opted to write it in the form of a formal letter.

**FORMAL-LETTER EXAMPLE:**

The Cell Block, Inc.
P.O. Box 1025
Rancho Cordova, CA 95741

www.thecellblock.net

Beat-em-Down Productions
P.O. Box 211
Sacramento, CA 95826

Date: May 20, 2013

Re: PRODUCTION AGREEMENT

Dear Mr. Jimenez:

The purpose of this letter is to document the terms of agreement that we made over the phone on May 18, 2013, as well as a few other specifications that I have.

• You have agreed to produce, to the best of your ability, our mixtape titled, "Mike Enemigo: Lyrical Intoxication." The mixtape consists of: 15 songs, 5 of which will need original beats to be produced by you; 5 skits; and hosting.

• In return for producing this mixtape in its entirety, we have agreed to pay you a flat fee of one thousand dollars ($1,000) in the following increments:

1. $200.00 for the first group of 4 songs.
2. $200.00 for the second group of 4 songs.
3. $200.00 for the third group of 4 songs.
4. $200.00 for the remaining 3 songs.
5. $200.00 for the skits, hosting, final mix, etc.

• It is agreed that after you receive a group of songs, you will complete the songs, and you will send them to us within fourteen (14) days after receiving payment.

• It is agreed that by signing this letter, you are giving a sworn declaration that you are the true creator and owner of the original beats that you contribute to this mixtape.

• It is agreed that since you are being paid a flat fee for this "work made for hire," we will own one hundred percent (100%) of the copyrights to the original beats that you produce, as well as all other creative contributions that you make toward this mixtape, and no royalty will be paid to you.

• Upon completion of this mixtape, it is agreed that you will send us a copy of the complete "e-file," as well as any other type of data-storing system you may have used to produce, mix, etc., containing all the information relevant to this mixtape and its contents.

Sincerely,

X

Michael Werth, President
The Cell Block, Inc.

X

Roy Jimenez, Producer
Beat-em-Down Productions

AGREED TO & ACCEPTED

## INSTRUCTION-WRITING EXAMPLE:

RE: COVER-ARTWORK INSTRUCTIONS FOR "CONSPIRACY THEORY" BOOK...

STORY SYNOPSIS:

1998. Kokain (Eminem) is an upcoming rapper in the Sacramento, CA underground scene. Nicki (Jessica Alba) is his girlfriend.

One night in October, using Kokain's 1970 Cougar, Nicki's brother and his best friend attempt to rob a house of its $100,000 marijuana crop. It goes wrong; a man is murdered with bullets from a 9mm Ruger and a .38.

Later, when investigators begin closing in on Nicki's brother and his best friend, they, along with the help of Nicki and a few others, conspire a way to make Kokain take the fall.

COVER IDEA:

I would like Eminem to be in the center; the main image. Jessica Alba should look as if she's standing behind him. Around them, I would like a collage of the following images, as they are relevant to the story:
- Studio speakers
- Microphone
- Money wad or roll
- Detailed bud(s) or weed plant(s)
- .9mm Ruger
- 38 revolver
- Sacramento capitol building
- Silhouettes of plotters in a group
- 1970 Cougar on spoke rims
- House with crime scene tape, maybe even a cop car out front

COLOR SCHEME:

I would like Eminem and Jessica Alba to be in color. I'd like the rest of the graphic -- the collage -- to be mostly black and white with some green. (I prefer the amount of different colors used to be minimal.)

NOTE: These are the actual instructions I wrote to get the artwork done for the cover of my book "Conspiracy Theory." Like a formal letter, the instructions are very clear and to the point. You want the person you are instructing to have all the information necessary to do what you want them to do, but you want to give them all the information in the least amount of words as possible; this is to avoid confusion. For this particular set of instructions, since they are for the artwork of a book cover, I began by giving the graphic artist a synopsis of what the actual book itself is about. I wanted the artist, who has not read the book, to get a general feel for the story, so he then could transfer the concept into the graphic on the front cover. You will notice, in the synopsis, I made sure to mention very specific key words: "1998," "rapper," "1970 Cougar," "$100,000 marijuana crop," "9mm Ruger," and ".38." I did this to make sure the artist understood the importance of them, as they are all things very specifically relevant to the story, and had the artist not been aware of them, I risk the possibility of the artist doing something that won't make sense. For example, had I not mentioned the year 1998, which is when the story takes place, I risk the possibility of the artist including something in the graphic that wasn't even around until 2008. That, obviously, would not make sense. Had I just mentioned "car," the artist might've put a 1970 Malibu. That wouldn't make sense to the story. The main character doesn't drive a 1970 Malibu, he drives a 1970 Cougar. Had I not made clear the importance of a "9mm Ruger" and a ".38" of having been the guns used, and instead just mentioned "guns," or that a guy had been "shot," I risk the artist putting a .45 and an AK-47 on the cover of my book. That would not have made sense, and we would've had a problem (or 2 or 3 or 4) to fix. I do not want a problem, so I must do all I can in the beginning to avoid one. I had to be very clear and to the point, using the least amount of words as possible, while at the same time very thorough.

After the synopsis, I explain my basic idea for the cover artwork in just a few sentences, followed by a clear, specific list of the things I'd like included in the graphic, and the color scheme I want.

**INTRODUCTION-LETTER EXAMPLE:**

Hello,

My name is Michael and I'm from Sacramento, California. I enjoy reading, writing, learning, working out, listening to music, laughing, having a good time and making new friends. Despite life's ups and downs I keep a positive attitude and remain optimistic. We only live once, so I believe it's important to maximize the opportunities and experiences life has to offer; one of the most important being that of genuine friendship.

I divide my days up by doing the things I enjoy, though I spend a large portion of them working on a book I am writing. I've written a few already; trying to get something going with that. Though I'm physically inside a cell and recognize my reality for what it is, I do my best to mentally escape this bleak environment through my creative writing.

Now, however, I would like to expand my little world by meeting people and making friends from all over, all walks of life. I'm interested in learning about as many different people, cultures, lifestyles and perspectives as possible, including yours, which is why I've decided to post this profile.

I'm open-minded and have no specific expectations with this. Though I hope to make great friends, learn, feel and have fun, I'm also open to sharing my experiences and giving a true, insider's perspective on prison life — for those of you interested in that kind of thing.

I hope you decide to contact me and I look forward to hearing from you soon. (For more info/photos: facebook.com/michaelwerth1)


NOTE: Though there is no exact way to do it, this is how an introduction letter should look. It's well-written, and it covers all the basics; it gives the reader an idea of who I am, what I'm into and what I'm looking for in a pen pal, all without giving away too much. It's positive and upbeat and it's inviting to everyone — people from all over, all nationalities, and all walks of life. That was my goal with this particular intro.

   Also with this intro, however, was the objective of possibly finding someone who would be interested in my writing; someone who may help me with my books. And so that someone who's interested in learning about a prisoner's experience – someone who's researching for an article, book, etc. – would hopefully pick me for their study, as that kind of connection would be valuable to my network, I made sure to specifically invite them as well.

## INTRODUCTION-LETTER EXAMPLE

Hello,

My name is Mike. I'm a California boy, from Sac-town, the city of kings. I'm a 6ft, cut-up dude, with the business. I'm a dedicated, determined, passionate, ambitious and creative person. I spend most of my time working out, reading, writing and drawing. I enjoy laughing and having fun. I strive to make the best out of every situation. We only live once; it is important to maximize our experience and staying positive is key.

I'm looking for a woman to correspond with the old-school way: snail mail. I'm not trying to lock anybody down and have 'em doin' this time with me. We all got enough problems of our own, no sense in adding someone else's to the mix. I'm just trying to kick it with somebody cool who's capable of holding a decent conversation. I've always believed that a man with unrealistic expectations is prone to bypassing realistic opportunities, so I have no outrageous expectations with this. I don't need to lie or be lied to. There's always a girl trying to convince a dude she can hold him down and be faithful while he does his time, but that's an unrealistic expectation! Only the rarest of circumstances allow such a thing! I don't even need all that! I'm just trying to find a friend who will appreciate me for the man I am, my mind and my spirit, and take it from there, come what may. So, hit me up, I'm looking forward to hearing from you.

NOTE: This intro is well-written and covers all the basics; however, it's a little more relaxed than the other example and geared specifically towards finding a female "friend" to pen-pal with.

Made in the USA
Lexington, KY
30 September 2017